Immigration and Refugee Policy

Immigration and Refugee Policy

AUSTRALIA AND CANADA COMPARED

EDITED BY
Howard Adelman, Allan Borowski,
Meyer Burstein and Lois Foster

VOLUME I

UNIVERSITY OF TORONTO PRESS
Toronto and Buffalo

First published in Australia 1994
Designed by Lauren Statham, Alice Graphics
Typeset by Syarikat Seng Teik, Malaysia in 11/13pt Sabon
Printed in Australia by
McPherson's Printing Group for
Melbourne University Press, Carlton, Victoria 3053

First published in Canada and the United States in 1994 by
University of Toronto Press Incorporated
Toronto and Buffalo
ISBN 0-8020-7608-4 (Vol. I)
ISBN 0-8020-7609-2 (Vol. II)

© Bureau of Immigration and Population Research, Australia, and
Employment and Immigration Commission, Canada 1994

Canadian Cataloguing in Publication Data
  Main entry under title:

  Immigration and refugee policy: Australia and
  Canada compared

Includes bibliographical references and index.
ISBN 0-8020-7608-4 (v. 1) ISBN 0-8020-7609-2 (v. 2)

1. Australia—Emigration and immigration—Government policy.
2. Canada—Emigration and immigration—Government policy.
3. Refugees—Government policy—Australia. 4. Refugees—
Government policy—Canada. I. Adelman, Howard, 1938–   .

JV7225.I55 1994   325.71   C94-931008-5

Foreword

Australia and Canada have much in common. Both countries have a history of early European settlement, association and institutional inheritance; large land areas (with diverse but harsh climates) endowed with rich natural resources; and populations which are small relative to the size of the countries. For decades, Australia and Canada have also shared a policy of planned immigration, including a strong refugee and humanitarian component.

The natural similarities of Australia and Canada have encouraged a series of comparative studies of social and other public policies in our two countries. With a view to understanding policy-relevant lessons and implications, these analyses have sought to explain why, how and with what effect Canadian and Australian governments have developed often different but sometimes convergent responses to similar problems.

Since Australia and Canada each possesses a planned immigration and refugee settlement program, it is useful and productive to examine the various relative aspects of these policies. For this reason we welcome the publication of *Immigration and Refugee Policy— Australia and Canada Compared*.

A joint initiative of the Australian Bureau of Immigration and Population Research, Citizenship and Immigration, Canada, and the Centre for Refugee Studies, York University, this book is published by the University of Melbourne and the University of Toronto Presses. Its distinguished editors and authors are drawn from a wide variety of disciplines and institutions in Australia and Canada.

The contributors were chosen on the basis of their expertise and their ability to draw policy-relevant inferences from their work. The editors took care to ensure that the authors represented a wide range of professional disciplines and approaches. Two seminars brought the contributors together—one in Melbourne in September 1991 and another in Toronto in May 1992. These meetings were followed by considerable collaborative activity among the authors.

Another distinguishing feature of this study is its scope. *Immigration and Refugee Policy: Australia and Canada Compared* comprises two volumes and deals in depth with a wide range of both immigration and refugee issues. Volume I begins by placing population movements to Australia and Canada in an international context. It then turns attention to the immigration and refugee policy-making and implementation processes in the two countries. Volume II examines settlement policy and the economic, environmental and social impacts of immigration.

By virtue of the contributors' expertise and the breadth and depth of the content of these two volumes, the editors have ensured the production of a landmark comparative study on immigration and refugee policy in Australia and Canada.

Without endorsing any particular conclusions, on behalf of the Governments of Australia and Canada, we therefore have pleasure in welcoming the publication of *Immigration and Refugee Policy: Australia and Canada Compared*. It is a tribute to collaborative and fruitful policy research by authors in Canada and Australia.

Nick Bolkus
Minister for Immigration and
Ethnic Affairs

Sergio Marchi
Minister of Citizenship and
Immigration Canada

CONTENTS

Contents

Contents

Contents

Preface

With a view to enhancing the 'user friendliness' of the volumes, each one includes an editors' introduction that seeks to serve as a 'first reader'—to provide an overview of the content of each chapter found in the volume as well as a 'glimpse' of the content of the companion volume.

The material prepared for this landmark comparative study is presented in two volumes, each of which is comprised of several parts. Part 1 of the first volume contains three chapters which seek to provide a context for the entire study. Three further parts of Volume I contain chapters which are devoted to an analysis of the two countries' policy-making, immigration policy implementation and refugee policy implementation processes respectively. The second volume has a completely different focus. It is concerned with the settlement of immigrants and refugees in Australia and Canada as well as the various impacts of immigration—economic, environmental and social—on the two countries.

Volume II is concerned with the issue of immigrant settlement (Part 1) as well as the economic, environmental (Part 2) and social (Part 3) impacts of immigrants. The first chapter of Part 1 examines the settlement policies and programs of Australia and Canada. This is followed, in Chapter 2, by an analysis of the ways in which both countries have responded to the increased ethnic diversity stemming from their immigration policies. The last chapter of Part 1 is a case study of immigrants from Hong Kong who have settled in Australia and Canada. Part 2 of the second volume deals with the economic impacts of immigration (Chapter 4) the labour market experiences of immigrants (Chapter 5) and the environmental impacts of immigration (Chapter 6).

Part 3 of Volume II, comprised of five chapters, is devoted to an examination of immigration's social impacts. The relationship between immigration and racism is the subject of Chapter 7, while Chapter 8 focuses upon the relationship between immigrants' English language proficiency and their economic and social integration. The impact of immigration on the education system is the subject of Chapter 9. Chapter 10 examines how migrants have experienced ageing in Australia and how efforts to respond to the needs of the ethnic aged have 'spilled over' into constructive responses to the needs of the Australian-born aged. In the final chapter (Chapter 10) the supposed relationship between immigration and crime is carefully scrutinised.

Volume I, Part One

The Context

As noted above, the introductory chapters to Volume I seek to provide a context for all of the other contributions to this comparative study. The first chapter provides an overview of Australian and Canadian migration patterns and policies while the second chapter examines international population movements more generally. The third chapter turns its attention to issues of justice in immigration and refugee policy.

In their overview of Australian and Canadian migration patterns in Chapter 1 Inglis, Birch and Sherington describe the contributions of net immigration to population growth, the geographic distribution of immigrants, the growth in temporary migration and the changing ethnic composition of the two countries. They then trace the evolution of each country's immigration policy and describe and analyse how these policies operate today. They conclude their chapter by exploring some of the challenges confronting immigration policy-makers in Australia and Canada.

The immigrants and refugees who settle in Australia and Canada in any one year represent only a very small proportion of international population movements. In their examination of these movements in the second chapter of Part 1, Borowski, Richmond, Jing Shu and Simmons begin by considering recent trends in international population movements (between and within regions) and the types of movements (permanent migration, refugee flows, temporary labour migration, tourism, and illegal immigration). The authors then present and evaluate some of the major explanations that have been offered for these movements (push–pull theory, social network theory, structural theories, involuntary migration theory), giving particular attention to what these explanations imply for understanding current and future international migration trends which may affect Australia and Canada. This is followed by a close examination of emerging changes in global economic and cultural relations between countries and how these are shaping Australia's and Canada's immigration policies and patterns. Chapter 2 concludes by speculating about the future movements of people around the world and to Australia and Canada.

Because some of the most fundamental issues facing a society are who is to be admitted and on what grounds such decisions should be made, one of the key problems immigration and refugee policy-makers must consider is that of justice. Admission policies and decisions directly affect the conception of justice governing a society. In Chapter 3, the last contribution in Part 1, Adelman reviews and critiques some conceptions of justice. He also develops a 'justice framework' for making immigration and refugee policy. With a view to ascertaining the usefulness of the framework he applies it to a select number of immigration and refugee issues. In doing so, he further clarifies how issues of justice can be applied to immigration and refugee policy.

Volume I, Part Two

Policy Making

The three chapters comprising Part 2 of this volume are devoted to an analysis of aspects of the immigration and refugee policy-making process in Australia and Canada.

The first chapter in this Part (Chapter 4) examines the roles played by political institutions and interest groups in shaping Australian and Canadian policies. Hardcastle, Parkin, Simmons and Suyama begin their analysis by presenting seven hypotheses which provide differing descriptions and explanations of the sources of influence on immigration policy-making. The authors' intent is to try to reach some conclusions concerning the adequacy of these hypotheses as explanations for the policies adopted in the two countries.

The seven hypotheses presented by Hardcastle et al. are: (1) responsible government, (2) bureaucratic dominance, (3) nation-building statism, (4) cosmopolitan élitism, (5) pluralism, (6) business dominance and (7) populism. Before attempting to draw any conclusions about their adequacy, however, they examine the role in policy-making played by formal constitutional and institutional structures and interest groups. Their analysis of political institutions involves an examination of the roles played by federalism and national–state/provincial relations, legislative–executive relations, Cabinet and the prime minister, the bureaucracy, the judiciary and international relations considerations. The analysis of the roles played by interest groups in influencing immigration and refugee policy encompasses political parties, organised labour, business interests, ethnic-minority interests, humanitarian groups, environmentalists, and ethno-centric groups opposed to immigration. Hardcastle et al. also give some consideration to the role of public opinion, a subject dealt with in much more detail in the following chapter.

In a rich and fascinating analysis that affords considerable insight into policy-making processes, they clearly show that Australia and Canada share many commonalities. They argue that an understanding of the sources and strength of the influences that come to bear upon the making of immigration policy is perhaps best captured conceptually as a tension between statist (hypothesis 3) and pluralist (hypothesis 5) dynamics.

As noted above, the role of public opinion in the policy-making process is dealt with in the second chapter of Part 2 (Chapter 5). Holton and Lanphier's analysis of the role of public opinion involves three central questions: (1) Does public opinion speak with one voice with respect to immigration policy? (2) How far has policy 'led' public opinion? and (3) To what extent has public opinion driven policy formulation?

In addressing the first question, Holton and Lanphier begin by pointing out the complexity and heterogeneity of public opinion. They disaggregate public opinion into the opinions of the 'active' public (those who have first-hand contact with immigrants), the 'interested' public (those for whom immigration is a salient but not necessarily predominant concern) and the 'general' public (which is involved in a much more diffuse and episodic manner with immigration issues). They then examine the opinion poll evidence on attitudes towards both the level and the composition of the immigrant intakes to Australia and Canada. Their conclusion is that public attitudes in general have hardened in both countries. At the same time, general public opinion is far from being uniformly hostile.

Indeed, before turning to the latter two questions Holton and

Lanphier describe the continuum of attitudes towards immigration policy. They also explore some of the reasons behind the hardening of attitudes (they argue that the economic recession is a major contributing factor) and the role of the media in shaping public opinion.

With regard to the relationship between public opinion and immigration policy Holton and Lanphier argue that Australian policy is not driven by 'interested' or 'general' opinion and that policy has led, rather than followed, general public opinion. At the same time, the weight of public opinion (particularly in response to specific events or perceptual images) may moderate the leadership role of government in the policy-making process. Such moderation seems to be more likely to occur in Canada than Australia (one of the few points of divergence between the Australian and Canadian experience in relation to public opinion and immigration). Holton and Lanphier suggest, however, that in the future it is unlikely that Australian and Canadian governments will continue to be able to exercise their traditional leadership role in immigration policy-making.

In the third and last chapter of Part 2 (Chapter 6), Fincher, Foster, Giles and Preston focus upon a dimension of immigration policy-making that has received scant attention, viz., gender. As Chapter 2 of this volume points out, women play a major role in all types of international population movements within and between the regions of the world (for example, they now dominate labour migration and refugee movements). With a view to examining the implications of immigration policies for women, in Chapter 6 Fincher et al. compare Australian and Canadian policies from the perspective of gender relations. On the basis of this comparison they identify an implicit gender inequity in the policies in terms of the general constructions of the ideal male and female immigrant. They examine the implications of this inequity for immigrant selection policies and the forms of settlement assistance.

Chapter 6 is divided into four sections. The first section examines the major themes found in the international literature on women in migration and then considers the extent to which these themes are also reflected in the Australian and Canadian literature. In the second section Fincher et al. turn their attention to identifying the visions of the ideal male and female immigrant which seem to have shaped recent policies in the two countries. The authors focus upon immigrant selection but also show how certain settlement policies, although not explicitly discriminatory on the basis of sex, place immigrant women at economic and social disadvantage. In the third section the authors present a case study of one form of settlement assistance, viz., language training, both to highlight the linked immigrant selection and settlement process and to illustrate how it confirms the view implicit in immigrant selection policy that the work done by immigrant women is less valuable than that done by immigrant men. In the concluding section Fincher et al. argue that a major gender inequity in immigration policy is its devaluation of the significance of women's and, thus, immigrant women's work.

Volume I, Part Three
Immigration Policy Implementation

Part 3 of this volume is comprised of two chapters which examine how the immigration policies of Australia and Canada are implemented in practice. The examination of the implementation of immigration policy largely involves an analysis of, first, the immigrant selection and control systems employed by Australia and Canada and, second, the business migration program of the two countries, one of the categories of the Australian and Canadian migration programs.

In the first chapter of Part 3 (Chapter 7) Burstein, Hardcastle and Parkin examine the immigration selection and control systems employed in Australia and Canada in recent years to achieve the annual immigrant intake levels established by the governments of the two countries. A central thesis of this chapter is that these systems are not only the means to regulate immigration but that they also produce and reflect a distribution of the power to select immigrants among various parties, government and private.

Chapter 7 is divided into five sections. The first section describes Australia's and Canada's immigration selection and control systems. The authors distinguish between four general categories of admission (family relationship, humanitarian, occupational and miscellaneous), some of which are 'demand-driven' and some of which are 'controlled'. They point out that the desire to manage an overall immigration program can be very difficult where demand-driven admission categories exist.

In the second section the authors argue that with the demand-driven components the selection of immigrants is effectively devolved to applicants and/or their sponsors while the power to select immigrants under the other categories is vested in government officers. From this observation, Burstein et al. postulate a 'privatisation hypothesis', viz., that over time effective control of immigrant selection has tended to pass from the government arena to the private arena. If confirmed, this hypothesis would suggest, first, a shift favouring private over national interests and, second, that immigration planning by government increasingly involves forecasting anticipated patterns of entry rather than controlling entry according to some overall plan.

The third and fourth sections are devoted to an examination of the extent to which the privatisation hypothesis is supported by the recent experiences of Canada and Australia respectively. This largely involves an analysis of data on the numbers, composition and characteristics of the immigrant intake and decisions about annual planning levels and qualifying standards. Burstein et al. conclude that the Canadian experience strongly supports the privatisation hypothesis. In Australia privatisation is also an important factor shaping the immigration program. However, Australia's more tightly controlled program seems less ceded to private initiative than the Canadian program. Nevertheless, in their concluding section, Burstein et al. point out that the privatisation hypothesis should be treated with some caution because the relative impact of privatisation is shaped by the particular policy and management approach of the immigrant receiving nation.

Chapter 8 is the second of the two chapters which make up Part 3. Here Borowski and Nash compare and contrast the development, achievements and problems of the business migration programs in Australia and Canada with a view to drawing some policy-relevant lessons.

The authors divide their chapter into five sections. The first section traces the history of the Canadian and Australian business migration programs. It also describes the provisions of Australia's new Independent-Business Skills migration category which replaced the Business Migration Program early in 1992. Borowski and Nash then turn their attention to an examination of the scale of business migration and the source countries which have yielded the largest numbers of business migrants. They point out that the level of business migration has been higher to Canada than it has to Australia, at least in part because of the increasingly inclusive definition of a business migrant adopted by Canada.

In the third section the authors review the research that has been conducted to date on the extent to which the business migration programs of the two countries have achieved their goals. Although research carried out in both countries is limited in volume and scope and, to varying degrees, suffers from methodological limitations, it suggests that the business migration programs have, generally speaking, been successful.

The research findings notwithstanding, recent years witnessed increasing challenges to the business migration programs of the two countries, particularly in Australia where the challenges resulted in the abandonment of the program and its replacement with the new Independent-Business Skills category. In the fourth section, Borowski and Nash review some of the major challenges to business migration. They also describe and account for the differential responses of the Canadian and Australian governments to these challenges. The concluding section draws out several lessons for immigration policy-making and implementation from the Canadian and Australian experiences of business migration.

Volume I, Part Four

Refugee Policy Implementation

The final Part of Volume I deals, in three separate chapters, with select aspects of refugee policy implementation.

Chapter 9, by Adelman and Cox, focuses upon overseas refugee policy, i.e., the selection abroad of refugees. It begins by pointing to the dilemma that nations face in seeking to be compassionate, humanitarian and protective of refugees while simultaneously seeking to exercise control on the number of asylum cases spontaneously arriving on their doorsteps. Adelman and Cox argue that the two approaches are often antithetical.

They then turn their attention to the nature of the relationship between immigration and refugee policy. Much of the rest of Chapter 9 is devoted to depicting how the dualism between humanitarianism and control is expressed in five areas of overseas refugee policy, viz., (1) emergency and long-term aid; (2) international intervention; (3) bilateral, multilateral and international mechanisms for coordination; (4) legal and bureaucratic mechanisms, and (5) special assistance programs for refugees designed to facilitate their coming to Australia and Canada. They conclude from their analysis that both countries have responded to the tension between humanitarianism and control by emphasising control.

The regulation and control of illegal immigration and refugee claims is the subject of Chapter 10. Cox and Glenn distinguish between two regulatory models—the administrative, which reflects the current position of Australia, and the adjudicative, reflecting the Canadian situation. The authors argue that the adoption of a particular regulatory model has important consequences for the relative number and treatment of illegal entrants and overstayers, change of status requests and refugee claims. On the basis of their analysis Cox and Glenn observe that the adoption of a particular model is not based on its anticipated consequences. Rather it is dictated by underlying assumptions as to the nature of the state, the role of executive authority, and the nature of international population movements. The authors conclude their chapter by considering which is the more effective model and whether the Australian and Canadian systems conform with the requirements of justice as expressed in human rights conventions.

The final chapter of Part 4 and of Volume I, prepared by Harris and Weinfeld, focuses upon three areas. The first is the current international regime which affects the world's refugee population and the Australian and Canadian responses within the international system. The second is the option of a regional approach and the elements of solutions around which discussions are taking place internationally. The final area is the possible challenge to the principle of state sovereignty arising from the forces of regionalism and ecological imperatives.

PART ONE

Context

CHAPTER 1

An Overview of Australian and Canadian Migration Patterns and Policies

Christine Inglis, Anthony Birch and Geoffrey Sherington

Introduction

At the end of the twentieth century, Australia and Canada find themselves in a rapidly changing world in which old policies of immigration that played such an important role in the development of both countries are coming under close and critical examination (Richmond 1991b). Many comparative studies of Australian and Canadian migration and policy were completed before these changes became evident in the late 1980s (Burnley & Kalbach 1985; Hawkins 1989; Rao, Richmond & Zubrzycki 1984). Whether international developments associated with increasing globalisation herald a watershed in Australian and Canadian responses to immigration is uncertain. However, the impact of such developments will clearly be influenced by the part which immigration has played in the formation of both nations.

Immigration and growth

Australia and Canada share a common history both as dominions of settlement within former French and British Empires and as modern industrial economies that have depended upon the inflow of population for growth and development. Until recently, they have thus sought to promote themselves as societies of immigration. But the geopolitical contexts of both societies have also led to some major differences in how each has framed its immigration policies. Much of this difference relates also to the role of the state. In Australia, state policies have been a crucial factor in social and economic development. As such, the politics of immigration have been at the forefront of discussion on the nature of Australian society since the mid-nineteenth century. In Canada, the central state has traditionally been a broker of economic growth rather than a determinant of social development. If anything, immigration policy in Canada (despite greater numbers of immigrants) has played a secondary role to the more central issue of the relationship between the founding 'charter' groups of colonial French-Canadians and English-Canadians. In Australia, immigration policy has been at the forefront of the construction of a national identity and development. Thus not only demographically, but in other more fundamental ways, immigration has been a contributor to the composition of the population.

In 1788 when non-Aboriginal settlement of Australia began with the arrival of the First Fleet, the indigenous population was estimated to be in excess of 300 000 (Jupp 1988a p. 17). Immigration has been a significant factor in the subsequent increase of the population to its present figure of greater than 17 million. Since 1860 the decennial rate of population growth due to migration only fell below 25 per cent following the 1890s Depression and the 1930s Depression (see Table 1.1).

In Canada since Confederation in 1867, the contribution of immigration to population growth, in contrast, has been as great only in the first decade of this century and, again, since 1961. For much of the late nineteenth century and during the 1930s, Canada actually lost the potential benefit of (often substantial) immigration because of emigration, especially to the neighbouring United States. Even in the decade after 1901 when Canada recorded the highest net population gain from migration, the number of emigrants was nearly half (48 per cent) of all those who immigrated (Beaujot, Basavarajappa & Verma 1988, p. 2).

Following World War II, Canada was somewhat slower than Australia in experiencing substantial net immigration. Whereas Australia's overseas-born population rapidly increased from less than 10 per cent in 1947 to 20 per cent by 1971, Canada's immigrant population, which was 14.7 per cent in 1951, had changed little by 1986 when it was 15.6 per cent (see Tables 1.2 and 1.3). However, since the trough in immigrant arrivals in both countries in the mid-1980s, Canada's immigrant intake has continued to grow so that it now outstrips that of Australia in both absolute and relative importance (see Table 1.4). The long-term effects of this increasing immigration

Table 1.1 Migration and population growth in Australia and Canada, 1860–1990

	Australia					Canada			
Year	Pop ('000)	Increase ('000)	Net migration ('000)	Net migration as a % of increase	Year	Pop ('000)	Increase ('000)	Net migration ('000)	Net migration as a % of increase
					1851	2 436	–	–	–
1860	1 146	–	–	–	1861	3 230	794	182	23
1870	1 648	502	167	33	1871	3 689	459	–150	–33
1880	2 231	584	192	33	1881	4 325	636	–54	–8
1890	3 151	920	383	42	1891	4 833	508	–146	–29
1900	3 765	614	25	4	1901	5 371	538	–130	–24
1910	4 425	660	118	18	1911	7 207	1 835	810	44
1920	5 411	986	222	23	1921	8 788	1 581	311	20
1930	6 501	1 089	304	28	1931	10 377	1 589	230	14
1940	7 078	577	30	5	1941	11 507	1 130	–92	–8
1950	8 307	1 230	361	29	1951[a]	14 009	2 141	169	8
1960	10 392	2 084	819	39	1961	18 238	4 229	1 080	25
1970	12 800	2 408	944	39	1971	21 568	3 330	722	22
1980	14 807	2 008	647	32	1981	24 343	2 775	793	29
1990[b]	17 211	2 403	1 086	45	1991	27 297	2 954	928	31

[a] Newfoundland is included for the first time.
[b] Australian data for 1990 is preliminary.

Sources: **Australia:** BIR 1991b, p. 8. For full details of changes in the time series consult this publication.
Canada: Beaujot, Basavarajappa & Verma, 1988, p. 2.
Also unpublished data from Statistics Canada for 1981–91.

rate for Canada may, however, be minimised because of the continuation of extensive emigration estimated between 1981 and 1986 as being approximately 47 per cent a figure in excess of the Australian level which, for example, in 1990–91 was at the relatively high level of 26 per cent (Michalowski 1991, p. 29, DILGEA 1992d, p. 3).

A further contrast in the migration patterns of Australia and Canada is that the immigrants have been far more evenly distributed across Australia than is the case in Canada. The disparity in the foreign-born population between Tasmania and Western Australia (10.1 per cent vs. 27.5 per cent in 1986) is far less than between the extremes characterising the Atlantic provinces and Ontario (3.6 per cent vs. 22.1 per cent) as shown in Tables 1.2 and 1.3. Not only are immigrants now more numerous proportionately in Australia than Canada, but their social, economic and political impact is more evenly

Table 1.2 Percentage of immigrants (overseas-born) in Australia by states, 1911–86

State	1911 % Immigrants	1947 % Immigrants	1986 % Immigrants
NSW	16.4	10.2	20.9
Victoria	15.7	8.7	22.8
Queensland	26.3	10.3	15.0
W. Australia	25.9	18.2	27.5
S. Australia	14.3	6.7	22.3
Tasmania	9.8	3.8	10.1
ACT	12.6	11.6	23.3
NT	54.5	12.6	18.4
Total	**17.2**	**9.8**	**20.8**

Source: ABS Census data 1911, 1947, 1986.

Table 1.3 Percentage of immigrants in Canada by province, 1901–86

Province	1911 % Immigrants	1951 % Immigrants	1986 % Immigrants
British Columbia	56.9	29.2	22.1
Prairies[a]	48.7	22.9	13.3
Ontario	20.1	18.5	23.2
Quebec	7.3	5.6	8.2
Atlantic[b]	6.1	3.4	3.6
Yukon[c]	n.a.	17.9	11.5
Northwest Territories	32.0	6.5	5.5
Total	**22.0**	**14.7**	**15.6**

[a] The figure for immigrants in 1911 and 1951 is for those born outside Canada. In 1986, the figure is that for the 'Immigrant' population.
[b] Newfoundland is included in the Atlantic Provinces from 1951.
[c] In 1911 the Yukon and Northwest Territories were grouped together.

Sources: ABS Census 1911, 1951, 1986.

spread in a country characterised by a higher density of urban settlement than Canada's. Hence post-World War II immigrants or their Australian-born children together constitute some 40 per cent of the population and immigration is very much a part of the everyday experience of all Australians.

In both countries the contribution of immigration to population growth has been related to periods of boom and bust. For Australia

Table 1.4 Immigrant arrivals in Australia and Canada, 1981–91

Australia		Canada	
Year	*Number*	*Year*	*Number*
1981–82	118 699	1981	128 618
1982–83	93 177	1982	121 147
1983–84	69 808	1983	89 157
1984–85	78 087	1984	88 239
1985–86	92 410	1985	84 302
1986–87	113 309	1986	99 219
1987–88	143 490	1987	152 098
1988–89	145 316	1988	161 929
1989–90	121 227	1989	192 001
1990–91	121 688	1990	214 230
1991–92	107 391	1991	230 781

Sources: **Australia:** BIR 1991b; 1992c; 1993b.
  Canada: EIC 1992c, p. 3, and unpublished data.

the discovery of gold in the mid-1800s and the economic growth of the 1880s were followed by the 1890s and the 1930s Depressions which produced a major decline in the overseas-born population—from 22.7 per cent in 1901 to the historic low of 9.8 per cent in 1947. For Canada, the effects of variation in the percentage of overseas-born in the population have been less dramatic and have occurred at a somewhat different time. Canada, like the USA, thus experienced its major peak of immigration in the first three decades of this century when the overseas-born population increased from 13 per cent in 1901 to 22 per cent (reached in 1911 and sustained for a further two decades). The subsequent decline in the 1930s to a low of 14.7 per cent was less dramatic than Australia's. The economic climate is, however, insufficient to account for the variations in their experience of immigration, as illustrated by their most recent experiences of immigration at the end of the 1980s, a period characterised by levels of unemployment in excess of 10 per cent in both countries. Canada has implemented its expansionary Five Year Immigration Plan which has resulted in a steady increase to an annual intake intended to reach 250 000 by 1993, Australia's initially similar intention to expand the immigration intake following the 1988 report of the Committee to Advise on Australia's Immigration Policies (CAAIP 1988) has undergone major revision in that the proposed intake for 1992–93 was reduced to 80 000. Such disparity in their immigration programs highlights the need to examine the political and social, as well as economic, context within which immigration policy has developed in both countries. Before examining this context in more detail two related aspects of migration require attention. These are the relationship between permanent and temporary migration and the effects of immigration on the dominant patterns of ethnic diversity.

Temporary migration

Since the 1970s, major changes in technology, economic structures, political and educational institutions have been associated with a process of globalisation which has involved the development of extensive patterns of temporary movement by tourists, workers, businessmen and students. In both Canada and Australia these temporary migrants far outnumber permanent migrants. In 1989, immigrants were less than 1 per cent of the 101 million arrivals into Canada. While two-thirds were returning Canadian residents, the remaining 38 million were tourists and other short-term visitors (EIC 1991e, p. 6). Similarly, in Australia the 121 000 immigrants who arrived in 1989–90 were only 2.7 per cent of the 4.4 million total arrivals; 2.2 million were either short- or long-term visitors (BIR 1991a, p. 9).

The growth in temporary population movements has important implications for permanent immigration patterns and policies (Sloan & Kennedy 1992; Stahl et al. 1992). After arrival temporary visitors often seek to obtain permanent resident status. Furthermore, through their participation in the labour market or in business they may replicate or substitute for the input of permanent residents. During their period in the country they also increase the population base. This has implications in the areas of increasing demand for goods and services and utilisation of resources.

Migration and changing ethnic composition

The most dramatic impact of immigration on the ethnic composition of white settler societies such as Canada and Australia has been the effect on the indigenous population which, by 1986, was less than 2 per cent of the total population in both countries. In 1986 nearly half of all Australians described themselves as being of British ancestry while a further one in five, nearly all resident for at least three generations and hence likely to be of British ancestry, described themselves as 'Australian' (ABS 1990; Price 1989). Of the remaining 30 per cent of the population, 3.6 per cent were Italian, 2.2 per cent German, 2.1 per cent Greek and 1.2 per cent Chinese and Dutch ancestry. Even in the nineteenth century, Chinese and Germans had only been a slightly larger component of the overall population (although their concentration in certain areas gave them greater prominence).

In Canada the French have a prior claim to being the major ethnic group and share with the British the status as the two founding or 'charter' groups. The continuing influence of early French settlement is still evident in that quarter of the population, mainly concentrated in Quebec, who described their ethnic origins in 1986 as 'French'. Just over a quarter of the population described themselves as 'British' while of the 29 per cent who said they were of 'mixed' ancestry, 8 per cent were from a variety of Anglo-Celtic ancestries (Statistics Canada 1990). The remaining 20 per cent of the population included 3.6 per cent Germans, 2.8 per cent Italians, 1.7 per cent Ukrainians, 1.4 per cent Chinese and 1.1 per cent South Asians. The key distinction, then, between the ethnic composition of contemporary Canada and Australia is the existence in Canada of the large, and long-established, French population.

Until the 1950s, the French had for a long period constituted 30 per cent of Canada's population (Palmer 1991). With the subsequent renewal of extensive immigration, though little from France, in conjunction with the demographic changes of the 'quiet revolution' in Quebec which has involved a major decline in birth rate, the French-origin population has declined to the present quarter of the total. In both Australia and Canada, the major effect of post-war immigration has been to reduce the predominance of the population of British or 'Anglo-Celtic origins'.

Initially, 'new' immigrants were from Europe, particularly Britain, and, in the case of Canada, from the United States, and from New Zealand to Australia, thus continuing the patterns operating in the first half of the century.

In 1966, the United Kingdom was still the major source of immigrants to Australia and Canada but changes were already apparent in the Eurocentric patterns of immigration. Hong Kong had joined the ten major source countries to Canada, while India and Lebanon were among the ten major Australian sources (Health and Welfare Canada 1990, p. 32; BIR 1992b). A decade later the increasing diversity of source countries and the declining importance of Britain was even more evident. In Canada, Hong Kong had been joined as a major source by Jamaica, Lebanon, India, the Philippines and Guyana, while Australia's major sources now also included Malaysia and the Philippines (Health and Welfare Canada 1990, p. 32; BIR 1992b). The pattern of diversification has continued unabated throughout the 1980s with non-European sources, especially the Asian region, becoming ever more important (see Tables 1.5 and 1.6). At the same time, the major source countries no longer contribute such a large proportion of the intake. Whereas in 1966–67, 86 per cent of Australia's immigrants were from ten countries, by 1991–92 they accounted for less than two-thirds of all arrivals and a similar trend is evident in Canada (BIR 1993, p. 20).

Critical in the diversification of the immigration sources was the abandonment by both Canada and Australia of their restrictions on non-European migration embodied in the White Australia and White Canada policies. In 1967, Canada was the first to formally abandon all immigration restrictions based on race, colour or religion, after abolition in 1962 of most of the discriminatory restrictions. By the mid-1960s Australia had also eased restrictions considerably, although it was not until 1973 that the White Australia Policy was formally replaced by a non-discriminatory policy similar to Canada's. Oppor-

Table 1.5 Ten major source countries of Australian immigrants, 1981–91

	1981–82			1990–91	
Country of birth	*Number*	*%*	*Country of birth*	*Number*	*%*
United Kingdom	36 994	31.3	United Kingdom	20 746	17.0
New Zealand	11 637	9.9	Hong Kong	13 541	11.1
Vietnam	11 088	9.4	Vietnam	13 248	10.9
Poland	5 732	4.9	New Zealand	7 467	6.1
South Africa	3 332	2.8	Philippines	6 388	5.2
Philippines	3 251	2.8	Malaysia	5 744	4.7
Germany	3 089	2.6	India	5 081	4.2
Netherlands	2 408	2.0	Taiwan	3 491	2.9
Malaysia	2 393	2.0	Sri Lanka	3 271	2.7
Cambodia	2 154	1.8	China	3 256	2.7
Sub-total	82 078	69.5	**Sub-total**	82 233	67.6
Other	35 953	30.5	Other	39 455	32.4
Total	118 031	100.0	**Total**	121 688	100.0

Source: BIR 1993b, p. 20.

Table 1.6   Ten major countries of Canadian immigrants, 1981–90

Country of birth	1981 Number	%	Country of birth	1990 Number	%
Great Britain	18 912	14.7	Hong Kong	23 134	10.8
China	9 798	7.6	Poland	16 536	7.7
India	9 415	7.3	China	14 193	6.6
USA	8 695	6.8	Lebanon	12 954	6.0
Vietnam	8 163	6.3	Philippines	12 590	5.9
Philippines	5 978	4.6	India	12 572	5.9
Poland	4 093	3.2	Vietnam	9 175	4.3
Hong Kong	4 039	3.1	Portugal	7 740	3.6
Haiti	3 700	2.9	Great Britain	6 897	3.2
Portugal	3 292	2.6	USA	5 067	2.4
Sub Total	76 085	59.2	**Sub Total**	120 858	56.4
Other	52 533	40.8	Other	93 372	43.6
Total	**128 618**	**100.0**	**Total**	**214 230**	**100.0**

Source: EIC 1982; 1991f.

tunities now existed for new source regions to supply immigrants at a time when European development and economic growth was reducing the numbers of European seeking to emigrate. The impact of increasing numbers of immigrants from non-traditional sources has meant that long-established patterns of ethnic diversity and dominance in Canada and Australia are changing. A reflection of this change is the terminology used to describe the newer groups: 'non-English-speaking background' (NESB) in Australia; 'visible minority' in Canada. The use of 'language' in Australia and physical characteristics or 'race' in Canada as a symbolic marker of the differences between newer and older groups reflects other complex differences in the responses of both countries to new immigration. Visible minority refers to those of 'non-white' or 'non-Caucasian' background which is loosely defined to include those from the Middle East, Asia, Africa and Latin America who now account for some 70 per cent of Canadian immigrants (EIC n.d.). In Australia, the term NESB is applied to those who come from countries other than Britain, Ireland, North America, New Zealand and South Africa. The increasing diversity in immigrants to these countries has added an additional dimension to the factors influential in the formulation of immigration policy in both countries.

Immigration policy in Australia and Canada

Historically, both Australia and Canada have been important receiving societies of people since their colonial foundations. Beginning in the seventeenth century the modern diaspora of peoples from Europe focused first on the American continent. Most of the current population of modern Quebec are descendants of those who settled in New France in the seventeenth and eighteenth centuries. The War of Independence of the thirteen British colonies brought to present-day Ontario and the Maritimes the Empire Loyalists, many of whose forefathers had been immigrants from Britain or Western Europe. These events in North America also led to the settlement of Australia as the British Empire swung away from the Atlantic and towards the Pacific and Indian Oceans. During the nineteenth century Canada had the advantage of being in relatively close proximity to Europe, and being part of the Atlantic trade in peoples. But it also had the disadvantage of the proximity of its large southern neighbour which continued to attract even recent immigrants across the border. For Australia, the 'tyranny of distance' would be a continuing disadvantage with the high costs of travel from Europe. Only with the discovery of gold did the Australian population begin a major increase. In contrast immigration into Canada languished during the mid-nineteenth century, while many new settlers simply crossed the border. Australia's neighbour New Zealand did not provide the same counter-attraction as the United States did for Canada.

The late nineteenth century marks a watershed in the development of policies in both nations which still have influence today. Following Confederation, the National Policy of Canada focused on immigration as part of overall economic development, particularly of the Western Provinces. Indeed, settling the West became a major economic aim of the national government. Immigration policy was thus associated with economic growth and expansion (Burnet and Palmer 1988). In contrast, the experiences of the gold rush period and the lack of perceived opportunities for the sons and daughters of the gold rush generation led to a greater attention to immigration controls in Australia. In part this also reflected different patterns of settlement. Outside parts of Ontario and Quebec, Canada would remain very much a society of rural and provincial small-town communities until well into the twentieth century. Australia had become predominantly an urban society from the mid-nineteenth century with a focus on providing for those already settled in the new colonial environment. As such, the labour movement in Australia soon developed policies

12

aimed at restricting rather than encouraging immigration. In contrast, the division within the Canadian labour movement prevented the development of any coherent policy on immigration. Indeed, the major opposition to increased immigration numbers into Canada often came not from Canadian labour but from Quebec politicians who feared the effect of the growth of non-Francophone settlers on the 'compact' between the two founding races.

The differences are seen partly in the changing views of the 'preferred immigrant'. Such categories have involved both preferences on grounds of ethnicity and skill. Thus early nineteenth-century embryonic restrictions on Asian immigration were developed as part of the policies that would be enshrined in the 'White Australia' policy on Federation. Canada also developed its 'White Canada' policy but this was principally designed to satisfy the electorate on the West Coast. In other ways, ethnocentric views in Canada had to come to terms with the need for economic development to compete within the North American context. By the 1890s Canadian policy was prepared in part to abandon a search for British immigrants in preference for rural settlers from Eastern Europe and other parts of Europe to develop the Western Provinces. Those from European peasant backgrounds prepared to work the soil were even preferred to labourers from British cities. A particularly large contingent of migrants came from the Ukraine, settling in Alberta. In contrast, Australian immigration policy of the early twentieth century still favoured the 'British first' as the ways of maintaining ties of kith and kin; Australian policies of economic development in the early twentieth century still sought to attract British settlers into land development. More generally, as a British Dominion state, Australia rather than Canada became the major supporter of the policies of inter-war Empire settlement which sought to tie the British Empire together through both trade and population policy. For Canada, Empire settlement was only part of a wider policy of encouraging economic growth through immigration. For Australia, Empire settlement seemed to have the attraction of unifying ethnic and economic ends.

It was only after World War II that Australia and Canada emerged as modern industrial states with apparent preferences for population growth and specific skills that could assist industrial expansion. As such, the policies of the two nations actually moved closer together in the two decades after World War II. In part this reflected new historical circumstances. In Australia it was significant that the earlier post-war policies were designed and carried through under a Labor Government. The traditional opposition of the Australian

Labour movement to increased immigration was now muted in the climate of post-war economic expansion from 1945 to the early 1970s. Rather than immigration providing a 'reserve army of labour' it appeared initially that the Australian-born sections of Australian labour could benefit from the economic growth that resulted from immigration. It was also significant of the different national economies, however, that Canada moved more quickly than Australia in the 1960s to select immigrants on grounds of skill rather than background (Economic Council of Canada 1991a, pp. 13–14). This was partly a recognition of the changing world economy as Europe recovered from World War II and Western European economies sought out their own supply of 'guest workers'. Canada also was first to abandon the vestiges of preference on grounds of race, although by the mid-1960s even White Australia was virtually defunct as a policy. It was finally officially buried in 1973 by an incoming Labor Government with an agenda for social reform focused on social justice and equity. In response to growing concerns that the high levels of the migration intake were placing considerable strains on both the welfare, social and physical environment, it also reduced the intake levels (Wilkes 1971).

Following the dramatic replacement of the Labor government in 1975, Australia reverted to a policy based on a high level of immigration intake, despite the international economic recession which was then occurring. Only briefly in the recession of 1982–83 was there a reduction in the commitment to high levels of immigration. This strategy was reinstated under a new Labor Government committed to major reforms of the Australian economy. Although demographic arguments advocating the use of immigration as a means of overcoming the aging of the population had some currency they were not sustained and economic arguments were critical in support of the expansion of immigration (Young 1988). Economic arguments for the stimulatory effects of immigration on economic growth and development were most explicitly developed in the Report of the Committee to Advise on Australian Immigration Policies (CAAIP 1988) which drew on earlier studies such as that by the Committee on Economic Development of Australia (Norman and Meikle 1985).

In Canada, even higher levels of immigration also occurred throughout the 1980s except for the recession in the earlier part of the decade. From a low of 84 000 in 1984, the intake climbed to 214 000 in 1990, whereas in Australia the peak figure of 145 000 reached in 1988–89 was only double the decade low of 69 800 (see

Table 1.4). This growth reflected governmental commitment to expanding the immigration program and, in particular, involved an expansion of the economic component of the program (see Table 1.8). As in Australia, demographic arguments for sustained immigration were common (Economic Council of Canada 1991a, p. 17) although the actual impact was questioned by a Demographic Review initiated in 1986 (Health and Welfare Canada 1990). In 1990 the Government announced a Five Year Immigration plan which confirmed its commitment to a high level of immigration by providing for an increase in the intake to 250 000 by 1993. In announcing the Plan the Minister referred to the need to increase the overall level of immigration as a way of maintaining the balance between three competing objectives of the policy: the social, embodied in family reunions, the humanitarian and the economic (EIC 1990c, p. 5).

Unlike Australia, Canada has maintained its high level of immigration into the early 1990s in spite of being in a recession similar in severity to Australia. By 1989–90 Australia's plans for high levels of immigration into the 1990s had been abandoned in the face of extensive criticism of the social problems and costs of maintaining high levels of immigration in a recession joined with vocal opposition to the impact of high levels of immigration on the environment. By 1992, the Government announced that its planning figure for the 1992–93 *intake* was to drop to 80 000, a figure similar to the figure for *net immigration* of 50–70 000 advocated by the Opposition. In reducing the planned numbers it also found it necessary (as did the Canadian Five Year Plan) to balance the demands of supporters for the social, humanitarian and economic elements in the immigration program. This was done primarily by reducing the two points-tested categories, that is, the Concessional Family category was reduced by 68 per cent and the Independent Category was reduced by 55 per cent.

Extensive Australian debates over immigration throughout the 1980s indicated that the long post-war consensus on the desirability of extensive immigration no longer existed. This period also coincided with the growing prominence of Asian source countries. The change ensured that the debate over high levels of immigration very rapidly degenerated into debate over the predominance of Asian immigrants. The 'Asian migration' debate was sparked in 1984 by comments by a prominent historian, Geoffrey Blainey, which rapidly highlighted the demise of the former bipartisan approach to immigration (Markus and Ricklefs 1985). Following the Government's moves to reduce the levels of the 1992–93 immigration intake and to adopt changes reducing social support provisions for new immigrants, there is an indication that bipartisan party policies are re-emerging.

Australia's rapid abandonment of its high immigration policy is indicative of the more prominent and sensitive role of immigration in Australian politics than it has in Canadian politics. Immigration issues, in particular those relating to refugee claimants discussed later in this chapter, have been present but not normally prominent in Canadian public debate. The greater prominence of immigration in Australian politics reflects not only the far greater contribution of immigration to population growth but the major historical role which the state has played in the development of immigration. Indeed the desire to control Asian immigration was an important factor leading to federation of the Australian colonies in 1901. In Canada, the relationship between Francophone and Anglophone and especially between Quebec and the other provinces has been far more significant for the future of the nation. Under the *British North America Act* all provinces retain concurrent jurisdiction with federal authorities over immigration matters. Yet the only province with which a formal agreement concerning the regulation and harmonising of policies on immigration has been signed is Quebec, a reflection of Quebec's distinctive concerns about its place within the Canadian nation.

By the 1990s both Canada and Australia find themselves in a changing world economic and political order where former colonial and neo-colonial ties are being replaced through the emergence of new economic forces, especially in Asia, and through the political collapse of the Soviet bloc. The concept and reality of the nation state, constructed in the nineteenth century, is now under challenge. Immigration policies now reflect only parts of the earlier traditions. In Canada, a national policy of immigration, first formulated in the mid-nineteenth century as the basis for national economic growth, is now subject to the specific interests and demands of particular provinces, especially those of Quebec. In Australia, where immigration policy was closely related to policies of social development, opposition to new settlers comes now not so much from the traditional labour movement, reduced as it is by policies of economic change, but from a collection of environmentalists and academics joined in concern for the impact of population on scarce resources. These anti-immigration groups are supported now by many on the Right of politics who recognise that the international movement of capital, rather than people, may be the major determinant of development in the twenty-first century.

Migration and control

Despite the changing emphases and influences on the formulation of immigration policy an enduring issue remains the mechanisms of control and promotion which ensure the effective implementation of policy decisions. Immigration's importance for the existence of contemporary Australia and Canada has not meant that either country has maintained an 'open door' policy for entry. Coexisting with a long history of official attempts to encourage immigration by preferred groups, especially in Australia, has been a concern by government to also control and restrict entry. The White Australia Policy and the White Canada Policy are among the best known and earliest examples of restrictions on entry. The administrative methods to control and manage migration have become increasingly complex and extensive as both countries seek to retain control over entry in a situation where migration's role in national social and economic policy is becoming ever more complex. Population policy, human resources development, economic growth and foreign affairs are among major national policy areas which immigration affects and which are seen as necessitating attention to both the numbers and the type of immigrant admitted. This is occurring at the very time when cheap and rapid transport facilitates the international movement of a growing world population with the resources and incentive to travel internationally in search of work, security or a better lifestyle.

In comparison with the United States the legislative bases for Canadian and Australian immigration policies are far less detailed and prescriptive. The legislation (*Australian Immigration Restriction Act* 1901 and *Migration Act* 1958; in Canada, *Immigration Act* 1976) has tended to be general with details of implementation embodied in government regulations or, very commonly in Australia, in administrative practices. Matters such as numbers, categories of migrant and selection procedures are hence extremely flexible. As a correlate they are also the potential target for political debate and lobbying on an ongoing basis, although such debate is far more extensive in Australia than in Canada.

By the end of the 1980s, the advantages of flexibility inherent in policy administration was being seen by officials in both Canada and Australia as outweighed by the potential it created for legal challenges to the decision-making process. In Australia, extensive ministerial discretion not only allowed for specific individual pleading, but also judicial intervention overturning such individual judgements

17

(Hawkins 1989, p. 122). Canada's Charter of Human Rights provides an even more specific legal reference point for challenging specific immigration policies as has been shown in a range of decisions especially in matters relating to claims for refugee and humanitarian status. Both countries have responded to this perceived 'lack of control' by introducing new legislation.

In Australia, the move towards greater codification and specification of regulations, together with the reduction in ministerial discretion, resulted in new regulations being introduced in December 1990 and the Migration Laws Amendment Bill 1992. In 1987, two bills, C-55 and C-84, introduced into the Canadian Parliament and subsequently adopted in 1988 were specifically designed to deal with refugee claims from increasing numbers of those seen as economic, rather than political refugees. In 1992 major amendments to the *Immigration Act* were introduced into the Canadian Parliament with the intention of providing more effective tools for the management of the immigration program in areas including selection, the determination of claims for refugee status, and the control of illegal entrants.

The administrative control of immigration, which has become the key to the implementation of contemporary policy, has two major aspects. The first is the devising of selection procedures which ensure that the type of immigrant selected will realise the aims of the policy. The second is the development of procedures to control and exclude the entry of those not officially selected for permanent residence.

The control of selection

Australia and Canada share an immigration selection process which provides three main bases for selection of immigrants: family ties, humanitarian need and economic skills and resources. In the immediate post-war period of immigration Australia's and Canada's selection policies relied extensively on family migration to realise simultaneously the aims of population growth and industrial expansion requiring large inputs of unskilled labour. The decision in both countries to abandon racially and ethnically discriminatory entry policies was accompanied by the establishment of specific criteria emphasising educational and economic factors for the selection of those who neither had close family ties nor specific humanitarian claims as a basis for selection. The details of the criteria, the weighting given to them in the 'points' system and the procedures for selection have varied over time and between the two countries. Consistently, however, the third type of criterion for selection has been used to obtain the skilled labour and economic resources now considered necessary for economic development in a world economic system where labour-intensive manufacturing industries are no longer competitive with those in countries with lower wages.

In 1992 Australia and Canada had immigration programs which included family, economic and humanitarian components, as well as other special-entry categories such as the Canadian Retiree category which is being phased out (see Tables 1.7 and 1.8). While the criteria for the various categories are not precisely comparable, both countries select some family members solely on the basis of their close relationship to a permanent resident (the Preferential Family and Family Class) and other, more distant, relatives who meet additional criteria including occupational and educational qualifications (Concessional Family and Assisted Relative). Refugee and Humanitarian categories exist, although again the criteria differ for non-Convention refugees. The economic component of the programs, which is now referred to as 'Skill Migration' in Australia, makes provision for business people bringing in capital to establish a business or, in the case of Canada, to invest. Since 1992 Australia has also made provision for those with experience in large corporations. The Australian program distinguishes between those with an approved job offer (the Employer Nomination Scheme) and others who obtain the requisite points; Canada does not make this distinction though a job offer is a basis for obtaining points.

Despite the similarities in their selection categories, since 1984 Australia and Canada have come to differ substantially in the 'mix' of their immigration programs (see Tables 1.7 and 1.8). In particular, the economic/skill component in Australia has increased at the expense of the refugee component. Also, the non-points-tested Family Class in Canada is far more prominent than the comparable Preferential Family in Australia. For 1992–93 the significantly reduced Australian intake more closely resembled Canada's. Nearly half were preferential family members, the percentage of refugees increased although the Concessional Family and Independent categories were reduced with the skill category providing 29.7 per cent of the total intake. Both countries now operate a planning framework which sets the relative mix of those admitted under particular immigration programs. Variations between the mix of entry components is thus a reflection of a series of political decisions made by the Canadian and Australian governments in response to an assessment of national needs and the influence of diverse interest groups concerned not only

Table 1.7   Eligibility category of settler arrivals in Australia, 1984–92

Category	1983–84	1988–89	1990–91	1991–92
Family migration				
Preferential	30.9	21.6	25.9	25.4
Concessional	17.7	19.4	18.5	19.9
Total	48.6	41.0	44.3	45.3
Skill migration				
Employer nominees	5.1	5.6	5.5	3.4
Business migration	2.1	6.9	6.7	6.0
Independent*	9.5	17.5	27.5	28.1
Other	0.1	0.1	0.1	0.1
Total	16.7	30.1	39.8	37.6
Refugees/Humanitarian	21.2	7.5	6.4	6.7
Other	13.5	21.4	9.9	10.5
Total	69 808	145 316	121 168	107 391

* In 1983–84 and 1988–89 Independent includes those admitted under the Occupational
Shares Scheme.

Source: DILGEA 1992c

Table 1.8   Eligibility category of Canadian landed immigrants, 1984–92

Category	1984	1988	1990	1992 (planned)
Family class	49.6	31.7	34.3	40.0
Assisted relative	9.3	9.6	11.8	10.2
Entrepreneur/Business	9.2	9.3	8.6	11.2
Independents	14.0	30.8	25.0	16.6
Refugees	17.4	16.6	18.5	20.0
Retirees	2.6	2.0	1.6	2.0
Total	88 239	161 929	214 230	250 000

Source: EIC 1990b; 1991f; 1992c.

about the size of the intake but also about the characteristics of the
immigrants. The far greater role of refugees in the Canadian program,
indicating the influence of non-governmental lobby groups such as
churches and a long-standing governmental humanitarian commitment evident in the extensive intake of Indo-Chinese refugees, also

reflects the greater geographical ease of access of asylum seekers to Canada resulting from its lengthy border with the United States.

While the basic rationales for the family, humanitarian and economic selection of immigrants are clear, difficulties inevitably develop when an attempt is made to specify criteria for selection which will assure that the aims of the different segments of the immigration policy are realised. Although Australia has not had the same public debate over the definition of 'family' as has occurred in Canada, widespread debates have occurred in both countries about the selection of individuals who do not meet the United Nations Convention definition of 'refugee'. The major official response has been to develop *ad hoc* country or regional humanitarian programs providing entry under less restrictive conditions than apply to refugee status. Even more difficult than establishing entitlement to entry on the basis of family or refugee status is the selection of those for economic purposes. For the economic selection to achieve its purpose in the short term it is necessary to ensure that prospective immigrants not only have the necessary skills and resources but use them after arrival. This does not always happen because of often rapid changes in the economy which affect the labour market or investment opportunities. A consideration with far-reaching implications is whether such immigration is at the expense of skills development for the locally born. The longer term effects of 'economic' immigrants have proven even more difficult to establish and remain a topic of considerable debate. In a recent report the Economic Council of Canada (1991) concluded that the general economic effect of immigration was limited.

Apart from the difficulties inherent in actually determining whether particular selection criteria achieve their aims, the situation is further complicated by the way, regardless of the intentions of the policy-makers, potential immigrants may adopt their own strategies when seeking to immigrate. In particular, those entering in family reunion categories may be highly skilled, just as those entering in various economic categories may have close relatives already living in the country (see Chapter 3, Volume 2, the companion volume to this book). To ignore such 'overlap' when considering the likely effects of particular selection decisions is to oversimplify the selection process.

A further difficulty confronting those seeking to control the selection process is that not all those entering the country for lengthy periods are required to obtain permission to immigrate permanently. As part of the close historical and economic ties between Australia and New Zealand there is no barrier to New Zealanders settling permanently in Australia. Indeed, since the early 1980s, a substantial number have done so (shown in Table 1.7 where they constitute the majority of those in the 'Other' category). Although reciprocal freedom to visit across their border exists for Canadian and United States residents it does not extend to immigration. Under the US–Canada Free Trade Agreement and the yet to be ratified North American Free Trade Agreement (NAFTA) limited special provisions exist for professionals, businessmen and investors to move temporarily between Canada, the United States and Mexico for work purposes. The rationale for this arrangement is the need to facilitate economic co-operation and trade between the countries. Even in the absence of specific free trade and economic agreements, changing international patterns of economic relations and investment place growing demand and pressure on governments to facilitate the movement of businesspersons and employees of multinational and local enterprises. Often this involves granting temporary entry, albeit for extended periods of time. Although Australia, in particular, has historically avoided the use of 'guest workers' and temporary labour, there has been a substantial increase in the numbers of those granted temporary residence including working holiday makers, as well as those with specialist skills and executives of overseas companies (DILGEA 1992d, p. 15). Students and tourists are other major groups whose entry on a short-term basis governments seek to encourage for economic and diplomatic purposes, not by limiting or controlling entry but by facilitating it. However, Australia is more restrictive than Canada insofar as it requires all visitors, other than those from New Zealand, to obtain entry visas. It also has no scheme comparable to the Canadian Live-In Caregiver Program which offers permanent resident status after two years of temporary residence. Such relatively 'open' entry policies for temporary residents constitute a challenge for maintaining high levels of control over permanent immigration since, after entering legally, individuals then seek permanent resident status through processes which remove much of the initiative from officials in charge of immigrant selection.

Control of illegal immigrants

Internationally, governments are experiencing major difficulties in coping with large and growing numbers of illegal immigrants seeking to escape from the effects of political disruption and war or to find better economic opportunities. Despite their relative geographical isolation, especially in the case of island Australia, Canada and

Australia have not been immune to pressures from illegal immigrants and others seeking asylum. They have undertaken a variety of measures to handle what is seen as a growing problem. Canada's lengthy and readily permeable land border with the United States and its extensive experience throughout the 1980s of substantial numbers of those seeking refugee status have made its concerns for the control of illegal entry and refugee status seekers somewhat greater. This is evident in its long series of debates and legislation throughout the 1980s. An unanimous decision by the Canadian Supreme Court in 1985 that existing administrative discretion in respect to claims of refugee status was inadequate under the 1960 Canadian Bill of Rights and the 1982 Charter of Rights and Freedoms, which allegedly 'sent shock waves through Canada's Department of Employment and Immigration' hastened the legislative changes (Greene 1991, p. 133). In Australia, the increasing number of on-shore applications for refugee or humanitarian status (in 1992 approximately 23 000), and the reappearance of 'boat people' is reviving public concerns about the social justice aspect of the program's administration. There is more limited concern about the potential which exists for such 'unplanned' applications to affect the administration of the policy (National Population Council 1991b).

The Canadian experience is that some 30 000 individuals per year will seek asylum or refugee status (EIC 1992e, p. 10). In Australia, extensive media attention is given to the relatively small numbers of 'boat people', predominantly from Southeast Asia and China, who arrive illegally. Far more numerous, however, are those who arrive legally but then overstay the period allowed in their visas. The numbers of overstayers has grown since 1986 with a dramatic increase of 50 per cent between 1989 and 1990 to 90 000, a year later the number had declined by 13 per cent following a hardening of government policy (Borowski & Shu, 1992, p. 48). This period co-incided with the Tiananmen Square massacre and many overstayers were students from the People's Republic of China who were allowed to extend their temporary entry visas for a period of four years and to bring family members from China. The question remains as to why such special treatment should have been given to them (in early 1994, permission to remain permanently was granted) but not to other illegal immigrants who may be from situations of equal danger. In 1990–91 13 954 applications for extensions to a four-year temporary visa were received while a slightly smaller number of individuals applied to change to permanent resident status on the basis primarily of family ties (DILGEA 1992d, pp. 12–13).

In Australia and Canada the legislative measures to provide greater control over the procedures for handling applications from illegal entrants and the numbers of legal entrants who apply for permanent residence status after arrival have already been referred to. Supplementing these internal measures designed to provide more control of those who have actually landed, both governments have also moved to penalise companies which provide transport to passengers without valid entry documents. A furher development has been participation in a variety of international diplomatic initiatives designed to limit the extent of unauthorised departures. Such an important initiative has been the United Nation's Comprehensive Plan of Action for Indochinese Refugees. In many of these initiatives they also are working with countries of Western Europe, which are experiencing major inflows of illegals especially from Eastern Europe and North Africa.

Challenges for the future

After two centuries in which immigration has played a major part in their shaping, Canada and Australia are confronting a dramatically changing world order. The political alliances and economic relations which have dominated the international scene in the half century since the end of World War II are transformed. International population movements are increasing rapidly in size and complexity. Australia and Canada have, in general, been well served by their immigration policies. But those policies will not necessarily be appropriate for the next half century. While prediction is always a hazardous activity, a number of major issues confronting Canada and Australia can be discerned.

An 'open door' or a 'fortress'?

The first is the extent to which an 'open door' policy is maintained for permanent or temporary migrants. Since it is many years since either Canada or Australia had an 'open door' policy for permanent immigrants this issue primarily relates to temporary entrants. Economic and diplomatic imperatives have ensured that the temporary entry of tourists, students and business people is encouraged and allowed on a reasonably unfettered basis. With the emergence of regional trade groupings such as NAFTA and the encouragement of international firms (especially in the financial and services sector) to locate in Australia and Canada, the conditions exist for freer movement of skilled professional and technical workers and managers. This can often be done on the basis of long-term, but temporary, entry visas. While this may suit the needs of both business and government, the effects of such arrangements, which are likely only to increase in numbers, cannot be isolated from the impact of permanent immigration. Policy makers will need to factor in the effects of such long-term temporary migration when considering future levels of permanent migration and the provision of settlement services.

The experience of Europe, and indeed Canada and Australia, is that legal temporary migration may be used by individuals as a basis for gaining entry and then remaining, often applying for permanent resident status on humanitarian or other grounds. Although Australia has sought to prevent this happening by extensively vetting applicants for student visas from countries such as China where this has often occurred, such procedures are only possible where reliable records allow such patterns of overstaying to be established. More generally, the millions of visitors annually would make detailed vetting an impossible task. For this reason alone, a relatively open door policy for temporary entrants is likely to continue. This has proved to be the case even in Europe where there is widespread support for stronger measures to reduce the numbers of asylum seekers and illegal entrants. 'Fortress Europe' appears more as a goal and attitude than a realisable strategy. Hence, alternative methods of handling those 'overstayers' and asylum seekers who do enter will become critical. It is important that the dimensions of the problem of overstayers and illegals is understood since the significance of the numbers in Canada and Australia may well be less than the public and media realise.

The goals of immigration

The goals of any social policy are critical both in establishing its legitimacy and public support and in determining its implementation. There has been a tendency in Australia and Canada to view immigration as an end in itself and an immutable part of the social fabric. Even if such a view were sustainable it provides no guidance as to how the policy could be implemented. There is also increasing public questioning of such an assumption since many of the old justifications for migration based on population need are now seriously questioned. If immigration is not an end in itself what other social objectives can it serve and are there other ways of meeting them?

Among demographic arguments for immigration population growth has been the most prominent. The time is past when sheer numbers of people were needed to settle and claim large tracts of land or to provide a stimulus as consumers for a domestically oriented economy. There are serious questions as to the optimal population size especially in Australia (National Population Council 1992). Work in Canada and Australia has also demonstrated that immigration can do little to solve difficulties associated with the age structure of a 'greying' population. While demographic arguments for immigration have lost much of their force, immigration nevertheless has important implications for population policy.

Economic arguments for immigration are linked with policies on economic development and human resource development. Australia and Canada have already adjusted their policies in the direction of attracting skilled migrants seen as vital to the restructure of their economies for post-industrial knowledge-based industries. At the same time they have sought to attract business immigrants with knowledge and capital. Hence both labour and capital have become important objectives of their immigration policies. The challenge will be to effectively utilise the skills and capital brought by immigrants. This requires that the impact of immigration on the labour market and educational and training provisions for the existing population receives careful attention, both from a social justice and community relations perspective.

Humanitarian considerations have played an important role in the immigration policies of both Canada and Australia. In a period when the numbers of those fleeing persecution, civil unrest and poverty is increasing daily, the potential for immigration to assist some of these people is considerable. The challenge lies in determining which groups or individuals should be singled out for permission to immigrate. Already the moral dilemmas are apparent in Australia and Canada as on-shore applicants for asylum status vie for an inevitably limited number of places with those waiting outside the country. In the past, the tendency has been for the selected refugees to be those with a shared background or perceived as having most to offer in terms of skills or from a country to which there is some diplomatic responsibility. Should, perhaps, refugee status be provided for those who are most disadvantaged?

The founding of Canada and Australia are examples of how foreign policy aspirations become entwined with immigration. Foreign policy considerations were also important reasons for both

Australia and Canada abandoning their discriminatory immigration policies two decades ago. In the post-colonial world the foreign policy implications of immigration have become far more complex. Australia's relations with New Zealand are closely bound with the freedom of movement between the two countries while Canada's involvement in NAFTA and the US–Canada Free Trade Agreement is predicated on the facilitation of temporary movement. Willingness to accept refugees from particular regions may also serve foreign policy objectives associated with establishing goodwill in a region or with a valued ally. Immigration entry policy is, however, far too indirect a tool for use in developing specific foreign policy objectives. However, the immigrant population can play an influential role in the formulation of foreign policy. Events in Eastern Europe have affected Australian and Canadian communities which have been prominent in lobbying governments for diplomatic support to particular regimes or in seeking consideration for facilitating immigration from those regions. Also, existing communities may be seen as able to assist in the development of improved trading and diplomatic relations with their home countries. Especially in Australia which is seeking to develop closer ties with Asia, the local Asian communities are offically viewed as a potentially valuable resource in this endeavour. As this example indicates, migration patterns may be more influential on foreign policy than vice versa.

The social goals which immigration can achieve are diverse but rarely offered as major rationales for an immigration program. The exception is family reunion, to which both Canada and Australia have a long-standing commitment, not least because of the benefits in terms of stability and growth which it is seen to offer for the receiving country. Widely held social benefits of the diversifying of immigration sources has been the creation of more interesting and culturally enriched societies in Ausralia and Canada but this is not proposed as a goal for the formulation of immigration policies. The contrary is, however, sometimes advocated as a means of sustaining 'traditional' groups and their cultures whether these are of British, French or more recent origin. It is also offered in support of arguments that the migration policy must not threaten the 'social cohesion' of the society. Immigration has clearly altered the ethnic composition of both Australia and Canada since the very first period of European settlement. More recent attempts to ensure the entry of migrants of 'preferred' ethnic origin have proved to be only partially successful. Furthermore, within the present commitment of both Canada and

Australia to non-discriminatory entry policies, any move to target specific ethnic groups would produce international and local objections. Given the diversity of their populations, both Canada and Australia have actually achieved an enviable record internationally for social cohesion and harmony which many other countries would like to emulate. An important element in the achievement of this success has been settlement policies.

In Canada and Australia there is varied support for the diverse rationales for immigration. No one rationale is universally accepted although there is a generally high level of social acceptance for immigration 'in principle'. The different rationales for the program are reflected in the components into which it is organised: family, economic, humanitarian. Since neither country espouses an 'open door' policy for immigration limited numbers of places need to be allocated in a way which satisfies the various lobby groups. Ultimately this is a political decision, albeit one with ramifications for many areas of economic, diplomatic and population policy. Establishing the political legitimacy of the program and the ultimate mix is extremely important. Where, as in Australia, immigration is a major area of public policy the challenge is especially great.

The management of the immigration program

Australia and Canada both operate their immigration programs with wide latitude as to its size, nature and administration. The size of their immigrant intakes has varied dramatically over the last half century in response to domestic and international circumstances. Contrary to the views of the Economic Council of Canada, there is extensive agreement that the actual numbers immigrating may be far less important for the intended outcomes of the policy than the composition of that intake. Clear-cut criteria that can be used to determine the precise requirements of the intake have eluded policy makers, for the processes influencing immigration are ever-changing.

Despite difficulties in eliminating the uncertainty involved in formulating an immigration program, a major challenge now exists to ensure that selection and processing procedures are handled as expeditiously, fairly and humanely as possible. Demands that the 'integrity' of specific areas of the immigration program are not impaired are becoming increasingly common. Such expectations of accountability have increased dramatically for all areas of government, especially those involving critical personal decisions. There is little reason to expect them to decline.

Settlement policies

The ultimate effectiveness of any immigration program depends on whether its outcomes match the intentions of the policy makers. These intentions often differ from those of the individual immigrants whose motivation for migrating is personal rather than serving the national needs of their new home. The challenge for settlement policy is to ensure that both the individual migrant and the nation achieve their goals.

A major factor underlying the success of Australian and Canadian immigration policy has been a realisation that, to maximise the benefits to both the country and the nation, it is necessary to provide support for the new arrivals so that their potential contribution to the country can be realised. Both nations have been fortunate in having a developed social welfare tradition which is responsive to such needs. In a period of budgetary constraint considerable pressure exists to reduce the role of these welfare systems, not only for immigrants but for all citizens. The challenge will be to ensure that, in the process of restructuring which is underway, the benefits which have been gained through ensuring immigrants access to appropriate services and support mechanisms are not lost. The development of a migrant underclass would do little to contribute to social harmony.

A further challenge will be to ensure that as the composition of the immigrant population changes to include more skilled professionals, services needed by this group are available. Such services include ways of determining how best to evaluate their qualifications and expertise and how to assist them in gaining language skills and other cultural information necessary to work in an appropriate occupation.

Another even more critical challenge, especially at a time of economic recession, is to ensure that tolerance exists in the community. Given the major changes immigration has brought to Australia and Canada, both countries have displayed very high levels of adaptability in incorporating the diverse population. This, in itself, constitutes an important resource which needs to be built on in a period of severe recession such as both are now facing.

Many nations are finding that their own identity is being challenged and that the nature of their identity and ability to respond is affected by processes which bypass or ignore the role of the individual state. The extent and fluidity of population movements is increasing and for many of those involved the notion of permanent immigration may be irrelevant. For these individuals too 'citizenship', while it may be a valued legal resource, will not necessarily have the same connotations of attachment as once it did. How nations such as Australia and Canada, which have grown out of a mixing of diverse peoples, will be affected by such developments is problematic. While neither Australia nor Canada have made citizenship a basis for participation by permanent residents in most areas of society, any development in settlement policy will need to take into account the changing international salience of 'citizenship'.

Despite the many striking similarities between Australia and Canada in their experience of immigration, differences also abound. As both face the challenges posed by the rapidly changing world order these differences may be as significant as the similarities in determining their immigration policies.

CHAPTER 2

The International Movements of People

Allan Borowski, Anthony Richmond, Jing Shu and Alan Simmons

Introduction

International population movements are 'an enduring component of the world economic, social and political landscape' (Papademetriou 1988, p. 237). This chapter examines important recent changes in the scope and persistence, origins and destinations, and composition of international migration. Our analysis gives particular attention to the implications of global trends for Canada and Australia.

The chapter is in three parts. Part one reviews the 'facts'—what is known about world-wide migration trends. While there are many gaps in the facts, what is known confirms that the number of men, women and children 'on the move,' either for temporary reasons or for permanent settlement, has increased dramatically over recent decades in all parts of the world, such that international migration has become 'a preeminently global phenomenon' (Tomasi et al. 1989, p. 400) with corresponding implications for Canada and Australia. Part two reviews various theories that have been advanced to explain international migration. We note that current migration trends and patterns are the result of combined economic, cultural and social forces operating at the level of nations, communities and households. Part three explores a number of specific hypotheses on the effect of new global forces and their implications for Canada and Australia. Particular attention is given to the inter-linked trends toward post-industrial economy, globalised trade and consumption patterns, and post-modern patterns of social interaction and culture. These global transformations, we argue, fundamentally shape acceleration and

31

diversification of international movement. They also fundamentally shape Australian and Canadian immigration policies and flows.

Recent trends in international population movements

International population movements are by no means a new phenomenon. Massey (1990) distinguishes between four major periods in the history of international migration over the last 500 years. During the first period, from 1500 to 1800, international migration patterns were dominated by relatively modest but cumulatively important outflows from Europe to its overseas colonies. The period from 1800 to 1925, the second period, was characterised by a massive transfer of people from the industrial countries of Europe to a few former colonies. Of the more than 48 million emigrants who left Europe, 85 per cent went to Argentina, Australia, Canada, New Zealand, or the United States. Except for a small amount of return migration there was little movement during the 1930s and the 1940s: international migration was virtually stopped during this third period by restrictive immigration laws, the Great Depression and World War II. The fourth period, after World War II (the 1950s), was a time of resettlement migration among the industrialised countries.

To these four periods can be added a fifth. This last period witnessed an increase in the number and variety of both sending and receiving countries and major transformations in the pattern and composition of population movements resulting in migration becoming a global phenomenon. Temporary labour migration grew in the 1960s. This was followed by the growth in family reunion in the 1970s. The 1980s were characterised by a rise in refugee movements and economic migration (Salt 1989), a movement pattern that has continued into the 1990s. Women continue to move as part of family units, but increasingly they also migrate independently. These trends have been overlapping and cumulative. Today, more people cross national borders than ever before. International migration, involving an estimated 45–50 million persons per year (Segal 1991), has emerged as one of the most challenging issues affecting nearly every part of the world.

But as Koehn (1991) has pointed out, some of the most recent and challenging pressures have more often stemmed from the temporary movement of nationals out of their country of origin than from the permanent migration of immigrants. Temporary movement includes temporary labour migrants, tourists, transilients (skilled and professional workers, entrepreneurs, business persons, etc.), students, the victims of environmental disasters, and political refugees. Indeed, this chapter is concerned with both permanent and temporary international population movements.

Fundamental political, economic, social and cultural changes have given rise to emergent migratory movements. These changes are considered in later sections of the chapter. Here we outline the major patterns of international population movements since World War II. We consider movements both between and within the regions of the world.

Movements between regions

South–north population movements

The contemporary pattern of international migration can be generally characterised as involving heavy flows from less developed countries (mostly in the 'south') to the more developed countries (mostly in the 'north'). On the whole, the developed countries now have a positive net migration balance (United Nations, 1989). It has been estimated that in the 1980s there may have been as many as 50–55 million people living in countries outside their country of birth. Of this total about 60 per cent originated from developing countries. However, these flows have changed in terms of their volume, composition and direction with the fluctuating economic and social circumstances of particular sending or receiving countries (Hall, 1989).

East–west population movements

After World War II more than 10 million people left Eastern Europe for Western Europe (Widgren 1991). In more recent times, however, South–North migration has been supplemented by East–West migration. The political changes that have taken place in Eastern Europe and their effects on the movements of people have become the centre of attention in many West European countries. Eastern European countries have experienced very substantial population outflows. Although there has been an upsurge in various forms of short-term migration (for example, temporary labour migration), there has also been a revival of permanent migration.

For instance, the then Federal Republic of Germany (West Germany) reported a net migration of 1 million in 1989, mostly immigrants from what was then the German Democratic Republic

(East Germany). West Germany's population growth rate, 0.11 per cent in 1988, soared to a level of 1.58 per cent in 1989 (Monnier 1990). During the 1980s some 120 000 persons emigrated from Eastern Europe to Canada, chiefly from Poland and the Soviet Union. About 400 000 Soviet Jews moved to Israel between the end of 1989 and the end of 1991. It has been estimated that perhaps 2 million people a year could leave the Soviet Union following the new emigration law of 1993 (*The Economist* 1991; OECD 1991).

South–south population movements

There are two broad types of South–South movement: the first involves the movement of refugees; the second involves the movement of temporary labour migrants or guest workers on fixed-term contracts from one region (or country) of the South to another.

It has been estimated there are 30 million refugees and internally displaced people in the developing world. Unlike earlier involuntary migrations that were resolved by overseas resettlement, Third World refugees today typically find only temporary asylum in neighbouring states. The majority of these people languish in refugee camps or survive illegally without any hope of resettlement or eventual return home. To use just one example, the plight of the Kurds and Shiites of Iraq in the wake of the Persian Gulf War has received global attention but few offers of resettlement.

The considerable South–South movements of temporary labour migrants—a major means by which developing countries become involved in international migration—is discussed below.

Intra-regional movements

International population movements since World War II have also been characterised by extensive movements between the countries of the same region.

Western Europe

Between the 1950s and early 1970s the rapid industrial growth of Western Europe was greatly assisted by the flow of labour from Mediterranean countries. While Germany paved the way with the introduction of its guest worker program in the 1950s, during the following decade Sweden, France, the United Kingdom and Switzerland were the main poles of attraction. During the 1970s and 1980s family reunion and the steady growth in numbers seeking political asylum ensured large increases in foreign population stocks of such countries as Germany, Sweden, Switzerland and the Netherlands.

It is of interest to note that in Western European there have been marked differences between countries and over time in the rates of both immigration and emigration. For example, countries which were once major sources of emigration have more recently become countries of destination. Thus, such countries as Italy, Greece and Spain, which yielded large numbers of emigrants in the 1950s and 1960s, have recently become countries of destination (Salt 1989).

The Middle East

Developments in the oil industry led to flows of skilled technical and professional workers from the United Kingdom and the United States and manual workers from the Indian sub-continent to the Middle East in the 1940s. After World War II, this pattern continued. As the oil economies developed in the 1950s and 1960s migrant labour was drawn increasingly from the Gulf States and other Arab states. After 1973, rising labour demand required new sources of labour migration and Asian countries became major suppliers with contractors playing an important role in labour recruitment. This recruitment has typically been highly regulated involving restrictions upon the admission of migrants' dependants.

The scale of temporary labour migration has been such that in some of the Gulf States migrants outnumber the native population.

North America

During the 1950s the United States and Canada were major destinations for emigrants, particularly from Europe, seeking to permanently settle elsewhere. Since the 1960s and 1970s, the scale of movement to North America has grown and the major sources have become the countries of the South. Thus, at the beginning of the 1980s Mexico and the Caribbean countries were increasingly joined by the countries of Central America as major sources of immigrants.

Asia-Pacific Region

More recently, the continued rapid growth of the Japanese economy and the newly industrialised countries (NICs) of Asia have led to a growing amount of temporary labour migration within the Asian region. Taiwan is presently experiencing both emigration to more developed countries and immigration from less developed countries.

Immigration to Australia was mainly European until the 1970s. However, the introduction of a non-discriminatory immigration policy in 1973 and the extension of assisted immigration schemes to refugees have resulted in many more immigrants from Asian sources. Changes in the mix of the countries that yield immigrants to Australia have matched those of the United States and Canada.

South Africa and West Africa

South Africa has long been a magnet for migrant workers. In 1973 80 per cent of its gold-mining workforce was foreign (Appleyard 1988). However, changes in the flow patterns over recent years have been determined by the political relationships between South Africa and its neighbouring states.

With regard to coastal West Africa, economic growth in this area has attracted workers from the less developed areas of inland Africa. There has also been movement along the west coast. Thus, for example, during the 1970s and 1980s there was substantial movement to Nigeria (Salt 1989).

Types of international migration

As the discussion in the third part of this chapter shows, the relationship between population movements on one hand, and the globalisation of economic and political relations (and the increasing pervasiveness of a global culture) on the other, renders the distinction between types of international migration increasingly problematic (Castles 1992). Nevertheless, in tracing the international movements of people it is possible to distinguish between five major types of international migration, namely, permanent migration, refugee movements, temporary labour migration, tourism and illegal immigration. These are not necessarily mutually exclusive categories. Nor do they capture all types of movement. Cross-border commuters and students studying abroad are, for example, not included in these five types.

Permanent migration

Permanent migration refers to the movement of persons to another country for the purposes of long-term settlement. Although significant numbers of immigrants may be entering, residing, and even remaining permanently in many other countries, only four countries—the United States, Canada, Australia and New Zealand—would be considered permanent immigration countries insofar as they have policies which explicitly provide for permanent settlement. Subject to meeting selection criteria, successful applicants for migration are granted permanent residency status upon admission in these countries. Israel and Germany also accept immigrants but base their immigration policies largely on religion (Judaism) and ethnicity (German ancestry) respectively.

Migration with the intention of permanent settlement has continued to decline. The four traditional immigrant-receiving countries have together accepted a total of fewer than one million immigrants a year in recent years. Although these countries have long favoured immigration and the number of permanent immigrants admitted to Canada and the United States has risen in the last few years, the immigration policies of these countries have generally become increasingly restrictive, giving preference to migrants with assets, education, English proficiency and specific skills.

Essentially there are three criteria for admitting immigrants in these countries: family reunification, skill and occupation, and refugee status. It is likely that selection criteria will become more, rather than less, specific in the future (Kritz 1987; Hall 1989).

The countries of origin of permanent immigrants have shifted since the mid-1950s when the majority came from Europe or developed countries. All traditional receiver countries have experienced changes in immigration policy and increasing immigration from developing regions in recent years. As a result, the source countries and composition of recent intakes have changed dramatically. For most of the 1980s Europeans accounted for only about 10 per cent of immigrants to the United States. About 43 per cent of legal immigrants came from Asia and another 43 per cent from Latin America (McFalls 1991). In Australia, the Asian-born also represent an increasingly significant proportion of recent overseas immigrants. In 1990–91 27 per cent of all settler arrivals were born in Europe and 50 per cent were born in South-east, North-east and Southern Asia.

Refugees, displaced persons and asylum seekers

Refugees are people who have fled their country of origin for fear of being persecuted because of their race, religion, nationality, political opinion or membership of a particular social group. Displaced persons are those who have been displaced, either within or outside their own countries, by war, civil strife, extreme poverty or natural disaster. Asylum seekers are those who move from their own country to another where they claim protection (DILGEA 1991d and 1991a).

According to the Office of the United Nations High Commissioner for Refugees (UNHCR 1991a) there are some 17 million refugees and persons of concern to the UNHCR world-wide. The largest concentration is in the Middle East and South Asia (9 797 200), with 5 443 450 in Africa, 737 600 in Europe and North America, 592 100 in East Asia and the Pacific, and 118 950 in Latin America and the Caribbean. Most refugees are located in Third World countries and 80 per cent of them are women and children (DILGEA 1991d and 1991a).

In any discussion of refugee movements, the influence of international migration, world population patterns, war and famine must be considered. In the mid-1950s refugee problems were concentrated in Europe. Since then not only Northern Africa but the Congo, Ghana, Togo, Burundi, Uganda and Senegal have been involved in huge refugee movements. In 1970, a massive refugee problem emerged in South Asia when Bangladesh was created (Widgren 1989).

South-east Asia is a region that has suffered protracted warfare in the last several decades. Escaping from war, civil conflict, political persecution and economic hardship, millions of people in the region have been displaced from their own countries. Since 1975, some 2 million Indo-Chinese have left Vietnam, Laos and Cambodia (UNHCR 1991a) and more than one million have been resettled from South-East Asia to Western countries (Widgren 1989).

The invasion of Kuwait by Iraqi troops in August 1990, in addition to its military, political and economic consequences, sparked an exodus of more than three million people. Before the war began in January 1991, more than 700 000 people fled Iraq and Kuwait. Over the next two months another 65 000 people, mostly foreign workers, sought refuge in Iran, Jordan, Syria and Turkey. In the aftermath of the war the Iraqi refugee population in Iran skyrocketed from 50 000 to 560 000 in a two-week period in April 1991. The movement of Iraqi refugees to Iran was the 'fastest refugee movement in the 40-year history of UNHCR' (UNHCR 1991b).

In Western Europe, the number of asylum applications rose from about 70 00 in 1983 to 442 000 in 1990. The major political changes in Eastern Europe, which have made travel significantly freer, have had a further significant effect on these numbers, most noticeably in Germany. In 1989, the number of asylum-seekers entering that country was 121 000. This number rose to 193 000 in 1990, with Eastern Europeans comprising a large per centage of the total. In addition, Germany has absorbed large numbers of ethnic Germans who have a right of return under the German Constitution (397 075 in 1990 and some 260 000 to September 1991) (DILGEA 1991a; Loescher 1991). The vicious civil war (1992 and into 1994) between the Serbs, Croats and Muslims in what was formerly Yugoslavia precipitated substantial refugee flows.

Temporary labour migration

Temporary labour migration has become an important component of modern migration. As many as 30 million migrant workers, mostly from poor countries, could at present be working outside their homelands on a 'temporary' basis (Purcell 1991).

Western Europe

After World War II the countries of Western Europe received large numbers of immigrants but much of this immigration was seen by many of the countries as temporary labour or 'guest worker' migration rather than permanent migration. Western European countries recruited guest workers to ease their tight labour markets during the 1960s and 1970s. The intention was that all temporary migrants would eventually return home. However, there were strong economic incentives for employers to renew the contracts of temporary workers to avoid the need for training programs. Further, combined with economic and political instability in the Third World, some 5 million of the 30 million migrant workers who came to Western Europe remained in the labour force and were subsequently joined by more than 8 million immediate and extended family members. Thus, the 'temporary' labour migration to Western Europe, despite rigid rules designed to ensure that the guest workers merely worked in Europe but lived elsewhere notwithstanding, resulted in the permanent migration of approximately 13 million people (Teitelbaum 1985, p. 90).

The Middle East

A new era of labour migration emerged in the 1970s as the oil countries of the Middle East sought to attract large numbers of temporary foreign workers, first from neighbouring Arab states and then from South, East and South-east Asian countries. It was estimated that, overall, there were three million migrant workers together with one million dependants in the countries of the Middle East in the 1980s (Hall 1989). Until the Gulf War, Asians made up well over half the labour force in some Gulf States (*Australian*, 10 March 1991). However, as a result of the Persian Gulf crisis (which eventually led to the Gulf War in 1991), large numbers of temporary labour migrants fled from Iraq and Kuwait into Iran, Jordan, Saudi Arabia, Syria and Turkey between 1989 and 1990.

Asian Region

Temporary labour migration is now an important source of labour in many Asian countries. Thus, for example, the construction sector of the Malaysian economy employs several hundred thousand Indonesians while Taiwan, Singapore and Japan have all become receivers of sometimes clandestine migrant workers.

Africa

Intra-continental flows of workers are also important in Africa. For almost a century the development of South Africa's agricultural, mining and industrial sectors has attracted foreign workers from nearby less developed countries in southern and central Africa. Zimbabwe has attracted foreign workers, principally form Malawi and Zambia. In West Africa, Nigeria, the Ivory Coast and Gabon have drawn workers from countries elsewhere in West Africa (Stahl 1992).

International tourism

The volume of international tourism has increased dramatically in recent decades. According to World Tourism Organisation (WTO) statistics (1990a, 1991a and 1991b), the number of international tourist arrivals increased from 25 million in 1950 to 160 million in 1970 and to 425 million in 1990. Tourism receipts increased from US$2 billion in 1950 to US$18 billion in 1970 and US$230 billion in 1990. International tourism recorded its highest growth rate of arrivals and receipts during the period 1960–1980. From 1970 to 1990 arrivals more than quadrupled and receipts rose by a factor of nearly seven.

Europe and the Americas accounted for 84 per cent of arrivals and 79 per cent of receipts in 1990, compared to 96 per cent and 93 per cent in 1950. Although Europe still attracts the largest number of tourists, in 1990 it recorded the smallest percentage gain in arrivals and the second lowest gain in receipts.

The East Asia and Pacific region experienced the largest gain in market share of world arrivals and receipts in 1990. The newly industrialised countries of Hong Kong, the Republic of Korea, Singapore and Taiwan, along with Japan and Malaysia in particular, achieved the highest rate of growth among all regions in terms of tourist arrivals (for business and holiday purposes) and receipts from 1985 to 1990.

Based on the 1980–89 trend line in international tourist arrivals, WTO has estimated an annual average growth rate of 4.2 per cent during the 1990s and forecast 637 million arrivals by 2000. Global receipts (in 1989 US dollars) from international tourism will rise by 8 per cent a year and reach more than US$527 billion during the same period. Growth in international business travel is expected to exceed that of leisure travel by two or three points. Domestic tourism will grow rapidly in developing countries in line with their improving economic performance (WTO 1990a).

The growth rates in international tourism underscore the accelerating pace of population movements. Thus, in 1990 about 2.2 million people visited Australia on a short-term basis—an increase of 150 per cent compared with 1980. Most of these visitors were tourists. In addition, there were 56 000 long-term visitors (an increase of 51 per cent since 1980) (Borowski & Shu 1992, p. 32).

In the case of Canada, the 1989 statistics on air travel and border crossings to and from the United States and from overseas indicate that there was a record number of 106 million border crossings. (The equivalent number for Australia—all arrivals and departures—was 8.4 million and has risen since.) Trans-border aircraft movements in Canada rose from 259 647 in 1980 to 356 218 in 1990. Although the number of non-resident person-visits to Canada from abroad (including road and rail movements) remained between 35 and 40 million throughout the decade, the numbers from countries other than the United States rose from 2.1 million in 1980 to 3.3 million in 1989 (Aircraft Movement Statistics 1990; Statistics Canada 1990). Thus Canada and Australia experience a daily ebb and flow of travellers entering and leaving the country. In contrast to Australia, however, cross-border shopping adds greatly to the great wave of people moving back and forth across the Canadian border with the United States. Amid this throng, immigrants, temporary workers and asylum seekers constitute a relatively small proportion of the total movement.

Illegal immigration

A number of countries have experienced, and continue to experience, large and persistent flows of illegal immigrants. These flows have been fostered by the demographic imbalance between the developing and the developed countries (rapidly growing Third World populations), differentials in economic growth, employment opportunities and wages differentials and a demand for low-wage workers in a number of developed countries.

Although some countries have sought to strengthen the sovereignty of their frontiers through such measures as the extension of visa requirements and increased checks on employers to ensure they have not hired illegals, illegal immigration still continues (OECD 1990). It has been estimated there may be between 10 and 15 million illegal migrants in different parts of the world (Hall 1989).

The country experiencing the largest inflow of illegals appears to be the United States. Indeed, the scale of illegal immigration to the United States is massive. About 3 million illegals enter the United States successfully every year; perhaps 25 per cent of them remain permanently (Behar, 1990). In early 1987 it was estimated that the illegal resident population of the United States stood at between 4 and 5 million. After the *Immigration Reform and Control Act* (IRCA) legalisation program ended in late 1988, the illegal population was estimated to have been reduced to approximately 1.5–3 million (Borowski 1990; US Department of Justice 1989). However, the numbers of illegals in the United States appears to be again increasing and thus calling into question the effectiveness of the IRCA legislation.

Canada, Australia and New Zealand incur the problem of over-stayers who enter on a tourist or student visa and fail to abide by the conditions of their admission. European countries also experience a considerable amount of illegal immigration: the United Kingdom from South Asia, the Caribbean and South America; France from North and West Africa; and Germany from Turkey, Greece and Yugoslavia. In Asia, many foreign workers in Singapore, Hong Kong, Malaysia, Taiwan and, increasingly, Japan are illegally recruited. Indeed, it has been estimated that there about 300 000 illegal migrants in Japan from countries such as India, the Phillipines, Thailand and Iran. In Latin America the flow of labour from Colombia to Venezuela and from Bolivia to Argentina is for the most part undocumented (Appleyard 1992; Stahl 1992).

Implications for Canada and Australia

The acceleration and diversification of international population movements have profound implications for virtually all nations. In the case of wealthy nations, particularly those with a past history of nation-building through immigration and settlement and of humanitarian support of refugee programs, the implications are evident in the large and rising number of potential immigrants and refugee claimants. Western Europe has become an important immigrant receiving area and now sends few emigrants abroad. In this context, immigration and refugee flows to Canada and Australia now come predominantly from Asia, and also (particularly in the Canadian case) other regions, such as the Caribbean and Latin America. Illegal and undocumented flows to both Canada and Australia are relatively small compared to such flows to some other wealthy regions, but pressures for such flows may be rising. In the following section, we examine some of the major explanations of the causes of international population movements, giving particular attention to what these theories imply for understanding current and future trends in international migration which may affect Canada and Australia.

The causes of international population movements

Theories that explain the causes of various phenomena are crucial if the very practical goals of science, understanding and prediction, are to be realised. Indeed, the last part of this chapter speculates about the future of international migration based on contemporary understandings of its causes. These understandings have their sources in the theories of international migration developed over the years by social scientists working in such disciplines as sociology, economics, anthropology, demography and geography.

As shown below, theories of international migration have undergone major changes. They have grown in number and complexity. New theories have replaced older ones which were found wanting in their explanation of a phenomenon which has become increasingly multi-faceted in the light of ongoing changes in the world at large. In this respect, the history of the evolution of theories of international migration parallels the history of sociological theory concerning the causes of other social phenomena. Theories of the causation of international migration and, for example, aetiological theories of crime and delinquency have, over the years, become progressively more complex and moved from relatively simple, sometimes mono-causal explanations to explanations involving a multivariate approach which acknowledges the influence of more and more contributing and interacting factors.

The theories

In this part of the chapter we overview some of the major theories of international migration. Ideally a theory of international migration needs to be able to explain ' . . . the scale, direction and composition of population movements . . . the factors which determine the decision to move and the choice of destination, the characteristic modes of social integration in the receiving country and the eventual outcome, including remigration and return movements' (Richmond 1988e, p. 7). The intent here is not to canvass all theories of international migration. Rather, what follows is an overview of a select number of contributions which capture some of the major themes and key turning points in theorising about the causes of migration. The body of literature on theories of migration is quite substantial. Because of the rich theoretical assortment several writers have attempted to create a semblance of a typology. Thus, for example, Stahl (1988) distinguishes between supply side theories (those explaining why people seek to move) and demand side theories (those which explain how the levels of immigration that are acceptable to immigrant-receiving countries are determined). Massey (1990) distinguishes between economic and social foundations of migration. And Papademetriou (1988) differentiates between the 'classical' school of migration theory and the 'conflict' school. The former attributes the decision to migrate to individuals' rational cost–benefit calculations while the latter views international migration as part of the international process of capital accumulation. He argues that modifications to both schools provide a richer, 'converged' explanation of international migration.

The theories considered here are push–pull theory, social networks theory, structural theory, and the theory of involuntary migration. Consideration is also given to the role of gender in the migration process. This part of the chapter concludes by considering the current state of migration theory.

Push–pull theory

Push–pull theory represents one of the traditional explanations of the 'voluntary' movement of people from one place to another, normally for the purposes of permanent settlement. First popularised by Lee (1966), it takes as its departure points global inequality and differential opportunities. The theory is centred on the notion that people move in response to some combination of social, political and economic push and pull factors—some remote, others proximate—in the countries of origin and destination. Thus, migration is seen as the result of the decisions of individual actors who, in pursuit of economic benefits, social mobility or family reunion, engage in a rational cost-

benefit calculation. This personal calculus leads them to leave countries of often low or insecure socio-economic status (and/or countries
experiencing violence) and migrate to the more affluent and stable
immigrant-receiving countries.

The criticisms of this theory are many. They have their origins
in the changing pattern of migration in Europe and the Middle East
from the 1960s onwards: supposedly temporary labour migration
resulting in permanent settlement, illegal immigration, and the movement of workers from Third World countries to the Middle East and
other newly industrialising Third World countries (Boyd 1989; Richmond 1991c). For example, the theory has been criticised on these
grounds.

- its inability to explain why similar movements do not arise out of
  other equally 'poor' countries;
- its inability to explain why certain regions within a country produce large outflows while other regions of the same country
  produce little or none;
- its limited ability to predict the origins of and changes in migrant
  flows;
- its inability to explain the large flows of people between the more
  advanced countries of the world, and
- its inability to explain the persistence of migrant flows even when
  the original pull factors lose their salience.

Portes and Borocz (1989) also highlight the first two criticisms
of push–pull theories. They go on to point out that addressing the
first criticism demands that consideration be given to the macrostructural determinants of the differences in migration patterns among
nation states. Addressing the second, according to Portes and Borocz,
demands consideration of the microstructural causes of the differences
in migration patterns among individuals within the same country of
region. The macrostructural determinants—the features of the larger
social structures which either constrain or facilitate the choices of
individuals—have their source in the history of past economic and
political contact and power asymmetries between sending and receiving nations, a matter which we return to below. The microstructural
causes have their source in the transnational social networks that
develop as a result of migration. Indeed, these networks permit immigration theorists to address the fifth criticism of push–pull theory:
the persistence of immigration even when some of the pull factors
(for example, better employment opportunities) may have substantially weakened.

Social network theory

Migrant social networks are 'sets of interpersonal ties that link together migrants, former migrants, and non-migrants in origin and destination areas through the bonds of kinship, friendship and shared community origin' (Massey 1990, p. 69). These ties are often rooted in a very strong sense of obligation to those family, friends and community members who live in other countries. Social networks can facilitate migration because they lower the costs of travel, information and job search costs, opportunity costs while engaged in job search, and the psychic costs of relocating (Massey 1990).

However, the existence of networks and push and pull factors are insufficient to explain migration to the major immigrant-receiving countries. All of these countries have selection criteria which are typically restrictive and, in times of economic downturn in particular (when some of the pull factors have weakened), they are often keen to limit the numbers of immigrants entering. The continued immigrant flows in these circumstances and the selectivity of the destinations chosen is explained by the notion of 'chain' migration, that is, migration that is mediated through migrant social networks (Birrell 1990, p. 1). Where family reunification is provided for under the immigration laws of a country the extent of previous immigration and the size and distribution of social networks of previous immigrants can have a major bearing on the potential for future immigration (Arnold et al. 1989).

Perhaps the major criticism of social network theory, as previously noted, is its inability to explain the origins of a given migration flow, only its persistence. Snowden (1990) also criticises it for its inability to include the role of the state. However, Snowden is not quite correct. Social network theory represents an important advance on push–pull theory in two respects. First, since it underscores the importance of linkages between countries for the understanding of population movements it represents a 'structural' approach to explaining immigration. It thus belongs to the genre of immigration theory that accommodates the role of the state. Second, it represents an approach to understanding the causes of migration that seeks to link the structural and individual determinants and emphasises their interaction.

Structural theories

Reference was made earlier to Papademetriou's 'conflict' school of migration theory which views migration as part of the international process of capital accumulation. Mention was also made of Portes and Borocz's (1989) explanation of migration in terms of the economic and political contacts and power asymmetries between sending and receiving nations. At the heart of both explanations is the notion of linkages between the sending and the receiving countries.

The migration trends of the 1970s and 1980s described in the first part of this chapter, particularly the trends in international labour migration, resulted in the development of new theories to explain the size, direction and persistence of migration flows. These theories viewed migration as structurally determined: that is, stemming from migration systems in which countries are linked by flows (such as those facilitated by social networks) and counterflows of people as well as economic and political relations between countries (Boyd 1989). Because structural theory views sovereign states as part of a global system of interacting states that are influenced by transnational and international political and economic linkages, it can also be described as a 'globalist' explanation of international migration (Zolberg 1989).

The various structures which generate international migration include, for example, the interrelationships between the economies and societies of former colonialist powers and their former colonies, international trade and tourism, study abroad, and transnational business practices. These practices may involve the movement of capital to less developed countries by multinational corporations seeking to take advantage of cheaper labour. Indeed, a perspective on international population movements (the 'new international division of labour' perspective) underscores the dependency between countries for capital and labour stemming from the restructuring of the world economy (Inglis & Wu 1992).

Transnational business practices also include the relocation of people by transnational recruitment agencies from poorer countries to meet unskilled labour needs in advanced countries, a process which resulted in the then 'periphery' countries of Spain, Italy, Greece and Turkey becoming the suppliers of labour (guest workers) to the industrialised core of France, Germany and Switzerland between the 1950s and early 1970s (Pedraza 1991, p. 307). Transnational recruitment agencies also facilitate the exchange of 'transilients'—skilled and highly qualified migrants between advanced countries (Richmond 1988b).

Involuntary migration

A distinction between 'voluntary' and 'involuntary' migration is widely used, the latter referring to forced movements (such as the slave trade) and to refugees. However, there are theoretical grounds for regarding the dichotomy as inappropriate. Thus, Richmond (1988a; 1991c; 1993) points out that all individual decision-making is constrained by structural influences, but the degree of freedom available to individuals in their decision-making is often a function of the situation in which they find themselves. He suggests that it is better to think in terms of a continuum between proactive and reactive decision-making. The overwhelming majority of migrants, both economic and political, fall somewhere between the two extremes. By the same token, the distinction between economic and political determinants is also harder to make as they combine with developmental and environmental factors to produce strong inducements to migrate (Richmond 1988e; Shenstone 1992).

An enduring feature of international movements since World War II has been the successive waves of refugee flows. These flows are likely to continue unabated during the course of the 1990s. The notion of 'forced migration' is typically associated with refugee flows and migration theorists have also sought to account for this type of international movement.

In Zolberg's (1989) view refugees in the developing world arise mostly as a by-product of two major historical processes which, when combined, generate violent conflicts and refugee movements. These two processes are the formation of new states and confrontations between the dominant and subordinate classes over the social order in the new states. They result in even greater refugee concentrations when external intervention spurred by superpower rivalry is an added dimension, for example, Afghanistan and Central America (Gibney 1991). Similar processes are also at play in parts of the developed world, for example, in some of the newly independent states of the Commonwealth of Independent States.

The power of these forces to generate refugee flows is starkly and recently exemplified by the former six-republic federation of Yugoslavia. Between June 1991 and the middle of 1992 2.3 million people fled their towns and villages in the wake of the civil war arising from Serbia's efforts to resist the moves towards independence by Croatia and Bosnia-Herzegovina. Of this number almost 400 000 found their way to Sweden, Germany, Switzerland, Austria and Hungary. Together with the large numbers seeking asylum in Europe, the wave of Yugoslav refugees has confronted Europe with its largest refugee crisis since World War II (Reuters and *The New York Times* 1992).

Ecological disasters can also generate involuntary movements. These disasters are not always natural ones but can be induced (man-made)—a consequence of the processes just described, for example, the Sahel region of Africa and the Ethiopia.

It should be noted, however, that political turmoil (including civil strife) and/or ecological disaster do not necessarily result in refugee flight across international borders. Whether those affected by these conditions become refugees is largely a function of their mobility, location in relation to international borders, existing migratory networks and whether the governments of neighbouring countries will permit border crossings. Where political and/or ecological conditions result in the *internal* displacement of people who may, as a result, have to endure precarious living conditions such people may not, from a purely legal point of view, be recognised as refugees (Nef 1991; Zolberg 1989). A recent example of massive internal displacement is offered by Croatia, Serbia and Bosnia-Herzegovina where, by mid-1992, 1.4 million people were internally displaced (Reuters and *The New York Times* 1992).

Gender and migration

Any discussion of the causes of international migration would be incomplete without some consideration being given to the role played by gender in population movements. The conventional wisdom is that the migrant is typically a young, economically motivated male who makes the decision to migrate.

The young male is either accompanied by a female partner or, at some subsequent time, is followed by her in a movement that is secondary to the original migration decision and movement of the young male.

The conventional understanding of migration decision-making, however, does not stand up to close scrutiny. As Pedraza (1991) points out in her review of the literature on women and migration, there have been and continue to be large international migrant flows that are female-dominated. These include, for example, legal migration for the purposes of permanent settlement to the United States, refugee flows which, initially at least, are commonly dominated by women and children (for example, from the former Yugoslavia), and the flow of Filipina domestics to Canada and other countries. In Australia's case women now make up just over 50 per cent of permanent migration (Young & Madden 1992, p. 5).

These flows can be the result of gender differences in economic and social roles which influence the process of migration decision-making. Thus, female migration flows may be the result of decisions taken independently by women or they may be the result of decisions taken by households in which gender looms large in the decision-making process. The latter is especially so in households characterised by 'normatively prescribed kinship and gender roles as well as a hierarchy of power ....' (Pedraza 1991, p. 308). As Boyd (1989) points out, gender differences in roles can also, for example, modify the conceptualisation of household strategies as necessarily being predicated on rational economic behaviour. They can also influence the sex composition of labour migration and the formulation and implementation of immigration policy, for example, where it is assumed males are breadwinners and females are always dependent spouses. (How gender differences in roles have influenced immigration policy in Australia and Canada is discussed in Chapter 6.) Clearly, then, gender differences in economic and social roles can have a strong bearing on the determinants of migration and, indeed, its consequences.

The current state of theory

Although the discussion so far has captured only some of the major themes and turning points of international migration theory it should be evident that the body of theory is quite varied. A much more detailed analysis of the literature reveals, for example:

- theories steeped within different disciplines;
- theories emanating from the same discipline but steeped in different ideological outlooks resulting in widely divergent explanations of migration;
- theories which differ in terms of their unit of analysis. Some seek to explain the migration behaviour of individuals, others focus on the family and still others treating the household as the appropriate unit of analysis;
- as noted above, theories concerned with the persistence of migration flows over time rather than their causes in the first instance, and
- theories which look at only some types of movement, for example, involuntary/refugee movements, and exclude others.

Given this range of theories, which represent the most adequate explanations of international migration?

Many social scientists fail to stipulate the criteria for assessing their own theories. The advantage of this reticence is that critics are certain to employ the wrong criteria and, for the theorist, 'it is better to be perennially misunderstood than found wanting by one's own standards' (Gibbs 1972, p. 59). Nevertheless, it is possible to identify several criteria for assessing the adequacy of a social theory. These criteria include the scope or 'fertility' of theory, its parsimony or simplicity, and its clarity, logical consistency and precision. Perhaps the most important criterion, however, is that of predictive power or agreement with observations (Valentine 1982). But an adequate explanation of international migration needs to do more than meet these criteria. It also needs to be comprehensive enough to deal with the diversity of international migration. No current theory appears to be able to meet all of these requirements. In fact, it may be impossible to develop a comprehensive theory that is widely sub-scribed to, especially in light of the dynamic nature of international population movements.

Promising directions

Although there is currently no single model or approach to inter-national migration which can adequately account for the complexity of contemporary international population movements, this does not mean that we lack useful hypotheses for understanding broad trends and their implications for specific countries. A consensus is devel-oping among scholars of migration theory that explanations of international migration for any given historical case must link social–structural constraints to, and opportunities for, movement at the global, national and local levels in the sending and receiving countries ('macro' determinants) and individuals' plights, roles, mo-tivations and decisions to move ('micro' determinants) (Koehn 1991; Pedraza 1991). As Boyd (1989) points out, migration decisions by individuals or groups (families, households and communities) are made within the context of certain constellations of structural fac-tors ranging from the international politico-economic system to the emigration and immigration policies of the sending and receiving countries.

From the above perspective, the identification of new structural factors shaping international migration is therefore a key step, although not the only step, in explaining emerging immigration pat-terns. The next part of this chapter pursues the structural dimension by examining emerging transformations in global economic and cultural relations between countries and how these are shaping immigration policies and patterns in the Australian and Canadian cases.

Global transformation

World migration patterns and the place of Canada and Australia in them are being transformed by three closely connected forces: the emergence of post-industrial technology; the globalisation of production, trade and consumption; and the rise of post-modern patterns of social interaction and culture. What is often referred to as the 'fifth industrial revolution' (Chirot 1990) in computers and communications plays a pivotal role in the transformation of international economic, social and cultural relations. These technological changes—and their social and cultural correlates—are not autonomous; rather, they arise from the search for profits within the international capitalist system, as well as from military and economic competition between nations.

In the last twenty-five years population movements, and the role of migrants (men and women) in the international division of labour, have been transformed by the global developments described above (Richmond 1969; Petras 1981; Sassen 1988; Simmons 1990). The new global forces have led to various specific changes in immigration patterns to Canada and Australia, including the following: a diversification of short-term movements (tourism, students studying abroad, workers in visas); rising numbers of individuals in poor countries seeking asylum and employment in Canada and Australia; a countertendency for both countries to tighten their control over permanent immigration and settlement from abroad by raising admission criteria (re schooling and work skills, etc.) for worker immigrants, increasing capital and other requirements for business immigrants, and defining more precisely those eligible to enter as refugees. Illustrations of these trends and the effect of global forces on them are provided below.

An accelerating diversity of movement

The accelerating pace of population movement is exemplified by the rapid growth in international tourism described earlier in this chapter. Even the category of 'landed immigrants' under-estimates the actual number of persons entering Canada who meet the UN approved definition of an 'immigrant'—a person remaining for one year or more. In the last decade (1981–90) the number of long-term visitors has risen from 60 000 to over 224 000. When added to the 'landed immigrant' series this represents an increase in the number of UN-approved definition 'immigrants' from 188 800 in 1981 to 437 700 in 1990. (The equivalent Australian statistics—permanent and long-term settlers and visitors—are 152 790 in 1981–82 and 177 960 in 1989–90.) Canadian and Australian estimates are gross figures, excluding returning residents.

Reflecting global changes and Canada's place on the Pacific rim, by 1990 more than half of the landed immigrants, and 44 per cent of those arriving as non-permanent residents, were from Asian countries. Hong Kong, the Philippines, mainland China, Sri Lanka and India being the main source countries (Michalowski 1991). Not all of these necessarily enter the labour force. Some of those admitted for a year or more are students. A substantial proportion of those arriving as landed immigrants are dependents, or sponsored family members and assisted relatives, who are not intending to seek employment, at least at first. However, an increasing proportion of those who enter the labour force on arrival, or soon after, do so with temporary employment authorisations. The number and duration of these authorisations has been rising steadily since they were introduced in 1973. At the beginning of the decade (1980–89) immigrant workers arriving annually exceeded the person years of employment provided by temporary workers, but by 1983 the reverse was the case. (In contrast to that of temporary workers, the labour force contribution of landed immigrants, if measured in person-years, is cumulative. However, it must be adjusted for emigration and subsequent withdrawal from the labour force.) In the 1980s, three out of four temporary workers were male but there was a greater propensity for female workers to remain in Canada more than a year, particularly those in domestic service. However, as the number of asylum applicants grew in 1980s, an increasing number of employment authorisations were exempt from prior validation. That is, they were issued without regard to whether Canadian residents were available for employment and without restriction as to the nature of the job sought. Males predominated among the asylum applicants who were more likely to remain in Canada for extended periods of time than those who came with prior authorisation (Richmond 1991b; 1991c; Michalowski 1991).

Post-industrial economy

The increasing use of temporary employment authorisations is one aspect of the structural changes that have taken place in the Canadian economy which, in turn, reflect the effects of demographic shifts, technological change and globalisation. In terms of employment, primary and secondary industries have declined while the tertiary and quaternary sectors of the economy have grown. In the period 1981–86, industries with above-average rates of growth in terms of employment accounted for 63 per cent of employed persons in 1986. The fastest growing industries were business, personal and other services including recreation, accommodation and food, together with health and social services. Over a quarter of the labour force was employed in declining industries, the most severely affected being primary textiles, leather products, machinery, and metallic and non-metallic products including paper. There was a differential impact of these structural changes on men and women, as well as on immigrants and non-immigrants. A third of all men were in declining industries compared with 13.5 per cent non-immigrant women and 17.7 per cent immigrant women. Recently arrived (1981–86) women from Europe were more likely to be in declining industries than others. However, overall Third World and other recent immigrants were more likely to be found in the expanding sectors than the Canadian-born and earlier cohorts of male immigrants (Economic Council of Canada 1991b; Seward & Tremblay 1991).

However, many of the jobs created in the expanding sectors are in the relatively unskilled traditional areas of food and personal services. Furthermore, the process of 'de-industrialisation' has led to a decline in traditional blue-collar employment in relatively well-paid and unionised locations. The labour market is stratified and largely segregated by gender. The result is a process of 'segmented structural change' in which immigrants and temporary workers are incorporated at various levels depending upon gender, ethnicity, length of residence, education, qualifications and entry status (Richmond 1992a). When 1991 census figures are available it is likely that decline in the secondary manufacturing industries will be even more evident, accelerated by the effects of the Canada–US–Mexico Free Trade Agreement and the deep economic recession since 1989. Recently-arrived immigrants invariably have higher unemployment rates than the Canadian-born and the foreign-born who are longer established (Beaujot et al. 1988b; Richmond 1988a). The same is true of recently-arrived immigrants to Australia (Jones & McAllister 1991).

The more 'dynamic' industries in the service sector were those where technological change is important and there was greater involvement in international competitive markets (Economic Council of Canada 1991). They accounted for 22 per cent of the labour force in 1986 (24 per cent males and 20 per cent females). Altogether, immigrants were slightly under-represented in these sectors and this was due to the smaller proportion of the most recent arrivals in fields such as transportation, communications and business services and their greater representation in traditional services. Recently arrived immigrant women from Third World countries with low levels of education were over-represented in low-paid jobs and declining industries (Seward & Tremblay 1991).

Globalisation of production and consumption

The term globalisation refers to the process through which economic and cultural forces organise communities around the world into a unitary system of production and consumption. Through such globalisation of industrial production final consumer goods, such as automobiles, are assembled in one country from component parts which are produced in several (even many) other countries. This method of organising production has led to significant relocation of labour intensive manufacturing to low wage (less developed) nations and to other changes that are leading to the 'new international division of labour' with consequent implications for employment opportunity and international migration. Through the globalisation of consumption, products assembled in one country are then advertised and sold throughout the world. This promotes the spread of similar consumer and life-style values from developed to under-developed nations, a cultural globalisation process which in turn also has implications for migrant motivation.

Globalised production and consumption are both very dependent on advanced technology. High-speed and accurate satellite communications are essential for co-ordinating production schedules of component parts. Similarly, sophisticated computers permit control of inventory, shipping, and other management tasks required for the international assembly and distribution of products. In addition, complex but inexpensive computer chips lower the purchasing price of radios and televisions, and the wide diffusion of these receivers in turn facilitates consumer access to the media and advertising. Finally, expanded high-speed aeroplane travel allows managers, technical experts and consultants to meet at different production sites at short notice. The high demand for increasingly efficient technology promotes technological change and further expansion of the global system.

International migration patterns affecting Canada and Australia have been significantly shaped in recent years by the forces of globalisation. The shift to the new international organisation of production and consumption has affected migrant motivation in countries where Canadian and Australian immigrants originate. It has also affected Canadian and Australian policies on immigration.

The impact of globalisation on countries where migrants originate is extremely complex (see Simmons 1990). While it is difficult to generalise across countries, some international trends may be noted. Perhaps the most significant trend is the way in which nations around the world have adapted their national economic planning to adjust to global trade and competition. Globalisation promotes a 'restructuring' of production and trade and policies toward export-oriented development. The exported products may be of any kind—agricultural goods, forest products, services in banking or tourism, or industrial goods—provided that they correspond to the country's comparative advantage in international trade. Countries which previously relied on import-substitution industrialisation have discovered that inward-looking polices of this kind fit poorly with the new globalisation. Protected by tariffs, their industrial products are often too expensive to compete internationally. Both market forces and international agencies, such as the International Monetary Fund, have obliged poor, indebted Third World nations to restructure their economies in an effort to be more efficient and to be more export-oriented. Wealthier nations, such as Canada and Australia, have tended to pursue this restructuring based on the logic of international markets, without external pressure from the IMF.

Structural adjustment over the 1980s in most Third World countries has been associated with rising pressure for emigration, but the mechanisms and outcomes have varied substantially from one country and region to another. Many countries in Latin America, the Caribbean and South Asia have experienced a net withdrawal of foreign investment and rising unemployment (World Bank 1991). These trends have tended to sustain and even increase economic pressure for Third World workers to emigrate. Where more attractive migrant destinations have been available, such as has been the case for many small countries in the Caribbean which had established important migration bridges with the United States and Canada, the outflow of migrants over the 1970s and continuing into the 1980s has been massive (Simmons & Guengant 1991). Where such destinations have been restricted, the increasing potential for international movement has tended to promote illegal and undocumented movement (for instance, in the cases of North African migrants in Europe, or Haitian and Mexican migrants in the United States).

In other world regions, such as Southeast Asia, a number of newly industrialising countries had already established themselves as attractive sites for labour-intensive, export-oriented industrial assembly. In some countries, such as Malaysia, labour demand has been high and pressure to emigrate low. In others, such as the Philippines, assembly plants and other export-producing firms have provided few jobs relative to labour supply, so the pressure toward emigration has continued to be high, as is evident particularly in high levels of movement to the United States (INS 1991), considerable movement to Canada (EIC 1991) and a Filipino diaspora in Australia and even Japan.

The impact of these changed world conditions has been similar for Canada and Australia. In the Canadian case, the number of applications for immigration has risen steadily and created long waiting periods, in some cases approaching three years, for a final decision (Simmons 1990). In this situation of high interest in immigrating to Canada, the government has introduced significant application fees to cover costs. In addition, the number of refugee claimants arriving to Canada as visitors then claiming asylum after arrival rose dramatically toward the end of the 1980s, in part related to the increase in numbers of refugees around the world and expanded communications and travel networks, and (in the case of claimants from countries such as Trinidad, Guyana and Brazil) in part related to economic crisis in their home countries. In 1989, the Canadian government introduced new legislation to tighten control over refugee admissions and to discourage those who sought to help claimants enter the country without approval (Simmons & Keohane 1992). However, some aspects of the legislation (such as the power to return claimants to a 'safe' third country) have been difficult to enforce. Other provisions may run counter to the national Charter of Rights. In any case, large numbers of claimants continue to present themselves. Some 30 000 or more asylum applicants have arrived annually over recent years (Simmons 1990).

New legislation introduced in 1992 (Bill C-86) is designed to achieve more effective control over immigration and refugee movements into Canada. It is part of a 'harmonisation' process arising from inter-governmental consultations between the European Community (EEC), Canada, the United States and Australia. It is complementary to the Schengen and Dublin agreements (1993), which regulate entry into Europe. The sixteen participating states have agreed to act in concert according to a 'strategy platform' developed in 1991, which deals with economic development, asylum and migration policy, regional stability and security (Blumenthal, 1991; Intergovernmental Consultations 1991; Widgren 1991).

Australia has also experienced a large increase in the numbers coming to Australia for a temporary stay and then applying to remain permanently. Between 1986–87 and 1989–90 the numbers seeking permanent residence after their entry to Australia doubled to 33 000. In 1990–91 just under 13 000 people were granted resident approvals. Among the permanent resident applications are a growing number of refugee claimants. The number of on-shore refugee applications has grown from 3590 in 1989–90 to 13 950 in 1990–91 (Borowski & Shu 1992, pp. 33, 35–36).

Globalisation has also affected labour demand in Canada and Australia and, through this, led to shifts in immigration policy. Canadian structural adjustment is evident in a new (1989) Free Trade Agreement between Canada and the United States and the North American Free Trade Agreement (NAFTA) between the United States, Canada and Mexico, which was originally signed in August 1992. The idea that Australia enter into a free trade agreement with the United States and/or some of its more proximate neighbours has been floated at times but more store has been placed on global tariff reduction within the General Agreement on Trade and Tariffs (GATT) (Boswell 1992). Structural adjustment is also evident in lower import tariff levels. Industries which had been developed since World War II on the basis of protective tariffs are undergoing a massive restructuring. Large numbers of plants are closing down. In Australia, the footwear, clothing, textile and automobile industries have been especially hard hit. In Canada, some plants are moving to the United States. In both countries, thousands of jobs have been lost. These national trends cannot, of course, be fully separated from a more general restructuring of international industry, the declining fortunes of North American automotive and other industrial producers, and a general recession in North America and Australia over the period from 1990 to at least 1993. The growth industries in Canada and Australia, such as banking, computer software, telecommunications, and advanced technology industry (for example, in bio-technology, the production of plastic tapes, etc.) benefit highly skilled workers primarily.

Immigration has always been viewed in Canada and Australia as an important tool for national economic development. Within the current era of global competition, this strategy has led to a preference for particular kinds of immigrants. In the early 1980s, for example, Canada adopted policies favouring two new classes of immigrants who would promote Canadian economic growth: entrepreneurs (who had business experience and an investment plan), and investors (who committed themselves to making investments in Canada). Australia has also had a business migration program in place since 1981. This was replaced by a new business skills category at the beginning of 1992. Currently, relatively few worker immigrants are admitted to Canada (see below), and in addition the criteria for accepting such independent immigrants have been modified in order to encourage only those with very high skills. For example, as of early 1992, applicants who wish to come to Canada as college or university professors in certain high technology fields (computer science, for instance) are no longer required to have proof from their employers that qualified Canadian residents are not available. The list of occupations which are favoured in the selection system has been 'tightened' (that is, reduced and defined more precisely).

In Australia's case, there has been a steady rise over the last decade in the skill profile of immigrants. Thus, the proportion of the total migrant intake classified as professional, technical and related, and skilled trades increased from 22.8 per cent in 1981–82 to 32.4 per cent in 1989–90. The increase in the skill level in recent years has been achieved by the increased selectivity of the immigration program, that is, through refinements in the points test used for selection. This increased selectivity was recommended by the FitzGerald Report (CAAIP 1988).

In the Canadian case, very recent changes in policy (since 1990) reflect both globalisation and the recession of the early 1990s. Following the pattern in the previous recession (early 1980s), relatively few workers are currently being admitted. In 1990–91, only about 10 per cent of landed immigrants were 'selected workers' (that is, workers themselves, excluding accompanying family members), such that the bulk of the inflow consisted either of sponsored relatives of previous immigrants or of refugees. A related trend is the rise in visitor visas over recent years which reflects the search for 'flexible' arrangements in a globalising economy: employers (and the government) want to meet current labour demands while reducing long-term social welfare commitments, and many workers abroad see their employment in Canada as a short-term venture in any case.

To summarise trends in Canadian and Australian immigration policy, we may say that in selecting immigrants on the basis of job skills, the two countries are following a long tradition. In showing an increasing preference for workers on permits, and in selecting immigrants on the basis of high technology and entrepreneurial criteria, both countries are adapting long-standing concerns regarding economic impacts of immigration to a new global context. The concern with and importance of family reunification and refugee issues in Australian and Canadian policy, in this context, may be viewed as the humanitarian response to the way in which globalisation also creates enormous family strains and the potential for political conflict and economic turmoil in migrant-sending countries.

Future prospects

What of the future movement of people around the world? The continued international movement of people is likely to be fostered by chain migration processes, a 'pull' factor that stems from the kinship and friendship structures and networks each new migrant creates between the country of destination and their country of origin. These expanding networks cause the costs and risks of movement to fall and the probability of migration to rise. They tend to build into the migration process somewhat of a self-perpetuating momentum that leads to its growth over time (Massey 1990).

With regard to temporary labour migration and permanent migration, in a recent study of the world labour market Johnston (1991) concluded that there would be a substantial increase in the mobility of people around the world during the decade of the 1990s. According to Johnston, the world labour force will grow by 600 million between 1985 and 2000. Of this number, 570 million people will be added to the workforce in developing countries. However, although much of the skilled and unskilled human resources are being produced in the developing world, most of the well-paid jobs (with attendant opportunities for providing services to an affluent society) are being generated in the industrialised countries, countries with ageing and slowly growing labour forces. This mismatch between the demand for labour on the one hand and its geographic location on the other will result in pressures for the massive relocations of people. The process of relocation will be facilitated, for example, by the decline in the real cost of international travel (especially air travel) and the relaxation by some governments of immigration and emigration barriers for selected categories. For example, from 1993 movement of EEC nationals within the Community area will be easier and the

Canada–US–Mexico free trade agreement (NAFTA) provides for easier movement of business and professional persons.

There seems little doubt that the temporary movements associated with tourism will continue to grow, and the rate of growth will be shaped largely by prevailing economic conditions in the developed countries of the world, the countries which yield the largest numbers of tourists. Travel, trade market segmentation, consumer interest/lifestyle changes and aircraft technology (making long-haul travel more readily accessible and less expensive) will combine to create continued moderate expansion in overseas travel (WTO 1990).

At the same time, however, it is important to note that some industrialised countries may actually raise their barriers to movement. For example, Western Europe is facing strong migratory pressures from 'economic refugees' from former Soviet bloc and Third World countries. In response to these pressures, Britain and Germany have either actually introduced or foreshadowed the introduction of stronger controls on refugees (*The Age* 5 July 1991). Domestic political considerations, including major social tensions, are also placing great pressure on European Governments to bring the 'refugee problem' under control. The harmonisation of immigration and refugee policies by the most economically developed countries has been described as a form of 'global apartheid' designed to protect their privileged status in the face of overwhelming demographic and political pressures from less affluent societies in Africa and Asia (Richmond 1992b).

We may conclude that the emerging world system of advanced technology, globalised trade, and post-modern social relations has major implications for both Australian and Canadian immigration patterns. The world system, once centred on Europe, has now become multi-centred, and includes the interlinked economies of Japan and the newly industrialising nations of Southeast Asia. Since the reunification of Germany and the collapse of the Soviet Union, Western Europe has its own vast source of labour to tap in Eastern Europe. The European Community is developing plans to co-ordinate efforts in all countries to control, limit or even exclude migrants from outside Europe. If NAFTA is ratified, the inclusion of Mexico into the existing Canada-US Free Trade Agreement will create a hemispheric migration system. Continental and multi-nation trading blocs are linked to a rise of inward-looking protectionist sentiments, and even to xenophobic and neo-fascist movements. Both conservative and liberal-minded politicians are responding to reactionary pressure to restrict immigration, and to deport those deemed not to meet narrow definitions of eligibility. These restrictive sentiments, in turn, run directly counter to the aspirations of, and increasing pressures on, those in certain Third World regions to migrate to the post-industrial global cities in other countries. It remains to be seen how Australia, Canada, and other traditional immigrant-receiving countries will respond to these contradictory pressures. Australia and Canada have traditionally seen themselves as open societies with democratic traditions, essentially egalitarian and committed to human rights. Immigration, in both countries, has been historically viewed as an important element in national development, including the international relations component of this. These factors will tend to guide the range of policy options open to consideration. Neither country can barricade itself against immigration altogether, nor is a completely 'open door' compatible with the maintenance of a viable economy, high levels of employment, and high minimum wages and other features of an advanced welfare state in a world in which the gap between the wealthiest and the poorest nations is widening. It is likely that selective immigration controls will be applied, as in the past, but the admission criteria will change. The tendency is to favour higher skill levels for workers and greater assurances that business immigrants will indeed make an economic contribution. In addition, one observes a rising general trend to favour temporary movements. Even those who settle retain close links with their former country. Admission criteria, short-term settlement, and long-term 'integration' policies will have to come to terms with the new globalisation. Moreover, it is increasingly evident in the new global order that states do not function autonomously, but must work within the framework of the United Nations, and other international forums, to achieve the goals so eloquently expressed in the International Declaration of Human Rights.

CHAPTER 3

Justice, Immigration and Refugees

Howard Adelman

Introduction

When someone knocks on the door of your country and asks to enter and become a member of your community, are you justified in saying no and turning him or her away? If so, on what grounds do you base your decision? And if you allow that individual to enter, on what grounds are you justified in accepting that person and not the many others seeking entry? Do you ask whether those grounds favour males rather than females, and, if they do, whether those grounds are fair? Is conditional admittance acceptable—conditional on good behaviour or obedience to laws or working in a particular area and/or in a particular field of endeavour for a specified period? Once admitted to membership in your community, however gradual that admission process may be, are you obligated to provide full formal membership? If temporary workers have contributed to society for a number of years, should they be allowed to become citizens? Further, are you obligated to go beyond formal membership and guarantee equal opportunity, not only between immigrants and the native-born, but between different types of newcomers, including men and women? If you are not obligated to do so, does this mean that newcomers will be disadvantaged by the inequality between them and the native-born, or that female newcomers will be disadvantaged in comparison to male newcomers?

These questions begin the discussion on why there is an issue of justice and a philosophical debate about issues of justice applied to immigration and refugee policy. The chapter then proposes a category framework for making immigration and refugee policy. The third section relates the debate concerning justice to the debates on immigration and refugee policy. Finally, the various concepts of justice are applied to a few specific immigration and refugee issues to illustrate the applicability of the framework while clarifying how issues of justice can be applied to immigration and refugee policy.

On justice

Justification. Obligation. Justice or injustice. The issue of justice is fundamental to policies on immigration and refugees. One of the most fundamental issues of a society is who we admit as members and on what grounds do we base those decisions. Formulators of immigration and refugee policy *must* consider the problem of justice because admission policies and decisions directly affect the conception of justice governing a society. As Michael Walzer (1983) noted, the decision to give membership in one's prosperous state is entirely the responsibility of the existing members. 'Individuals may be able to give good reasons why they should be selected, but no one on the outside has a right to be inside. The members decide freely on their future associates, and the decisions they make are authoritative and final' (p. 41). It is one of the most important decisions members of a state make.

The canonical text for reintroducing the question of justice into modern political theory is John Rawls's contractarian vision, set forth in *A Theory of Justice* (1971), in which justice is rooted in individual consent based on individual self-interest (Held 1976). Actions, even collective acts, are initiated by the individual through the exercise of his/her will based on cognitive and moral reflection; those acts are presumed to be rational. That is, the individual has epistemic and moral responsibility and, given what she or he knows and believes, must make decisions based on that knowledge and those beliefs and take moral responsibility for them. Collective decisions are a product of the negotiated compromises of individual rational agents. In making those decisions, the value of individuals transcends those of nations and states.

Questions of rights are at the heart of such decisions. Basic to those rights is the right of the individual to use his or her own knowledge and beliefs to make decisions. The individual has the right to engage in private reflection necessary to this decision making, the right to gain access to and communicate information necessary to engage in this reflection and the right to try to influence the decisions of others.

Rawls also attempted to root justice in universal theory, in the sense of providing abstract principles from which concrete issues could be adjudicated. 'My aim is to present a conception of justice which generalizes and carries to a higher level of abstraction the familiar theory of the social contract as found, say, in Locke, Rousseau and Kant' (Rawls 1971, p. 11). However, if the theory claimed universality, it not only had to be abstract, it had to address questions about the fair allocation of goods worldwide, including the allocation of one of the scarcest goods of all, the right to acquire membership in a rich, prosperous and democratic state.

Thus, questions of justice are applicable to immigration and refugee policy. The three foundation stones of a Rawlsian approach to adjudicating justice issues are its individualism, its foundation in rights theory and its abstract theoretical character, claiming universality in both the abstract and global senses.

Are current Australian and Canadian immigration and refugee policy goals just? Are the norms for regulating and controlling entry just? Do the consequences of those policies raise or lower the standards of justice in the world? To ask such questions is to assume we possess three key factors in order to answer them. It assumes first, that a principle of justice can be abstracted from the political, economic and social context and used to assess historically and politically rooted policies; second, that the agents formulating policy utilise the abstract principles and make policy on the basis of conscious goals, norms, anticipated consequences and a perception of reality; and third, that those assessing the policies assume that a knowledge of those goals, norms, consequences and perceived circumstances give rise to existing policies so that those policies can be assessed in terms of a prescriptive concept of justice.

Finally, to ask such questions may also assume that the principle of justice regulates other needs or goods, such as survival, the economic well-being of the individual, the social welfare of the whole or even the demands of a divine will. That is, a concept of *right* rooted in a concept of justice has priority over and is independent of any *good*. Rights trump needs or utilities. Right rooted in justice also regulates other rights, whether they are considered necessary to achieve certain goods, or are considered as rights independent of the good to be achieved by them. Such rights might include the right of nature to maintain itself in a balanced way, egalitarian rights, rights to security of persons and property, and even the collective rights of the chosen, whether they are those of a particular nationality, an aristocratic or intellectual elite or the working class.

Given these foundation principles, why, then, in creating a universal system of human rights, do individuals *not* have an *inherent* right to move anywhere? Why is the right of free individual movement restricted by state borders and regulations? Because the rights were asserted, not on behalf of individuals everywhere, but on behalf of the individual members of a state. Thus, recent United Nations initiatives, in articulating rights of movement, affirmed 'The Right of Everyone to Leave any Country, Including his own, and to Return to his Country' (UN 1991). Rights were set out to justify placing limits on state action, action which was to be dependent on citizen consent while allowing individuals to pursue their various goals unimpeded. State actions not based on consent of the governed were illegitimate.

This general principle is true of modern rights theories as well as the classical contractarian theories of Locke and Rousseau. Thus, an ideal rights theorist, such as Rawls, depicts society as a closed and isolated system (1971, p. 8), or 'a nation-state [which] controls a connected territory' (1980, p. 536) and which is a self-sufficient association. Movement from one state to another is only permitted at the sufferance of other states. The right to move between and among states is only granted as a result of the contracts and covenants between and among states. The only inherent right an individual has is the right to return to a state in which he or she holds legitimate citizenship.

In other words, rights are supposedly universal, but (a) those rights only belong to members of liberal states; (b) those rights are not universal in extending to individuals when they leave their liberal states; and (c) on the basis of rights theory, there is no right to claim the protection of, let alone membership in, a liberal state if an individual's 'universal' rights are abused by the state in which they habitually live. Yet the latter is precisely what has happened in the evolution of refugee law since the signing of the refugee convention after World War II (Adelman 1988). Whatever the merits of a Rawlsian position in creating a system of justice for those who are already members of a state, it seemed to provide no basis for adjudicating decisions about who should be allowed to become new members of that state and how to adjudicate the rights of the members of a state versus the rights of immigrants and refugees. Thus, Rawls (1980) is concerned with the 'freedom and equality of *citizens* (my emphasis) as moral persons' concerned with the 'just form of basic institutions within a democratic society' rather than a 'conception of justice suitable for all societies'. Therefore, as a thesis restricted to liberal democratic states, it did not seem to provide a means for adjudicating needs issues on a global level either. Nor did Rawls seek to provide a theory for determining issues concerning the distribution of goods and services over the whole globe, including the distribution of access to membership in the wealthier states (cf. Pogge 1989, ch. 3).

Thus, at least two fundamentally different critiques have been aimed at the universal abstract theory of Rawls: first, the theory is rooted in a state—it is not global in its foundation or applicability; second, the theory ignores history and is too abstract when, in reality, history and socialisation, not human nature, are the key determinants of immigration as well as other policies. In other words, Rawlsian theory is synchronically parochial and not spatially universal, it is diachronically abstract, making it too universal and historical and ignoring its rootedness in history and a particular type of society.

From those who believe that justice theories concerning immigration are rooted in the state, and those who believe that justice theories concerning immigration are rooted in history, two different critiques have been put forth which are aimed at the individualist rather than the universalist postulates of Rawlsian theory. One is a realist statist critique. Individuals do not make immigration and refugee policy. Nation-building elites and/or the state itself make policy. And that policy is made in the interests of the state no matter how moral questions and concerns enter the policy-making progress.

The problem is that morality does enter into state making policy with respect to individuals. Even the realism of George Kennan (1954, p. 49) allows for justice to be applicable to the state treatment of individuals outside the state. In realpolitik, morality is still applicable first to individual behaviour within a state (particularly in setting standards for individual virtue in a civil society); second, to state behaviour towards its own citizens; and, finally, to state behaviour to individuals outside the borders of the state even when interests of state enter into immigration and refugee decisions. It is only in state to state relations that amorality reigns.

The second critical perspective, focused on the individualism of Rawls (paralleling the historicist critique of the abstract universality of Rawlsian theory), is a communitarian critique which claims that Rawls's theory says nothing about preserving the identity of the nation, such a concern providing one criterion for adjudicating decisions about who could become a member of one's state. Since Rawls himself in his later essays restricted his theory of justice to a specific community, a liberal democratic society, critics claimed that his individualistic theories were built on communitarian premises. Others have argued that communitarianism was inherent in the theory itself. Liberal societies entail shared values about legitimacy based on consent of the governed, rules for adjudicating when consent has been obtained and rules for accepting the decisions of those who are considered to have legitimate authority, in other words, patterns of principles and values based on reciprocal interdependency (Flatham 1976; Sandel 1982; Shapiro 1986). Garry Wills, in *Lincoln at Gettysburg: The Words that Remade America*, went even further. He depicted one of America's greatest political leaders as an individual who both articulated these universal liberal theories within the framework of a classical idiom of eternal verities and polarities while shifting the substance of the premises of the American enterprise from a compact between states for their mutual convenience and defence to a thesis of perpetual union decided by the people (not states) where the function of the state was viewed as forging a national (communitarian) identity, thereby creating a unique meld of universal liberal theory and American exceptionalism.

Should immigration policy be rooted in the will of the individual members of the state or in inherited community values, particularly since essential values and the character of our society are affected by immigration and refugee decisions and the rationale behind them? This is the issue which appears to divide liberals and communitarians, while both are united in the belief that the members of states make the decisions. If, however, the decisions are really made by a nation-building elite (a mixture of politicians, mandarins, judges and an 'active' public, the latter a very small minority of those citizens) or, as in statist theory, the state itself considered as the prime actor, this may not only relocate the locus of the decision, but the type of ethical theory appropriate, though not the applicability of questions of justice to those decisions. For example, Simmons and Keohane (1992) argue that the state in formulating immigration policy is engaged in an hegemonic project, monitoring, garnering support and minimalising criticism by the control it exercises in setting the context for discourse with ethnic groups, humanitarian organisations and provinces.

Statist critiques are aimed at the gap between reality and the theory of popular sovereignty, that is, the myth of popular control of government (Morgan 1988) which is basic to Rawlsian justice; communitarian critiques are aimed at the gap between the ideal conception of contract theory and the reality of community control, that is, the fact that a set of essential values define the character of a particular society and have an impact on immigration and refugee decisions and the rationale behind them. Hence, there is a perceived need to ensure that immigration and refugee policy preserves those values while recognising that those values are determinants of immigration and refugee policy, even if they only set the parameters within which the statist elites operate.

Finally, if both the universalist and the individualist theses of Rawls are both attacked from two very different directions, so is the postulate that rights are the basis for a moral theory of the modern state. From this critical vantage point, needs, not the rights of individuals, are basic to immigration and refugee policy. The key measurement is either the needs of one's own society, or the needs of the immigrants and refugees, or some combination of both. From one set of critics, utilities trump rights; rights do not trump utilities.

This perspective raises its own problems. It is difficult to agree upon a universal framework, such as the greatest happiness of the greatest number, to use as a relevant universal utility from which to assess immigration or refugee policy. There is no single end to adjudicate the conflicts among the various conflicting goals. There are a variety of ends, such as survival of the group or the human race, or economic well-being or interests of state. And each goal has different applications dependent on whether the reference is to an individual or to a specific group. Not only are there questions about a transcendent rights theory; there are also questions about a transcendent utility or needs theory as a basis for immigration policy.

From the opposite angle, we find an Aristotelian attack on Rawlsian ethics as a basis for immigration and refugee policy. It is the capacity of the state and the society within it to absorb immigrants and refugees that provides the key foundation for determining how many immigrants and refugees a society can take. Neither rights nor needs provide such a basis.

The choice, however, may not be selecting one principle—such as individual rights—to rule over the other two—needs or the absorptive capacity of society. All three may be applicable. Thus, although justice issues are a constant aspect of justifying and legitimating immigration policy, such justifications take into account the rights of the existing members of a state and the rights of refugees who are not members of the state, but only those who are already on its territory. When refugees overseas are allowed entry, the *needs* and *capacities* of the state granting entry, combined with both the *needs* and *capacities* of the refugees, seem determinate (Adelman & Cox, Chapter 9 in this volume). The *needs* of the society are used to determine which immigrants are to be selected and the *capacity* helps to determine the overall number. There appears to be something very inadequate about discussing immigration and refugee policy in terms of a justice theory rooted in rights alone.

The critics who attempt to ground a Rawlsian abstract justice theory with respect to immigration can be divided into those who are synchronically oriented and those that are diachronically oriented. Those who attempt to root justice issues concerning immigration in space focus on either the interests of state or in the hegemony of the decision makers who control the state, on the one hand, or the absorptive capacity of the state on the other. Those who attempt to root justice issues concerning immigration in time focus on either a set of historically transmitted values (communitarians) or a current assessment of needs relative to some historical teleological goal of equity (utilitarians). The various criteria of justice applicable to immigration and refugee policy, using Rawlsian theory as a centerpiece, can be summarised as shown in Chart 3.1:

Chart 3.1: Summary of Rawlsian theory and its critique

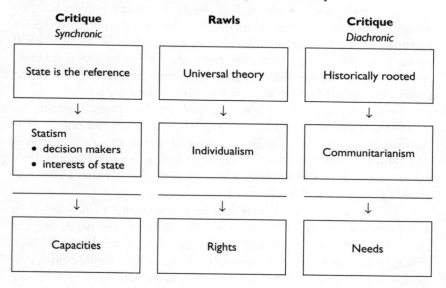

This chapter argues that in immigration policy, justice is achieved by adjudicating among various utilities and normative rights criteria, as well as the capacity of the society to absorb those immigrants and refugees. In refugee policy, communitarian liberalism has extended rights to include the right to move as a universal right, and applied it to those who feared being persecuted for claiming such rights and who have fled to a country that protects such rights. There is no right independent of the communitarian base in which such rights are articulated. On the other hand, within the liberal tradition and communities, a universal right to move and resettle has emerged for those who (a) lack membership in a state that guarantees the protection of liberal rights, (b) have been persecuted by their former state, and (c) have arrived on the territory of a liberal state and requested its protection. Refugees have been granted a right to move and, further, receive protection and become members of a state. The mandarins and politicians who make immigration and refugee policy with the interests of their own state as primary must take these rights seriously as a fundamental value in policy formulation.

However, in immigration, as distinct from refugee policy, no independent prescriptive conception of justice abstracted from history exists to regulate the choices and to assess needs served by immigration policy. Rather, various rights as means are correlated with specific kinds of needs as ends.

Further, in both immigration and refugee policy, justice is not an abstraction but a concept rooted in historical development. Moral rules do not arise from a deductive rational moral science, akin to classical geometry, but arise out of the interaction of precedent with experience. The task of applying these principles globally is one of negotiation and development rather than a direct product of the abstract theory.

To assess whether any of these theories of justice are, in fact, applicable to reality, we must ask what principles of justice, if any, are entailed in the current immigration and refugee policies of Australia and Canada? Are there any principles entailed at all, just or unjust? Are the policies merely ad hoc, determined by multiple and various circumstances, with neither coherence nor any principle of justice governing them, or do they reveal an emerging concept of justice? In other words, the question of justice vis-à-vis immigration and refugee policy cannot be examined by comparing an 'ideal' model of justice with the second-rate world we live in, but rather by examining our world and how questions of justice, in the context of immigration and refugee policy, have actually been adjudicated. To do that, we must go beyond deliberations about abstract justice to elucidate the categories in which actual policy decisions in this field are made.

A category framework

In order to clarify existing policies, it is helpful if we create a map outlining the range of policy decisions. What are the possible goals and objectives of immigration and refugee policy? One objective may be protecting and enhancing economic growth by importing capital and expertise, and, perhaps, labour to maintain a balanced proportion between workers and the retired. Another goal might be demographic—to obtain a larger, more stable or even a smaller population by balancing emigration with trends in reproductive rates and government programs for encouraging or discouraging couples from having children. Immigration driven by a population policy might be based on a desire to increase the number of consumers to improve domestic productivity through economies of scale or to improve the state's ability to defend itself from threats to its national security. On the other hand, such a population policy used as a basis to determine immigration totals might be driven by a sensitivity to the country's ecological system leading to a demand to restrict immigration. But there may also be a need to reduce ecological pressures in overcrowded countries and, hence, increase the immigration intakes of less crowded ones.

A different goal might be to maintain and enhance, or, alternatively, to alter a cultural system of values that characterise the nation. If those national values are considered to be genetically inherited or transmitted by the traditions and practices of a dominant ethnic group, a goal of immigration and refugee policy may be to maintain or even enhance the dominance of that ethnic group within the population as a whole. If, among those values, the unity of the family is highly regarded, both for the stability it creates for society as a whole as well as society's inherent respect for the family, then family reunification programs will be lauded, regardless of the immigrants' countries of origin. On the other hand, if the survival of the language and culture of a dominant ethnic group is threatened, then that group might scrap even some of its most cherished values to ensure group survival.

Finally, the goals of immigration and refugee policy may not be driven primarily by domestic considerations. Foreign policy concerns, for example, might have been one of the factors in Australia's rejection of its traditional White Australia Policy. Asian xenophobia may still be an influential factor in Australian and Canadian immigration policy. On the other hand, humanitarian concerns and recognition of the rights of the suffering, the persecuted and the dispossessed might counter such influences. Such policies may be rooted in humanitarian or religious values dictated by divine commandment.

This depiction of possible goals for an immigration and refugee policy regime intermixes the conceptual basis of such policies rooted in different ideas of justice with various realms—nature, the civil society, the nation-state and the divine or supernatural—that are the repositories of such values. It may be helpful to distinguish the values central to those realms from their goals.

Each of the above four realms has two aspects. Nature may be viewed parochially from the perspective of the nation-state's territory and the ability of the ecology to support the existing population. Nature may also be viewed globally from the perspective of world ecology and the right of all individuals, including future generations, to have access to the essentials of life. In either case, the pre-eminent value in determining justice claims is the preservation of an ecological balance. The goal sought is survival.

The civil society, the second realm in which individuals and groups advance their own interests, may be considered either from the perspective of equal rights for all individuals or from the need to guarantee equal opportunity for various disadvantaged groups. The pre-eminent value, equality, may be the same, but from the individual perspective it limits the state's right to interfere with or restrict an individual. From the group perspective, equality demands interventionist and affirmative action by governing institutions. The civil society's interest in advancing the economic well-being of its members may encourage a business investment program that invites immigrants who wish to invest substantial capital in Australia and Canada and create jobs for Australians and Canadians. At the same time, based on principles of equality, but applied to group rights, that same program may be opposed by some because it gives one group, those with capital, a separate entrée, thereby appearing to undermine the principle of equal opportunity for all groups. But the goal, whether advanced by affirmative action or by laissez faire, is always to advance economic well-being.

The governing institution, the nation-state, is the third realm. As a state, its main concern is the security of its citizens. As a nation, its main concern is securing and enhancing the identity of the dominant nation which the state was created to protect. On one side, the security concerns are physical. Entry shall be denied people who would threaten that security in any way. On the other side, the nation-state is concerned with protecting the spirit of a people and the language, culture and values which define that spirit. By what means and to what extent should a country admit into membership individuals from other societies who may not share the dominant language, culture and values, if the overall goal of the host society is to secure and preserve its own physical and spiritual well-being?

The fourth realm refers to some transcendental source for determining human value issues. Those transcendental commandments may demand individual self-sacrifice to help others in need. Or they may command acting so that one's actions reveal and enhance the inherited values of one's community. In the latter context, salvation is perceived to be communal rather than a product of individual acts. In either case, a pre-eminent value of self-sacrifice and charity (in contrast to preserving a natural balance or guaranteeing equality or security) is espoused in order to enhance the prospects of replacing the messy human order with a transcendent universal one.

Each of these realms has a universalist and a particularist aspect as well as a common value applied to both. There are very different implications for immigration and refugee policy, depending upon whether the universal or the particular is given priority. Thus, global ecology, concerned with giving all individuals access to the essentials of life, might direct immigration policy in Australia and Canada to take greater numbers of immigrants to reduce the pressures on the rain forests of over-populated countries. On the other hand, domestic ecological concerns focused on the physical survival of one's own community might indicate a need for reduced immigration inflows to preserve the small areas of habitation among the vast territories of Canada and Australia, little of which is good for sustained population support.

Currently, a more common basis for determining immigration and refugee policy, particularly where the liberal ethos has become dominant and the concept of economic man holds sway, is economic well-being. It is possible to develop an immigration policy that offers as many individuals as possible from the Third World an opportunity to enhance their personal well-being as long as such immigration enhances the well-being of the members of the Australian and Canadian states. This does not mean that uniform immigration policies result. A policy may guarantee equal opportunity to every individual or, alternatively, enhance the opportunities of disadvantaged groups.

The economic self-interest of individuals with equal rights to pursue economic gains is not the only aspect of a civil society. The interests of groups may also be relevant. A society may wish to ensure that disadvantaged communities are guaranteed equal opportunity once they become constituent members of the society. Such equal opportunity may focus on education, job mobility, the right to acquire the language skills, technical tools and the formal recognition needed to participate in the society. But group rights not only affect settlement policies for immigrants and refugees once they are admitted; they may also affect the right to entry itself. Thus, women may be disadvantaged by some immigration policies, while their entry (though not their situation once they enter) may be facilitated by other policies, such as the women-at-risk programs of both countries or the special program for the admission of female domestics into Canada. Similarly, disabled individuals or those with treatable illnesses, such as tuberculosis, may be discriminated against by immigration policies. Other groups may be disadvantaged when applying for entry because they may have very limited access to immigration officers, given the very uneven distribution of those officers around the globe. In Australia, economic self-interest and a foreign policy concerned with overseas links through increasing the educational levels of the citizens of its neighbours may have combined to produce an educational program for overseas students who could pay fees and enter special educational institutions. However, when those entrants on student visas from China asked for asylum because of the events in Tiananmen Square, many saw this use of educational visas as a method of purchasing entry into Australia by providing those students with a way of circumventing the immigration queue. This form of entry ran counter to the principle of equal access.

When goals such as protecting and enhancing the import of skills and capital are cited, we may develop a policy of importing temporary workers or, alternatively, allow immigrants to enter but place restrictions on the numbers and the type. We may attempt to balance age groups so that the proportion of retirees to the work force does not become distorted; this may lead to age restrictions on entry or, alternatively, attempts to use financial incentives for women and families to bear more children to offset a dependence on immigration for maintaining the population size. Immigration may also be decreased to offset increases in unemployment in the belief that large-scale immigration cannot be continued when there is a great deal of unemployment during an economic recession. In this respect, Australia and Canada appear to have followed opposing policies in the 1990–91 period; Australia reduced immigration intakes as the recession took hold, while Canada increased its immigration intake, thus introducing an immigration pattern running contrary to the business cycle based on evidence that immigration, even in a recession, if anything benefits the economy.

On the other hand, establishing a larger population base to create economies of scale within one's domestic market, or allowing the entry of immigrants from existing or potential significant trading partners, or even importing workers who are more self-sacrificing, disciplined, harder working or more motivated to earn a living and succeed, usually lead to more expansionist and less restrictive immigration policies. When any of these restrictive or expansionist arguments are used for determining immigration policy, the appeal is to economic self-interest as the basis for adjudicating justice. The reference realm is the civil society and the economic self-interest of its members. Justice is defined solely in terms of what is in the best interests of one's existing membership.

In addition to ecological balance in the quest for survival, and to equality when concerned with economic self-interest, security is a third value reference for determining immigration and refugee policy. The physical security of the population is the state's responsibility. This should not be surprising since, in the social contract version of modern state theory, issues of security became the monopoly of the state, which, in return, was obliged to protect the right of individuals to pursue their own interests.

The concern for security is related to a variety of very different goals vis-à-vis immigration policy. The security issue might be used to argue for a large population increase so that a state has the population base to protect itself against more powerful neighbours; but it could also be used to argue against immigration in relation to national security. The import of 'foreigners' might be viewed as building a fifth column within the state, one undercutting the ethnic homogeneity or majoritarian status of the society and the mutual loyalties among its members.

The White Australia Policy of the past is an example of grounding immigration policies to secure the continued dominance of one national group defined by racial criteria. The desire and importance any community or nation places on ensuring its own survival may be a prime determinant of immigration policy. When the survival of a nation and its language and culture is threatened, restrictionist rules governing entry and resettlement may be perceived as more acceptable than the racist policies of the past. Thus, the primacy given to the survival of the Quebecois may be accepted and may constitute one of the most important determinants of immigration policy for Canada.

The dilemma is to distinguish an argument used for discrimination from one used to preserve a nation's language and culture. In fact, these very same arguments can be used to drive people out of one's state and or conquer adjacent territory populated by one's own ethnic group. Croats can attempt to drive Serbs from Croatia or Serbs from Serbia can attempt to annex portions of Croatia and Bosnia and drive Croats and Muslims out of the latter area. Armenians can be driven from Nogorno-Karabakh in Azerbaijan. The other ethnic groups are cited as threatening the security of those respective nations. The conquest of territory or expulsion of populations out of one's territory are complementary territorial-based security policies related to restrictive immigration policies lest the entry of those who do not belong to the dominant ethnic group endangers state security.

The security of the state and the nation's continuity is not to be confused with the rights of a nation to preserve, protect and enhance its inherited values, even if a restrictive immigration policy is sometimes the outcome of both rationales. However, the concern with national rights and values is not necessarily related to restrictive immigration policies. For example, an expansionist immigration policy might be defended by such mundane arguments as a way of introducing more interesting and perhaps tastier cuisines into the national repertoire, or introducing more variety into a culture that is perceived as staid and stagnant. Expansionist immigration policies are defended in relation to the inherited values of the nation, not simply to preserve those values, but to transform and enlarge them.

Nor do arguments for preserving traditional values necessarily lead to restrictive policies. An inherited respect for the protection of individual rights and the obligation to respect international human rights treaties form part of the current national heritage of most democratic western liberal states, so that the institutional basis has been developed for guaranteeing a refugee claimant a right to protection, a right to due process in the adjudication of such claims and hence, in most cases, to membership in the state in which a claim is successfully made. There may be different degrees of achieving justice based on this criterion, a criterion rooted in rights and obligations related to the inherited values of a community that celebrates individual rights. But it effectively results in an expansionist immigration policy.

Inherited humanitarian values rooted in the ethos of a nation rather than a narrower concern for the protection of individual rights may have led to large Australian and Canadian intakes of Indochinese refugees. But the obligations assumed may be rooted neither in a respect for individual rights when individuals make refugee claims, nor in the right of a national group to preserve, enhance or transform its values and beliefs. Instead, the obligations may be rooted in supranational or transcendental responsibilities unrelated to any rights whatsoever.

Thus, there is a final and distinct value reference for justice claims as a basis for influencing those immigration and refugee policies not rooted in the principle of natural balance or in equality of opportunity for individuals or groups or in security for either the state or the nation. This reference to justice is built on categorical imperatives or moral commandments related to some transnational, transcendental or even supernatural realm and frequently claims to have a monopoly on justice.

For these defenders of universal justice, barriers created by the state may be anathema to those who consider the right to move around God's globe as the most basic right of all. Allowing a state to exercise restrictions in this area, restrictions that may lead to suffering, is akin to giving ethical responsibility to an institution which, by the very definition of its creation in contract theory, has no ethical responsibilities to anyone else except its own members. Even if the foundation stone is not security, even if it is not the rights and obligations based on equal opportunity to pursue individual or group economic self-interest, even if it is not a quest for natural balance in the ecology, as long as the adjudication of any justice claim is left in the hands of the state, there can be no justice.

For many with transcendental convictions, placing the responsibility in the state's hands for the most basic freedom of all, the freedom to move around the globe, or the most basic issue of security, the continuity of one's family and nation beyond one's own life span, is an act of sheer folly that can only lead to the most severe restrictions on both. Surrendering the adjudication of ethical issues to the state is akin to locking oneself in a prison, vast though its territory may be, and turning the keys over to one's jailer. And the danger is that not only does one restrict one's movements arbitrarily, but one gives the jailer control over what one may think. The state then becomes an object of idolatrous worship. Faith in the state and loyalty to it is presupposed to guarantee the individual's freedom to move to ensure the security of one's family and nation over time. From such a perspective, immigration policy based on self-interest or nation-state security should not be replaced by any immigration restrictions whatsoever. In an extreme situation, all state intervention restricts a fundamental right, the right to move.

Those who hold such a position regard debates over migration as blasphemy, particularly when it comes to refugee cases. For when lives are at risk, debates about humane deterrence, burden-sharing, inequitable allocations to those who have developed the most advanced principles of protection and so on appear akin to reducing fairness and justice to a pact with the devil in which justice is merely the equal allocation of responsibilities and duties, the very root of envy and resentment and, further, one that willingly sacrifices the individual at the stake while bureaucratic norms of a fair allocation of responsibilities are sorted out.

The framework for deciding what is just when assessing immigration and refugee claims is summarised in Chart 3.2. There are four categories: realm, goal, normative value and appreciation. Four realms have been distinguished: the transcendental, the civil society, the national state and nature, and also four goals, that is, ideal justice, individual economic well-being, the well-being of the totality and general survival. The normative values divide into four sets: self-sacrifice, equality, security and balance. Finally, the reference of applicability of the system of justice is rooted in a number of differential dichotomies: to strangers or just nationals, to individuals or to kin, to citizens of the state or members of the nation, and finally, to the ecology of the territory of the state or to a global ecology.

Justice and policy

Refugees

In conceptualising the emergent values of justice that have developed in immigration and refugee policy in western liberal states, and in Australia and Canada in particular, my first thesis is that the refugee issue is one that runs primarily through the vertical axis (between the transcendental ideal state and nature) in Chart 3.2. That is, the right to move, which is applicable to refugees under the United Nations Convention, and the protections afforded a refugee by a liberal state, are aspects of the state's ideal values and the effort to universalise those values and make them transcend the state. They articulate the ideals of the liberal state. Rather than being rooted in the pursuit of self-interest, those ideals are, in fact, rooted in a normative rule of humanitarianism and self-sacrifice for others.

That self-sacrifice has two dimensions. One is a priority for those who are considered kith and kin. Thus, Germany takes in Germans

Chart 3.2   A justice framework for migration policy

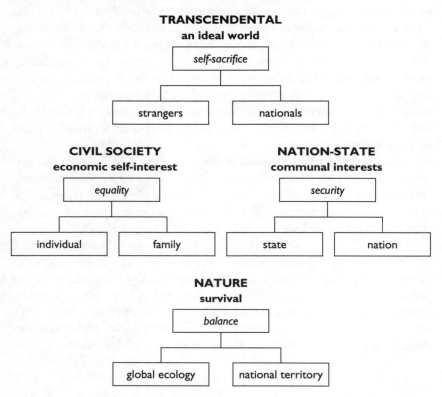

even though they may not have lived in Germany for generations. Israel accords rights to Jews under the Law of Return. Hungary may give priority for refuge to Hungarians in Romania or Yugoslavia.

The other dimension includes those who are strangers but who want to uphold the values of a liberal community and fear persecution because of that. As a result, they have fled a country that was unwilling or unable to protect such values. The justice in such cases is universally applicable because there is no distinction based on kinship or the ideology actually held by the refugee claimant. The only reference is to the transcendent values inherent in a liberal community itself.

When those refugees are not on the territory of the state offering refuge, they may be selected by a combination of immigration criteria (the needs of one's own civil society and, therefore, the ability of the refugee to resettle successfully) and the needs of the refugees who are only selected for resettlement when the prospect of return seems non-existent. The quest is not only for balance in nature, but for a balance between the needs of one's own society and the needs of others in the world who lack the protection of a state. Rights are only accorded refugees *not* on state territory who are considered kith and kin.

Notice that if refugees are not on state territory, unless they can claim to be kith and kin with rights under a Law of Return, the only refugees with rights are those on one's native soil. In addition to rights granted to others **not** on state soil on the principle of *jus sanguinis* (descent) as an expression of the self-definition of a nation constituting the state, and as an extension of a state's transcendent values extended to strangers on one's soil who are given rights to claim refugee status, protection may be accorded to others who, though neither strangers nor kith and kin on the one hand, nor complete strangers on the other hand, help distinguish the national persona from that of the state they fled.

As an example, Canada admitted over 100 000 Americans who fled because they did not want to fight, or did not want their children to fight, in the Vietnam War. At the same time, though not called refugees, they were allowed to become landed immigrants *within* Canada after their arrival. Though not ethnic kin, they were the closest ideological kin to English Canadians, for English Canada had been founded by United Empire Loyalists who either refused to join the American revolution in the first place or who were rejected by the United States of America when the revolutionaries won.

The result yields a trifold application of rights applied to refugees on the basis of transcendent values, where 'R' refers to Rights and 'S' and 'O' refer to Self and Other respectively depending on the relationship of the subjects to be protected.

Rights
R–S   rights of self determine that which is granted to others on the principle of *jus sanguinis* (descent)
R–O   rights of others who are given protection under the law
R–S/O   rights of self-definition in relation to the significant other

However, in analysing refugee policy and the debates over the issue, the actual issue of refugee claimants is much more complicated. It results in a colour-coded taxonomy for refugees, which is quite separate from the issue of those who try to use a refugee claims system without any justification whatsoever. Legitimate refugee claimants can be classified as follows:

(a) red   — those individually targeted for persecution;
(b) blue   — those members of groups targeted for persecution;
(c) yellow — those fleeing from violent situations;
(d) green   — those fleeing from environmental disasters;
(e) brown   — those fleeing from a disastrous economic situation;
(f) black   — warrior refugees.

There was a growing realisation that the refugee claims system was attracting and allowing entry not only for those in the red and blue categories, but also for those in the yellow, green and brown categories for whom the program was not intended. Put in the abstract framework of categories for policy making, the question of refugee claims and assistance is the degree to which the right to move should be extended to those who flee, not so much because they are victims of a demonstrably illiberal state or because they share an ethnic or historical kinship with the citizens in one's own state, but because they have fled in order to survive. What protections ought to be accorded to refugee victims of an assault on basic survival as opposed to refugee victims of an assault on transcendent values?

Put in a more philosophical way, if victims of civil war, environmental calamities or economic disaster flee to one's state, what are one's obligations? Convention refugees are protected by the values extended by a liberal contractarian state, applied universally, when territory *not* under the jurisdiction of a state is no longer available to which to flee, and when a victim arrives within the jurisdiction of a liberal state, or where the victims are assumed to be part of the original contract because of shared kinship or values. But the contractarian liberal state was also based on an imaginary assumption that humans had equal rights to self-preservation as well as the right to be governed by a government that ruled with their consent. The current debate about refugee law and protection is first about the degree to which protection ought to be accorded to those who flee states that breach liberal principles and, second, about the rules to be developed within liberal states to ensure such protection. There is also a debate about whether to extend such protection to those who flee territory where there is no effective government, territory reduced to a state of nature which can no longer ensure there is enough and sufficient for all. The debate is whether refugee policy should encompass all the protective rules, given the liberal rights guaranteed by western states, and utilised for the victims of states with illiberal policies, and further, whether that policy should be extended to those appealing for protection on the basis of a 'natural right' of self-preservation. The refugee regime has been extended to such victims under the Charter of the Organisation of African Unity and the Cartagena Agreement in Central America. Should such an extension be made universal, and, if so, by legislation or by the extension of case law?

Note that on the (ascend) vertical refugee axis, as well as on the horizontal immigration axis, *rights* of both kith and kin are given priority. The only strangers who have *rights* are those who lack state protection and need it, and they only have those rights if they are on state soil to claim them, a claim which must be proven. Refugees chosen abroad are selected based on balancing the needs of the refugees with the needs of one's own society.

Immigrants

The debates over justice in immigration, as distinct from refugee policy, occur on the horizontal axis of Chart 3.2 above. That is, in immigration policy the civil society's self-interests and the state's security are primary criteria. Immigration policy, on the one hand, entails decisions made in the self-interest of Australian and Canadian citizens, either because it advances the economic self-interest of the respective countries through the admission of capital investors, entrepreneurs and skilled or needed labour, or because families are allowed to sponsor relatives in the belief that the integrated family unit is the backbone of the civil society. Immigrants who have been admitted based on their skills, labour or capital contribution to the growth of Australia and Canada were admitted because of the host country's *needs*.

The other major source of immigrants, those who enter under family reunification programs, were admitted based on a concept of the *right* of individuals in Canada to be reunited with members of their immediate family. The reunification programs are rooted in the *self-interest* of both individual Canadian citizens and Canada in general in promoting family life and the happiness of its citizens. Enforced separation of family members would be detrimental to such goals.

But immigration policy is also decided on the basis of state and national security (excluding criminals and potential subversives). This dimension is well illustrated in the divisions within Canada between the French of Quebec and the English of the rest of Canada where refugee policy is considered the exclusive prerogative of the federal state, whereas immigration policy has been devolved to Quebec while preserved within federal jurisdiction for the rest of Canada. For

Quebec, control over immigration is central to the preservation of the Quebecois ever since the birth rate in Quebec fell steeply following the Quiet Revolution in French Canada during the 1960s. That is, a primary consideration of immigration policy for Quebec is the security and survival of the Quebecois, which must be balanced against the economic self-interest and family unification premises of immigration policy applied to the civil society.

For the Reform Party on the right of the political spectrum in the rest of Canada, particularly Western Canada, immigration is also a central issue for preserving the inherited values and culture of English-speaking Canadians. But for those who were part of the Quiet Revolution that permeated English Canada in the 1980s, where the incorporation of the Charter of Rights and Freedoms into the Constitution (a variation of a key element of the American secular religion) became the basis for a renewed English Canadian identity, the Charter became a statement of the common rights of all Canadian citizens by which they would weld their attachments to the Canadian polity (Russell 1983; Knopff & Morton 1985; McRoberts 1991). On 5 April 1985, the Supreme Court of Canada in the Singh case used the Charter of Rights and Freedoms, in particular, its clauses requiring fair treatment, to apply to non-citizens claiming refugee status to require that refugee claimants be given an oral hearing. In this decision, the Charter of Rights and Freedoms became applicable to non-citizens on Canadian territory. This decision radically transformed the protections and the legal basis for those protections for refugee claimants in Canada. In addition, refugee rights became a central concern of the internationally oriented 'new nationalists' of English-speaking Canada while remaining a matter of indifference to the nationalists of Quebec. Control over immigration and enforcement of the French language for immigrants to Quebec, even if it meant overriding the Charter of Rights and Freedoms, was the central issue for French Canadian nationalists of all stripes.

On the (assumed) immigration horizontal axis, excluding family class immigrants, the presumption is that needs rather than rights have priority. Further, it is not the needs of others which have priority. Neither Canada nor Australia determine who to select as immigrants based on the applicants with greatest need so that the needs of others which are greatest determine who are selected as immigrants. The Singers (1988) argue that it is the interests of all those affected, rather than self-interest, that is, universal interests versus self-interest, which ought to determine immigration policy on the basis of a needs theory—the more pressing the need, the greater the attention to it.

In reality and fact, the needs of one's own society determine who are allowed to enter.

Justice theory applied to specific cases

To ascertain the utility of applying this justice framework to specific immigration and refugee issues, we will take up four problems in determining refugee and immigration policy—a request by the UNHCR to resettle Shiite Iraqis who fled the repressive suppression of the southern revolt against Saddam Hussein following the end of the Gulf War, the adjudication of claims of refugees fleeing violent wars rather than a fear of persecution, the proposal to give priority to children and spouses in the family class and the problem of dealing with immigrants with special needs or, alternatively, using the special needs of Canada or Australia to set conditions for immigrants who come to these countries.

About 20 000 Shiites fled to Saudi Arabia following the Gulf War and the suppression of the Shiite revolt in the south of Iraq. Sunni-dominated Saudi Arabia would not let them become working contributors to that society; the refugees are confined to camps. (Saudi Arabia was already following the Kuwaiti lead and, though much more slowly, undertaking a process of replacing Arab guest workers—largely Palestinian and Egyptian—with Muslims from Pakistan and Bangladesh and even Christians from the Philippines, to offset a perceived security threat from other Arabs.)

If Saudi Arabia, a rich state, would not take in fellow Arabs who had fought against its own enemy, why should a country like Canada (whose citizens have little connection with the Shiites from southern Iraq) do so? Further, although the refugees did have a well-founded fear that, if they returned, they would be persecuted by Saddam Hussein, they were not in danger where they were; even though Saudi Arabia was not a signatory to the Convention, the refugees seemed to be at very little risk of imminent refoulement. There was also the continuing prospect, although one which receded day by day, that Saddam Hussein would be ousted and they then could return.

The Shiites were a collection of refugees with internationally recognised rights, but without a way to gain access to a state that would adjudicate those claims while trapped in a state that not only was not a signatory to the Convention, but granted few rights to its own citizens. Further, the Convention imposed no obligations on states towards Convention refugees unless those refugees were on the soil of the signatory state, and, in a minimalist interpretation, the only obligation the Convention imposed was not to refoule the refugee to his or her native land from which the refugee had fled. In this case, refugees had rights but ones which could not be exercised in any procedural sense because the state in which they found refuge was not threatening to deny them the minimal right of avoiding refoulement but, at the same time, provided none of the other rights which might allow the refugees to move beyond the bare and boring conditions of camp life.

Australia and Canada had no legal obligations to accept the refugees under the Convention. Did they have a moral obligation to assume some responsibility? It is my argument that both countries did have such a moral obligation, but it was not unequivocal. The obligation was not clear and absolute because the refugees were neither in danger nor posed a danger to the state in which they found themselves. Urgency was absent. There were potential alternatives in the near future depending on the course of history. Further, there were other groups of refugees in parallel positions in parts of Africa. Would Australia and Canada be asked to resettle them? The refugees did not have the requisite skills that would induce Australia or Canada to volunteer to make space for them in the annual immigration quota nor do they have many, if any, family connections that would create a domestic pressure for their entry. Some might have argued, very erroneously, I believe, that an intake of Shiites opened the possibility of a radical fundamentalist Iran using the refugees for subversive purposes.

The obligation arose neither because of the needs of the refugees nor the needs of either country, but because both countries, particularly Canada, sets the pace and marks the standard for defining obligations to refugees internationally. And refugees with rights that only allow them to remain in limbo year after year belies that those are rights in any real sense of the term. If refugee rights were to move towards a universal and transcendental standard, then some country had to take the initiative and ensure that the refugees had *de facto* though not merely *de jure* rights. Since the UNHCR was only asking the West to resettle a total of 35 000 refugees that year, and Canada's annual quota for government selected refugees traditionally hovered around 13 000 (a quota which it had not come near to filling that year), taking in twice its normal allocation of 10 per cent of the 20 000 Shiites, that is 4000, would not make a significant dent in its program or interfere dramatically with intakes elsewhere, and the deed could be accomplished in one fell swoop. Canada could make the moral gesture, demonstrate its support to the UNHCR's resettlement program and all at little cost to itself.

Rights as developed historically to that moment created some moral pressure and the Canadian definition of itself created additional incentive, but no legal or even clear cut immediate moral obligation to take in the refugees. Since this weak source of moral pressure was not supplemented by any incentive based on Canadian needs or pressures by a moral constituency, such as humanitarian organisations, churches or mosques, and since new Canadian immigration law was to be introduced in the near future and the government did not want any criticism from its right for being too generous, it was unlikely that the sense of moral obligation would become strong enough to offset all the negative factors against Canada taking a lead on this issue. And internationally no other volunteers seemed apparent.

The situation merely demonstrates a need to clarify and strengthen the international obligation and to develop a true sense of burden sharing with formal obligations when refugees do not fulfil all the requisite conditions (such as being on the soil of a country which is a signatory to the Convention). Otherwise moral pressures will remain insufficient to create action let alone an expanded legal protective mechanism.

What about refugees who flee violent wars or totalitarian regimes but are not themselves subject to a threat of individual persecution? Tamils from Sri Lanka and Iranians in flight from the fundamentalist Shiite regime in power are cases in point. In these cases, Canada in particular does have both a legal obligation since refugees from Sri Lanka and Iran who have made claims in Canada have had high success rates before the Refugee Board. Case law in Canada has provided a broad interpretation of who can qualify as a Convention refugee. Further, Canada has a moral obligation not to return claimants to Sri Lanka and Iran unless we can verify that we are not putting the rejected claimants in danger, something easier to do in Sri Lanka than in Iran. The incentive to fulfil these moral obligations is helped by the fact that both the Tamil community and Canadians from Iran provide a small but forceful lobby on behalf of both groups. The numbers are not large enough to threaten other intakes or dramatically alter the population balance in Canada. The character of the civil society combine with the rights already won and recognised in Canada for refugee claimants, and the moral responsibilities Canada has customarily assumed towards those who are not qualified Convention refugees but whose lives might be endangered by sending them back to their home countries.

If we move from the issue of refugees to that of immigrants, Canada, in its new immigration act, Bill C-86, passed at the end of 1992, gave virtually automatic rights to quick entry to spouses and dependent children of those already landed in Canada. This group received preferential treatment over other applicants to immigrate. Of course, Canada was in a position to legally and practically do so, but can such a position be morally justified? I argue that such preferential treatment is not only morally justified but that justice itself demands preferential treatment simply on the basis of the greater needs of those already in Canada as well as the greater needs of immediate family members compared to any other class of immigrant applicant. Further, it is in the interest of society as a whole to encourage and reinforce family life and stability. In this case, needs to trump rights and dictate that this class of immigrant applicant be given effective automatic rights of entry.

Are we not guilty of imposing western concepts of the nuclear hetero-sexual family on the issue of needs rather than taking into consideration the broader concept of the family in traditional societies and the evolving change in the family concept in the postmodern era to include homosexual couples and single-parent families? Yes, but it is not an imposition; it is merely the fact that Canadian standards as they evolve and change (that is, Canadian community values) will dictate the definition of the family and not the source country. Communal interests and values combine with the needs of some members of the civil society to dictate that it is indeed just to give priority for entry to immediate family members.

Finally, can justice limit entry for persons with special needs or utilise specific regional needs to make entry conditional? As an example in the former case, could Australia and Canada deny the entry of a person requiring renal dialysis when the facilities for undertaking renal dialysis are in short supply? The answer here is unequivocal; Canada can not only deny such entry but must do so if it is to live up to its obligations to its own citizens. Here, parochial country needs trump over any universal rule of distributive justice.

In the case of the latter, the Canadian Immigration Act (1992) intends to allow entry for immigrants with specific skills needed in a particular area of the country provided the individual agrees to reside in that area for at least two years. Such conditional admittance has little difference in principle from the conditional admission of domestic workers or the older programs for agricultural workers that used to be an integral part of Canadian immigration programs when the country was predominantly an agricultural nation. For that matter, there is no difference in principle from requiring doctors after graduation to serve the state for several years, either in the armed forces or in areas with a shortage of medical professionals if their tuition was financed by the state. Provided the conditions are clear, reasonable and known in advance then conditional admission into membership in a state offend no rights and are based on a contract of mutual need where both parties benefit.

Thus far, all the cases proposed have been consonant with existing or proposed state policy; the analysis endorses the actions of the state as satisfying various criteria of justice. I now want to analyse one proposal that I consider offends principles of justice. The existing Canadian legislation provides for a safe third-country provision. If a claimant arrives at the Canadian border after sojourning in another country where the refugee could have made a refugee claim, and that country was a signatory to the Convention and has a reasonable (not perfect or even one that lives up to Canadian standards) refugee determination system, then the law provides that the claimant can be denied entitlement to make a claim if the country in which the refugee claimant had sojourned had been proscribed as a safe-third country by Cabinet. The new legislation reinforces this provision at the same time as it allows Canada to enter into bilateral and multilateral agreements for 'shared responsibility' concerning refugee cases.

Shared responsibility can be an opportunity to develop a multilateral system for reasonable refugee determination with responsibility for predetermined numbers of refugees allocated to the various countries on a per centage basis based on a formula which takes into consideration the abilities of the various countries to handle the responsibilities of resettlement. On the other hand, shared responsibility can be a euphemism to enter into agreements on the European model which compensate countries financially if they carry a disproportionate portion of the refugee flow, but, in reality, discourage a generous approach to refugee determination. In fact, the system encourages countries to enact very restrictive legislation lest that country, through a generous or even fair system, attract too many claimants.

If the latter pattern is followed, then what we have is a beggar-thy-neighbour policy and not one of real shared responsibility. In addition to visa controls and carrier sanctions, it is but another device not only to prevent the entry of unwanted arrivals, but also to inhibit access to a country's refugee determination system for genuine refugees. We have a system which may be reasonably fair if one can gain access to the system, but one which is also designed to deter such access and also create pressures to ensure the determination system remains relatively restricted lest it become a magnet for claimants. As a complementary measure, the legislation penalises carriers harshly for bringing individuals with improper documents (necessary for many if not most genuine refugees) but provides no provision for refunding the penalties if those claimants prove to be genuine refugees.

In sum, the legislation does provide reasonably fair protection for refugees who gain access to the system but, at the same time, provides many barriers to prevent genuine refugees from gaining entry to make a claim and proposes to strengthen some measures, such as the safe third-country provision and carrier sanctions to greatly limit access to the system. Though such provisions satisfy the perceived self-interest of some political groupings, those perceptions cannot mount much of a defence on any reasonable needs criteria; they also fundamentally assault the principle of rights for refugee claimants which Canada is both legally and morally bound to uphold. Since rights trump needs in the arena of refugees in any case, such provisions offend the principles of justice applicable to immigration and refugee issues set forth here. Since Canada does not even carry its fair share of refugee asylum claims in the West (1 claimant per 1000 of population compared to an average of 1 per 850 of population) let alone any reasonable share of the world burden which is mainly born by Third World countries, one cannot even make the argument that Canada is so overburdened with responsibilities that it is impelled to offend principles of justice for the sake of self-interest.

Conclusion

The right to move that has emerged has not been equated with a fundamental right. It has become more and more extensive, but it is not an abstract universal right. If the right to move is considered fundamental, and yet the right to move is rooted in history and changes over time, then such a thesis is predominantly communitarian. Rights are considered an offshoot of the development of society and of state and interstate law and practice. Though the rights of individuals have been granted increased recognition by the international community, states retain exclusive control over the rights granted to those individuals. Under a communitarian presumption, no abstract principle of justice exists independent of history. There is no abstract principle of justice by which to adjudicate the choice of which needs have priority. But rights are not reduced to historical practice. Rather, rights have emerged to advance and satisfy certain needs as well as to universalise the communitarian values of a liberal society, including not only the right to have a government that enjoys the consent of the people, the right to be protected by the rule of law, the freedom to speak and publish, or the freedom to belong to a group of one's choice, but also to move and claim such rights in a liberal state if, in the effort to stand up for such rights, one fears persecution.

This paper was not intended to adjudicate migration and refugee issues in terms of justice. Rather, it was intended to assist policy makers in such adjudication by trying to show that immigration and refugee issues occupy different planes of justice and to set out the importance of taking such justice claims seriously while providing a category matrix in terms of which the adjudication will be more careful, thorough and self-consciously done.

PART TWO

Policy Making

The Making of Immigration and Refugee Policy: Politicians, Bureaucrats and Citizens

Leonie Hardcastle, Andrew Parkin, Alan Simmons and Nobuaki Suyama

Introduction

This chapter investigates and compares the process by which immigration and refugee policy decisions are made in Australia and Canada. It is particularly concerned with the distribution of influence over the policy-making process by government actors, political institutions, interest groups and citizens. The chapter limits its analysis to the formulation of policy, such as the making of policy decisions about the size and composition of the immigrant and refugee intake, and does not directly consider implementation and management matters. Neither does it delve deeply into details of legislation or regulations. Rather, its purpose is to provide a broadly based interpretation of the overall patterns of policy making in the two countries.

In its first section, a number of hypotheses are put forward which provide alternative descriptions and explanations of national immigration policy. Then the constitutional and institutional framework within which authoritative policy decisions are produced with respect to immigration and refugee matters are discussed. Subsequently, we contrast Canada and Australia with respect to the impact of political parties, organised labour, business interests, ethnic-minority interests, and other societal forces on immigration and refugee policy. This informs a re-examination, in the concluding section, of the alternative hypotheses.

While there are obviously some important differences between Canada and Australia, the immigration and refugee policy-making processes in the two countries do reveal substantial similarities. At the broad level of explanation invited by the alternative hypotheses, the chapter concludes that the situation in both Australia and Canada can be characterised by the tension between two embedded dynamics: a 'nation-building statism', involving the management of policy by governmental elites according to an agenda which legitimates state action and promotes national goals, and a 'pluralistic' social and political structure which enables particular societal pressures to bear on the process. The 'statist' dynamic is most dominant within Canada's policy-making process, and was likewise dominant in Australia in the 1950s and 1960s. In more recent decades, the policy-making process in both countries has been more vulnerable to 'pluralist' intrusions, most notably in Australia since the late 1970s.

Patterns of influence over policy-making: alternative hypotheses

It is useful to identify a number of hypotheses which provide alternative descriptions and explanations of patterns of influence over immigration and refugee policy-making. Each of the hypotheses enjoys some currency in the general Australian and Canadian social science literature as well as in the specific literature dealing with immigration and refugee policy. The chapter does not attempt to provide a rigorous 'test' of these hypotheses. Their purpose is rather to provide an organising and argumentative framework for the information and analysis which follow by suggesting broad lines of enquiry and explanation. The hypotheses are by no means exhaustive nor mutually exclusive.

Hypothesis 1: Responsible government

Both Australia and Canada are federal parliamentary democracies built around the notion of 'responsible government' (Mallory 1984; Ward 1987; Summers 1990). Political parties contest national elections on the basis of specified platforms, and the national government is formed from the party or coalition that wins a majority of seats in the Lower House of the national Parliament. That government can claim an electoral mandate to implement the platform which has received voter endorsement. Once in office, the government continues to be responsible to Parliament in the sense that it must continue to enjoy the confidence of a Lower House majority. In practice, the relatively disciplined political parties of the Westminster variety which are a feature of both countries (Epstein 1964, 1977) ensure that governments are rarely if ever forced to resign. Nonetheless, ministers remain responsible to Parliament in the sense that they are answerable for their conduct in their portfolio, and in particular they are expected to provide leadership to their Departments in carrying out the policies of the government.

Applied to the immigration and refugee field, this 'responsible government' scenario suggests that, in both Australia and Canada, national elections provide an opportunity for political parties to present alternative platforms to citizen-voters. The electoral victory of a party or coalition can be taken as endorsing the immigration policies contained in that platform, and the Minister for Immigration proceeds to direct his or her Department towards their implementation.

Hypothesis 2: Bureaucratic dominance

A standard critique of the conventional 'responsible government' model is that it understates the real power exercised over the policy-making process by the departments and their officials. Ministers and governments may come and go, but public servants tend to remain and their departments develop more or less permanent spheres of authority and interest. Contrary to the Westminster assumptions about the neutrality of public officials and the amenability of Departments to the policy platforms of incoming governments, political scientists in both Australia and Canada have suggested that bureaucratic agencies develop particular value-orientations towards their mission, and have an interest in maintaining and enhancing their spheres of influence (Campbell & Szablowski 1979; Wilenski 1979; Atkinson & Coleman 1985; Thompson 1990).

This interpretation has been applied to immigration policy in both countries. In Australia, Birrell and Birrell (1981, p. 231) have argued that the Department of Immigration 'has never been just a passive arm of Government, faithfully implementing Government policy'; rather it has 'actively promoted the goal of population expansion and the cultivation of public support for this'. In Canada, Abella and Troper (1983), Abella (1988) and Schultz (1982) argue that bureaucrats had tremendous influence in maintaining the racially-discriminatory policies of the past, while Whitaker (1987) has a similar interpretation of the role of senior officials in creating what he maintains were distortions and biases in Canadian refugee policy throughout the post-War period.

Hypothesis 3: Nation-building statism

'Statist' theory has developed within the social sciences in recent years in response to the insight that state institutions can be a repository of power independent of societal forces (Nordlinger 1981; Skocpol 1985). This perspective contends that policies pursued by state institutions are best explained by the interests of those institutions and of the 'state managers' who inhabit them, and thus by a process of decision-making internal to those institutions, rather than by a political process which links state institutions to societal pressures. In particular, these state institutions and managers have an enduring interest and goal of nation-building: using the legitimacy and leadership of national government to strengthen the nation's economic and infrastructural basis, and to enhance its position in the international arena. This statist perspective has been particularly influential in Canadian social science (Cairns 1977; Nossal 1985; Keating 1987). It has been noted in the Australian literature (Bell 1992) and a recent analysis has proposed that the Australian national public sector has constituted, at least until recently, a 'nation building state' (Pusey 1991).

Simmons and Keohane (1992) and Suyama (1991a) have explored an explicitly state-centred explanation for Canadian immigration policy. While there appears to be no self-consciously 'statist' interpretation of immigration policy in Australia, aspects of the argument in Blainey (1984b) and in Birrell and Birrell (1981) are consistent with the view that the state elite has formulated and implemented policy in pursuit of its own vision for the nation, relatively insulated from societal pressure.

Hypothesis 4: Cosmopolitan elitism

Some social theorists have suggested that modern 'post-industrial' societies such as Australia and Canada are distinguished by the hegemony of a professionally credentialled, cosmopolitan 'new class'. The 'new class' wields authority through its ownership of what Gouldner (1979) calls 'cultural capital'. Its values—of internationalism, universalism and liberalism—contrast with what are characterised as the parochial and ethnocentric values of other sectors of society. The cosmopolitan values predominate because 'new class' members—academics, teachers, journalists, media managers, public servants, human service professionals—constitute an elite which controls the major organs of education and mass communication.

Betts (1988) argues that the 'enlightened' pro-immigration and pro-multicultural values of the liberal–cosmopolitan elite are crucial in explaining immigration policy development in Australia, while Hawkins (1988, 1989) and Dirks (1980, p. 13) at least implicitly posit a similar argument for Canada.

Hypothesis 5: Pluralism

The pluralist model envisages the policy-making process as shaped by pressure from mobilised societal interests, with policy outcomes understood as bargained and brokered compromises reflecting the relative strengths of these interests. Because, it is argued, many different interests arise with respect to important policy questions and because power resources are relatively dispersed throughout society, the outcomes rarely represent a domination of one interest over others. Pluralism is widely recognised as one of the conventional interpretive models of political science. Its general explanatory utility has been canvassed in both Australia (Parkin 1980; DeAngelis & Parkin 1990) and Canada (Riddell-Dixon & Riddell-Dixon 1987).

With respect to immigration policy, Parkin and Hardcastle (1990, p. 315) have argued that 'immigration policy formulation' in Australia can be explained in part by 'the dynamic pluralist interaction among mobilised interests'. A number of analyses of Canadian immigration and refugee policy have also pointed to important pluralist influences (Simmons & Keohane 1992).

Hypothesis 6: Business dominance

Australia and Canada are both capitalist societies, with private capital accumulation and investment for private profit providing the basic motor of the economy. There are prominent interpretations in the social sciences which accord a pre-eminence to this economic basis as the fundamental determinant of public policy. Governments, it is argued, are bound to pursue policy strategies which are in the interests of the business sector. Otherwise, private investment fails to occur, economic stagnation—and electoral unpopularity—follow. There are Marxist and non-Marxist variations on this theme, with an extensive general literature both in Australia (McEachern 1991) and Canada (Panitch 1977).

The interpretation is also prominent in the immigration literature, with some theorists interpreting immigrant labour as serving the interests of capitalism by providing cheap labour and diluting the influence of organised trade unions. In Australia, Collins (1984) has portrayed post-war immigration policy along these broad lines, depicting the mass of unskilled immigrant workers as constituting a 'reserve army of labour' in the Marxist sense. In the Canadian literature, the so-called 'Staples Approach' to Canadian political economy suggests a form of business dominance: immigration policy is interpreted as an instrument for Canadian business leaders and investors, and their class allies in Britain and the United States responding, to reap profits from business expansion, such as in agricultural production early in the century (Corbett 1957) and in urban manufacturing industry after World War II (Green 1976). Del Negro (1984) and Stafford and McMillan (1988) have similarly argued that recent Canadian immigration policy can also be understood almost in its entirety from the perspective of a business-dominated economic interest.

Hypothesis 7: Populism

While 'public opinion' is a rather amorphous concept, there are some purported measures, namely national opinion surveys, often used by political parties, governments and the media as guides to overall public sentiments. 'Public opinion' is sometimes conceived as a latent force capable of being mobilised, through a 'populist' appeal to the values of the citizenry, if public policy moves beyond the parameters of acceptability. Historians have noted elements of a recurring populist dimension in Australian political life (Brugger & Jaensch 1985). The latent potential for populist mobilisation might thus represent a broad societal influence on public policy not through the formal procedures outlined under the Responsible Government hypothesis but through 'public opinion' setting the general parameters of acceptable policies.

The populist hypothesis thus suggests that immigration and refugee policy is shaped by the necessity for widespread popular support, in the absence of which a populist appeal to public opinion would be an effective strategy for policy change. Of particular concern in this context would be a populism based on ethnocentricity. Populist appeals to majority cultural groups based on perceived threats by immigrant minorities to their hegemony have occurred in some democracies, with examples including the American 'nativist' movements (Higham 1955) and Le Pen's influence on contemporary French politics. When Blainey (1984a) warned, in criticism of Australian immigration policies in the 1980s, that 'it is public opinion which ultimately decides whether an immigration program will succeed', he appeared to be especially concerned about a possible populist reaction by what he termed the 'old Australians' against ethnically distinct (and especially of Asian origin) new arrivals (see also Blainey 1984b). In both Australia and Canada, the racially restrictive immigration policies and the assimilationist settlement policies of the past are commonly attributed to the effects of an allegedly pervasive racism or ethnocentrism in the general population (McQueen 1970; Satzewich 1991).

Political institutions

An examination of the institutions and processes of policy formulation, and the role played within them by particular interests, is necessary before credible conclusions can be drawn about the relative utility of these hypotheses. The analysis here begins with formal constitutional and institutional structures, since these provide the legitimate framework within which the policy-making process is constituted. Some of the hypotheses—such as the Bureaucratic Dominance and Statist interpretations—place particularly strong emphasis on the behaviour of some of these institutions.

Federalism and national–provincial relations

Australia and Canada are distinguished by their federal governmental arrangements, with the authority and sovereignty of the state divided between a national government and State/Provincial governments. In general, the national governments have jurisdiction (though not necessarily exclusive) over obvious national matters, with the States/Provinces responsible for most of the basic services delivered to citizens. In both countries, especially in Australia, local government is relatively insignificant and, especially and most passionately in Canada, the distribution of powers between the national and the provincial level has been a matter of historical contention and contemporary debate.

At the time of federation (1867 for Canada and 1901 for Australia), Canada's national government was probably envisaged as relatively more powerful than Australia's, being granted not only jurisdiction over specific national policy matters but also significant general authority under the 'Peace, Order and Good Government' clause of the Constitutional Act. The Australian national government was granted simply a list of specified powers, with all other powers (unspecified) remaining with the States. Ironically, however, subsequent developments have strengthened the relative position of the Provinces in Canada and the national government in Australia. While judicial review was an important causal factor in both countries, so were idiosyncratic features.

In Canada's case, these include its strong regional diversity, the impact of natural resources in strengthening the financial position of some Provinces and, probably most important, the 'distinct society' in Quebec which, especially since the 'Quiet Revolution' of the 1960s, has been a force for specific recognition and autonomy at the provincial level (Suyama 1992). The intensity of the debate about national–provincial relations is such that 'for the Canadian state, the politics of federalism are the politics of survival' (Black 1975, p. 1).

While the politics of Australian federalism are not so lethal, they have also been contentious. Dominance of the public finance system and conditional grants to the States provide a potential avenue for significant national influence over policy areas formally under State jurisdiction. The position should not, however, be overstated: the States retain a significant political strength which belies their weakened Constitutional and financial status (Sharman 1990).

Immigration powers are particularly interesting in this federal context. In both countries, immigration is a concurrent Constitutional power with national law predominating in the case of conflict. The immigration program in Australia is firmly under the control of the national government, though this was only gradually accomplished after federation with separate State-based promotion and recruitment schemes continuing for some time and persisting, on a small and selective scale, into recent decades. The national Immigration Department accepts some responsibility for post-arrival services, but State governments necessarily assume a major responsibility for providing services to expanding immigration-driven populations. Most States adapt their mainstream services in education, welfare, health and other human services, though some have Ethnic Affairs agencies which oversee the process.

Most of these Australian arrangements would be familiar to the Canadians, though Canada has produced more central–Provincial tension in the past and is likely to feature much greater Provincial input in the future. Most Provinces gradually and uneventfully ceded immigration management to the national government in the period after federation. However, British Columbia's repeated attempts to restrict Asian immigration conflicted with attempts at the national level to placate China and Japan. Provincial legislation was repeatedly annulled by the national government until, by the 1920s, British Columbia had finally ceded *de facto* control of the immigration program. More recently, Quebec's concerns with maintaining its Francophone viability have been exacerbated by its declining birth rate. The national Canadian and the Quebec government have entered into various agreements to the effect that Quebec now controls its own immigration selection and post-arrival programs, with shared Federal/Provincial financing. In recent negotiations, Quebec has been demanding that it receive its proportionate share (around 25 per cent) of immigrants to Canada. Other Provinces have now also expressed a greater interest in participating in the shaping of the overall immigration program. The national government consults with Provinces before proposing new annual intake targets. Other provinces, such as Alberta, have reached specific short-term agreements with the national government though with far less decentralised effects than the Quebec agreement. Provinces are particularly active participants in the selection and initial supervision of immigrants admitted under the 'business immigration' sub-program (Simmons & Keohane 1992).

Legislative–executive relations

Both Australia and Canada feature the strong executive branch and weak legislative branch typical of Westminster-style Parliamentary democracies. Policy initiatives arise in the executive branch, co-ordinated through Cabinet (itself drawn from the party or coalition with a Lower House majority), and Parliament generally plays a passive or subordinate role in the policy process. The implementation of immigration policy may often require legislation and hence Parliamentary approval, such as the Canadian refugee legislation (Bills C-55 and C-84) of early 1989. However, party discipline generally ensures that government bills are guaranteed passage through the Lower House of the Parliament.

The impact of the Australian parliamentary process is strengthened by the existence of an elected Senate with powers virtually equal to those of the House of Representatives. This can provide an impediment to untrammelled executive dominance, since the electoral system almost ensures that neither of the potential governing parties can win a Senate majority. Thus passage of legislation through the Senate often involves negotiation and compromise. In Canada, by contrast, the Senate—an appointed chamber—has been relatively ineffective (Uhr 1989; Suyama 1991b), though it managed to delay and insert some minor amendments to the refugee bills in 1988 (Nash 1989, pp. 56–64). Important changes to the Canadian Senate, proposed in 1992 as part of a major constitutional reform, will, if fully implemented, transform that body's structure (making it smaller, with equal Provincial representation) but not necessarily make it stronger.

Even in the Lower Houses, it would be misleading to dismiss Parliament's role altogether. In both countries, the parliamentary forum is the arena in which ministers are required to answer in public for their policies and the work of their departments. Parliamentary questions and debates, while generally playing little role in the shaping of legislation, provide a forum for the Opposition to criticise government action under the gaze of the national media. Political leadership credentials are often established by performance in the Parliamentary chamber. Parkin (1987) has argued that the Parliamentary forum played an important, even if only cathartic and symbolic, role during the intense and passionate debate in Australia in 1984 over the issue of Asian immigration. A wide range of views was able to be aired, and the process led to a convergence on both sides of the chamber towards a more conciliatory public position. It contributed to the replacement of the then Leader of the Opposition (Andrew Peacock) by a rival (John Howard) who had performed particularly creditably in the immigration debate.

Parliamentary committees also have the potential for some independence in scrutinising executive action. The Canadian Parliament has a Standing Committee on Labour, Employment and Immigration which oversees executive activity in the portfolio. A Joint Parliamentary Committee was closely involved in the drafting of the 1976 Immigration Act; its work was praised by some observers (Dobell & d'Aquino 1976) though Richmond (1975) argues that it achieved a prominence only by default because the government was unsure of its strategy. In Australia, investigations by the Joint Committee of Public Accounts into alleged problems with the business migration program precipitated the suspension of the program by the government in July 1991. A relatively new Joint Standing Committee on Migration Regulations has also investigated some specific immigration issues; its first two reports, for example, dealt with illegal immigration and with problems pertaining to change of immigrant status due to marriage or *de facto* relationships.

Cabinet and the Prime Minister

The locus of policy initiative is within the executive branch. Cabinet is the heart of executive government in both Australia and Canada. It is chaired by the Prime Minister, and individual ministers (such as the Minister of Immigration) participate in two capacities: one as a corporate member of Cabinet bound by conventions of collective responsibility and the other as the member with specific responsibility for matters under his or her portfolio.

Cabinet's potentially overwhelming workload is typically managed by delegating most routine or uncontentious matters to lower levels in the executive branch. In both Australia and Canada, the sort of immigration and refugee matters which are likely to reach Cabinet would include: major policy reviews (example: the establishment in 1987 of the FitzGerald Committee in Australia); proposals for major policy changes (example: the extensive Canadian governmental review of immigration targets in 1991, leading up to significant legislative proposals in 1992); the designated intake targets for forth-coming time periods (example: the Australian 1992–93 immigration target announced in April 1992); and particular 'crisis' situations (example: the extraordinary Canadian public reaction to the 1987 arrival in Nova Scotia of a boatload of Sikhs seeking refugee status).

In both countries, the prestige of Prime Ministerial office provides the incumbent with considerable policy latitude. In Australia, Prime Minister Hawke seemed to identify himself closely with some refugee issues, and his announcement of generous asylum provisions for Chinese students in the wake of the Tienanmen Square incident appeared to surprise his Cabinet colleagues and bypass Immigration Department recommendations. The allocation of portfolios to particular Ministers is also a Prime Ministerial prerogative and can influence policy direction: for example, Hawke's designations in 1986 of Mick Young and in 1991 of Gerry Hand as ministers for immigration were widely interpreted as promoting policies more favourable to the expressed interests of ethnic minority communities. There are, however, limits to this Prime Ministerial latitude. Under the Australian system, the Prime Minister needs to retain the confidence of a majority of his caucus colleagues. Bob Hawke failed this test in December 1991. While probably not decisive in this contest, some of Hawke's caucus critics drew attention to his pre-emptive announcements on the Chinese students and his alleged partiality towards the so-called 'ethnic lobby' as examples of his declining credibility.

Crisis refugee situations also saw Canadian Prime Minister Mulroney acting relatively independently of his Cabinet colleagues. In 1986, he authorised admission to the Sri Lankan Tamils dumped off Newfoundland but a year later declared—with a new election looming—that the Sikh refugees would be subjected to rigorous individual tests. Because the Canadian Prime Minister is chosen in a national party convention, not in the parliamentary caucus, the policy latitude attached to the office is probably even broader than in Australia (Weller 1985, p. 69).

Individual ministers also appear to have some latitude in putting their own particular stamp on the portfolio to which they are allocated, though again there are political limits. The Immigration portfolio is regarded as one of the more onerous in both countries, since it can involve responsibility not only for determination of broad policy but also for individual decisions about particular cases of admission and deportation.

Immigration has been described by an Australian journalist as 'the killer portfolio' (O'Reilly 1988), and indeed there has been a rapid turnover of Ministers under the Labor government since 1983: seven incumbents in less than ten years. Most of these seven have, during their relatively brief periods of tenure, pursued distinctive policy agendas (Parkin & Hardcastle 1990, pp. 318–25). For example, Stewart West (1983–84) was a former trade union official who favoured intake cuts to preserve job opportunities. His successor Chris Hurford (1984–87) consciously and successfully worked for an expanded intake; however his efforts to increase the proportion of skilled entrants at the expense of family reunion applicants upset organised ethnic minority interests, whose attitudes were interpreted as influencing his removal by the Prime Minister. Mick Young (1987–88) was regarded as more acceptable to those interests, while Clyde Holding (1988) was not in office long enough to make a distinctive impact. Robert Ray (1988–91) pursued an agenda of administrative streamlining and the minimisation of discretion in the selection process, while Gerry Hand (1991–93) was seen to have been a more conciliatory appointment with respect to ethnic minority interests; his successor, Nick Bolkus, appointed after the March 1993 election, may follow a similar pattern.

The Mulroney government in Canada also had a succession of Ministers for the Labour and Immigration portfolio—Flora MacDonald (1984–86), Benoit Bouchard (1986–88), Barbara McDougall (1988–91), and Bernard Valcourt 1991–93)—supported by a succession of junior Ministers—Walter McLean (1985–86), Gerry

Weiner (1986–88), and Monique Vezina (1988–91)—who, under the portfolio arrangements, have taken responsibility for immigration matters. The Immigration portfolio is probably of lower status than in Australia, though a respectable performance can produce the reward of promotion to a more senior portfolio (for example, McDougall was elevated to External Affairs).

Concern has been expressed by both Canadian (Franks 1987, pp. 23–26) and Australian (Weller & Grattan 1981) commentators that rapid Ministerial turnover, which is probably not limited to the immigration portfolio, may have the effect of strengthening the influence of permanent officials.

The bureaucracy

The location of administrative responsibility for immigration within the bureaucracy reveals something of the purpose and priority attached to it by governments. In Canada, the Immigration Branch has been successively attached to such Departments as Agriculture, the Interior, Mines and Resources, and Citizenship, before arriving at its present configuration within the Employment and Immigration Commission. Immigration is, however, the 'junior partner' within the Commission, accounting for only about 10 per cent of employees. (It should also be recalled that Quebec now administers much of its own immigration program.) In Australia, a freestanding Department of Immigration handled the massive post-war program until 1984. It was then located with Labour for the 1974–75 period during the latter stages of the Whitlam government, at a time of a substantially reduced intake and after the previous Minister had lost his parliamentary seat following a local campaign with uncomfortably ethnocentric elements. An independent Department was reconstituted in December 1975 under the Fraser government as Immigration and Ethnic Affairs. This nomenclature has been retained ever since (with the inconsequential addition of 'Local Government' in 1988; it was dropped in 1993).

Birrell and Birrell (1981, p. 231), as noted above, have attributed to the Australian Immigration Department a mission of 'actively promot[ing] the goal of population expansion and the cultivation of public support for this'. The Department's capacity to fulfil this mission is, however, potentially constrained by other executive branch influences and structures. The situation of its Canadian counterpart is very similar.

The impact in both countries of direct Prime Ministerial intervention in refugee policy has already been discussed. Central financial agencies (the Treasury Board in Canada, the Treasury and Finance Departments in Australia) also potentially have an impact through constraining budget allocations (though in practice this is not a costly portfolio area in comparison with other human services) and through general macro economic policy determination. The Australian Treasury and Finance Departments appear to have argued in recent years, against the position taken by the Immigration Department for reduced immigration intake levels (Walsh 1991a, 1991b).

There are other agencies whose policy interests overlap with immigration. While in Canada the same agency has jurisdiction over both immigration and employment, these have been divided in Australia (except for the 1974–75 period) so that, for example, the designation of occupations deemed to be in short supply becomes an inter-Departmental communication. Canadian immigration officials abroad are attached to the Department of External Affairs. The External Affairs Department tends to have a somewhat different perspective on immigration policy matters from the Employment and Immigration Commission, being more attuned to Canada's relationships with other countries (Dirks 1990). In the 1950s and 1960s, for example, it was External Affairs which pushed for Canadian accession to the UN refugee protocol while the then Department of Citizenship and Immigration resisted (Dirks 1980, Hathaway 1992). These contrasting missions undoubtedly also exist for Australia, where (for example) the Foreign Affairs Department was apparently alarmed at the implications for Australia's relationship with Beijing of the decision to extend visas for Chinese students.

Foreign student entry creates other bureaucratic complications in Australia. From 1986, the Department of Employment Education and Training has encouraged tertiary educational institutions to market their courses on a full-cost fee-paying basis to foreign students, with the Immigration Department's role restricted to the issuing of temporary visas. Immigration Department warnings about abuse of this program resulting in illegal overstaying in Australia, particularly by large numbers of Chinese students recruited by English-language training institutions, went largely unheeded elsewhere in the executive branch for several years (Matheson 1990, p. 92).

Both countries have created independent agencies to oversee 'multicultural affairs'. Canada had (since 1992) a Minister for Multiculturalism and Citizenship and previously had a Minister of State (namely a junior minister) for Multiculturalism. In Australia, an Office of Multicultural Affairs was established in 1987 within the Department of Prime Minister and Cabinet, and there is some evidence that its advice on immigration policy has differed from the Immigration Department (being more sympathetic to ethnic community concerns for family reunion and less impressed by arguments for a stricter economic focus). Holton and Sloan (1990, pp. 328–9) also point to 'the gradual shift in responsibility for the determination of the parameters of settlement policy from the Department of Immigration to the Office of Multicultural Affairs'. While policy ownership may thus be disputed in Australia, immediate post-arrival services still tend to be the responsibility of the immigration agency in both countries, though some language programs are provided under other agencies.

Even within the immigration departments, the administrative and policy process is not monolithic. Both countries have refugee-status determination panels and appeals committees which exercise some quasi-judicial autonomy and provide a significant check on agency decision-making in individual cases. There has been substantial reform of these bodies since 1989, creating for Canada a Immigration and Refugee Board and for Australia a Determination of Refugee Status Committee and an Immigration Review Tribunal (IRT). While the intention of the Australian reforms was to minimise ministerial discretion and thus correspondingly increase the scope for departmental decisions, the new bodies have displayed substantial independence to the point where the Australian Minister of Immigration has appealed to the Federal Court over IRT decisions.

Also characteristic of the immigration arena has been the occasional establishment of major *ad hoc* enquiries into various policy matters. In Australia, the Borrie (1975), Galbally (1978), Jupp (1986) and FitzGerald (1988) Reports have been landmarks in the policy debate even if their recommendations have not always been implemented. Of the four reports listed, it is the Galbally Report which has been most influential in shaping subsequent developments (in this case the establishment of multicultral services and policies). While obviously the Immigration Department made detailed submissions to these enquiries, the reports have been genuinely independent exercises. The FitzGerald Report, indeed, was very critical of administrative and professional aspects of the department. More permanent, but also influential, investigations have been carried out through the National Population Council and, since its creation in 1989, the Bureau of Immigration Research.

Canada seems to have resorted less often to such enquiries, though it is worth noting influential independent reports by Sedgwick (1966), Ratushny (1984) and Plaut (1985). Some recommendations of the Sedgwick Report (on procedural fairness in immigration cases) were subsequently adopted (Hawkins 1988, p. 149), while the other two reports (dealing with the determination of refugee status) had some influence though the process finally adopted was rather different from that recommended.

The judiciary

In the past, judicial intervention in the administration of immigration policy has been only of limited relevance in Australia. With no constitutional Bill of Rights, the courts have generally not intervened significantly. Even new developments in administrative law tended to bypass immigration and refugee matters because nearly all immigration and refugee decisions (excepting a few matters such as deportation) were exempted from the purview of the Administrative Appeals Tribunal established in 1975. However, appeals to the Federal Court under the *Administrative Decisions (Judicial Review) Act* of 1977 have been increasing, with immigration matters in recent years constituting the largest single category of applications to the Federal Court under this Act (DILGEA 1989, p. 4).

The entrenchment of the Charter of Rights and Freedoms in the 1982 Constitution makes judicial interpretation potentially very important in Canada. The Supreme Court's landmark decision in the Singh case in 1985 established that anyone physically in Canada is protected by the Charter and that, in this case, refugee arrivals were therefore entitled to an oral hearing. The decision alarmed immigration authorities. It spurred greater efforts to intercept refugees before arrival, and the Federal Court later somewhat weakened the impact of the decision when it agreed that the hearing could be 'preliminary' rather than an official Refugee Board hearing. In 1990, the Federal Court also made a ruling which required the setting of new guidelines for the exercise of ministerial discretion on 'humanitarian and compassionate' grounds. Overall, however, the impact of judicial review seems less dramatic in practice than anticipated a few years ago.

International relations

National governmental institutions not only legitimate a framework for domestic political decisions but also represent the interests of the nation in dealings with other nations. Immigration and refugee policies by definition have international implications, and international considerations have had an impact on national government policies in both Australia and Canada.

Historically, both countries adopted defensive immigration postures. Australia's misgivings about its regional location were a major factor both in the 'White Australia Policy' and in the mass European migration program in the post-war period. Canada has a similar history of racial exclusion and a preference for Europeans. More recently, however, defensive postures (though far from nonexistent given that immigration regulations effectively preclude far more applicants than they include) have been considerably tempered by broader foreign policy considerations. The removal of Australia's racially based policies and the recent marked increase in immigration from Asia is in part explained by the perception that these policies were offensive to Asian states and, more recently, an impediment to intra-regional trade. Canada has probably had a broader agenda, seeing itself as a promoter on the world stage of humanitarian policies (including with respect to refugees). Both countries now actively promote immigration through business programs targeted at the Asian region.

The mobilisation of interests

In this section, discussion moves beyond formal institutions and their interests to examine the manner in which broader societal interests are organised and expressed, and their degree of influence on policy making. Elections are structured around individual citizens expressing individual preferences, but what is sociologically striking about on-going political activity is its aggregation and organisation. Political parties are commonly identified as the principal vehicles for organising and transmitting societal interests into the political arena. As open liberal democracies, Australia and Canada also feature a myriad other interest groups which organise and articulate various sectional or ideological preferences (Pross 1986; Warhurst 1990).

Political parties

Though having no special constitutional status in either country, political parties are in practice the central organising mechanisms in national political life. Under the responsible government hypothesis, competition between parties for popular support is the mechanism for maintaining the responsiveness of government to the governed. This model assumes that the parties present alternative policy packages between which voters are able to choose. What is noteworthy in both Australia and Canada, however, is that bipartisanship is the norm with respect to immigration and refugee policies.

The effective electoral contest in Australia is between the Australian Labor Party (ALP) and the Liberal–National Party coalition. The ALP has close organisational and policy links to the trade unions and its platform identifies it as a 'democratic socialist' party. The Liberal Party platform extols the virtues of free enterprise, while the National Party (whose voting base is in rural electorates) combines advocacy for rural interests with social conservatism. Ostensibly, therefore, this Labor versus non-Labor contest has the hallmarks of a clear partisan choice between Left and Right. The parties are less polarised in practice, however, than this simple characterisation suggests, though interpretations in the political science literature vary from claims of close convergence (Jaensch 1989, pp. 20–22) to arguments that significant policy differences remain (Head 1989).

Whatever these broader arguments, party groupings have normally been very close on immigration matters. The basic thrust of policy development—from the so-called 'White Australia Policy' through the mass post-war immigration schemes to the present non-discriminatory intake criteria, and from assimilationist to multiculturalist domestic policies—has been bipartisan (Parkin & Hardcastle 1990, pp. 315–18). There have been brief periods when inter-party contention has occurred—including several in the 1980s—but these have been remarkable because they are atypical, and characteristically strenuous efforts have ensued to restore bipartisanship.

In the early 1990s, the Opposition (Liberal and National Parties) have advocated a large, though temporary, cut in the intake target. Though some of Prime Minister Keating's remarks in response have had the flavour of partisan criticism, it is remarkable how quickly these have been tempered and how uncomfortable many of his Labor colleagues—and his own Minister of Immigration—have felt with their tenor. The government has implemented its own moderate reductions in annual targets, thus essentially preserving a bipartisan approach.

Bipartisanship has also generally prevailed in Canada, where the major national parties—the Liberals and the Conservatives—are in any case more 'centrist' in their ideological orientation and are less influenced by extra-parliamentary organisation than are, for example, the Australian Labor Party or the Canadian New Democratic Party, both of which have links to organised labour. The Liberal and the Conservative parties both appeal broadly to diverse national interests, and are subject to policy changes over time which make it difficult to distinguish them categorically. Often policy initiatives taken up by one party become later the platform of the other. Yet, at any given moment they compete with one another and can have markedly different policies. For example, from the late 1980s to the early 1990s, the Conservatives strongly endorsed the US–Canada Free Trade initiative on the premise that it would lead to economic competitiveness and growth, while the Liberals opposed free trade on the grounds that it would erode national autonomy, particularly in the area of industrial strategy.

Similarly, the Liberals and Conservatives in Canada have differed in immigration and refugee policy, yet these differences at any point in time seem to be based not on any fundamental different principles. Rather, their approaches seem to differ in response to the conditions and opportunities present during their periods in government. The Liberals established Canada's contemporary immigration policy during long periods in office from the mid-1960s through the 1970s, while the Conservatives largely continued the same general policies over the 1980s. Yet on specific points they have differed. For example, they clashed on many aspects of the refugee legislation (Bills C-55 and C-84) passed by the Conservative government in 1988, with the Liberals arguing that the legislation threatened human rights (Abu-Laban 1988). In sum, there is evidence that both parties arrive at their policy positions while in government through balancing similar factors—Canada's economic interests, pressures from the Provinces (especially Quebec), and the expressed interests of ethnic voting blocs.

In both countries, smaller parties, being less bound to the necessity for compromise in building majority support, tend to have tighter and more distinctive platforms. There seem to be direct parallels between the Australian Democrats and the Canadian New Democratic Party. Both are somewhat 'centre-left' in orientation and tend to favour more 'humanitarian' goals. Both are therefore particularly sympathetic to liberalising refugee intake procedures. Their position on broader immigration matters is, however, less clear: they are caught among various conflicting 'leftist' concerns including environmental protection, population control, internationalism, respect for human rights, support for multiculturalism, and so on.

Canada has two quite distinctive but significant other parties. The Bloc Quebecois favours Quebec's control over its own destiny and hence supports the current decentralisation of immigrant selection and settlement programs to Quebec, even though it would prefer to see this taken a large step further in an independent Quebec. The

Reform Party, based in the west but becoming in 1993 a national contender, articulates a populist hostility to current levels of immigration and to cultural diversity. Substantial national support for the Reform Party would be a challenge to bipartisan norms in immigration policy, though it is likely that its policies would need to be moderated in order for it to win substantial support beyond its western base.

Organised labour

There are good reasons for expecting organised labour interests to be quite active with respect to immigration policy. The importation of workers can be perceived as a potential threat to jobs and working conditions, and is likely to lead to downward pressure on wage levels. Historically, trade unions in both countries have supported restrictive immigration policies. While historians still debate their relative influence, unions were certainly an element of the national consensus in Australia about the 'White Australia Policy' (Curthoys & Markus 1978). General support from organised labour has been an important ingredient in the post-war immigration programs in both countries. This support was underwritten, in Australia, by the centralised wage-fixing system and, in both countries up until the 1980s, by the adjustment of the target intake in relation to the demand for labour.

More recently, the leaders of organised labour have reconciled themselves to relatively large intakes even during economic downturns. There appear to be several reasons for this: first, the ethnic diversification of the workforce has produced a greater sensitivity among these leaders to pro-immigration sentiments among their constituents; second, these leaders probably see some merit in the argument about the long-term benefits of immigration for economic stimulation and job creation; third, the leaders (themselves increasingly likely to be professionally educated) have absorbed elements of the cosmopolitan ideology (Quinlan & Lever-Tracy 1990; Simmons & Keohane 1992).

Australian professional associations, not normally associated with 'organised labour' but in practice sharing some of the same concerns, have become increasingly critical of the admission of immigrant professionals. Organisations representing engineers and doctors have recently been quite vocal, with the latter successfully persuading the Keating Labor government severely to cut back the admission of foreign doctors.

Business interests

'Business has generally favoured high levels of immigration': this submission by the Business Council of Australia to the FitzGerald Committee (Matheson 1990, p. 92) could apply equally to Canada. For the business sector, relatively high immigration intakes produces a larger supply of potential workers, reduces upward pressure on wages and creates a larger consumer market for business products. In general, therefore, the reasonably consistent pro-immigration thrust of post-war policies in both countries has furthered the interests of the business sector. This does not mean, however, that business organisations have consistently lobbied for such policies or that their lobbying has been decisive. In fact, in Canada business constitutes one of the less visibly vocal lobbies (Simmons & Keohane 1992).

There are several possible reasons for the low public profile of business in public debate on immigration. At a general level, the government's own interest in economic prosperity makes a concerted expression of business concern at that level somewhat redundant. As in other policy areas, business interests are probably promoted less by overt lobbying than by the natural directions of public policy in a capitalist society. At a more specific level, there is no reason to expect a pro-immigration unanimity of views among established businesses. Immigration may facilitate the creation of rival firms or alternative market-place products. To the extent that it facilitates a more international and export-oriented business sector, then some domestic industries will feel threatened by free-trade pressures to reduce tariffs and other protection. In Australia, restrictive immigration and restrictive tariffs were packaged together as part of the grand compromise between labour and capital that shaped the country over more than half a century (Castles 1988). There are differing business interests with respect to intake composition. While the housing, construction and retail industries are probably indifferent, composition is of the utmost importance to some traditional manufacturing industries which want a supply of low-skilled labour and to other businesses needing employees trained in specific occupations.

In the past decade or so, business organisations have generally supported provisions for increasing the 'skilled labour' intake. Yet, in both Australia and Canada, governments have continued to give strong support to a substantial 'family reunion' component, wherein workforce skill levels are below average (Hugo 1988), and the 'skilled' component often bears the brunt of cutbacks. Thus it appears that the business voice is not necessarily very strong with respect to policy details.

Business operators are also taxpayers. Like other taxpayers, they have an interest in minimising the welfare budget and hence would not be expected to favour high intake levels at a time of very low demand for labour and high unemployment. They probably also, on average, display a conservative social profile. It is likely therefore that the business sector might contain a disproportionate group sceptical of multiculturalism and state programs which support it.

Ethnic minority interests

The increasingly prominent and vocal activities of ethnic minority organisations have been a feature of immigration politics in both countries, particularly in the last decade or so.

In Australia, it was common up to the late 1970s for political scientists to observe that immigrant-based minority groups were relatively quiescent in terms of political involvement (Parkin 1977, Wilson 1980), though occasionally they had expressed views about particular policies or controversies. From the late 1970s, however, the so-called 'ethnic vote' and the 'ethnic lobby' have become common phrases in the political lexicon.

There are several reasons for the increased political prominence of ethnic minority groups. First, the passage of time since the major post-war influx of non-British immigrants has been sufficient to ensure greater economic security and familiarity with the political system (Mistilis 1980). Second, a considerable number have acquired professional education and requisite political skills. Third, the numbers who have taken up Australian citizenship and have hence acquired voting rights increased over time. Fourth, for this reason ethnic groups have begun to be directly wooed by the major political parties. Fifth, under the multicultural policies introduced in the 1970s, modest amounts of public funding have been channelled to ethnic organisation, thus underwriting their viability. Sixth, Southern European ethnic communities in particular seem disproportionately concentrated in some key marginal Parliamentary seats.

Jupp (1988b, p. 173) argues that the ethnic communities now form 'an element of the electorate . . . too large, vocal and well organised to be ignored by parties hoping to govern'. The Labor Party seems to have been particularly assiduous in courting the 'ethnic vote' and with some apparent success: McAllister (1988) concludes that the disproportionate pro-Labor vote among Australians of Southern European origin has been an important element in the ALP's electoral coalition in recent years, to the extent that the party would otherwise have lost the 1987 election.

The phrase 'ethnic lobby', like the phrase 'ethnic vote', is perhaps misleading since it exaggerates the unity of ethnic minorities (Jupp 1988b). Nonetheless, there is substantial coordination of political input through State-based ethnic umbrella groups, with a national voice through FECCA (the Federation of Ethnic Communities' Councils of Australia). FECCA and its allies are particularly concerned about immigration policies and have strongly lobbied for liberalised family reunion procedures. This lobbying is widely recognised as quite successful. The creation of the Office of Multicultural Affairs has also been interpreted as initially a concession to, and now an avenue for, ethnic minority interests (Jakubowicz 1988, p. 967).

While there have been some suggestions that the increased immigrant intake targets in Canada in recent years are in part attributable to governments trying to court the 'ethnic vote', the influence of ethnic community organisations in Canada seems much stronger with respect to the provision of community services than with immigration policy itself. A major exception to this is the special arrangement with Quebec which is expressly designed to protect Francophone interests, though from the Quebec perspective the French-speaking community within its borders are no 'ethnic minority'. The peculiarity of Anglophone-Francophone relations in Canada, for which there is certainly no Australian equivalent, may be a factor inhibiting the stronger expression of ethnic minority interests within the English-speaking majority elsewhere in Canada.

Humanitarian interests

Whereas ethnic-minority organisations seem more prominent in Australia than Canada in making representations about immigration policy, the reverse appears true with respect to such humanitarian groups as churches and refugee advocacy organisations. In Canada these play a role disproportionate to their size. They are very well organised and feature some highly articulate spokespersons (community leaders, lawyers, academics) who have considerable communication skills and access to media (Simmons & Keohane 1992). Their influence, however, is not necessarily substantial. The 'humanitarian lobby' lost badly in its campaign against changes to refugee determination procedures in the late 1980s. Australia's equivalent groups are considerably less vocal, though there has been an important, mainly church-based, lobby on the refugee issue. Forthcoming government efforts to deport a large number of long-term refugee claimants may provide a good test of their ability to mobilise opposition.

Environmental interests

Environmental organisations are in many respects the most prominent pressure groups in contemporary Australian politics (West 1991). On the question of immigration, however, their voice has been somewhat muted and discordant. While there are some activists who regard continued population growth as environmentally unsound (Day & Rowland 1988; Smith 1991), others are more neutral. The stance of prominent organisations such as the Australian Conservation Foundation is somewhat ambivalent. Political and ideological linkages on the Left explain something of this muted voice: scepticism about immigration does not easily fit into an alliance between environmentalism, humanitarianism and multiculturalism.

Environmental groups appear even less involved in Canada. A small Zero Population Growth group and some members of the Ontario Conservation Council promote the idea that Canada's environment is threatened by immigration but these arguments have little impact in the policy debates of the 1980s (Simmons & Keohane 1992).

Ethnocentric anti-immigration groups

In contrast to other democracies like France and Germany, no well-organised anti-immigration movements based on ethnocentric or 'nativist' ideas have developed in either Australia or Canada. In Australia, there have been some minor attempts to mobilise Anglo-Celtic opinion against immigration from non-traditional sources, ranging from fairly ritualistic expressions of opposition from some elements of the Returned Services League (the main war veterans association) to the activities of a few very tiny and blatantly racist fringe groups. The lack of influence of such groups suggests that the not uncommon interpretations of Australian society as embodying inherent racism need considerable revision (Denoon 1985; Arndt 1988). Such groups appear to be even less prominent in Canada.

Public opinion

As noted above, 'public opinion' is a rather amorphous concept in the absence of an explanation of how it can be interpreted and politically mobilised, though opinion polls are a common purported measure. For Australia, Betts (1988, p. 53) argues that 'surveys and opinion polls on immigration since World War II document growing opposition among the majority of respondents'. Goot (1990) is somewhat more cautious and warns that survey results seem very dependent on context and wording. Nonetheless it is clear even from Goot's analysis that there has been substantial (though variable and not always majority) opposition to current or higher intake levels for many years, with opposition increasing during the 1980s. Canadian polls show similar results, with very recent polls showing particularly high levels of opposition (Angus Reid Group 1989).

For most of the years covered by these polls, however, reasonably high levels of immigration have in fact occurred in both countries with relatively little social friction developing. The situation may represent either a classic case of the common social–psychological distinction between attitude and behaviour, or a not inconsistent coexistence of opposition to a general policy with tolerance for the people admitted under the policy. In any case, it demonstrates that 'public opinion' of this sort has had little impact on policy in either country. At best, as Hawkins (1989, p. 248) concludes in her comparison of Australian and Canadian immigration policies, 'Government leads the way and cautiously brings the public along with it.' Certainly Blainey's contention, noted earlier, that 'it is public opinion which ultimately decides whether an immigration program will succeed' (Blainey 1984a), appears unconvincing.

The alarmed public reaction to the small boatload of refugee claimants off Nova Scotia in 1987, which led to statements from senior politicians and bureaucrats about the need for stricter controls, may seem an exception to this conclusion. However, some observers suggest that the incident had been considerably exaggerated in order to bolster support for tougher legislation already contemplated (Simmons & Keohane 1992).

Broader perceptions of 'public opinion' seem to have been influential historically in affecting the official style and pace of immigration programs. Certainly both Australia and Canada were conforming to the broad precepts of public opinion in their racially restrictive intake criteria of the past, while the official emphasis on assimilation with respect to new settlers was probably more directed at reassuring the domestic population than at realistically effecting a transformation of recent immigrants.

Conclusion: The making of immigration policy

The similarities between the policy-making processes in Australia and Canada are far more striking than the differences. The basic institutional structures, the array of interests which mobilise with respect to immigration and refugee matters, and the broad patterns of policy response display many common features.

We began with a sketch of seven alternative broad hypotheses about the distribution of influence over the policy-making process with respect to immigration and refugee matters. In the light of the subsequent analysis of political institutions and mobilised interests, how do the hypotheses now stand?

As initially acknowledged, the hypotheses are not mutually exclusive, and elements of each provide insights into the situation in both countries. At the outset, however, the first and last of these hypotheses—responsible government (Hypothesis 1) and populism (Hypothesis 7)—seem to have least to offer, though they are the two propositions most closely associated with conventional democratic norms. The responsible government model is based on political parties presenting clear alternative platforms to the voters, with the winning party implementing that platform on the basis of the electoral mandate. In both countries, however, general bipartisanship means that alternative immigration platforms are not in fact presented at elections. Even when, as in Australia in recent years, occasional partisan differences have emerged, these have in no case persisted until an election period. In fact, an approaching election has seemed to spur on the search for a bipartisan consensus. Likewise, the Populist interpretation does not fit the weak relationship between 'public opinion' and public policy, and the minimal influence in both countries of ethnocentric populist movements.

The evidence in both countries for the importance of bureaucratic institutions is considerable, but it suggests less a picture of bureaucratic dominance (Hypothesis 2) than one of bureaucratic politics. Undoubtedly, inertia and mission combine to give the immigration agency considerable influence on policy as well as administration, but there are also plenty of other influences within the executive branch—Prime Ministerial discretion, ministers with their own agendas, semi-judicial appeals boards, other agencies with somewhat different missions, and so on—as well as external societal influences.

While immigration policies have generally coincided with long-term business interests, this seems best explained in ways other than simple assertions of business dominance (Hypothesis 6). As discussed above, business groups, while not inactive, are not especially vocal with respect to immigration issues and are not consistently successful in shaping the details of the policies.

There is a degree of plausibility in the proposition that cosmo-politan elitism (Hypothesis 4) describes the prevailing dominant ideology in both countries. The pervasive bipartisanship about poli-cies which do not seem to have consistent popular endorsement and the general support accorded to those policies by business elites and the leadership of organised labour is consistent with this hypothesis. Probably also supportive, though not able to be analysed in this chapter, would be the prevailing attitudes among opinion leaders in the universities, the churches, professionals in the public service and perhaps the media. Whether this constitutes a decisive level of expla-nation for the policy process is, however, less uncertain.

The evidence appears most convincingly to suggest that the policy-making process in both Australia and Canada is shaped by a tension between the dynamics of nation-building statism (Hypothesis 3) and pluralism (Hypothesis 5). The statist framework encapsulates much of the process in both countries: state actors (ministers, bureau-crats in various agencies, party elites once in government) seem intent on pursuing national goals, such as economic growth, control of border movements, trade opportunities and international respect-ability, and can often do so with relative insularity from other domestic influences. The state sector does not have complete auto-nomy—for example, it cannot afford seriously to offend business interests—but in its own self-interest it is unlikely to attempt this anyway. Neither is it necessarily internally robust or coherent, as exemplified by the major concessions to Quebec and indeed by the questions hanging over the future configuration of Canadian feder-alism, and by the evident inter-agency dissonance in Australia. 'Statism' in this sense seems particularly applicable to Canada (Simmons & Keohane 1992) and to Australia especially in the forma-tive decades of the 1950s and 1960s when state institutions not only sponsored unprecedented levels of mass immigration but also care-fully managed societal acceptance of the social consequences.

Yet as Simmons and Keohane (1992, p. 1) observe with respect to Canada, 'the state [is] not simply an all-powerful hegemonic leader, but [is] also . . . a grouping of worried actors, always looking at contingencies and seeking strategic solutions. In other words, the state appears both powerful and vulnerable.' What is also particularly notable about the policy process in recent years in both countries is its 'vulnerability', in this sense, to pressure from mobilised interests. The extensive consultations in which ministers in both countries now engage prior to announcing major policy decisions such as intake targets are an acknowledgement of the necessity for this vulnerability to be recognised and, if possible, managed.

In Canada, the policy process is far more 'pluralistic' in character now than it was several decades ago. Although Simmons and Keohane (1992, p. 9) conclude that 'state policy is probably less influenced by [organised lobbying] than it is by its own calculations on actions which would strengthen its own legitimacy', these actions include 'the mediation of major social conflicts' and pre-empting 'challenges from oppositional social movements' which effectively mean some acknowledgement of and adjustment to the concerns of organised interests.

In Australia, the pluralist dynamic seems to have developed further (Parkin & Hardcastle 1990). It is striking how frequently program targets, selection criteria, composition components and Ministerial appointments have been apparently influenced by real or perceived lobbying pressure. The success of ethnic minority interests in defending family reunion opportunities has been frequently highlighted, though events in the past few years suggest that countervailing forces—in the bureaucracy, in the trade unions, among intellectuals—are also able to exert pressure when immigration levels seem to be getting too high.

The policy result in both countries is somewhat less stable than the steady policy development implied by the 'nation-building statist' ideals. In Australia, immigration policy formulation since the early 1980s has been described as 'uncertain' and 'inconsistent' with 'frequent changes in policy direction' (Parkin & Hardcastle 1990, p. 315). In Canada, Simmons and Keohane (1992, p. 27) similarly note that 'policy can change quickly, contain major internal inconsistencies, and appear to vary with the whims of the current government (or Minister of Immigration) rather than with any systematic long-term interests in Canadian society'.

The 'statist'–'pluralist' tension provides a useful perspective on the bipartisanship towards immigration and refugee matters which prevails in both Australia and Canada and the importance of which, given the pre-eminent role of party politics in organising public life, bears repeating and underlining. Each side of this tension promotes bipartisanship: 'statism' incorporates the party elites into the process of maintaining and legitimating state control while 'pluralism' induces a convergence by the parties towards a policy package congruent with the prevailing balance of mobilised interests.

The party system may help to explain why pluralist features seem more pronounced in Australia than in Canada. Whereas the conservative (Liberal and National Party) coalition in Australia is somewhat analogous in structure and behaviour to the major Canadian parties, there is no Canadian equivalent to the Australian Labor Party (ALP). The ALP is, at least in form, a classic 'mass party' (Parkin 1983). It is thus peculiarly open to membership influence and ideological struggle through its extra-parliamentary organisation. It has been the ALP which arguably has been most assiduous and most successful in courting the so-called 'ethnic vote', to the extent of having ethnic-specific local branches in some States (Allan 1984), and it has been ALP figures who have been most passionate about the maintenance of relatively high intake levels and non-discriminatory selection criteria. It has also benefited, as outlined above, from disproportionate and perhaps decisive voting support from Southern European ethnic communities. Yet the ALP is also a repository, at least historically, of some trade-union based scepticism about immigration and, more recently, some of its leadership has promoted an 'economic rationalist' critique of current policies. Thus within the ALP itself there is encapsulated some of the pluralist pressures which impact upon national policies. Not only has the ALP been Australia's governing party nationally and in nearly all of the States from the early 1980s to the early 1990s, but it has arguably set the agenda in immigration and multicultural matters since the early 1970s. For electoral reasons, the Liberal/National Coalition has been forced to adopt much of the same agenda (Hawkins 1989, p. 117).

Another explanation for Australian pluralism might explore the suggestion that the Australian governmental élite has become particularly divided over immigration policy matters, thus weakening 'statist' resolve and providing an opening for pluralist alliances. Some parts of the bureaucracy (such as the Immigration Department) appear to favour relatively large intakes based on economic selection criteria, others (such as the Office of Multicultural Affairs) appear to champion large intakes based on generous family reunion criteria, while the 'economic rationalists' (prominent, for example, in the

Department of Finance) appear somewhat unconvinced by both arguments and are sceptical of traditional 'nation-building' justifications for state intervention (Pusey 1991).

In conclusion, there are many institutional and procedural similarities between Australia and Canada in their policy-making processes with respect to immigration and refugee matters, and in both countries an understanding of the distribution of policy influence seems conceptually portrayed by a tension between 'statist' and 'pluralist' dynamics. Within this broad pattern of similarity, Australia's policy process seems somewhat more open, at least at present, to external pluralist-style representations while Canada's governmental elites appear more successful in defending their 'statist' predominance. These differences may explain the divergence in policies in the early 1990s: while the Canadian state moves (at least according to officially projected targets outlined for the five-year period 1990–95) in the direction of higher intakes, the outcome of Australia's pluralist interaction is in the opposite direction.

CHAPTER 5

Public Opinion, Immigration and Refugees

Robert Holton and Michael Lanphier

Introduction

Canada and Australia have experienced some of the highest rates of immigration in the post-war world. In both countries the composition of the immigrant intake has featured very significant numbers of refugees by world standards. The development of non-discriminatory immigration policies has also contributed to cultural diversity. Both Canada and Australia have sought to manage the settlement of this culturally diverse immigrant intake through policies of multiculturalism rather than assimilation. What is less clear is the relationship between public opinion and these shared features of immigration and settlement policy. How far do these policies reflect or fly in the face of public opinion? And what basis of popular consent is there for the continuation of such policies?

Migrant settlement in both Canada and Australia involves both a philosophical rationale, and a set of administrative and operational practices to assist and to regulate the pattern of refugee and immigrant integration. Public opinion may address either or both of these.

A key element in the rationale of settlement policy is an ethic of immigrant entitlement. Despite a past which involved a strongly selective bias toward peoples of white Christian Anglo-European background, recent years have witnessed only occasional and isolated lapses from a non-discriminatory philosophy. More impressive by far is the variety of guises under which the ethic is realised.

Of first importance appears the humanitarian impetus of duty toward displaced peoples. The theme usually runs that a rich country should treat newcomers with the same type of consideration and accord the same rights as those enjoyed by citizens, with few exceptions (vote, run for elective office in government). The same universalism should apply to immigrants in general. Second, citizenship should become accessible after a reasonable time period to allow for completion of the immediate settlement process, and a demonstrable commitment of immigrants to remain as permanent settlers.

For the ethic of entitlement to operate successfully it is assumed that there be the consent or at the very least compliance of all citizenry and institutions with the overall policy. Put another way, there should be no inhibitions, structural or interpersonal, to the efforts of newcomers to resettle. Compliance with a universalistic policy rationale is also assumed at a practical level. Federal governments require that settlement plans and policies are implemented at federal, state/ provincial and local levels with only small tolerance for variation. In other words all immigrants should have similar basic entitlement regardless of their origins or destination, and secondary migrants should have the same entitlement at their new destination as they enjoyed at the place of landing. The degree to which this type of public consensus genuinely exists or persists over any length of time is, however, not at all clear.

Delivery of immigrant settlement services through salaried professionals in the public sector can in most respects proceed on the basis of enacted legislation and statutory instruments irrespective of public consensus. Another important but often neglected aspect of service delivery is the attitude of volunteers in the non-government sector. Government depends upon non-government organisations (NGO) to deliver a variety of services. In Canada these include orientation, counselling, some language provision, some housing, and host family schemes. In Australia a similar NGO involvement embraces some initial settlement services, a community refugee support scheme, some basic welfare provision and immigrant information services.

The voluntary sector for its part has to depend upon volunteer personnel. Some of these will come from immigrant communities, but others from the general population. It is particularly among volunteers that continuing commitment to the ethic of entitlement must be maintained to keep volunteer-dependent service delivery active.

Immigration and public opinion: the research agenda

In pursuing the elusive relationship between public opinion and immigration policy it is worthwhile to outline the considerable scope of the research agenda involved. This can be outlined as follows:

1 *Does public opinion speak with one voice with respect to immigration and settlement?*
• If not, what is the range of voices to be heard?
• What do the opinion polls tell us about public opinion? What other sources of public opinion are there?

2 *How far has policy 'led' or remained ahead of public opinion, and how far has public opinion driven policy formation?*
• Is there one consistent pattern here or is the relationship between public opinion and policy a shifting one?
• What are the mechanisms by which public opinion and policy interact?
• How far do policy-makers construct, manage or manipulate public opinion?
• How far does public opinion generate its own autonomous effect on policy determination?
• How far does public opinion exert an influence through focus on images that may affect sentiments, and how far through deployment of arguments that may be translated into policies and programs?
• Is the influence of public opinion greater in some areas of immigration policy (e.g. intake) than others (e.g. settlement)?
• What is its role in relation to refugee issues?

Public opinion and immigration: some conceptual and methodological issues

It is well known that public opinion is a complex and heterogeneous rather than unitary and organic phenomenon. It is also an entity grounded as much in emotion as rational calculation, especially where public access to relevant information is scarce. Politicians and leaders of interest groups typically invoke an intimate relationship with public opinion in their rhetoric on immigration.

For the social scientist there are, however, many pitfalls in trying to determine and measure the true nature of public attitudes with any degree of precision. These include the effect of the survey instrument itself on responses given. In a recent Australian study on immigration and social cohesion, Bill Cope and his colleagues argue that many variations in the findings of opinion polls on immigration can only be explained in terms of the way questions are framed (Cope et al. 1991).

Notwithstanding such difficulties the notion of public opinion can usefully be disaggregated. First there is the 'active' public who have first-hand contact with immigrants. This is generally the group among which consensus as to the rightness of the ethic of entitlement is strongest. It is also the group with the highest degree of personal and organisational investment in assuring the efficacy of such an ethic in operation.

The other two components of public opinion have less frequent, more remote or simply non-existent contact with immigrants and refugees. The first of these is the 'interested' public, for whom immigration is a salient but not necessarily predominant concern. Finally there is the 'general' public which is involved in a more diffuse and episodic manner with immigration issues. While detached from policy making, members of the general public provide the context of consent or resistance upon which the general thrust of policy rests.

These distinctions can be translated into empirical terms for both Australia and Canada as follows. In both countries we can locate an 'active' public associated with interest groups seeking to influence policy (for example, refugee support and humanitarian organisations). The 'interested' public is largely outside organised opinion but can be mobilised to express individual views on immigration to political leaders or newspapers. The 'general public', whose aggregated responses are summarise in opinion polls, might be thought of as the least influential segment of public opinion. After all, occasions of determinative affirmation or veto for the public are extremely rare. Nonetheless general currents of opinion can radiate more widely both through public opinion polls, talk-back radio shows and more informal community and workplace networks. Most scholarly research on general opinion is, however, based on polls.

Attitudes to immigration levels and immigrant characteristics

Salience of the issue

Evidence from both Canada and Australia suggests a limited level of public interest in, and/or awareness of issues relating to immigration.

In Canada, for example, recent polls found that 56 per cent of the public indicated being either 'somewhat' or 'very well' informed on immigration and refugee issues during 1991, although males reported slightly higher level of awareness (61 per cent) than females (51 per cent). And in an earlier poll conducted in 1989 only 30 per cent indicated interest in issues relating to refugees (Longwoods 1991).

In Australia, the polls have focused far more on levels of support for immigration than on levels of concern for immigration and refugee issues. Poll evidence from the 1980s, reviewed by Goot (1988), indicates that less than 10 per cent of respondents typically mention immigration as one of the three main issues facing the country. Even when prompted to do so by explicit questioning, levels of concern typically reached no more than 30 per cent.

Situational salience

Important events and the imagery that surrounds them can increase the salience of immigration as a public issue. In Canada, for example, the arrival in 1986 of Sikhs seeking refuge off shore of Nova Scotia created a heightened awareness. This owed much to agitation by the then-Minister of Immigration, who demanded the recall of Parliament to effect legislation to protect against a perceived influx of ships of fortune about to disembark clandestine cargoes of humanity on Canadian shores. In such an instance apprehensions are aroused both on the part of the general public as well as the interested public of federal politicians and near associates.

A more diffuse wave of concern was current in 1990 when the Royal Canadian Mounted Police training college announced that it was about to graduate its first Sikh member who requested for religious reasons to wear his turban instead of the traditional headgear (Stetson hat or peaked cap). A group circulated leaflets protesting against the breaking of Canadian tradition of uniform which had become a national symbol. To this nationwide campaign was added the distribution of cartoons and buttons depicting Sikh costume in derisive imagery, juxtaposed against Canadian symbols.

In Australia, the events and images that have had most impact on the immigration debate in recent years involve the arrival of Indochinese 'boat people' on Australia's northern shores in the late 1970s. The arrival of the first boat people in April 1976 sparked an intense period of public debate dominated as much by emotionally charged perceptions as by informed analysis (for further details, see Viviani 1984).

It should be emphasised that only a very small proportion of the Indochinese refugees that were to be settled in Australia over the next decade actually arrived by boat. Nonetheless, the unplanned and unauthorised arrival of the boat people served to dramatise feeling on refugee policy in a manner quite unlike the immediate post-war intake of 'displaced persons' from Central and Eastern Europe. For many, especially those who had lived through the wartime threat of Japanese conquest the new Indochinese arrivals reawakened anxieties about an 'Asian' invasion across Australia's unprotected northern coastline. This viewpoint was often overlaid with outright anti-Asian sentiment, including the perception that those fleeing from the Vietnamese war would become troublesome residents, unable to integrate and preoccupied with freeing their homeland. These fears coalesced with racism in the notion of Indochinese refugees as 'yellow Croatians'.

Levels of immigrant intake

Within Australia, opinion poll evidence suggests a hardening of attitudes towards current immigration intake levels and to the refugee component within the intake. Recent polls indicate that a clear majority of a respondents (69–73 per cent) favour reducing or cutting immigration altogether (Morgan Poll May 1990, Saulwick Poll October 1991, cited in *Sydney Morning Herald* 4 Nov. 1991). These figures are significantly higher than the 46–58 per cent favouring reduction recorded by polls during the 1980s.

In Canada, attitudes to immigration levels are not nearly so hostile. Since 1989 from two-thirds to three-quarters of the public perceives the intake of immigrants to be increasing, yet less than half of all respondents (43 per cent) judges that the numbers admitted are 'too many' (Longwoods 1991). Slightly more females (48 per cent) are inclined to feel this way than males (39 per cent). Given recessionary constraints, it is possible that women view newcomers as increased competition that will add to the structural disadvantages women already face in the paid labour force. As in Australia, however, there is a clear trend towards increasing opposition to current levels, with the proportion rising from 31 per cent in 1989 to 43 per cent in 1991 (Longwoods 1991).

A poll for Multiculturalism and Citizenship Canada (1991) also found that tolerance for immigrants was waning. Only 39 per cent of respondents indicated that recent immigrants should have a say in Canada's future (p. 34) and only 24 per cent maintained that employers should place special emphasis on hiring 'qualified minorities' (p. 37).

Composition

Preferred category

In Australia, the most preferred category of immigrant remains the economic immigrant. Immigrants with skills are consistently preferred by over half of respondents (56 per cent), while those with 'money to invest' are also most favoured by 15 per cent (Saulwick Poll October 1991, cited in *Sydney Morning Herald* 4 Nov. 1991).

In Canada, the position is more complex. The overall ideal image of immigrants appears to be people who have some attachment to Canadian society before arrival and who will 'fit in': some 64 per cent think that family reunification should be a major selection criterion and a similar proportion (63 per cent) think that immigrants should be selected to 'fit into society'. Somewhat fewer (58 per cent) feel that the economic contribution (demand for skills and investment) should be a selection criterion, although a larger proportion (between 61 and 73 per cent) feel that attracting investors is indeed an important factor (Longwoods 1991).

Refugees

In Australia, preferences for refugees show some fluctuation. There has been a marked decline from the 23 per cent of Australians who preferred this group in 1981 in the context of an increased intake of Indochinese refugees, to a low of only 10 per cent in 1991. General public opinion concerning refugees seems to have hardened even though the specifically Asian element has not increased during the last decade.

Nonetheless, the late 1970s and early 1980s was no 'golden age' of tolerance towards refugees, to be contrasted with the contemporary hardening of opinion against them. Australian governments acted very cautiously and with due deference to hostile elements in public opinion in agreeing to only modest increases in the refugee intake.

Yet, having said this, it is equally the case that general public opinion remained broadly in favour of modest increases in refugee intake from 1976 to around 1979. The image of the boat people was received by many in a very positive light—whether as a poignant human tragedy demanding humanitarian sanctuary, or as Australian allies driven out of their homeland by Communist oppression. It was only in 1979 as a result of a massive expansion of departures from Vietnam and external pressures from world opinion for Australia to do more, that calls for a greater intake began to erode general public support.

In Canada, as in Australia, attitudes toward refugees have recently hardened. In a three-year period, for example, there was a marked increase in negative attitudes toward the levels of refugee intake: in 1989, some 31 per cent indicated that 'too many' refugees were being admitted. The figure rose to 39 per cent in the next year; by 1991, the corresponding per centage was 49 per cent. This augmented negative judgement is accompanied by a near-unanimous perception that the number of refugees admitted has increased. Thus, despite a relatively low salience and level of interest in such issues, the Canadian public appears in the process of developing antipathy toward the continuation of existing policy and practice.

The Canadian public also makes some distinction among the refugee groups which they would prefer to come in lesser numbers. Refugees from the Middle East appear to be least welcome, with some 41 per cent in 1990 judging that fewer should arrive. Some 35 per cent judge that fewer should arrive from Latin America and from Southeast Asia. The corresponding figures for refugees from what was Eastern Europe and Africa are 30 per cent and 23 per cent respectively, in favour of fewer arrivals (Angus Reid Group 1990).

With respect to claimants for refugee status, attitudes are similarly reserved. Just over half (53 per cent) would not allow a claim if the refugee had previously been granted safe haven elsewhere; the same proportion upholds the existing determination process: that is, they do not favour amnesty or similar relief. And some two-thirds would not offer any civil entitlement until refugee status is granted (Longwoods 1991). Although direct comparisons cannot be made because of incommensurability of questions, it would appear that attitudes toward refugee claimants has also hardened over the past three years. Until 1991, no question yielded greater than a 41 per cent 'negative' position (Angus Reid Group 1990). Yet in that year similar questions show proportions between 53 per cent and 67 per cent (Longwoods 1991).

Asian immigration and public opinion

A significant component of the immigrant intake into both Australia and Canada in the last two decades has been of Asian origin. In Australia much debate has taken place as to the salience of increased 'Asian' migration to the increase in negative attitudes to immigration. Goot (1988), reviewing evidence from the 1970s and 1980s, found that levels of hostility to current levels of Asian immigration differed very little from levels of hostility to immigration in general. This tends to downplay any specifically anti-Asian or racist element in public opinion. Evidence from more recent polls, by contrast, suggests a growing divergence of popular opinion between attitudes to immigrants in general, and to Asian immigrants in particular. A review of a series of Morgan polls over the last decade indicates that opposition to Asian immigration has become greater than to immigration as a whole by a margin of around 10 percentage points (Morgan Poll Feb. 1990 and press release March 1990). This margin almost certainly widened between 1990 and 1992. Only 6 per cent of the respondents in the Saulwick Poll (April 1992) favoured Asia as the first-choice source, compared with 41 and 25 per cent choosing Britain and Europe respectively. A further 18 per cent were prepared, however, to accept immigrants from wherever they come, a significant element of non-discriminatory pragmatism, especially among university-educated and younger respondents.

These data cannot be taken to imply a massive intolerance within the general public to Asian immigrants currently settled in Australia. The recent Human Rights and Equal Opportunity Commission Inquiry into Racist Violence found that racist violence against Asians and other non-English-speaking background immigrants was a cause for concern. Yet its scale and intensity was neither as great as racist violence towards Aboriginal people, nor as great as racist violence on the basis of ethnic identity in many overseas countries (Human Rights and Equal Opportunity Commission 1991).

If we look for evidence of hostility to immigrants we can certainly find it. But what about evidence of tolerance? If we fail to look for this as well, there is danger of presenting a one-sided picture skewed to overt problems rather than quieter forms of positive achievement. Evidence from the 1988 poll conducted for the Office of Multicultural Affairs by AGB: McNair indicates that nearly 60 per cent of Australians would be prepared to accept an Asian person either as workmate, next-door neighbour, close friend or family member (OMA 1989, p. 170).

Further analysis of this survey by McAllister and Moore (1989) indicates that tolerance towards 'Asians' in general, or to specific groups such as 'Vietnamese', or 'Chinese' is lower than for immigrants in general. Nonetheless the scale of tolerance towards 'Asian' outgroups remains significant.

An area in which adverse comments on Asian immigrants arises concerns links with crime. In Canada 'Asian' news stories have often featured public apprehension about links between Asians and crime. At least two major metropolitan areas, Toronto and Vancouver, have experienced serious allegations about involvement of recently arrived Vietnamese and Chinese in gang-related criminal activity, especially with respect to extortion, robbery and victimisation (Cernetig, 1992).

In Toronto, a member of the public affairs department of the Metro (Toronto) Police alleged at a crime enquiry that two-thirds of all offences committed in 1990 by persons of Asian origin were attributable to those from Vietnam and China. Of a total of 3000 crimes presumably attributable to Asians (a scant 1.5 per cent of all crimes that year) some 1000 and 500 crimes were attributed to persons from Vietnam and the People's Republic, respectively. This information was greeted with mixed reactions in the Chinese community, as such collection of statistics runs counter to official police policy. No means exists for verification of such statistical allegations, even if definitional ambiguities on attribution of racial origin to incidents did not persist (Appleby 1991).

Shortly after the release of this information, the Metro Toronto Police reaffirmed its opposition to the collection of statistics on the basis of ethnic or national origin. This decision occurred in the context of considerable notoriety attaching to the issue of Asians and crime. There was not only widespread circulation of the allegations, but also front-cover publicity by a leading news magazine. With a caption 'Terror in the Streets' (*Maclean's*, 25 March 1991), a picture of an Asian holding a gun was printed.

General analysis of attitudes

The overall conclusion from this scan of attitudes toward immigrants and refugees is that a deterioration has taken place in levels of public acceptability. This applies both to Australia and Canada. While attitudes toward both immigrants and refugees have become increasingly negative, those relating to refugees appear to have attenuated in markedly greater proportion.

Nonetheless, general public opinion is not uniformly hostile. In Australia evidence of increasing tolerance to immigrant settlers of non-English-speaking backgrounds needs to be set against increasing levels of opposition to current levels of immigrant intake. In Canada too the picture is one of a segmentation of opinion rather than a unidimensional shift towards opposition.

Opinion profiles in Canada

Research on the segmentation of opinion has gone somewhat further in Canada than Australia. A recent analysis has identified the following segments of the Canadian general public (Longwoods 1991).

Protagonists (23 per cent)
This segment is composed of those having completed at least some post-secondary education, employed in predominantly white-collar occupations, with experience with cultures other than Canada: that is, born in another country or having acquaintance with recent immigrants. They are disproportionately male. They support increased levels of immigration and believe that immigrants have made notable contributions for the betterment of Canadian society. Additionally, they consider themselves well informed on immigration issues but consider that the such issues are of only 'average' concern.

Concerned supporters (22 per cent)
This segment appears demographically distinct in that it is found predominantly among people living in non-metropolitan areas who are older (age 55+), not currently employed outside the home. They disproportionately have mother tongues other than English/French. While this segment approves the current levels of immigration and the federal government's handling of the matter, it entertains concerns about negative social and economic effects, such as a perceived drain on social services, and the crowding of job market.

Indifferent (21 per cent)
This segment appears demographically somewhat indistinct except for having greater proportions of Quebec Francophones and those

currently unattached to the labour force. This segment appears neutral and rather unconcerned about immigration issues. Their attitudes about the contributions of immigrants and refugee is filled with ambivalence.

Reactionaries (19 per cent)

This segment is over-represented in the Canadian metropolitan areas, especially in Ontario, among people who are older and have lower levels of completed education. Few have direct acquaintanceship with recent immigrants. This segment expresses concern over immigration issues, especially with respect to recent waves, expressing reservation if not apprehension about social and economic effects attributable to immigrants. They feel that the federal government does not control the immigration flow well (Longwoods 1991).

The above typology represents an attitudinal continuum which represents gradations of favourability toward federal immigration policy. But it does not differentiate the Canadian general public into crisp, discrete strata so as to suggest a rivalry among classes. At present, attitudinal positions have not been socially crystallised.

Yet at the level of the interested public, signs of such crystallisation are emerging. Since 1981, the National Citizens Coalition has published large advertisements challenging immigration and refugee policy. The organisation has retained the issue as one among many which impair individual rights of freedom as the organisation interprets it. These occasional thrusts remain for the Coalition only as part of a larger agenda which attracts a certain portion of Canadians mainly from business and entrepreneurial backgrounds.

More recently, a new national political party, the Reform Party, has attracted growing numbers of adherents, including those disaffected by over-centralisation. Among many items in their platform is a concern only occasionally overtly expressed that immigration policy represents a danger through arbitrary admission of large numbers who have not been chosen or requested at the grass roots. Again this issue remains entwined with others reflecting disaffection with governmental interference in daily local life. To date an immigration policy has not been explicitly enunciated by the Reform Party.

Another group, the Heritage Front, explicitly protests incursions of immigration and refugee inflows which are non-white. These represent a threat to the present position of the 'white race' in Canadian society. The group is mixed in age, (including mid-years and younger, with some 'skinheads'), maintains a 'hot line' and is producing video cassettes to propagandise their position.

The above developments indicate that Canada may be witnessing the beginning of a counter-ideology, although the boundaries and overall impact of this incipient movement are presently indistinct. As characteristic of social movements in the early stage, the turn of specific events (technically, 'precipitating events') will likely determine the course. Although mobilisation of some support is evident, there would have to be a far greater infusion of resources, including both financing, influence and especially much more demonstrated support from larger numbers both of the interested and general publics. Additionally, the course of mobilisation would have to proceed relatively unobstructed. That case is far from assured, as established governments and NGOs (that is, the active public) presently show no signs of acceding to any demands.

Interested opinion in Australia

A confidential survey of 'community attitudes' by the Liberal Party in Australia reported a range of hostile attitudes to current levels of immigration, to Asian immigration, and to multiculturalism (Weekend *Australian*, 7–8 September 1991; *Australian*, 29 September 1991). Nearly half of those involved regarded immigration as a major problem.

Among other issues, respondents raised the spectre of Asian ghettoes as a pejorative image of social division. While the Liberal leader, Dr Hewson declared he was not 'locked into' the report's conclusions, a number of new policy emphases emerged in subsequent months. These included a significant cut in the immigration intake, but did not include any change to the ethnically non-discriminatory basis of immigration intake, or to the policy of multiculturalism.

This episode is of some importance to analysis of the relationship between public opinion and policy making because it draws attention to the 'interested' component of public opinion. This is the segment that lies somewhere between the 'active' members of immigration lobbies or members of immigrant-related NGOs, at one end of the spectrum, and the much more diffuse 'general public', at the other. The respondents to this survey were not drawn randomly as in a public opinion poll, but from a survey of 'families, church and pensioner groups, environmental groups, ethnic community groups, and businesses'. It is not known exactly how this group was selected, but it is reasonably clear that the survey was designed in part to tap opinion among those influential at the grass roots.

Towards an explanation of the hardening of attitudes

Public attitudes to immigration or any other issue are subject to temporal variation, reflecting the course of social and economic events. One of the main explanations for the recent hardening of attitudes in both Canada and Australia is the impact of the current economic recession. In Canada, for example, attitudes reflect a some-what more negative profile from early in 1990, when unemployment was notably high. In this context immigrants are somehow seen as being an unnecessary complicating factor.

Even so, the majority of poll respondents perceive immigrants favourably as economic assets (72 per cent see immigrants doing jobs rejected by Canadians). However, rather fewer respondents see them as social contributors, some 48 per cent expressing concern that immigrants represent a drain on social services (Longwoods 1991). This emphasis on fiscal drain may also be perceived unfavourably during a recession when the scope for public spending is tight and immigrants may be seen as competing with other types of claimants, including the unemployed.

In Australia, respondents both to opinion polls on immigration and to the Inquiry into Racist Violence point to the current economic recession as a major source of concern. The October 1991 Saulwick poll found that 76 per cent of those wanting cuts in immigration cited unemployment as their main reason, while only 10 per cent cited social tension (Saulwick Poll October 1991, cited in *Sydney Morning Herald*, 4 Nov. 1991). This economic focus confirms the finding of previous polls that many Australians believe immigration is bad for the economy and especially bad for employment (Morgan poll May 1990 cited, in Sydney *Sun*, 13 May 1990). It is also consistent with the preference for immigrants with skills, and the decline in support for refugees who are perceived to lack economically relevant skills. Large sections of public opinion appear not to accept the views of many economists that the economic impact of immigration is in most respects a positive one. It seems that public perceptions are out of line with reality here. But why should this be?

Is it because public understanding of economic mechanisms is very weak? There certainly does seem to be a deep-seated sense in which immigrants are publicly regarded solely as competitors for scarce resources, rather than as potential creators of economic wealth.

Or is it because immigrants are a convenient scapegoat for economic insecurity, a factor mentioned by the Inquiry into Racist Violence? And if immigrants are made something of a scapegoat is this the result of direct experience of economic deprivation including job competition with immigrants, or the effect of prejudiced attitudes?

What evidence there is suggests that there is no clear-cut correlation between direct experience of economic deprivation, on the one side, and hostility to immigration and immigrants, on the other. To take one striking finding hostility to immigration increases with age, yet youth unemployment rates are at unprecedentedly high levels. Other evidence discussed from the OMA survey suggests only very weak correlations between employment status and economic deprivation, on the one hand, and prejudice towards immigrants, including Asian immigrants, on the other. Available Canadian research also supports this view. Unemployment rates and other socio-economic factors seem to exert only a limited negative impact on public attitudes towards immigrants (Schissel et al. 1989).

The connection between the recession and attitudes to immigration is then rather complex. It is not so much that direct experience of unemployment or job competition with immigrants changes attitudes, but rather that the existence of the recession is interpreted by public opinion as rendering existing levels of immigration and refugee intake as untenable and irresponsible. This interpretation, it should be emphasised is held by many whose employment status is not threatened or who may not be intending any future labour force participation.

Another recent dimension to public opposition to current levels of immigration is the environmentalist argument which says that immigration puts too much strain on Australia's land and resources such as water. The October 1991 Saulwick poll reported that environmental pressure was mentioned by 13 per cent of those wanting cuts in immigration (Saulwick Poll October 1991, cited in *Sydney Morning Herald*, 4 Nov. 1991). The environmentalist opposition represents a new factor in the immigration debate, and has closer connections with Australian nationalism than issues of economic welfare. It has become active not only at the level of 'general' public attitudes, but also as a component of the 'active' public specifically concerned with immigration. There is now an increasingly vocal environmentalist lobby whose opinion is canvassed whenever the opinions of the 'active' segment of public are sought.

In Canada too, concern has been expressed about the possible threat of immigration to the environment through pollution and overcrowding. This has been mentioned by around 45 per cent of respondents in recent polls. Such concerns have had a long history in Canada, stretching back to the mid-1970s when the Federal Government tabled its 'Green Paper'. More recent incarnations of this view were stated in a National Health and Welfare report which suggested that population size is ultimately contingent on the environment's ability to support 'economic activity' (Beatty 1989). Nevertheless, this ongoing popular notion reflects a more generalised concern that immigrants, despite acknowledged contributions, may hasten worsening socio-economic and environmental conditions.

Impact of the media

It is hard to establish either for Australia or Canada how far the print and electronic media have acted as an independent factor in the determination of public opinion.

The press in Australia has certainly engaged in an active way in debates about immigration and multiculturalism. However there is little evidence of particular papers initiating or supporting particular campaigns to influence opinion. Instead one tends to find the representation of a mix of positions and the employment of columnists with a range of viewpoints.

Nonetheless, in both Australia and Canada, there have from time to time been complaints by immigrants about the media's portrayal of particular communities. In Canada, for example, members of the Chinese community in Vancouver have expressed concern over the effect of a five-part radio series, 'Dim Sum Diaries', broadcast in the spring of 1991. Media critics and Chinese community leaders prominent in the local area criticised some of the scenes in the quasi-historical but fictionalised account for having racist overtones and reinforcing unfavourable stereotypes about Canadians of Chinese origin.

The issue escalated to national attention in May 1991, when it was placed on the agenda of the National Congress of Chinese Canadians. A resolution was passed which severely criticised CBC for the production and requested remedial action including wide apology and production of another more positive series (Tan 1991).

The question remains one of debate among media specialists within the Chinese community. The print media has also portrayed Chinese immigrants, particularly from Hong Kong, in a negative light. Inflated housing prices in the Vancouver area prompted the media to run articles singling out rich immigrants as causing the high real estate costs. Rather than present the complex nature of market demands which govern land values, the press opted for a simple unicausal explanation where wealthy immigrants, referred to as 'Yacht People', were cast as unwelcome opportunists, unnecessarily driving up the price of Canadian property (*Economist* 1989 p. 43, Ungerleider 1991, p. 160). Other articles in the print media have focused on the need to stress 'traditional Canadian values' in the education system as a way of introducing immigrants to Canada, especially those from Pacific Rim areas (Ungerleider 1991). Thus the context of a heightened awareness of any sustained reference to customs and behaviour of a group of easily identifiable ethnic origin may arouse defensiveness and have wider implications for media diffusion than in past practice.

Public opinion and policy: past, present and future

It is not easy to produce a clear picture of the mechanisms which link public opinion to the determination of policy. Certainly both politicians and senior public servants watch the general public opinion polls, though usually only as guides to likely responses to policy options. Political parties also commission polls, though it is not clear whether the information gained has much effect on the substance as distinct from the public relations aspects of policy.

There is a sense in which politicians already know what active public lobbies are going to say. In seeking further information about public attitudes they may want more systematic data than available from general opinion polls. It may be hypothesised that the specific function of the 'interested public' may be that it enables politicians to orient their political programs to specific grass-roots concerns and to influential makers of opinion at the grass roots.

For Canada, influence of the 'interested' public is inferential: editorial opinion and 'op ed' articles do not hesitate to assume critical positions, but they also support ongoing policy interests. Federal Cabinet and Departments reserve the right to commission surveys and refuse to disclose their results until the policy formulation exercise is complete and often longer, presumably in anticipation of backlash.

There is no evidence in Australia, however, to suggest that either Government or Opposition policy is driven either by 'interested' or 'general' opinion. There continues, for example, to be considerable convergence between the policies of both parties. For example, the Labor Government proposed modest cuts in general intake for 1993.

This cutback represents a continuation of the policy of balanced objectives. It gives something to the popular mood that immigration should be cut in times of recession and avoids being outflanked by the Opposition, while not seriously alienating the ethnic lobbies or humanitarian concern for refugees.

For their part, the Opposition has avoided any overt break with bipartisanship thereby protecting their own ethnic vote. Bipartisanship is further underwritten by divisions of opinion on immigration within the political parties and the consequent advantage to party unity to be gained from adopting a cautious consensus approach. There are, in other words, both party political as well as opinion-based reasons for a balanced approach to immigration issues.

There is a good deal of evidence in Australia to suggest that post-war policy makers have led rather than followed general public opinion. This is reflected in attempts to pre-empt the formation of an independent agenda of public debate on immigration through close management of information and public imagery concerning immigration, and in the physical management of the settlement process.

Attempts at the management of opinion were built into post-war programs to increase immigration of those from non-English speaking backgrounds. Arthur Calwell, the first post-war Minister of Immigration, speaks in his autobiography of official manipulation of public imagery concerning the 'displaced persons' refugee scheme. The first arrivals under this scheme were in his own words 'a choice sample', featuring young single people including 'platinum blondes of both sexes', 'the blue-eyed and red-headed'. 'The men were handsome and the women beautiful, he goes on. 'It was not hard to sell immigration to the Australian people once the press published photographs of that group' (Calwell 1972).

Over the longer term, however, governments have generally avoided the blatant manipulation of imagery from above. This is partly a result of a generally bipartisan approach to immigration intake and settlement policy which, with few exceptions, has avoided direct and emotive appeals to general public opinion. Policy debate around party political circles has been dominated either by economic or humanitarian discourse.

The management of immigration by public servants has tended to be cautious, avoiding dramatic changes of direction in response to real or perceived shifts in public opinion. There have been some attempts to influence the imagery of immigration and immigrants, such as the discussions held by the Office of Multicultural Affairs with producers of TV soap operas over excessive stereotyping of 'ethnic' characters. These activities have been far more muted, however, than Calwell's more manipulative approach. The development of social imagery concerning immigration has therefore generally originated in a far more spontaneous manner from below, amplified in many cases by the print media.

Canadian television presents a range of messages about immigrants and ethnic minorities, but they often oscillate widely in accuracy. A few are blatantly discriminatory, while others transmit a 'counter-stereotype' which disregards the real problems faced by immigrants. The image of the upwardly mobile manager or professional presents a distorted view that racial barriers have been transcended in Canadian society. The viewing audience is left with the unrealistic notion that social structural impediments no longer exists for immigrants in Canada and with hard work they are able to rise to the top of the socioeconomic order. While politicians do not create and produce such shows, broadcast personnel at the Canadian Broadcasting Corporation (CBC) are indirectly influenced by federal policy. Thus, the development of social imagery concerning immigration has therefore generally originated in a far more spontaneous manner from below, amplified in many cases by the print media.

If policy makers have managed the immigrant intake and settlement process by means other than manipulation, the strategies involved have been numerous. They range from incorporation of many ethnic lobbies into the process of consultation that leads to annual immigration intake and composition targets, to attempts in Australia to prevent immigrant ghetto formation through dispersal of on-arrival hostel facilities across a range of physical locations.

Managing a potential backlash

While governments may in the past have been able to stay ahead of public opinion, this may no longer be true in the current epoch of hardening attitudes. While there are institutional insulators of policy making from direct public intervention, the longer-run likelihood of an unpopular policy remaining unchanged is remote. Both formal political process as well as informal influence militate for change along the lines of pressure group representation. Not only does parliamentary responsibility formally guarantee such responsiveness, but the dependence of government upon other agencies (local governments, NGO) for implementation virtually guarantees responsiveness to counter-opinion.

We may therefore outline the following sketch or scenario of the possible implications of a backlash drawing in particular on the Canadian experience. Presumably, alterations in level of intake as well as quality of intake could be adjusted. Adjustment, however, would represent a compromise between the advocate active public and the more numerous but less closely involved interested public, countering for greatly reduced numbers. It is no less possible for the quality of refugees, and to a far more limited extent, immigrants, to be similarly modified.

In the case of refugees, the Canadian annual Refugee Plan specifies target numbers according to world regions. One figure could be changed independently of others. In the case of immigrants, the quality of intake is a joint function of multiple determinants including the number of regional offices which Canada maintains, the sheer number of applicants from any origin, their 'points' score, as well as the type of provisions required by the several provinces.

Agencies and NGOs who depend upon volunteer service to deliver their mandated role will obviously encounter difficulties recruiting, especially among groups other than newcomers themselves. There is little incentive to offer time for work which appears socially irrelevant or worse, not in the Canadian interest.

Immigration and refugee issues may become situationally twinned with another political issue of the day: for instance, over-population and environmental degradation. Although no causal link can be tightly drawn between the two issues, the very juxtaposition invites hypothetical linkages which reinforces any initial (or previously induced) aversion toward immigrants and refugees. Similarly, the more issues with which immigrant- and refugee-related matters are so linked, the greater the probability that persons who may be neutral or previously favourably disposed toward Canadian immigration policy will be influenced negatively.

This process may be accelerated by a counter-ideological proliferation. In other words, organisations may promulgate types of counter-ideology which either directly or indirectly discourage immigration and refugee intake. Such ideological formation often develops by a process of incidental accretion.

If indeed the counter-ideology develops into a full-blown movement, several effects would ensue, all of which could develop a 'feedback' which would further erode support for the present policy of an increased immigration and refugee intake and a programmatic resettlement policy.

144

Among the refugee and immigrant population, a slower adaptation would likely follow if resources from orientation and especially English/French language classes were curtailed. Thus the general public would witness a self-fulfilling prophecy: the perception that newcomers do not adapt would be confirmed.

From political constituencies, signals would change from mixed to negative: no payoff would have been realised from a relatively generous intake and resettlement policy. Whether immigration and refugee issues would continue to be salient as a result of 'backlash' or simmer down to their characteristic status of being barely recognisable as a separate political issue cannot be predicted. Yet dubious political advantage could be realised in either outcome.

From the NGO community, an acute sense of betrayal would be experienced: it would receive no recognition for jobs well done as the conduit through which services to immigrants and refugees are delivered. The sometime partnership with federal and provincial governments, which frequently appeared contentious as NGOs advocate increased financial and infrastructural support, would be passively terminated. Whatever resources agencies could find from their own constituency resources might sustain some service deliveries, but at a much reduced level. They too would have been eroded by backlash.

Immigration backlash and multiculturalism

One of the most interesting yet elusive aspect of the debate on immigration concerns the relationship of backlash with multicultural policy debate. In particular, will the increasing hardening of attitudes to immigrants contribute to an undermining of the multicultural policies in place in both Canada and Australia?

Some opinion poll evidence in Canada indicates diffuse public support for multiculturalism. A survey conducted for Multiculturalism and Citizenship Canada (1991) found that 61 per cent of the sample supported multiculturalism, with support strongest among the young and the better educated. Only 43 per cent, however, believed that minorities should preserve their cultural heritages. Females were slightly more supportive of this policy than were males—47 and 38 per cent, respectively (p. 23). Public opinion on the issue of multiculturalism and national unity also seems to be divided between principle and practice. In principle, a large majority of respondents (79 per cent) felt that such a policy is essential to uniting Canada. However, in practice, less than half (47 per cent) believed that it will, in fact, help unite Canada (p. 32). Moreover, the perceived impact of multi-culturalism policy has both support and opposition. On the positive side, those sampled maintained that it would 'enrich' Canada (62 per cent), would provide greater equality (55 per cent), give all cultural groups a sense of belonging (55 per cent) and promote foreign trade (48 per cent). On the negative side, respondents stated that some groups would ultimately gain more than others (27 per cent), there would be increased conflict (23 per cent), the changes brought about would be too rapid (14 per cent), and it would eliminate the 'Canadian way of life' (12 per cent) (pp. 27–28).

Relevant government programs, in addition, have been limited in scope, with a considerable emphasis on 'creative' and performing arts, with funding being redirected into anti-racist educational pro-gramming beginning in the 1990s. Expansion of programs into other spheres of life seems unlikely. This is not only because of current fiscal restrictions on Government funding, but also because of the lack of explicit social and political support for such an expansion. Few if any incentives are evident for (provincial/municipal govern-mental, non-governmental or private) agencies to make provision for expanded multicultural facilities.

As immigrant settlement services tend to be 'front-loaded' for newcomers, the services are most prevalent immediately after arrival and become less frequent or accessible in successive months and years. In subsequent stages of settlement, by contrast, immigrants are expected to have learned to speak English/French and use mainstream services. While such arrangements do not exert formal or active 'pressure' upon newcomers to forsake their cultural heritage, its use becomes less and less relevant in the very instances of exchange between person and institution. At best, therefore, social arrange-ments foster increasingly passive and private forms of cultural retention. Occasions for overt and sustained expression of one's former cultural roots are therefore limited to those which can be promoted and sustained by the collective and individual means of newcomers themselves. In this scenario, multiculturalism would become a means to promote institutionally assimilative ends.

The potential impact on multiculturalism of a hardening of opinion against immigration was raised for debate in Australia during the deliberations of the Committee to Advise on Australia's Immi-gration Policies (CAAIP 1988). The report of this committee argued that 'community suspicion of multiculturalism is considerable' (p. 11). The main reason for this was the perception that multiculturalism is a policy for sectional 'ethnic interests', rather than Australians as a whole. Nonetheless the committee reasserted the argument that immigration policy is not driven by multiculturalism. While this judgement is an accurate one, the existence of perceptions that policy is driven by sectional 'multicultural lobbies' may have added to a hardening of attitudes to immigration itself.

Although a political and administrative division of labour in public policy-making has seen multiculturalism restricted to issues of settlement rather than intake, this arrangement is somewhat arbitrary. It smacks more of political expediency than any clearly separable policy divide. This is primarily because judgements as to the capacity of Australia to settle particular numbers of specific immigrant groups without social dislocation inevitably influence the scale and typology of immigrant intake policy.

What commitment to multiculturalism has done is to underwrite an unspoken assumption among policy-makers that a large non-English speaking background immigrant intake is compatible with social cohesion. Even though there remains serious public confusion and hostility to the perceived operation of multiculturalism as a 'sop' to special interests, policy makers committed to a non-discriminatory immigration policy have so far failed to come up with an alternative policy formulation. The problem with multiculturalism is not that it is incompatible with social cohesion. The problem is rather one of conceptual ambiguity between multiculturalism as a form of separatist cultural pluralism, and the current policy rationale for multiculturalism as a component of a liberal–democratic framework of social citizenship rights.

Conclusions

There seem to be several striking parallels between contemporary Australian and Canadian opinion concerning immigration policy and refugee intake.

First, there is evidence in Australia, as in Canada, of a recent hardening of attitudes among the general public to prevailing levels of immigration, and more specifically, to refugees. Economic immigrants with relevant skills are the preferred category of immigrant. Yet even allowing for this, public opinion is not uniformly hostile. The picture is one of complex differentiation.

Second, there is no clear evidence of stratification of general opinion along class lines, or in terms of economic deprivation.

Third, elements of 'interested opinion', including environmentalists, may be swinging against a pro-immigration position, but the political effect of this is unclear.

Fourth, public responses to the immigration issue are driven, to a significant extent by specific events and by perceptual images that form around them.

Fifth, policy makers in Australia as in Canada face a plurality of perspectives and constituencies. While general and interested opinion may currently be more negative than it was five years ago, the active lobbies appear fairly evenly matched.

Sixth, this plurality represents something of a dilemma for policy makers in terms of striking a balance between competing viewpoints and interests.

The post-war Australian achievement in settling a large, culturally diverse immigrant population in conditions of relative social harmony owes a good deal to a broad commitment by most politicians and most senior public servants at most points in time to avoid the of kind public polarisation on immigration policy that has occurred elsewhere in the world, notably in France.

It is far harder to find points of clear-cut divergence between the Australian and Canadian experience in relation to public opinion and immigration. It is not easy, for example, to determine whether an incipient anti-migrant or anti-refugee backlash is greater in one location than the other. Clearly neither country has witnessed the kind of overt anti-refugee backlash current in Germany. In the Australian case, at least, this reflects the lack of a strongly exclusive conception of national identity defined narrowly in terms of a particular ethnic core.

One area of difference between Australia and Canada may lie in the relative place of multiculturalism within policy debate and public opinion. Multiculturalism in Canada has been seriously constrained by funding limits, and increasingly limited to the 'creative' and performing arts. In Australia its scope appears somewhat greater and more vital. This is especially evident in the push to 'mainstream' access to and equity in participation for non-English-speaking immigrants over the full range of government programs and services. What remains unclear in Australia is how far public opinion accepts multiculturalism as one component of a universalistic social justice program, and how far it is perceived as a particularistic and divisive 'pro-ethnic' policy incompatible with social cohesion.

CHAPTER 6

Gender and Migration Policy

*Ruth Fincher, Lois Foster, Wenona Giles and
Valerie Preston*

Introduction

This chapter compares recent immigration policy in Australia and
Canada from the viewpoint of gender relations to examine the implications of the policies for women. It seeks to develop from this
comparison a commentary on the gender inequity implicit in the
policies, both in the general constructions of 'ideal male and female
immigrants' that underpin state actions on immigrant selection and
settlement and in the precise provisions that have been formulated to
affect specific aspects of peoples daily lives.

This chapter has three sections. First, a review indicates where
different and similar emphases have been placed in literature written
about immigrant women in Canada and Australia. In the second
section, a brief policy comparison identifies the general thinking on
masculinity and femininity that has guided recent immigration policy
in both countries, and then important aspects of selection policies
that define and influence men and women in different ways. The third
part of the paper is a case study of language policies in Canada and
Australia, which shows how the more limited opportunities for immigrant women (compared with immigrant men) to take up language
training cements their lowly labour force status, confirming the views
implicit in immigrant selection policy that the 'work' that is done by
immigrant women is less valuable than that done by immigrant men.

In conclusion we develop the argument that a major gender
inequity in immigration policy is its under-rating of the significance
of women's and thus immigrant women's work. Since much of

immigrant selection depends on notions of 'skill' in the paid work-place, and subsequent settlement assistance, especially in Canada, often depends on labour force status, this is a crucial flaw. Views of the relative lack of value of women's work that are present in immigrant selection policies and settlement provisions are in contrast to recent attempts by employment and training bureaucracies in Australia to recognise women's working competence and to record it.

Canadian and Australian literature on immigration, gender and women

To what extent have the gender relations of immigration policy attracted attention in Australian and Canadian writing and how have they been represented there? As these countries are among the few with active immigration policies currently, it is useful to have an overview of the aspects of immigration which have been studied and those which have been ignored. A further step is to position these national pictures against the international backdrop.

In our reading of the international literature, there are at least five main lines of exploration of women in migration.

1 The most striking feature of the international literature has been the transformation from a decided lack of interest in women in migration. Recently, multicultural, feminist, Marxist and other perspectives have been applied to the analysis of women migrants and their experiences. Lack of interest was manifested either by simply dealing with migrants as if they were without gender or by assuming that migration matters can be adequately covered without resort to details of the experience of women. Gender-blindness concerning migrants and migration and the apparent 'invisibility' of women in studies of internal and international migration have now become topics of interest in their own right (Camus-Jacques 1990; MacDonald & MacDonald 1972; Morokvasic 1981; Wilson 1978). Explanations of women's invisibility in part reflect the conventional wisdom that as females are not the initiators in the decision to migrate, their experience of migration can be adequately subsumed within that of males. There is a taken-for-granted view that women are the appendages of either protective males or the patriarchal state (see, for example, Allen 1980; Mama 1984, 1989; Simon & Bretell 1986).

A new body of literature is identifying and analysing migration as a gendered phenomenon. For example, one line of inquiry is concerned with understanding how state actions lead to the social construction of gender relations and migrant status (Ng 1988b, 1991, 1992). A second is the analysis of migration streams to detect where, when and under what circumstances there is conformity with one classic pattern in which early male dominance is followed at a later stage by female predominance (Thadani & Todaro 1978).

2 Examining the burgeoning literature on women in migration, Fincher et al. (1992) suggest that there are a small number of key aspects that appear and reappear constantly. Because they are important for many national and international settings, a range of analyses mediated by differing theoretical frameworks is accumulating around each. The aspects are: (a) emancipation or dependency as a legacy for women migrating; (b) the marriage–migration nexus in which women's movements are tied to men and their migration prospects to marital status; (c) the significance of gatekeepers (who intervene between the potential migrant and the immigration regulations) in channelling women's and men's migration experiences and (d) location-specific capital, resources such as kin networks (either in the country of origin or the country of migration) that increase or make possible women's mobility and options.

3 There is a large body of research embedded in an international literature that examines how 'difference', particularly that based in ethnicity, class, and race, affects the labour migration of women (Bottomley et al. 1991; McLellan & Sayers 1992; Morokvasic 1981, 1984, 1991; Phizacklea, 1983; Yuval-Davis 1991; Yuval-Davis & Anthias 1989). These authors have a strong interest in the question of emancipation and 'pseudo-emancipation' of women immigrants. They paint a generally pessimistic picture where there are wide differences in racial, cultural, and economic attributes between immigrants and host populations. Insights from the Australian but more especially Canadian work in this area, are taken up in the two later sections of the chapter.

4 Attempts to develop a theory of citizenship that addresses the varied treatment accorded different categories of ethnic minorities and women is the focus of much research on immigrant women world-wide (Bottomley et al. 1991; Bottomley & de Lepervanche 1984; Yuval-Davis 1991; Yuval-Davis & Anthias 1989). This literature is important in pointing out how state multicultural policies have constructed immigrant populations as collective groups, part of a community whose boundaries are ill-defined.

5 Unravelling the relationships among ethnicity, race, class, gender, and culture in the experience of migration and settlement has become a focus of interest. Variants on this theme are present in the other themes. For some, the issue is one of deciding salience (this is especially to be found in the writings of feminists of 'colour' such as Hooks (1982), Omalade (1980) and Ramazanoglu (1989), or others such as Pettman (1991, 1992). For other analysts, it is more a matter of pinpointing the nature and degree of the relationship among varying 'mixes' of these factors (Lees 1986; Martin 1988; Parmar 1982; Stasiulis 1990b).

Are these themes from the international literature reflected in the migration literatures in Australia and Canada? There is no doubt that a focus on gender, or explicitly on women in migration, is sparsely represented in Australian sources (with the exception of targeted reports—for example, DIEA 1981; DIEA 1986—and women's speakouts). It is only very recently that gender has received any scholarly attention with pioneering works by Bottomley and de Lepervanche, *Ethnicity, Class and Gender in Australia* (1984) and Bottomley, de Lepervanche & Martin, *Intersexions Gender/Class/Culture/Ethnicity* (1991). Even here, the major emphasis is not on immigration. As the editors state in the preface to the 1991 volume:

> Part of our intention . . . was to introduce a more comparative perspective into feminist . . . discussions about gender, class, ethnicity and culture . . . A second, and related aim . . . is to examine modes of representation-within social theory and discussions of capitalism and postcolonialism, as well as in dominant ideological notions such as caste, domesticity and 'success' (p. ix–x).

In fact, significant analysis of the role of women in Australian society from the beginnings of white Australia emerged only relatively recently. Today, only a handful of Australian social commentators such as Adam-Smith (1984), Bell (1983), Dixon (1984), Grieve and Burns (1986), and Summers (1975) have placed women at 'centre stage'. Immigrant women have remained largely 'in the wings'. Some attribute this situation to the Anglo-hegemony of Australian society and academia in which a sisterhood transcending ethnic boundaries is one of the casualties (Martin 1984, 1991; Tsolidis 1991). In the overseas literature, sociologists such as Anthias & Yuval-Davis (1983) have made the same argument.

Alcorso (1991) is critical of the Australian literature on women in migration for being less comprehensive and sophisticated than the international literature. In particular, she identifies four areas that are under-represented: (a) theoretical treatment of the topic; (b) detailed case studies of particular immigrant communities and/or groups; (c) attention to the social, cultural and economic context of women's migration; and (d) the presentation of a great variety of situations in the host society in which immigrant women participate.

The Canadian literature is larger, perhaps due to the greater number of researchers. It includes analyses of immigration policy and practice by community groups and policy analysts. Community groups have provided an important catalyst for research by pressing for strategic conferences that have addressed specific policy issues and by persistently pressuring government to address inequalities in provincial and federal policy (Adamson et al. 1991; Go 1987; Hernandez 1987; INTERCEDE 1983; Janke & Yaron 1979; McKee 1981; OCISO 1985; Wallis 1988). Policy analyses carried out by state institutions such as Multiculturalism Canada and the Canadian Advisory Council on the Status of Women and by individuals outside the government or organisations such as the Institute for Research on Public Policy have also provided valuable data (Arnopoulos 1979; Estable 1986; Seward & McDade 1988; Seward & Tremblay 1989; Seydegart & Spears 1985). Case studies that are either ethnographic or statistical are an important source of qualitative and quantitative historical data. Most ethnographic studies focus on specific groups of immigrant women in Canada and their struggles in both the workplace and the household (Burnet 1986; Gannage 1986; Lindstrom-Best 1988; Silvera 1986). Statistical research has described and compared the changing position of immigrant women in the Canadian labour force. Through examinations of the ways that state policy defines immigrant women and the differences among them, this research has attempted to deconstruct the migrant category (Boyd 1984; Preston & Giles 1991; Reitz 1990).

In both countries, there is interest in the insertion of migrants, men and women, into the labour force and other societal structures. Often the topic has been approached by examining cohorts of migrants and particular ethnic groups over time, especially using official statistics such as the Census. The Australian literature has tended to concentrate on tracing patterns of gross numbers and the skill composition of flows. Skill has been seen very much in masculine terms.

Themes explored have included union reactions to immigrant (male) labour, the costs of importing labour vis à vis skilling the Australian born and romantic versions of the exploitation of immigrant labour for early large-scale development projects such as the Snowy Mountains Hydroelectric Scheme.

The principal focus of Canadian research on immigrant women has been their economic situation, particularly their position in the labour force (Arnopoulos 1979; Boyd 1977, 1984, 1987, 1990, 1992; Estable 1986; Gannage 1986, Labelle et al. 1987; Lindstrom-Best 1988; Meintel et al. 1984; Ng & Estable 1987; Silvera 1986). This approach is closely allied to the international literature on immigrant women which examines migration as a response to an expanding market economy and its articulation with unpaid domestic work (Labelle 1990; Morokvasic 1984; Phizacklea 1983; Sassen 1988; Simon & Bretell 1986).

Both the Canadian and Australian literatures concerning women have responded to the shift in migration flows from mainly European and predominantly English-speaking origin groups before the 1970s to a migrant flow during and after the 1970s that has increasingly included Asians, South Americans and Caribbeans (Boyd 1990, 1992; DIEA 1986). This change reflects shifts in immigration policy that had favoured immigrants of European origin to a non-discriminatory policy directed towards family reunification, labour market skills and the admission of refugees. In response to the ethnic/racial inequalities that these new groups of immigrants confront in Australian and Canadian society, research has focused on the effects of region of origin as well as the economic and social conditions that shape social inequalities (Boyd 1990, 1992).

In Australia, the dearth of case studies about specific immigrant communities and/or groups is likely to be redressed more rapidly than some of the other omissions noted by Alcorso (1991). A growing number of Australian academics are studying demographic, social, educational and cultural aspects of groups of female immigrants including Greek-Australians, Latino-Australians, Turkish-Australians, Lebanese-Australians and many others (see Bottomley 1979, 1983, 1985; Elley 1988; Foster & Rado 1991; Kunek 1988; Langer 1991; Mackie 1981; Inglis & Manderson 1984; and Manderson & Inglis 1991). The work of Bottomley et al. (1984, 1991) is adding knowledge about the dimension of the relationships among the factors of class, gender and ethnicity in addition to culture.

The contemporary Canadian literature which examines ethnic difference arises out of international debates concerning citizenship status and takes a more theoretically informed approach. Much research is guided by the recognition that anti-racist and feminist discourses regarding citizenship 'have tended to treat both women and ethnic/racial minorities as homogeneous categories' (Yuval-Davis 1991, p. 64). Advocates of immigrant women have inspired a literature that has provided an important framework for criticisms of sexism and racism in state policy. However, theoretical and substantive progress is hampered by continuing disagreements concerning the relations among gender, class and ethnicity.

For immigrant women, the links between gender and class are still being debated. For example, Ng argues that 'the question of whether sex, ethnicity or class is more important to their [women's] real life situation is no longer relevant' (Ng, 1984, p. 31). She advocates focusing on 'everyday experiences' of people to describe the class location of ethnic women. Indra (1991) suggests an alternative view, criticising Ng (1984) for adopting a monolithic and stereotyped view of immigrant women.

Disagreement also exists regarding the relationship between class and ethnicity. Reitz (1990) defines ethnicity as separate from class, but as reinforcing existing inequalities in the labour market. Like Yuval-Davis & Anthias (1989), his work critiques both the reification of ethnicity as totally independent of other forms of differentiation and the reduction of national or ethnic groupings to some form of a class grouping. McAll (1990), however, states that ethnicity is neither a 'mask' that conceals class nor an alternative to class, but an integral part of class. Thus class and ethnicity form synonymously. In the Australian context, Martin (1991 implies that ethnic and sexual construction precede class construction as a biographical fact, and Misztal (1991) suggests that although economic implications of the labour market are at the core of migrant women's issues, they are not the only factors because the market serves as a vehicle for both political pressure and cultural values.

The dynamic nature of gender, class and ethnicity complicates research. The meaning of ethnicity, gender and class is being constantly created and recreated by immigrant women. They are not passive recipients of culture. Thus also the symbolic and mental 'boundaries' of their communities are dynamic (Cohen 1985).

Multicultural studies in Canada use the 'boundary' approach to avoid questions of power and to reinforce the idea of ethnicity as primarily a cultural phenomenon. Slogans such as 'unity in diversity' form the basis of an ideology devoted to avoiding discussion of social inequality. Various critiques of Australian multiculturalism advance similar arguments (see Jakubowicz 1984). As Li's research points out, there is 'a cost or benefit associated with each origin in the capitalist labour market' (1988, p. 135) to immigration authorities and employers. However, there is also a cost and benefit associated with sexual difference. Recent Canadian research by Breton et al. (1990), Li (1988) and McAll (1990) referred to the need to address issues of gender but omitted to do so in any systematic way.

Studies of ethnicity which have incorporated gender analysis have tended to focus on the work of social reproduction carried out by women (in Australia, see Martin 1984). Research has examined how state policies define women's access to resources such as housing, childcare, care of the elderly (in Canada, see Findlay & Randall 1988, Hamilton & Barrett 1986, Henderson et al. 1992). The manner in which women's ethnicity is constructed through the relationship between their reproductive and productive roles requires more exploration and definition (in Canada, see Ng 1992, Meintel et al. 1984, 1987).

In conclusion, the five themes isolated from the international literature find few echoes in the Australian and Canadian literatures. Partial exceptions might be the regular and systematic monitoring of labour force statistics by bodies such as the Australian Bureau of Statistics or Statistics Canada. These data can be reinterpreted to provide insight into the effects of migration on women's emancipation or dependency (see, for example, Boyd 1990; Casey 1992; Foster et al. 1991; Wooden 1990). In Canada and Australia, immigrant women have been described as triply disadvantaged: by their status as female, as foreign-born, and by their origins or race (Boyd 1987, 1990, 1992; Martin 1984). And as Labelle points out:

> Il faut raffiner l'analyse des relations sociales dans lèsquelles sont prisés les femmes designées comme 'immigrantes' ou 'appartenant à une minorité visible'. Les notions de 'double ou triple handicap' doivent, à notre avis, être analyseés dans le cadre de situations concrète afin d'éviter les genéralisations abusives (1990, p. 78).

Apart from the greater output of research on gender and migration in Canada, the foci of the Canadian and Australian literatures have also differed. We detect from the Canadian literature more frequent and possibly more productive interaction between community groups pressing for strategic policy research and academics and bureaucratic assessors acting in response to these pressures. A greater scrutiny of immigration policy from the viewpoint of gender relations has resulted in Canada, for example in the work of Monica Boyd (1977, 1984, 1986, 1987, 1990, 1991, 1992). Both literatures on women migrants and gender in migration have emphasised labour market outcomes for immigrants. In Canada, however, this topic has been cast more theoretically in terms of the intersections of class, gender and ethnicity and their role in the construction of immigrant women as disadvantaged citizens. If the number and variety of case studies on particular groups of immigrant men and women has been limited in Australia, and certainly it has been in comparison to the larger Canadian literature, then that situation is being rectified as more and more researchers become involved in such work.

Policy overview

In this section, two ways of comparing the immigration policies of Canada and Australia are attempted. First, a broad picture is presented of the visions of 'ideal male and female migrants' that have seemed to underpin recent policies. These are the notions of masculinity and femininity underlying the immigration program. Second, more precise indications of the implications for immigrant women of contemporary selection policies and the forms of settlement assistance directly linked to selection category are given. As an initial step, we have treated separately these two ways of analysing how immigration policy contributes to the gendered nature of migration, while recognising that accepted ways of thinking about gender roles play some part in defining the nature of all immigration policies.

The information used for the first part of this section's brief analysis is primarily Australian: the Australian authors have been working through old procedures manuals, (DIEA, DILGEA 1959, 1964, 1971, 1972, 1976, 1982, 1989), and interviewing immigration officers who have served in postings overseas, to try to gain understanding of the thinking about gender that has given rise to particular modes of implementing immigration policy and interpreting its rules 'on the ground'. The information used for the second section is primarily Canadian, both because the Canadian authors have relied on existing feminist critiques of particular migration policies, more numerous in the Canadian literature, to form their commentary, and because there are more ways that access to settlement assistance in Canada is linked to migration category to the detriment of immigrant women.

Visions of the masculine and the feminine in immigration selection

In the immediate post-World War II period, Australia's immigration intake rested on the image of the able-bodied, male manual worker of European origin, as the 'desirable' migrant. Officers of the Immigration Department posted overseas used their discretion to recruit such migrants. Immigrant women were defined in relation to the masculine ideal as dependents. Their stature as migrants rested on marital and familial status rather than their skills or physical strength, though the physical attribute of women's age was a significant eligibility criterion because it affected their capacity to give birth. In the 1970s, skill requirements began to define the desirable migrant, replacing the notions of physical stature that had privileged certain men in the previous two decades. Again, in the skill-based definitions of the ideal, migrant women were marginalised, because the desired occupational characteristics underpinning these notions of skill were, as those of physical stature had been before them, characteristics more readily fitting men. 'Migrant', then, has been a gendered category in Australian migration policy since World War II, as well as a racialised one for some of that time. The views of masculinity and femininity pervading immigrant selection are illustrated below by statements from files and comments from officers of the Immigration Department posted overseas at the relevant times.

A 1956 poster of an Italian cane-cutter with the caption 'There's a man's job waiting for you' captures the spirit of the Australian migrant recruitment effort in the 1950s. Australia was actively seeking young, able-bodied men from overseas to work in agriculture, mining and on major construction projects.

A disproportionate number of males in the early, post-war Australian migrant intake resulted from this preference, as a 1969 report of the Department of Immigration and Ethnic Affairs reveals:

> There was a preponderance of males in the early years of Australia's post-war migration programme due to the influx of refugees, mainly single males; to large-scale unassisted migration from Southern Europe which initially was largely male; and to early tendencies to recruit single men to build up the work force with minimum demands on housing and other services (File 69/70582).

Handbooks or manuals were produced to advise Australian immigration officers overseas, or Foreign Affairs representatives fulfilling immigration tasks, on the assessment of applicants. The handbooks became progressively more sophisticated, setting out general guide-lines for selection in the 1960s and 1970s, introducing numerical assessment in 1979 and providing increasing detail until December 1989 when selection criteria were formalised in legislation. But in the earlier post-war decades the manuals dealt mainly with personal characteristics. This was consistent with the emphasis on able-bodied, physically capable males as ideal migrants. All applicants, until the mid-1970s, were to be screened in case their height (or lack of it) prevented them from working or caused them to be scorned by the Australian public. The manuals recommended to interviewers that:

> For persons within the worker age group, the assessment should take into account . . .
> (b) general physique in relation to occupation. An applicant should not be of such diminutive size and/or poor physique as to be at a distinct disadvantage in competing in a new environment for employment in his normal occupation (*Migrant Entry Handbook*, 1971).

On the other hand, officers were advised in 1964 that the height limit could be disregarded if the migrant 'possesses a skill unaffected by a lack of height' or on compassionate grounds as long as:

> the person concerned must be of otherwise robust build and not such diminutive size as to provoke adverse comments in a normal Australian community; and where a family unit is involved the lack of height must be confined to one or two members depending on the number of persons in the family and it must be clear that the degree of shortness is not a familial trait (*Migrant Entry Handbook*, 1964).

Over these years, also, family breadwinners were males only. The pronouns used in departmental manuals made this quite clear. In the 1964 manual dealing with 'Dependants Unaccompanied By Breadwin-ner' for example, the following is stated:

> . . . a member of the family unit of an applicant or nominee should not be permitted to proceed to Australia ahead of the breadwinner but a breadwinner may be permitted to precede his dependants. The consent of a wife to the issue of a visa to her husband is not required in such cases.

It was not until 1989 that the concept of breadwinner sponsoring and supporting dependent wives and children was thoroughly altered in the migrant entry instructions and replaced by specifications that members of a principal applicant's family unit derive their eligibility for migration from that person and therefore cannot precede the principal applicant.

Economic goals have also guided Canadian immigration policies in the post-war period (Economic Council of Canada 1991; Hawkins 1989). First stated formally by Prime Minister Mackenzie King in 1947 and codified in the 1953 Immigration Act, the primary goals of Canadian immigration were to enlarge the Canadian population and improve the Canadian standard of living (Hawkins 1988). These goals are reiterated in Part 1 of the *Immigration Act* of 1976 which sets as its general purpose 'immigration policy . . . designed and administered . . . to promote the domestic and international interests of Canada'.

Two clauses refer explicitly to economic conditions, while a third refers to demographic goals in respect to the size and rate of growth of the Canadian population. Although economic goals appear to be less important than social and cultural goals such as facilitating the reunion of Canadian families, fulfilling Canada's international obligations with respect to treaties and enriching and strengthening the cultural and social fabric of Canada (*Immigration Act* 1976, Part 1). The interpretation of the Act in subsequent regulations has confirmed the economic thrust of Canadian immigration policy (Economic Council of Canada 1991). Parliamentary and public debate has concentrated on the economic merits of immigration. At the moment, the majority of immigrants enter Canada for the purpose of family reunification or as dependants of principal applicants (EIC 1989a). The growing number of 'non-economic' migrants has heightened public concerns that immigrants are taking jobs from native-born Canadians while simultaneously placing undue burdens on social services. Outside the immigrant communities themselves, there is little public support for those who advocate an immigration policy based on humanitarian concerns.

In both countries, the views of masculinity and femininity that underpinned migration thinking placed little value on the wife's potential for paid work. The perception is reflected in the Immigration Department's manual (1972) indicating that large families were not considered economically viable because such families would have only one 'worker':

> families with more than four children should not be accepted for assisted passages . . . unless . . . [they can arrange private accommodation or] . . .

(c) there is in a family with five children one worker among the children
and with six children there are two workers (preferably but not necessarily male—normally 16 years of age and over . . .) among the children.
The wife's earning potential is not to be taken into account when
determining the number of workers in a family.

Though policy makers of the day were aware that women migrating might have been workers in the paid labour force or wish to
join it in Australia, women were nevertheless largely viewed in terms
of their relationship to men migrating—as dependent wives, sisters,
daughters. Philip Lynch, then Minister for Immigration, in an address
to a commercial association spoke of how 'about half of these new
settlers will be workers, most of them married and accompanied by
their wives and children' (Lynch 4 April 1970). The rules of dependants migrating made many stipulations, until the early 1970s, based
on women's marital status. For example:

- married women were not to travel to Australia for permanent residence unless accompanied by their husband or unless they were
  joining their husband;
- if a married woman was 'legally separated' she was not to be
  sponsored as a fiancee and not to be allowed to enter for a de facto
  relationship unless there were already children of the de facto union;
- the only restriction on fiancees was that they were to be over 18
  years old and have bona fide intentions; fiances, on the other hand,
  were to be assessed under another migration category if possible,
  and often a bond was to be lodged by the sponsor (adapted from
  1959 *Migrant Entry Handbook*).

As well, especially in the 1960s but also into the early 1970s,
single European women were encouraged to migrate to Australia, as
long as they were of marriageable age (18 to 35 years). All criteria
designed to restrict or control entry of migrants were lifted in relation
to single women from 1959 in order to facilitate the entry of as many
as possible. The 1964 handbook stated that single women between
18 and 35 would be considered for migration irrespective of their
occupation. No literacy tests were required for single women of any
age. And once issued single women's visas, these women were not to
marry before migrating to Australia. There seems to be little doubt
that the push to introduce greater numbers of single women to
Australia was to provide wives for males already here. As one migration officer stationed in Europe at the time stated:

We were encouraging females to come into this country, there was an imbalance here among the migrants, to marry off the males in this country (interview transcript, unpublished, Fincher et al. 1992).

On the other hand, the Department of Immigration in 1972 refuted claims that it had sought young women migrants as 'marriage fodder':

... at no stage did the Embassy [in Peru] 'recruit' large numbers of single girls let alone encourage them to migrate with a view of ready matrimony in Australia. The girls apply voluntarily and do so in large numbers. Statistically, neither Australia nor Peru have an imbalance between the sexes to speak of ... (File 72/76644).

It should be noted, however, that in the mid-1960s, a period when masculinist notions of physical capacity dominated immigrant selection rather than the 'skill' definitions that have dominated since the late 1970s, certain worker requisitions were made by the Australian government on the basis of the birthplace of prospective migrants. The Department of Employment designated areas of labour shortage and the Immigration Department selected countries as recruiting sites for specific shortages (skilled trades, unskilled, domestic workers etc.). Immigration also determined the categories in which women could be sought as workers—and there weren't many, which is odd given that this was the time that single women immigrants were being sought—clearly an example of the limits to thinking about women immigrants, who were seen as breeders but not taken seriously as workers (see Departmental file 63/46044). These practices are good examples of the stereotypes about migrants that actually engineered, in a small way, their labour market segmentation once in Australia. So, for example, in 1963 female clerical and sales workers were recruited in small numbers from the UK, but only if they were under 35 years old; skilled tradesmen were recruited from Britain especially; female domestic workers and unskilled male workers were recruited from Greece and Spain but none from Britain.

After the early 1970s, the criterion of 'skill' assumed prominence in Australian migrant selection processes. Weight was variously given to level of education and occupation in assessing skill. Again, women were marginalised in that they were not recognised as having skills that characterised the ideal migrant. For skill, in Australia, has been constructed historically as a property of males. Certain tasks and jobs are seen to require 'skill'. Viewed as skilled individuals, men who have been disproportionately employed in those occupations have accrued political power over what has subsequently been defined as 'skilled' (Bennett 1984). Assessment of 'skill' has therefore been based on occupations that people have had rather than the competencies of people themselves. The definition of skill is slowly changing, as witnessed by the introduction of *skills audits* in the workplace.

The 1982 *Migrant Entry Handbook*, at item 20.4.4, indicates how 'points [determining migrant selection in the independent and concessional family categories] are awarded according to the skill level of an applicant as determined by his worker code'; ten factors, including skill but also age, education, English ability and occupational attributes, were used to rank a prospective migrant and the 'pass' score at the time was 60 or more points. The points awarded for 'skill' were made according to occupational designations as follows:

Professional and technical	10 points
Skilled (specified worker codes)	10 points
Professional, technical and skilled workers whose qualifications are not fully recognised	6 points
Service occupations	4 points
Clerical, commercial and administrative	3 points
Semi-skilled	2 points
Rural	0 points
Unskilled	0 points

At particular times, particular 'skills' were designated as in 'occupational demand' in the Australian labour market—28 points could be awarded a migrant intending to work in an occupation in 'shortage', and 24 if intending to work in an area of 'minor shortage'. Business migrants and employment nominees were always classified as in shortage—thus business migrants (usually men) would accrue more points than those in the 'clerical, commercial and administrative' designation (often women) on the above list. A further 10 points was available if the applicant had 'outstanding occupational attributes'; to accrue these points, the 1982 manual indicates:

> . . . an applicant would normally show all of the following attributes:
> - several years experience in employment in the occupation in which he proposes to work in Australia
> - a past record of employment which shows a stable, responsible approach to employment and a record of success and achievement

- good progress in his past career, where the occupation is one in which career advancement is possible
- personal qualities relevant to the proposed employment in Australia; these could vary widely from case to case eg for an applicant in a manual occupation involving heavy lifting they would include size and strength; for an applicant in a managerial occupation, they might include responsiveness, initiative and appearance (Item 20.4.24).

Now, clearly this material does not exclude women who satisfy the criteria. However, if the criteria are examined, it is also clear that women as a general rule will fit the requirements far less frequently than will men. With regard to points for 'skill' allocated to those with experience in certain occupations, the unskilled category includes domestic work or house duties in which women have often been occupied.

And the lowly rated service sector or clerical, administrative and semi-skilled tasks include many of the jobs in which women work in the paid labour force. (We noted already that business migrants who are disproportionately men receive extra points for being 'in shortage' that workers from commercial backgrounds do not get.) The 'outstanding occupational attributes' points are also unlikely to go to women, women being less likely to have completed continuous service in career-advancing jobs because of absences from the workforce due to child rearing. Furthermore, they ar more likely to be in jobs without prospects of career advancement. And if women applicants are expected to fit, with their personal qualities and aspirations, into the labour market for women in Australia, then they must be defined in terms of Australia's highly sex-segregated labour market right into the categories of worker least likely to generate points for skill in immigration selection. The difficulties for women to gain entry under these categories encourages them to apply through the preferential family/dependent spouse categories, even if they had intended otherwise.

The points test on which selection of independent and concessional family immigrants is based has continued to stress skill. In 1989, for instance, the preferred occupational and education characteristics could net the applicant far more points than any other item (like family relationship, age or language skills).

A masculine bias is also apparent in Canada where, until 1974, married women were not allowed to enter Canada as the principal applicant. Rather, their spouses had to be the main applicant regardless of the man's occupation and educational qualifications (Boyd

1991). Like its Australian counterpart, the Canadian Immigration Department also promulgated regulations intended to expedite the entry of male farmworkers and labourers from specific countries to satisfy various regional and sectoral labour demands (EIC 1989a).

Canadian evaluation of independent and assisted relative immigrants is also based on a points test underpinned by a masculine view of skill. Introduced in 1967, somewhat earlier than Australia's, the points system intended:

> to spell out in detail the principles governing the selection of Canadian immigrants . . . and . . . to provide an assessment system which permits immigration officers to apply the same standards in selecting immigrants in all areas of the world (Canada 1967).

The original system assessed applicants in terms of eight criteria that were assigned various weights. Twenty points were based on years of formal education or training, another 10 were given for occupational skill, usually reflecting years of experience in the paid labour force. Finally, another 30 points were granted on the basis of a definite job offer in Canada; Canadian demand for the occupational skill; and employment opportunities in the area of destination. Altogether, a total of 60 points were assigned on the basis of the applicant's perceived ability to participate in the paid labour force. In contrast, independent immigrants could obtain a maximum of 5 points if a relative in Canada was able to help the applicant become established.

The points system has undergone repeated amendments with major changes in 1978 and 1985 that have tended to increase the relative weight given to the applicant's perceived ability to satisfy current labour market demands. For example, the revisions in 1985 removed any points for independent applicants who had a relative in Canada who could assist with establishing the applicant. The minimum points for independent applicants also increased from 50 to 70 to ensure the selection of highly qualified workers (Hawkins 1989). The importance of skills and work experience in the paid labour force is highlighted in the most recent immigration plan that proposed to increase the number and proportion of skilled workers who qualify as independent immigrants while simultaneously reducing the number of assisted relatives and narrowing the definition of dependents who qualify for sponsorship under the family class (EIC 1990a). Indeed, provincial recommendations concerning occupational needs will be solicited annually to identify occupations in demand for which points will be assigned. With its growing emphasis upon skilled workers, immigration policy about independent immigrants will continue to reinforce existing gender inequities, favouring men over women in many cases.

In Canada, like Australia, gender inequities in the skill-driven selection of immigrants derive in part from the failure to value women's work which is often domestic work, paid and unpaid, and women's workforce participation which is often interrupted due to family responsibilities. At face value, the Canadian points system appears less biased than the Australian system, since it does not assign weights separately to each occupation under the categories of occupational skill or education and training. However, the number of points given for occupational skill are based mainly on experience in the paid workforce. The effect of this interpretation of skill is similar to that of the Australian system. Immigrant women enter Canada with the imprint of their countries of origin where women's opportunities to obtain formal training and employment are likely to be less than those of men (Boyd 1990). Women may also lack the same record of paid employment as men because of gender inequalities in the country of origin that limit their access to specific occupations. With the exception of the domestic workers' program, current policy discounts the value of women's domestic experience and skills unless they have been recognised in the formal economy of the country of origin. The biases in the assessment of potential immigrants are particularly onerous for single women. Married women may enter as spouses, avoiding the points system altogether, single women, who are unlikely to have had the same access to education, training, and the labour market in their countries of origin as men, are subject to the same criteria for admission to Canada.

In sum, the working capacity of men has largely defined the ideal migrant in Australia—either in terms of physical attributes to enable them to undertake heavy manual work (as in the early post-war years) or in terms of trades and professional skills and business acumen and experience (as in more recent decades). The same focus on the working capacity of men is implicit in the economic criteria used to assess many applicants to Canada. Associated with the model working male in both countries has been the nurturing, family-oriented female, the two together apparently viewed as the backbone of the ideal, economically viable immigrant family.

The important point to note in the contemporary situation is that in both Canada and Australia, skill is being pursued as the central characteristic of an ideal migrant, and the way in which skill is defined and measured disadvantages women applicants. Notions of what 'skill' consists of, and ways of measuring it, are biased to permit men to do better on assessments of 'skill possession'. We regard this as a general issue of gender equity, in which societal denigration of the sorts of work women commonly do, whether in•the home or in the paid workplaces of the clerical and services sectors, is reflected in the low value awarded such work in applications to migrate. The high proportion of women who enter Canada and Australia by virtue of their family ties reflects the failure of current policies to value women's work. Women qualify more easily for immigration as members of a family than as independent immigrants. Developing ways to perform 'skill audits' that are not gender-biased in this way is something the Australian Department of Employment, Education and Training is currently working on. There is need for a systematic assessment of the way that 'skill' and 'work' are interpreted in immigration selection policy, with a view to eradicating such gender biases.

Implications for immigrant women of selection policies and settlement policies tied to selection mechanisms

In this section, more specific policy issues from the contemporary period are addressed to ask how specific selection practices and policies affect women, and how settlement is affected by selection category. Does it make any difference to a woman immigrant under which category she entered Australian or Canada? The category of migrant entry seems to make a far greater difference to the settlement prospects of immigrant women in Canada than it does to immigrant women in Australia: in Canada, eligibility for many important settlement services depends on migration entry category and is less readily available to those categories of migrant in which women predominate.

Clearly, lack of access to social services can impede an immigrant's settlement. In Canada, immigration class affects access to social services, with social assistance and appropriate medical care, job training and employment counselling and pension policies being among the most important (Boyd 1987; Seward & McDade 1988). Language training is now accessible to sponsored immigrants but only since 1992. Canadian settlement policies favour those who are destined for the labour market, namely independent immigrants whose skills are deemed necessary to meet Canadian labour market demands. Since the majority of principal applicants in the independent class are men, settlement policies often favour men over women.

Critics have commented extensively on the general inadequacy of Canadian settlement policies that have been managed by several agencies in the federal government, administered through a plethora of federal–provincial agreements and often delivered by municipal and local agencies (Economic Council of Canada 1991; Hawkins 1988, 1989). At the federal level, the provision of services to immigrants has also been hampered by the division of responsibilities between two departments, that was introduced in 1966. The Ministry of Manpower and Immigration, now the Department of Employment and Immigration, has had primary responsibility for immigrant workers, paying for language training for adult immigrants in the labour force and providing reception, family and employment counselling. It works with voluntary agencies where necessary. The Department of the Secretary of State has been responsible for the social, political and cultural integration of immigrants (Hawkins 1988).

The division of responsibilities has proved particularly troublesome for immigrant women who are more likely to enter Canada as sponsored immigrants than as independent immigrants. As sponsored immigrants, women are ineligible for the services provided by the Department of Employment and Immigration, while those provided by the Department of the Secretary of State have in the past failed to take account of the need for immigrant women to earn an income while undertaking language and job training (Boyd 1987; Seward & McDade 1988).

Sponsorship also reduces women's access to income support (Boyd 1987, 1991; Seward & McDade 1988). Sponsors are obliged to support relatives for ten years after initial residence in Canada. To obtain social assistance within the ten-year time limit, immigrant women must demonstrate that the sponsorship relationship has dissolved. Misunderstanding the requirement, immigrant women may mistakenly believe that they are ineligible for social welfare programs. Limited access to income support may increase immigrant women's tendency to stay in abusive and unsatisfactory family relationships that impede their integration into Canadian society (Boyd 1987, 1991). Even among sponsored immigrant women who are eligible for income support, namely refugee women, there is pressure to become financially self-sufficient as soon as possible. Refugee women are often encouraged to take any available job, regardless of their previous training and academic qualifications (Moussa, Allmen & Ptolemy 1989). The importance given to financial self-sufficiency forces many refugee women to accept poorly paid unskilled jobs that reduce their abilities to take advantage of language training. The double burden of paid employment and family responsibilities leaves them with little time and less energy to devote to language training (National Working Group on Refugee Women 1989).

Access to job training and employment counselling is crucial for all immigrant women who have difficulty in having their credentials and work experience recognised by Canadian employers (Boyd 1987, 1990; Economic Council of Canada 1991a; Labelle 1990; National Working Group on Refugee Women 1989). There are no programs designed explicitly to improve the employment opportunities of immigrant women. Programs often have had restrictive eligibility criteria that reduced their usefulness to immigrant women. For example, people were eligible for training or work experience under the Job Development Program only if they had been unemployed for at least 24 of the last 30 months. As several authors have pointed out, immigrant women often could not afford to be unemployed that long (Boyd 1987; Seward & McDade 1988). There were similar problems with the Job Re-entry Program for which only women who had been out of the labour force for at least three years were eligible. Furthermore, Boyd (1991) argues compellingly that the success of all these programs depended upon the availability of support services such as child care that reduce the double burden on women.

Employment counselling to help immigrant women identify job opportunities and compete successfully for Canadian jobs is also inadequate. Immigrant men and women both have difficulty obtaining employment in Canada where their credentials and work experience are often not recognised by potential employers (Economic Council of Canada 1991a; National Working Group on Refugee Women 1989; Seward & McDade 1988). Yet calls for a national system of reviewing educational qualifications and professional accreditation have gone unheeded.

The cumulative effects of the inadequacies of language training, job training, and employment counselling place immigrant women at a disadvantage with regard to pension programs. Although immigrant women are more likely than Canadian-born women to be employed in the paid labour force, the majority are in low-wage unskilled and semi-skilled jobs (Boyd 1990; Seward & McDade 1988). As a result, immigrant women receive low pension benefits from the Canada/Quebec pension plan that is based on years of employment and wages. Full benefits from the universal pension scheme, the old age security program and the guaranteed income supplement are available only after ten years of residence in Canada. Otherwise, the benefits are pro-rated except where treaties allow for co-ordination of benefits between pension plans in the country of origin and the Canadian plans (Boyd 1987).

In Australia, the migration status of a woman as a preferential family migrant with a working husband would not reduce her eligibility for settlement services like language tuition, accommodation in migrant hostels, or access to the counselling services of Migrant Resource Centres or the Commonwealth Employment Service. There are limits to the government income support she could get—no unemployment benefits would be awarded if her husband is working, for example, the same as for any Australian married person with an employed spouse. Unemployment benefits are available to immigrants (women as well as men, as long as their spouse is not employed) within about a week of arrival in Australia—these are the same income support benefits available to unemployed Australians, and carry the same regulations about searching for work while receiving them, reporting all income earned, and only being able to earn a small amount without reduction in the level of the benefit. If an immigrant (woman or man) has entered Australia under an Assurance of Support arrangement, his/her family will be required to support him/her financially for a specified period. There are groups of immigrants for whom sponsors' assurances of support must be given—like adults within ten years of retiring age—but immigration officers have discretion over when and to whom other assurances apply. Immigrant women might be particularly likely to incur assurance of support restrictions upon entry, because more immigrant women than immigrant men are elderly—a demographic fact. But the direct implications of entry category for women's labour force status in Australia are less evident in the Australian case.

There is only one case we envisage in which, under present Australian practices, immigrant women might be disadvantaged by the manner of their entry to Australia in their subsequent employment prospects. This occurs when a family's application for entry in the independent category is being approved. In this circumstance, the educational qualifications and work experience of the principal applicant (usually the male) are formally assessed before approval of the migration application, to see what their equivalent is in Australian terms. Such assessment is a lengthy process, requiring the immigration authorities to send the applicant's papers to the relevant trades assessing bodies (for example) in Australia. If the principal applicant's qualifications have equivalents in Australia, generating enough points for the family to migrate, then the principal applicant has the advantage upon arrival of having his (as it very usually is) qualifications and experience already assessed. Other adults (often the female spouse) in the family, also admitted under the independent category with the principal applicant, would have to start the long process of qualifications assessment from scratch, after migration. In this situation, the principal applicant would be more likely than the 'dependant' adult to find suitable employment quickly. The Women's Issues Plan (DILGEA 1991b) has included some measures to try to reduce this potential disadvantage.

This section has illustrated how certain (more often Canadian than Australian) settlement policies that do not discriminate explicitly on the basis of sex nevertheless place immigrant women at economic and social disadvantage. Further, the chain of women's disadvantage starts at the point of their migration entry status. It makes a difference, in Canada, what migration category you enter under. It makes less difference in Australia.

A further point emerges in critics' questions about the patriarchal view of the family inherent in current Canadian regulations about who can be sponsored as a spouse (Boyd 1987). Only legally defined spouses and the dependents of legal unions may be sponsored under the family class. *De facto* marriages are not recognised. As a result, partners in common-law marriages are not admissible except as fiancees and their children may enter only as assisted relatives or independent immigrants. In Australia, by the end of the 1980s, despite the fewer points that family links could give an independent or concessional family applicant (as in Canada), the reuniting of families was still being stressed as an important component of migration policy. And the profoundly heterosexist and legalistic logic of the views of family and marriage embedded in previous Australian immigration selection was made more flexible through the 1980s when *de facto* marriages became accepted, and when homosexual relationships were condoned as a basis for migration on compassionate grounds until the introduction of the migration regulations in 1989 did away with this category. A similar category was reintroduced in December 1990. The first implication for women and also for men who are sponsored under the family category is that in Canada the definition of the family is very narrow; this is not the case in Australia.

Looking at further differences in Canadian and Australian policy for migrant selection, and how this affects immigrant women's subsequent settlement, it is notable that among immigrants admitted to Canada intending to participate in the labour market, women predominate in only one group, domestic workers. This is an entry category that Australia does not have. The Canadian foreign domestics program under which temporary visitors may become permanent residents after two years of Canadian residence is one of the few immigration programs that allows for a change of status. It also explicitly values domestic skills and experience, by targeting those willing to work as domestics of which there is a current shortage in Canada. In 1989 in Canada, 99.7 per cent of the 3596 people who qualified for permanent residence under the domestic workers program were women, while at least 80 per cent had migrated from non-European countries (EIC 1989b). The predominance of non-European women reflects the program's requirements. Domestic workers can enter Canada only after obtaining an offer of employment. The offer of employment can be made only after the potential employer has demonstrated that no qualified Canadians are available.

Domestic workers must have some prior experience of domestic work and be judged able to attain financial self-sufficiency. To obtain permanent residence, domestic workers must demonstrate that they can achieve financial self-sufficiency within a two-year period during which the worker is required to live in the employer's household and further their education through formal coursework. The requirement that domestic workers live with their employers means that they may not bring their children to reside in Canada. Indeed, the guidelines for immigration officers who are evaluating applicants under the foreign domestic workers program state that a women's marital status and number of dependants should be considered, although being married and having children does not necessarily disqualify an applicant (Boyd 1991).

The vulnerability of domestics who are dependent upon their employers to qualify for permanent residence has been of major concern (Arat-Kroc 1989, Calliste 1989). According to Boyd (1987, 1991), the dependency of domestic workers raises concerns about abusive working conditions, particularly low wages and very long hours. Several organisations are also concerned that high proportions of domestic workers are not obtaining permanent residence (Seward & McDade 1988). Approximately 60 per cent of domestic workers were landed between 1982 and 1985, raising concerns about the criteria for permanent residence. Several organisations have questioned whether employers are supporting domestic workers' efforts to upgrade their skills. They also question the ways in which immigration officers assess financial self-sufficiency on the basis of savings and earnings potential which may both be low for domestic workers who are often paid minimum wages (Seward & McDade 1988).

Recent proposals to change the Foreign Domestic Workers' Program have renewed these concerns. The proposed amendments include the following admissibility criteria: workers must have at least 6 months formal education as a domestic worker, paid experience as a domestic worker and fluency in one of Canada's official languages. These amendments are intended to ensure that domestic workers who become permanent residents can compete for jobs in the Canadian economy. Advocacy groups contend that the amendments will discourage non-European women from taking advantage of the program since they are often unable to afford specialised formal education and may have difficulty documenting previous employment as domestics in their countries of origin. They also note that the proposed legislation continues to undervalue domestic labour by assuming implicitly that women will compete for jobs outside the domestic sector once they become permanent residents (Oziewicz 1991). They argue that because domestic workers are performing jobs that are in high demand in the labour market, they should be given landed immigrant status from the outset of their employment in Canada (INTERCEDE 1992).

In Australia, the only evidence we have found of such a practice is from a Department of Immigration manual (1960), in which there are indications that non-European merchants could bring to Australia non-European maidservants and governesses or amahs, though rarely a manservant. Servants were not permitted to bring spouse or children. It is still the case that domestic workers can be sponsored to Australia as temporary residents by diplomats or company managers who are temporary residents themselves; the sex of the domestic workers is no longer specified, however.

From this brief review of ways that immigrant women's migration entry category can affect their settlement prospects, several recommendations can be made. There needs to be removal of the disadvantage that category of migrant entry imposes on women in Canada and to a lesser extent apparently in Australia. First, there is no gender equity in the fact that if women enter Canada as a 'sponsored' spouse in the family category, they should be denied settlement services, especially when the family is probably a unit migrating rather than a series of differentially 'worthy' individuals. What does 'sponsored' actually mean in this circumstance? In practice, it is being interpreted as an assessment that women family entrants are less worthy than their husbands, even if both will be employed in the paid labour-force after arrival (Samuel 1988). Many women would find entry under existing skill-based alternative provisions impossible, in any case, for the reasons of masculinist bias advanced in the first part of this section. Australian migrant approval procedures might be improved if the spouses of principal applicants had their experience and qualifications formally assessed before their applications were approved for migration (as has been suggested in the DILGEA Women's Issues Plan). This would not only remove any bias experienced upon arrival by the 'dependent' adult, but would also serve to advise those people planning on entering Australia thinking their qualifications would guarantee them work, that suitable work was more (if approved) or less (if unapproved) likely.

Second, there is no gender equity in the restrictions placed on domestic workers in Canada that place them at a disadvantage relative to other entry categories. It would be preferable to remove this category, and include recognition of the skills of women in this type of work as part of other entry categories—that is, if domestic and service sector work (unpaid and paid) were properly recognised in the 'skill' definitions underpinning migrant selection, there would be no need for such a category as domestic workers.

Language training: a case study in the 'gendering' of migration and settlement

In this section, we focus on one element of the linked migration entry and settlement process—language and language training—to highlight the gendering of that process. Language facility is crucial to the nature of the immigrant's insertion into the labour market; as employment itself is segmented on the basis of gender in both Australia and Canada, a language case study has much to offer in illustrating some of the gender issues in migration.

The politics of language is inherently more complex in Canada both because of the bilingual nature of the country and the earlier emergence of ethnicity as a salient socio-political factor in Canadian society. An official language policy can be said to have been put in place with the British *North America Act* of 1867; the nation's 'official' bilingualism became more firmly entrenched after the Bilingualism and Biculturalism Commission of 1967 when the Trudeau pronouncements of 1971 linked bilingualism to multiculturalism. Until 1987, Australia did not have an explicit official language policy. Prior to that time, English was *de facto* the official language and language policy was restricted to legislation which spelt out the responsibility of the federal government for the Adult Migrant

Education Program (AMEP) and the Child Migrant Education Program (CMEP); in both of which the teaching of English as a second language (TESL) was the central component. Australia, with a highly diversified population due largely to multi-ethnic immigration, approaches the twenty-first century with the domination of the English language basically unchallenged.

Government recognition of the importance of fluency in the dominant language, English in Australia and English or French in Canada, has affected immigration policy to varying degrees and at different times. Fluency may have been a positive factor in selection or, as has often been the case for women immigrants, the state has not required language facility for entry, but settlement imperatives have then come into play, with disadvantageous results. Through government control and assistance, both countries have tied language training closely to labour market participation. Language training schemes in both countries, claiming to be gender neutral, have often deserved the tag of being 'gender blind' and hence particularly disadvantaging to women. Even in cases where gender has been acknowledged, supporting services such as counselling or child care may still be inadequate. Some commentators even go so far as to say that constraints on access to language classes for NESB immigrant women in Australia (especially for other than new arrivals), and low level of English language skills attained from language classes, combined with scanty resourcing for mother tongue maintenance, ensure that language training for many such women is a sham. On the Canadian side, the arrangements for language training have actually denied many immigrant women language training opportunities.

Boyd (1984) has pointed out that it is not enough to describe the relative location and characteristics of immigrant women in the labour force. Rather, it is also important to understand why they are affected by gender, ethnic status and nativity. Language facility is one of the key mediating variables that allows us to link gender, ethnicity and place of origin with immigrant women's various positions in the labour market (Boyd 1992).

In Australia, there are some factors in the general social context that affect women immigrants in ways that may influence their capacity to gain access to language and other training. These factors are noted briefly before turning to the specific provisions for English as a Second Language (ESL) and literacy training which affect male and female immigrants differently.

First, despite a long-standing immigration program and the increasing proportion of women immigrants, including those of NESB, in the population and in the labour force, there has been a somewhat belated recognition of the importance of language and literacy provisions. This is surprising in a country which has relied so heavily on immigration for population growth generally and, more specifically in recent years, for skilled labour in building the 'clever country'. This raises the question of whether immigrants who arrived in earlier periods can benefit from the current improvements in language and literacy policy.

Second, Wooden (1990), reporting on occupational disadvantage for immigrant women, gives as reasons the occurrence of direct or indirect discrimination against immigrants and the greater disadvantage conferred by refugee status. He also emphasises such differentially distributed characteristics as pre- and post-migration education, recognition of overseas qualifications, length of residence in Australia, and English language proficiency. For instance, applicants for refugee status already in Australia have little or no access to social security benefits and, in many cases, no right to work while their cases are being assessed.

Third, analysing reforms aimed at restructuring industry, work organisation, training systems, union structures and wages policy along with streamlining of English language training programs and overseas skills recognition processes introduced by the Hawke government (and continued by the Keating administration since late 1991), Stasiulis argues that the combined economic and multicultural agenda is less likely to benefit particular groups of immigrants including the unskilled, semi-skilled, older and females. For example, she notes (1990a, p. 2):

> Changes in award restructuring are widely acknowledged to lead to the retrenchment of older, less skilled, non-English speaking, and frequently . . . female immigrants. The re-direction of resources in English language programs to new, skilled immigrants is likely to lead to further marginalization of these segments of the NES immigrant population.

Support for this view comes also, for example, from the Women's Employment Branch of the Department of Labour in Victoria (1990). In a report focusing on women and award restructuring, the authors warned that the potential of restructuring in respect of women workers is unlikely to be realised unless training and award restructuring strategies address specific issues, especially the lack of recognition and the undervaluing of the skills held by women. This problem is accentuated in the case of NESB women.

For instance, in spite of the passage of a Training Guarantee Scheme in 1990 requiring individual firms to spend at least 1 per cent of their gross wages bill on training, there has been no call for a proportion to be dedicated to combined ESL language and literacy and specific job-related skills training for NESB workers, male or female. Research evidence (for example, Foster & Rado 1991) has shown that NESB female workers are more likely to be bypassed in selection for on-the-job training including ESL courses than their NESB male colleagues.

Fourth, there is also the perennial problem for women workers generally and also for NESB immigrant women of child-care (DEET 1990, 1991). In spite of the ratification by Australia in 1990 of Convention 156 of the International Labour Organisation (ILO) which requires member countries to aim for national policies reducing the conflict between employment and family responsibilities, the progress towards a national strategy to implement the Convention, and the expansion of government-subsidised child-care facilities since 1983, affordable, quality and culturally appropriate child-care facilities provision remains inadequate. Mageean (1990) identifies lack of child-care in addition to factors of isolation, lack of educational resources and especially failure to cater for adult learners of a variety of non-English speaking backgrounds as barriers to participation in education and training by adult immigrants in rural Australia, in spite of DILGEA programs such as the Home Tutor Scheme.

The following are features of federally supported English language services in Australia. The program named the Adult Migrant Education Program (AMEP) is part of the Department of Immigration, Local Government and Ethnic Affairs (DILGEA 1991e). It costs over $100 million annually and more than half the clientele enrolled comprises women. Some access to child-care services is made available. Other federal departments, such as the Department of Employment, Education and Training (DEET) sponsor work-related training programs which include language components.

From the late 1980s, there has been an upsurge of interest in adult education, both continuing and mainstream, as part of labour market restructuring (ACTU 1990; Long 1990; McTaggart & Smyth 1990; Senate Standing Committee on Employment, Education and Training 1991). This and the nexus between language and literacy exemplified by the Australian Language and Literacy Policy (ALLP) (Dawkins 1991) have come at a time of renewed scrutiny of the AMEP.

In response to the FitzGerald Report (1988), which promoted a sharper economic focus for immigration and immigration-related policies, new questions have been raised about, and actual changes made in, the AMEP. Examples of questions are: is adult ESL education or solely labour market training; is adult ESL a solution to re-entry training for the victims of recession; is ESL to be an integral component of a range of programs (workplace, labour market, job-seeking) to be promoted because of the impact of award and industry restructuring? Intended changes include expanded provision for language and literacy funding and programs (as noted above). In addition, there are plans for revised Commonwealth/State funding relations in which the States and Territories for the first time would be obliged to invest heavily in English language and literacy provision. A five-year residence limit (and priority for less than three years) on the automatic right of immigrants to entry to English language and literacy courses without charge and in some cases with financial support is also proposed, as is putting cost recovery measures back on the AMEP Agenda. The 'privatising', to some extent, of English language and literacy provision is planned by enabling private (that is, commercial) ventures to tender to provide English language and literacy services. These were formerly totally funded and controlled by government, and implemented by the Adult Migrant Education Services (AMES) of the States and Territories, and selected higher education (such as University Language Centres) and college providers (DILGEA 1990a).

It must be acknowledged that, with the exception of the first, none of the intended changes has been fully implemented and, indeed, in some cases intense controversy has emerged; for example, there has been an acrimonious debate between the Commonwealth and the States over cost-sharing. Nonetheless, there has been considerable speculation about the intended and unintended consequences of the proposed changes. Overall, there is concern that the privatisation and cost recovery measures, the tightening nexus between work and language training opportunities, and the operation of 'market forces' among language and literacy training providers—all expressions of the sharpened economic focus of the Program—may disadvantage many immigrants, male and female alike (Moore 1991).

Particular concerns have been voiced regarding potential disadvantage for women immigrants. One arena in which these were made public was a national conference on Migrant Women, Settlement and Training held in Adelaide in 1991. Speakers endorsed a background paper (Hill et al. 1991) that highlighted the following points in relation to the changes to the AMEP and served as a serious indictment of the government's language and literacy and social justice policies. The charges against the AMEP were these.

- AMEP is underfunded (it has insufficient resources to cater for the backlog of longer resident immigrant women and new arrivals and to provide sufficient and appropriate child-care facilities).
- Inadequate levels of English competence result from limited amounts of free tuition (hence, with constraints on access for women as noted in the first point, women are likely to be relatively even more disadvantaged).
- The Plan discriminates against women, even within the 3–5 year period after entry, by identifying fewer resources for those who are not seeking work or not employed (women not oriented to work will not be able to gain access to the supplementary programs sponsored by the Department of Employment, Education and Training (DEET).
- Limitations on English language training for women will limit their overall chances of eventually obtaining skilled jobs (as women often have lower pre-migration skill levels than men and low English proficiency will limit their access to training in Australia).

Thus, these sources point to considerable constraints on the language training program which inhibit access and, importantly, may be expected to reduce outcomes. These problems must be seen in a context in which Immigration Department policy restricts free and financially supported English language training to new arrivals and Department of Employment, Education and Training (DEET) directions link language and literacy training to employment programs. The dice are loaded against older and longer resident immigrants and immigrants with family responsibilities. In all of these categories, women constitute a higher proportion than men (see Foster & Rado 1991; Tung 1992).

This conclusion has been reinforced by the major changes to adult ESL implemented in 1993 following the 1992–93 Federal Budget. In Tung's (1992) estimation, the changes such as the ceiling of 510 hours placed on tuition, the introduction of fee-paying services to be collected onshore and offshore, the administration of an English language test overseas and further emphasis on English language training directed only to registered job seekers are likely to disadvantage women immigrants more than their male counterparts.

In Canada, immigrant women are less likely than immigrant men to be able to gain access to language programs funded by the federal government. An inability to speak either French or English in Canada is associated with lower labour force participation rates for women, higher unemployment, occupational and industrial concentration and lower weekly wages (Boyd 1990, p. 289). Numerous reports by community groups, academics and the Federal and Provincial governments have documented issues concerning access to language training for immigrant women (Boyd 1986, 1987; Estable 1986; Giles 1987, 1988; Paredes 1987; Seward & McDade 1988; Seydegart & Spears 1985). In particular, Boyd has researched extensively, through analysis of census data, the effects of inability to converse in either official language. These data raise the following issues: (i) immigrant women confront systemic discrimination in federal language training policies; (ii) women in certain ethnic groups are less likely to speak English or French than other groups.

Immigration policy in Canada has a history of ethnic and gender bias (discussed in the policy review earlier). A new immigrant language training policy announced recently by the Canadian government continues this trend. In the previous policy, the implications of entry as a dependent were critical to understanding the systemic discrimination of the language training policy in Canada. The new policy further curtails women's access to training. And insofar as it is less likely to benefit unskilled, semi-skilled, older and female immigrants, thus leading to their further marginalisation (Stasiulis 1990b), the new policy seems to more closely resemble the current Australian language training policy.

The previous Canadian language policy had been repeatedly criticised because it limited women's access to language training. Boyd (1990) summarised these criticisms: first, those not destined for the labour force were not eligible for Canadian Employment and Immigration Commission (CEIC) language training programs (EIC 1986b). Many immigrant women are employed in the expanding informal sector of the labour force as domestic workers, cleaners and home workers. The work in this sector is often described as invisible and those women who work there are not counted as being part of the labour force. Second, if a knowledge of English or French is not necessary for employment, persons were likely to be ineligible for CEIC language programs. Many of the jobs held by immigrant women in the processing and service sector do not require that women speak one of the official languages to adequately perform the required work. Third, the CEIC language program provided economic support such as a living allowance only to independent immigrants. Thus women, who form the majority of sponsored immigrants, were not eligible for the basic training allowance and consequently were unlikely to participate in CEIC full-time language programs.

The most remarkable characteristic of the new policy is the total elimination of the basic training allowance in favour of promised significant increases in the number and flexibility of language training opportunities. Thus criticisms of the previous policy, encouraging an increase in the pool of those eligible for a living allowance to include women, have been superseded (EIC 1990d). In fact, the money for training allowances has been redirected into the development of more language courses.

The new language training policy is divided into two parts: Language Instruction for Newcomers to Canada (LINC) and Labour Market Language Training (LMLT). LINC is by far the more important program; most government language training funds (80 per cent) are dedicated to it. The goal of LINC is to provide 'basic communications skills', while the goal of LMLT is to 'provide specialized or advanced language training oriented to labour market needs' (EIC 1992b). However, both LINC and LMLT are mainly restricted to newly arrived non-citizens and government assisted refugees. Those who have been in Canada for more than one year, refugee claimants, and Canadian citizens are likely to be excluded (Metro Community ESL Coordinators Committee 1992).

The Ontario Council of Agencies Serving Immigrants (OCASI) estimates that 39 per cent of the present clientele from immigrant service agencies will be unable to obtain language training under the new program. Thus women who have given priority to settling their families and have worked in Canada for some time may not have access to federal language training, nor will those women who have been in Canada for more than a year and are escaping abusive relationships to establish an independent life. Women who have been displaced into the informal economy or into jobs where a knowledge of English or French was not required will also become the victims of this new policy. The irony of this situation is that many of these women do not speak English because of the previous restrictive language policy, as described above. Men will likely benefit more than women from the 'newly arrived' aspect of this program, as they have traditionally been less responsible for settling the family than their wives.

Child-care allowances have also been affected by this policy. While LINC allows that 'Some training arrangements will include support for babysitting . . . ' (EIC 1992b), the previous policy granted subsidies to women to make their own child-care arrangements. It is also thought by critics of the new policy that 'babysitting' will not conform to provincial child-care regulations (OWD 1992). As mentioned previously, adequate child-care arrangements are essential to the participation of women in training programs.

LMLT will provide training that combines the development of language and occupational skills. It has been instituted to specifically address the language needs of those who have labour market skills 'in demand'. Potential clients must also 'meet regular labour market program criteria regarding suitability for the relevant occupational objective' (EIC 1992b). It has not been made clear how this 'demand' and 'suitability' will be defined. It is feared that, in this program also, immigrant women will find access difficult and that most clients will be men (OCASI 1992, OWD 1992). Eligibility in this program will also depend on a relatively advanced language competency that is the equivalent of completion of advanced LINC levels. However, the maximum time allowable for language training in the LINC program is eight months and this is not regarded by educators as adequate learning time to make full use of skills training programs such as LMLT. In some instances, women are more than twice as likely as their male counterparts to be unable to speak one of the official languages (Boyd 1990, p. 280). It is therefore unlikely that immigrant women will have the same access as men to LMLT.

Further, in Canada an inability to speak English or French is linked to ethnicity, insofar as certain groups of immigrant women are more likely than others to lack fluency. Women who have recently arrived or were born in Southern Europe (Greece, Italy, and Portugal) or Asia are more likely not to be able to converse in English or French (Boyd 1990; Giles 1992). Boyd attributes this situation to several factors. First, the sex differences in language knowledge reflect sex differences in the ability of women to learn English or French in the home community. Second, the existence of institutionally complete communities in Canada (Breton 1973) may reduce the need for certain ethnic groups to learn English or French. Third, as described above, immigrant women experience particular problems in gaining access to language training (Boyd 1990, p. 280). Taken as a whole, these factors have likely resulted in the development of ethnic as well as gender differentiation in the uptake of language as well as skills training programs. Neither ethnic nor gender differences have been adequately addressed either in the previous or in the present language training policies.

Knowledge of French or English is strongly correlated with location in the labour market. While women who do not speak one of the official languages find themselves more likely to be employed full-time, they also work longer hours than other women on a weekly basis and earn lower wages than other women (Boyd 1990, p. 282). This is particularly the case for women from Southern Europe who are located in manufacturing, retail trade and personal services (Boyd 1990; Preston & Giles 1991) and Asian women (Boyd 1990). Women from Asia are a bifurcated group. Those who speak English or French are located in white-collar positions, are highly educated and earn high incomes. Those who do not speak English or French are located mainly in the service occupations and in the accommodation and food industries (Boyd 1990; Preston & Giles 1991). Boyd attributes this partly to recency of arrival and the heterogeneous nature of Asian migration as well as the more diverse and numerous countries represented in the Asian-born group compared to the Southern European group. Southern European women who do not speak English have 'lower levels of education, the lowest labour force participation rates, and the greatest amount of occupational and industrial concentration' (Boyd 1990, p. 288) as compared to Southern European men and Asian men and women.

Finally, there appears be some support from these case studies for the conclusion that, in both Australia and Canada, gender equity in official language(s), literacy and skills training is neither considered adequately in pre-planning of policy and programs nor actually delivered by existing provisions. One must acknowledge that there is *now* no *a priori* exclusion of immigrant women from language training in Australia or Canada, although many factors produce similar results. The previous Canadian language training policy did exclude women *a priori* from access to language training: sponsored immigrants, the majority of whom are women were not eligible for a language training living allowance whereas independent immigrants, the majority of whom were men, did. Nonetheless, the state in both countries has a case to answer that it is failing to provide equitable access for immigrant women to preparation for jobs, and by extension, to jobs themselves.

Conclusion

In this paper, we have described the views of gender roles that underpin immigrant selection policies in Canada and Australia, the links between the types of immigrant entry category in which women predominate and the disadvantage experienced by women in access to subsequent settlement services, especially in Canada. We have described the ways that official language policy in both countries disadvantages women because it is linked to limited notions of work in the paid labour force. Specific indications that current policies and practices disadvantage immigrant women in selection and settlement processes have been discussed, and practical measures to alleviate these effects have been proposed.

We wish merely, in conclusion, to reiterate our general point that the flaws in immigration and settlement policies that result in such damage for women are grounded in inappropriate and outdated views of what constitutes 'work' and 'skill'. Immigrant selection policies in both Australia and Canada, and language policies for newly arrived immigrants, have been profoundly linked to notions that paid labour force participation is the only 'work' worth rewarding with preferred immigrant selection status and with government-assisted language tuition. Furthermore, only certain types of paid work are 'skilled', and these are the sorts of paid work done disproportionately by men, not women. Immigration policies and practices seem to have been blind to major critiques of these notions of work and skill made by feminists over the last two decades. Quite why immigration policy has remained blind to its own masculinist bias, when other government departments (those associated with employment and social justice in Australia, for example) have recognised the bias and are starting the long process of correcting it, is unclear. Nevertheless, a thorough and critical review should be undertaken of the masculinist views of work and skill that guide contemporary immigration policies. Then the next step would be to ask how it is that only immigrants who are 'workers', however defined, need language tuition in order to participate in the general social practices of their new countries.

PART THREE

Immigration Policy Implementation

CHAPTER 7

Immigration Management Control and its Policy Implications

Meyer Burstein, Leonie Hardcastle and Andrew Parkin

Introduction

This chapter examines the impact of the immigration selection and control systems employed in recent years by Canada and Australia. It argues that these systems need to be understood not simply as means to regulate immigration. They also produce and reflect a distribution of selection power among various parties, government and private. The chapter explores a 'privatisation' hypothesis: that is, over time, that effective control over immigrant selection has tended to be transferred from the government arena to the private arena. This hypothesis suggests that there has been a shift favouring 'private' over 'national' interests and implies that government planning with respect to immigration increasingly involves forecasting anticipated patterns of entry rather than controlling entry according to some overall plan.

The first part of the chapter describes the immigration selection and control systems used in the two countries. The second part describes the implications of these systems for the distribution of selection power, and further explains the hypothesis to be explored. The third and fourth parts assess the degree to which the hypothesis is supported by the recent experiences of Canada and Australia.

Immigration selection and control systems

The authority to control and manage immigrant entry is clearly vested in the national governments of both Canada and Australia (though

187

the Canadian Province of Quebec also has limited authority over immigrant intake). Both national governments undertake careful annual planning exercises to set the framework for admissions in the forthcoming year. In each case, the framework specifies a total number of immigrant entries distributed over various designated categories or components.

Of particular interest is the distinction between categories under which applicants have effectively been given entitlement for admission in contrast to other categories where applicants have no such entitlement. Admission under the first set of categories can be described as 'demand-driven': the numbers admitted are simply the numbers of those *qualified* for admission who *seek* admission. It could be argued that only admission under the non-demand-driven categories can be regarded as effectively 'controlled' by government, in the sense that the total number to be admitted can be specified and precisely managed by the government. (At another level, of course, the question of why a government might authorise a demand-driven category needs to be addressed.)

There is an obvious tension between, on the one hand, a desire to manage an overall immigration program and, on the other hand, recognition of demand-driven categories of admission. As we will discuss, the particular management frameworks now utilised in both Canada and Australia have been shaped in part by past difficulties in handling this tension.

The immigration selection and control systems now employed in Canada and Australia display many basic similarities along with a few interesting and significant differences. Governments in both countries undertake formal consultations with various community interests before announcing an immigration plan or program for the forthcoming twelve months. In Canada, this is known as the 'levels plan' while in Australia it is simply termed the 'immigration program'. Each employs a hybrid system incorporating a specific numerical overall target for total intake along with the continuation of some demand-driven categories, with the buffer between the two consisting of other adjustable categories which contract or expand as required to meet the overall target.

The immigration management systems extend beyond this annual plan. There are various guiding principles of selection shared by both countries, such as the eschewing of any form of discrimination on the basis of race, nationality or ethnic background. There is also, of course, a necessity to aim for administrative efficiency and high-quality service.

At its broadest level, the immigrant management systems comprise a legislative framework within which the programs operate. The regulations made within this framework establish eligibility for admission, the designation of various categories, the annual setting of target admission levels, and the administrative devices used to control certain aspects of selection (such as the calculation of points within a numerical calculus to determine eligibility).

The system also incorporates decisions about where to locate administrative offices around the world, about the deployment of resources to these posts and about the relative priority to be given to processing various types of cases. In Canada, a 'work target' system was introduced in 1981 and has since become the principal tool for controlling the allocation of immigrant-processing resources and, hence, controlling immigrant volumes and characteristics. On a global basis, resources and targets are tailored to fit the annual 'levels plan' and (to the extent possible) its components. Resources are allocated to individual missions according to a formula that takes into account the volume of applications and the accumulated backlog. The formula seeks gradually to balance the backlogs at different missions around the world. As of 1992, the domestic system is being configured along similar lines to the overseas system but has not yet evolved to the same level. Australian immigration management operates along similar, though less formalised, lines, also seeking to allocate administrative resources to locations and categories of highest demand and highest designated priority.

It is useful to group the various admission classes in both Canada and Australia into several general categories according to the principal selection criteria employed. (In order to generalise across both Canada and Australia, the terminology employed here to designate and describe this classification does not necessarily correspond with that used in either country; indeed, to avoid confusion, terms with specific—but different—meanings in either country have been avoided.) For the purposes of this chapter, the general categories can be termed *family relationship, humanitarian* and *economic*. It is also useful to designate another *miscellaneous* category to cover some particular special or idiosyncratic classes of immigrants. Each of these requires further elaboration, focusing on how each of the two countries recognises and manages them.

Family relationship

For this chapter's classification purposes, the 'family relationship' category covers persons admitted primarily on the basis of their family relationship with persons already living in the destination country.

Both Canada and Australia recognise a category of very close family members whose admission is demand-driven. This category is labelled 'preferential family' category in Australia and simply 'family class' in Canada. In both countries it consists essentially of spouses, fiancees, dependent children and parents sponsored by a relative who is already a permanent resident of Australia or Canada. Since December 1988, a 'balance of family' test has applied in Australia for parents, who could enter under the 'preferential family' category only if more of their children were resident in Australia than in any other country. In both countries, sponsorship implies some guarantee of financial support for at least the initial years of settlement.

The demand-driven nature of this family relationship category means that the annual announced intake 'planning level' is essentially an estimate of likely demand, and the main management task is to allocate administrative resources in such a way as to prevent a build-up of unprocessed applicants. It has often been observed in the literature on human service administration that demand-driven systems are chronically faced with the problem of providing adequate resources, sometimes leading, in practice, to *de facto* attempts to manage demand through such devices as queues and delays (Lipsky 1980). While, with some services, this may lead some applicants to drop out of the queue or seek an alternative service, the impact of such devices on immigration applications seems to be the accumulation of a backlog. Immigration managers in both Canada and Australia appear to have been well aware of this potential problem. In the latter half of the 1980s, Canada was forced to shift resources from Europe to Asia to deal with an accumulating backlog. Australia seems to have had less of a problem with backlogs; there was a significant accumulation of cases from Indochinese applicants in Australia's Bangkok office in the late 1980s but a major reason for this were the delays in approval from Vietnamese authorities.

The management of demand-driven systems is assisted if eligibility standards are easily adjusted and if there is reliable information available about the number of likely applicants. Each of these is a potential problem for the demand-driven family relationship category. Information about the potential number of family relationship applicants is somewhat unreliable, because the program is global in scope and demand is subject to unpredictable political events in other countries. Attempts to tighten eligibility rules can face strong political resistance, though this does not mean that tightening is always precluded: Australia reimposed the 'balance of family' rule in 1988, while Canada, which had relaxed its rules in 1988 to permit the sponsorship of unmarried children of any age, tightened them again in 1992 following a sharp expansion in numbers.

Both Canada and Australia limit demand-driven family relationship admission to a defined group of immediate family members. Applications from other, more distant family members—such as siblings or non-dependent children—are subjected to a points test, under which points are allocated on the basis of such factors as the family relationship, educational qualifications, language ability, employment experience, age and occupation. This group is termed the 'concessional family' class under the Australian program and 'assisted relatives' under the Canadian.

The Australian 'concessional family' intake has been linked since 1989 to the 'preferential family' intake in that the annual program specifies a planned numerical level for the two family categories combined. The maximum number to be admitted through the 'concessional family' avenue is the residual left after all 'preferential family' demand has been satisfied (though an estimated 'planning level' is still announced each year). The pass mark in the points test is regarded as a 'floating' one, so that qualifying standards can, in effect, be raised or lowered to control intake. In management terms, this means that there must be careful monitoring of applications in the pipeline to ensure that the pass mark is set at the appropriate level.

The Canadian 'assisted relatives' intake has similar characteristics to the Australian 'concessional family' intake (primarily non-dependent children and siblings) and is chosen under a similar sort of points system. However, the numbers admitted in Canada are not related to the numbers admitted in the 'family class'. Rather 'assisted relatives' are regarded as a component of what this chapter has termed the 'economic' category. (Australia had a similar linkage in the 1986-89 period.) 'Assisted relatives' are subjected to the same test as other 'independents' (as described below) though, until rule changes in February 1993, they were awarded bonus points because of the guarantees provided by their sponsors. (From February 1993, the bonus for assisted relatives was reduced and the requirement for a guarantee by the sponsor has been eliminated.) Managerial adjustment of the number of points needed for admission, with the aim of ensuring that the numbers admitted correspond to the announced planning level, is a similar mechanism in practice to Australia's floating pass mark.

Humanitarian

This broad category comprises several distinct components which are managed in a variety of ways. There are again parallels between Canada and Australia as well as important differences. The most significant legal distinction in the humanitarian stream is between those admitted as refugees under the strict criteria set down in the Geneva Convention, and those admitted on humanitarian grounds outside the Convention. For the purposes of this chapter, however, a more important set of distinctions are those which relate to the selection process. In this sense, the intake can be divided between 'domestic asylum seekers', 'government-assisted humanitarian' and 'privately sponsored humanitarian'.

'Domestic asylum seekers' are the self-selected category of people who seek immigrant status from within Canada or Australia on humanitarian grounds. Most claim refugee status under the United Nations Convention on Refugees which has been signed by both Canada and Australia, and both countries have procedures for adjudicating such claims based on the UN Convention. Some applicants arrive at an official port of entry, some enter the country illegally (such as a landing of 'boat people' on the coast), while some enter legally on some other temporary basis (such as on a tourist or a student visa). 'Domestic asylum seekers' as understood by this chapter also include persons who are admitted on looser humanitarian grounds (including some who have unsuccessfully sought refugee status) including, in Canada, the beneficiaries of various status adjustment programs that have been used in recent years to dispose of large accumulated caseloads inside the country before the introduction of new legislation.

'Government-assisted humanitarian' designates entrants, without domestic sponsors, admitted on humanitarian grounds from a foreign country. The number of these sort of entrants can generally be managed with a fair amount of precision to accord with the announced annual planning level. Admission follows largely from selection or recruitment by authorised officers, either directly by Australian and Canadian officers or indirectly through international organisations such as the UN High Commission for Refugees or the International Organisation for Migration (sometimes within the framework of negotiated arrangements with other countries of resettlement). In Australia, for example, the 1991–92 intake included a 'Refugee Program' for UN-recognised refugees, a more broadly defined 'Global Special Humanitarian Program', and a 'Special

Assistance Program' targeted at East Timorese nationals resident in Portugal, at ethnic minorities in the former Soviet Union and at persons fleeing conflicts in Lebanon and in what was Yugoslavia.

'Privately sponsored humanitarian' refers to entrants, chosen from a foreign country, sponsored by Australian or Canadian individuals (such as family members) or by private organisations, typically church-based groups or ethnic associations. In Canada, this is effectively a demand-driven category: a sponsored applicant, provided that refugee status is confirmed, is admitted with no numerical limit to the intake. In Australia, however, where the distinction between privately sponsored and government-assisted entrants has little management significance, there is a designated planning level for the total humanitarian intake.

Economic

For the purposes of this chapter, the 'economic' category comprises various intake classes under which immigrants are admitted primarily on the basis of their business, investment or labour-market skills. (While, as noted above, Canada administratively links its 'assisted relatives' class with other 'economic' classes, this chapter has discussed 'assisted relatives' under the 'family relationship' heading.) Some 'economic' sub-categories are essentially demand-driven, while others involve more careful selection and management. For the purposes of analysis, it is useful to sort the economic sub-categories into three types: business, labour and open categories.

With respect to business, both Canada and Australia have operated programs designed to attract immigrants who offer business-related prospects. The Canadians distinguish between 'self-employed', 'investor' and 'entrepreneur' applicants. 'Self-employed' applicants face a points test in which self-employment gives them a considerable points bonus but which also tests language ability and education. Fiduciary considerations are important for the other two categories: 'investor' applicants are required to invest money in approved ventures or funds (and there has been extensive experimentation aimed at channelling investors into particular parts of Canada and into particular business activities) while 'entrepreneurial' applicants must provide evidence of previous successful business involvement.

Australia's business migration program, begun in 1981, operated under various criteria until its suspension in 1991. In the 1985–87 period, for example, there were 'investor' and 'entrepreneur' subprograms similar to the Canadian. In its final form, the program admitted applicants (and their dependants) with a successful business record, with a specified capital amount for investment in Australia and an intention to settle permanently. From 1988, the role of accredited private agencies in assisting (and perhaps effectively recruiting) applicants was officially recognised. The program was suspended after critical observations by the Joint Parliamentary Committee of Public Accounts (which reinforced concerns within the Department of Immigration) which suggested that there was insufficient evaluation of whether appropriate business investment actually took place. There were also allegations (never formally substantiated) about the recycling of funds back overseas and an influx of criminals. In February 1992, a new 'business skills' program based on a points test was announced.

With respect to labour-related programs, Australia has historically developed more varied and elaborate schemes. Under the 'employer nomination scheme', skilled applicants are nominated by Australian employers for specific employment positions for which they can demonstrate no reasonable likelihood of filling with a person already resident. Various other 'labour agreement' schemes have also operated (such as the Occupational Shares System operating for most of the 1980s) involving a more general admission of skilled people in an agreed set of occupations within industry-wide agreements negotiated between the government, employers and trade unions. A 'special talent' category permits admission to outstanding individuals regarded as having particular special occupational attributes. These Australian labour-related categories are all demand- driven: provided that applicants conform to the appropriate criteria, they are admitted. In Canada's case, applicants who are nominated by employers, or who fall into special categories identified by Provincial governments, receive bonus points within the points test. (The Province of Quebec undertakes its own selection using its own criteria.)

Beyond these specific business and labour-related categories, both Canada and Australia have a large, more open economically-related admission category which they label 'independent'. In both countries, a points test is used and either the pass mark (Australia) or the points that may be earned (Canada) are varied in order to control the intake numbers.

In the case of Australia, the number admitted is the residual left under the announced annual planning level 'Skilled Migration' after the demand under the other economic categories has been satisfied; that is, the number of 'independents' selected depends on how many 'business', 'employer nominee', 'labour agreement' and 'special talent' entrants wish to be admitted. (Until 1986, Australia had no such residual category: economic immigrants had to qualify under one of the specific sub-programs.) In the case of Canada, a separate annual target for 'independents' is set annually, with the intention being to bring supply (qualified applicants) into balance with demand (target requirements). In order to hit the target, adjustments to qualifying standards are made frequently, as often as every quarter.

Miscellaneous

A significant aspect of Australia's immigration *intake*, though outside its official immigration *program*, is the unrestricted entry into Australia of New Zealand citizens as part of the reciprocal arrangement between Australia and New Zealand which underpins the Closer Economic Relationship (CER). New Zealand entrants can be understood as an unregulated demand-driven category of 'immigrants' outside the immigration program. One component of the program, designated 'special eligibility', is nonetheless partly linked to New Zealand entry. 'Special eligibility' covers former Australian residents and citizens who have maintained ties with Australia, and the dependants of New Zealand citizens who intend to settle in Australia but who are not themselves New Zealand citizens.

Both Canada and Australia have, in the recent past, recognised self-supporting retired persons as a specific class of immigrants which, for the purpose of this chapter, can be allocated to the 'miscellaneous' general category. While neither country now admits such persons as immigrants (Australia, for example, having substituted a temporary-residence arrangement), both did so until recently so that they show up in some of the statistics later reported in this chapter.

Management and the locus of control: a 'privatisation' hypothesis

As noted above, immigrant management control systems need to be understood not simply as regulating immigration but also as producing and reflecting a distribution of selection power among various parties, government and private. The immigration categories described above vary in the degree to which selection decisions are made by governmental authority. With demand-driven components, selection of immigrants is effectively devolved to applicants and/or their sponsors, and the role of the annual planning levels is essentially one of forecasting the demand. Other categories feature a much more immediate power vested in government officers to choose both the number and the characteristics of immigrants.

From this observation stems a proposition, which this chapter examines in detail with respect to Canada and Australia, which can be termed a *privatisation hypothesis*: that, over time, effective control over immigrant selection has tended to be transferred from the government arena to the private arena.

In a purely descriptive sense, the hypothesis suggests that the categories which are demand-driven, self-selected and/or sponsor-selected have tended to grow increasingly dominant in terms of the volume of immigrants admitted. This dominance would also be apparent in the composition of the overall immigration program, with the kind of characteristics typical of demand-driven, self-selected or sponsor-selected coming to predominate over the kinds of characteristics typical of entrants over which there is 'government control'.

Behind this hypothesis is a suggested underlying causal dynamic: that the immigration management systems themselves promote privatisation by conferring on immigrants (whatever the category under which they are admitted) the opportunity—which might even come to be politically expressed or demanded as a 'right'—to be a new link in a demand-driven chain connected to other potential immigrants. The sponsorship of family members from abroad then competes with other applicants for immigration places. There is thus, according to the hypothesis, a predisposing gravitational bias towards a privatisation even if special efforts are made to select more 'government-controlled' applicants.

As already noted, this hypothesis, if confirmed, would suggest that there has been a shift favouring 'private' over 'national' interests and would imply that government planning with respect to immigration increasingly involves forecasting anticipated patterns of entry rather than controlling entry according to some overall plan.

The chapter now turns to an examination of the utility of the privatisation hypothesis with respect to Canada and Australia. The examination involves the analysis of data on the volume and composition of immigration, on decisions about annual planning levels (especially on which particular components are to be expanded or contracted), on decisions about qualifying standards and on the aggregate characteristics of the immigrants admitted. It also involves a more subtle evaluation of the interaction of different factors and decisions. Immigration management is a complex process, building up layers of changing circumstances and decisions over a wide span of time. Some of the determinants are independent of each other, some are mutually reinforcing and others are in conflict with each other. The determinants might include court decisions, rule changes, distant international conflicts or civil wars, and amnesties granted to illegal aliens.

The Canadian experience

The recent Canadian experience appears strongly to support the privatisation hypothesis. Immigration has expanded sharply in areas—family class, privately sponsored refugees and domestic asylum seekers—where the primary immigration decision originates with private individuals. This has arguably produced a substantial transfer of control from the government arena to the private sphere: that is, to Canadian sponsors, advocacy groups and self-selected migrants. The shift has meant that the annual 'levels planning' exercise increasingly emphasises components which are essentially forecasted over components that are truly planned.

A useful way of beginning the recent Canadian story is with Chart 7.1, in which immigration categories are arrayed along a spectrum from maximum private control at one end to maximum government control at the other.

Numbers

Immigration—its dynamic and its management—ultimately reveals itself in numbers. The statistics reported in Tables 7.1 and 7.2 report Canadian numbers from 1979 to 1981, arranged by categories following the same ordinal structure as for Chart 7.1.

The Canadian story begins on an expansionary note in 1979 when, over a two-year period, a special program for Indochinese 'boat people' brought in 60 000 refugees. At the same time, the Immigration Department was engaged in an ambitious program to expand points-tested immigration (including those classified above as 'independents' and as 'assisted relatives'). Both the Indochinese program and the expansion of points-tested entry ended in 1982: the Indochinese program was wound down as the political situation in Southeast Asia stabilised and points-tested immigration was halted in response to economic recession (though the shut-down was mistimed and the recession abated soon after immigration was curtailed).

Chart 7.1 Canadian immigration categories by locus of control

Maximum private control

        domestic asylum seekers
        family class
        privately sponsored humanitarian
        retired persons
        investors
        other business immigrants
        assisted relatives
        independent
        special programs
        government-assisted humanitarian

Maximum government control

What is interesting about the expansion of the early 1980s is that it was made up of elements from both ends of Chart 7.1's control spectrum. It was also very short-lived, lasting only two years. The numbers tell the story: privately sponsored refugees fell from 21 093 in 1980 to 4367 in 1981; the large points-tested categories ('assisted relatives' and 'independents') from 54 536 in aggregate in 1981 to 17 541 in 1983. Behind the scenes, the decline was even sharper, as indicated in Table 7.1: by the end of 1982, caseloads abroad for independent and assisted family admissions had declined by some 60 per cent only to be followed by a further decline of 22 per cent in 1983.

Neither the refugee flow nor the growth in the points-tested categories had much impact on the family class, which remained fairly steady over the cycle of expansion and contraction. The reasons are as follows. First, the political situation in Indochina mitigated against a large number of family sponsorships. Second, in the case of points-tested immigrants, many came from Europe, and European immigration does not carry with it the same propensity to sponsor as does Asian immigration. Third, sponsorship pressures were modulated in both directions, initially by constraints on processing capacity which prevented 'output' from rising as sharply as caseloads and then by the accumulated backlog of cases which cushioned the downturn as intakes fell. The result was a fairly flat family class pattern over the 1980 through 1983 period. Family class caseloads peaked in 1982 and then declined by about 16 per cent in 1983 as foreign posts began to run out of new business. By 1985, immigration had dropped below 85 000 persons, the lowest figure in more than a decade.

The turnaround was initiated in 1986 with a decision by the new government to again expand the number of points-tested immigrants. While this had little impact on arrivals before 1987, the case-loads (which anticipate arrivals) doubled in 1986, as shown in Table 7.2. The expansion in independents and assisted relatives was sustained through to 1990. In 1991, however, the volumes dropped, notwithstanding government plans for continued increases. The reason for this decline may be found in the changes that occurred in the 'privately-controlled' categories.

Between 1986 and 1989, the number of privately sponsored refugees rose fourfold as Eastern Europeans, chiefly Poles, took advantage of a confluence of factors: the political transformations in Eastern Europe, Canada's policy regime which classified all Eastern Europeans who were outside their country as refugees, and a well-organised sponsorship campaign in Canada. The family class also increased as both independent immigrants and refugees began to sponsor. This sponsorship chain was amplified by a new definition of dependency which enlarged the pool of eligible relatives. (The change, introduced in 1988 and since rescinded, expanded the family class from the spouse, parents and dependent children of Canadian residents to include never-married children and their dependants, regardless of age.) The increases in family and refugee immigration were so rapid that higher planning levels and a concomitant transfer of resources to Asian posts could not accommodate the expansion. The result was a squeeze on independent and assisted relative migration, and a fall in the numbers of each admitted to Canada.

Table 7.1 reveals the dimensions of the increase in immigration and the changing patterns. Domestic asylum seekers rose from 1500 in 1986 to over 10 000 in 1991; privately sponsored refugees increased from 5200 in 1986 to 22 000 in 1989, tapering off to 17 000 two years later after the Eastern European program was trimmed; and 'family class' immigration climbed from 42 000 in 1986 to 85 000 in 1991.

Another way to consider the change is to consider the ratio of arrivals between the three dominant privately sponsored categories (domestic asylum seekers, family class and privately sponsored refugees) and the two government-controlled categories (assisted relatives and independents). In 1986, this ratio was about 2.5:1. Two years later, in 1988, it had been reduced to virtual 1:1 parity. By 1991, it was back to 1.8:1, demonstrating the squeeze put on the government controlled categories by the privatisation of the intake. Even within the two government-controlled categories, the independents without relatives led the initial expansion but incurred virtually all of the cutback occurring in 1991.

Table 7.1 Immigration components over time: Canada 1979–91

Components	1979 No.	1979 %	1980 No.	1980 %	1981 No.	1981 %	1982 No.	1982 %	1983 No.	1983 %	1984 No.	1984 %	1985 No.	1985 %
Domestic asylum seekers	175	0.2	371	0.3	453	0.4	698	0.6	630	0.7	972	1.1	1 268	1.5
Family class	40 470	40.2	51 039	35.7	51 025	39.7	49 993	41.3	48 710	54.6	43 814	49.7	38 606	45.6
Private refugees	13 778	13.7	21 093	14.7	4 367	3.4	5 829	4.8	4 120	4.6	3 915	4.4	3 881	4.6
Investors	0	0.0	0	0.0	0	0.0	0	0.0	0	0.0	0	0.0	0	0.0
Retired	1 159	1.2	1 548	1.1	2 063	1.6	2 252	1.9	2 094	2.3	2 313	2.6	2 100	2.5
Other business	3 881	3.9	5 116	3.6	6 028	4.7	6 364	5.3	6 225	7.0	6 260	7.1	6 496	7.7
Assisted relatives	8 255	8.2	13 647	9.5	17 592	13.7	11 943	9.9	4 699	5.3	6 774	7.7	6 046	7.1
Independent	19 322	19.2	31 433	22.0	36 944	28.7	33 676	27.8	12 842	14.4	11 340	12.9	12 049	14.2
Special programs	0	0.0	0	0.0	0	0.0	12	0.0	670	0.8	2 486	2.8	2 463	2.9
Govt. refugees	13 564	13.5	18 884	13.2	10 160	7.9	10 399	8.6	9 182	10.3	10 365	11.7	11 796	13.9
Sub-Total	100 604	100	143 131	100	128 632	100	121 166	100	89 172	100	88 239	100	84 705	100
Special asylum clearance	0	0.0	0	0.0	0	0.0	0	0.0	0	0.0	0	0.0	0	0.0
Total	100 604	100	143 131	100	128 632	100	121 166	100	89 172	100	88 239	100	84 705	100
Planned Total	–		120 000		130–140 000		130–135 000		105–110 000		90–95 000		85–90 000	

Table 7.1 Cont'd

Components	1986 No.	1986 %	1987 No.	1987 %	1988 No.	1988 %	1989 No.	1989 %	1990 No.	1990 %	1991 No.	1991 %
Domestic asylum seekers	1 483	1.6	1 609	1.0	884	0.5	1 562	0.8	3 725	1.7	10 348	4.5
Family class	42 246	45.3	53 535	34.9	51 442	31.7	61 002	31.7	73 419	34.1	84 094	36.9
Private refugees	5 222	5.6	7 433	4.9	12 355	7.6	21 597	11.2	19 272	9.0	17 333	7.6
Investors	23	0.0	319	0.2	1 030	0.6	2 275	1.2	4 220	2.0	5 169	2.3
Retired	1 839	2.0	2 676	1.7	3 181	2.0	3 572	1.9	3 547	1.6	4 204	1.8
Other business	7 525	8.1	10 832	7.1	14 122	8.7	15 329	8.0	14 318	6.7	11 821	5.2
Assisted relatives	6 210	6.7	20 826	13.6	30 782	18.9	34 486	17.9	36 980	17.2	25 938	11.4
Independent	13 517	14.5	23 221	15.2	31 977	19.7	36 262	18.8	36 905	17.1	34 888	15.3
Special programs	2 501	2.7	2 738	1.18	2 012	1.2	2 428	1.3	3 285	1.5	2 353	1.0
Govt refugees	12 707	13.6	12 848	8.4	13 829	8.5	14 107	7.3	12 831	6.0	7 638	3.4
Sub-Total	93 273	100	136 037	88.8	161 614	99.5	192 620	100	208 502	96.9	203 868	89.4
Special asylum clearance	0	0.0	17 214	11.2	866	0.5	71	0.0	6 781	3.1	24 089	10.6
Total	93 273	100	153 251	100	162 480	100	192 691	100	215 283	100	227 875	100
Planned Total	105–115 000		115–125 000		125–135 000		150–160 000		165–175 000		220 000	

Source: EIC, adapted from unpublished figures, var. years.

Table 7.2 Cases in progress, Canada (as of December 31 in designated year)

7.2.1 Cases in Progress Abroad

Component	1981	1982	1983	1984	1985	1986	1987	1988	1989	1990	1991
Asylum refugees	0	0	0	0	0	0	0	0	0	0	0
Family class	18 785	20 189	16 979	16 892	15 407	15 308	15 247	18 577	31 414	44 510	50 639
Private refugees	732	1 434	1 091	1 008	1 339	2 404	4 278	6 703	14 004	18 530	13 912
Investors	0	0	0	0	3	87	217	656	1 731	3 370	4 281
Retirees	1 148	967	943	874	766	979	1 227	1 470	2 054	2 305	2 606
Other business	2 155	2 085	1 720	2 029	1 761	2 410	3 462	3 984	4 613	7 962	8 987
Special programs	1	48	198	178	211	157	385	409	741	1 018	963
Assisted relatives	4 996	2 967	3 624	3 886	3 223	6 278	9 936	11 629	12 650	15 448	14 962
Independents	14 513	4 387	2 223	2 169	2 283	5 869	11 901	12 854	11 954	12 443	12 279
Government refugees	2 523	2 475	2 666	3 187	4 372	5 872	5 574	5 907	5 782	3 464	2 696

7.2.2 Cases in Progress in Canada

Component	1981	1982	1983	1984	1985	1986	1987	1988	1989	1990	1991
Asylum refugees	369	505	623	737	933	844	906	1 173	1 418	907	699
Family class	13 046	10 416	9 779	7 062	9 897	10 897	12 210	16 637	21 100	29 052	20 318
Private refugees	33	63	46	34	29	68	47	130	241	217	158
Investors	0	0	0	0	0	0	0	0	0	0	0
Retirees	41	39	41	52	36	31	54	40	59	54	26
Other business	13	10	23	18	13	14	11	14	19	18	11
Special programs	8	229	955	1 044	1 116	927	844	596	293	217	167
Assisted relatives	1 170	819	559	509	493	548	623	763	763	1 146	1 413
Independents	879	2 910	4 509	5 128	4 324	3 296	3 208	3 718	12 350	16 247	9 761
Government refugees	388	300	459	483	436	435	296	570	619	452	321

Table 7.2 Cont'd

7.2.3 Cases in Progress Total

Component	1981	1982	1983	1984	1985	1986	1987	1988	1989	1990	1991
Asylum refugees	369	505	623	737	933	844	906	1 173	1 418	907	699
Family class	31 831	30 605	26 758	23 954	25 125	26 125	27 457	35 214	52 514	73 562	70 957
Private refugees	765	1 497	1 137	1 042	1 368	2 472	4 325	6 833	14 245	18 747	14 070
Investors	0	0	0	0	3	87	217	656	1 731	3 370	4 281
Retirees	1 189	1 006	984	926	802	1 010	1 281	1 510	2 113	2 359	2 632
Other business	2 168	2 095	1 743	2 047	1 774	2 473	3 473	3 998	4 632	7 980	8 988
Special programs	9	277	1 153	1 222	1 327	1 084	1 229	1 005	1 034	1 235	1 130
Assisted relatives	6 166	3 786	4 183	4 345	3 732	6 771	10 484	12 252	14 413	16 594	16 375
Independents	15 392	7 297	6 732	7 297	6 607	9 165	15 109	17 572	24 304	28 690	22 040
Government refugees	2 911	2 775	3 125	3 670	4 808	6 307	5 870	6 477	6 401	3 916	3 017

Source: EIC adapted from unpublished figures, var. years.

Plans

It is especially noteworthy that the compositional changes of the last five years occurred against a background of rising planning levels. Whereas in 1986, plans called for only 105–115 000 immigrants, by 1991, the planning levels had risen to 220 000 persons.

When the decision was first taken to expand immigration in 1986, it was based on a broad consensus among governments (Federal and Provincial) and the various interests in Canadian society—ethnic community organisations, immigrant advocacy groups, business interests and so on. There was widespread agreement that 'balance' needed to be restored to immigration by expanding the points-tested and business categories, though not at the expense of the family and humanitarian streams.

Much the same theme was repeated in 1987, 1988 and 1989. During this period, various groups consistently reaffirmed their support for a policy of moderate, balanced growth. Nevertheless, some differences in emphasis were apparent: while the governments wanted modest increases favouring the business and skilled labour streams, ethnic organisations favoured accelerated increases and were especially supportive of measures to expand the family relationship intake.

From 1986 onwards, the Federal government espoused balanced growth among family, humanitarian and economic immigrants. At the same time, however, a critical step was taken that contributed to that balance being upset. In response to pressure from interest groups and recommendations by a Parliamentary committee (the Parliamentary Standing Committee on Labour, Employment and Immigration), the government agreed to expand the criteria for the family class to include never-married sons and daughter (and their children) regardless of age. It also awarded extra points to 'independent' immigrants who were being sponsored by their relatives (that is, the 'assisted relatives' stream). The results were apparent shortly thereafter (as was evident in the statistical discussion above).

In 1990, after extensive consultations revealed broad support for moderate increases in immigration and for a balanced flow, the government announced a five-year immigration plan. The plan called for roughly proportionate growth in the family, humanitarian and economic categories. To achieve this, however, the overall size of the immigration movement had to be increased considerably to 'make room' for the growing family class and to proportionately increase the number of independent immigrants. This was made necessary because Canada's management system does not provide the legal authority to limit family and refugee immigration.

At the same time as it announced the new levels plan, the government also announced that it would improve the management of immigration. This was intended to support a gradual increase in the size of the independent category over the planning period and a shift in the direction of a more skilled intake. The measures were to include a review of selection criteria, a review of the 'family class' eligibility rules (in particular, the definition of dependency as it concerned children), a reassessment of the privately sponsored refugee program and closer monitoring and better management of the refugee asylum program.

Composition

The shift in control from the government to the private sector has produced, in addition to its effect on overall volumes and on the planning process, a change in the characteristics of immigrants towards lower educational, occupational and mainstream language skills.

With respect to educational qualifications, Figure 7.1 charts, for various intake categories, the ratio of persons with greater than secondary school education to persons with less. It is clear this ratio among 'independents' has been consistently higher than for any other group while the ratio for the family class has tended to be consistently lower. Since 1986 (the year in which the expansion began), the ratio for the 'assisted relatives' category has also exceeded all other categories. (The only anomaly surfaces with regard to the privately sponsored refugees: over the last few years, an influx through this category of Poles has brought in large numbers of immigrants with trade and with other certificates, resulting in a higher than expected ratio).

Differences are even more pronounced in terms of higher education: in 1991, for example, 12.1 per cent of 'independent' immigrants and 3.6 per cent of 'assisted relatives' were in possession of a Masters or doctoral degree. The corresponding figures for the family class and for the combined refugee categories were 2 per cent and 1.9 per cent respectively.

With respect to occupational skills, Figure 7.2 plots, for various categories, the ratio of managers, scientists and other professionals to all other occupations. (The data are based on the intended occupations

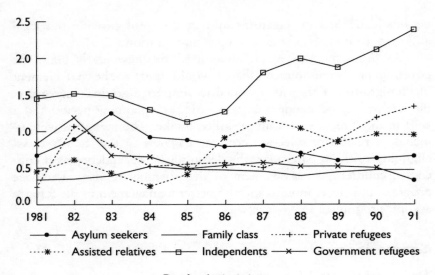

Data for plotting points

Components	1981	1982	1983	1984	1985	1986	1987	1988	1989	1990	1991
Asylum seekers	0.67	0.89	1.25	0.92	0.88	0.79	0.80	0.70	0.60	0.63	0.66
Family class	0.34	0.35	0.39	0.52	0.48	0.47	0.45	0.39	0.44	0.47	0.47
Private refugees	0.24	1.07	0.81	0.52	0.55	0.57	0.50	0.66	0.88	1.19	1.34
Assisted relatives	0.45	0.61	0.43	0.25	0.41	0.91	1.16	1.04	0.85	0.96	0.95
Independents	1.45	1.52	1.49	1.30	1.13	1.27	1.80	1.99	1.87	2.11	2.38
Government refugees	0.83	1.19	0.67	0.65	0.49	0.53	0.57	0.52	0.52	0.50	0.33

Source: Prepared by staff within EIC.

Figure 7.1 Educational attainment by category of immigrant: Canada 1981–91

Ratio of persons with more than secondary education to persons with less than secondary education

of immigrants and not on the actual jobs they obtain in Canada.) The discrepancy between government-controlled and privately controlled components is even more clear-cut than it was with education. The independent component consistently displays the largest proportion of professionals followed by the assisted relatives. The privately controlled components all have similar, far lower, proportions of professionals and show little change over time in the skill content of new arrivals. With most job growth likely to be in the professional and scientific categories, this evidence suggests that the shift in immigrant composition is producing a decline in the ability of immigrants as a whole to be absorbed into the labour market.

Interestingly, the declining 'professionalism' ratios for 'independents' after 1987, and the higher ratio for 'assisted relatives' in the late 1980s are a product of the overall expansion in immigration. Between 1982 and 1986, only persons with approved job offers from Canadian employers were accepted in these categories. Approval was rarely given for non-professional jobs. After 1986, the constraints were relaxed. The result was a 'dilution' of the 'independent' flow and, less obviously, the addition of an economic dimension to the 'assisted relatives' which had, for four years, existed as a quasi-humanitarian movement.

Mainstream language ability is important because it appears to be a key to successful settlement, both economic and social. Figure 7.3 charts the ratio of the number of speakers of either English or French to those without mainstream language facility for each of the intake categories. By far the largest proportion of persons with an ability in either English or French is to be found in the 'independent' category, which is to be expected because the selection test rewards language skills. The finding that asylum seekers also tend to have a facility in English or French is also not surprising because the majority have been in Canada for quite a few years before they are approved for permanent settlement. 'Assisted relatives' show only a small advantage over the other categories, because the bonus points they receive in the selection test for being sponsored by a Canadian relative offset the need for high points on other selection factors including language ability.

The decline in the language skills of 'independents' after 1986 followed by an increase in 1989 is explained by two trends. Before 1986, entry was restricted to immigrants with approved job offers. This meant that the majority of independents were recruited directly by employers and hence were likely to speak either English or French. When the numbers were expanded in 1986, Hong Kong immigration skyrocketed (due to the political situation and new computerised processing facilities). A significant proportion of these entrants spoke neither English nor French. After 1988, this movement was partially squeezed out by family migration and 'replaced' by 'independent' migration destined for Quebec. This in turn increased the number of French-speaking or bilingual immigrants and accounted for the increase in the ratio beginning in 1989.

Overall, the data on immigrant characteristics confirm the observation that the privatisation phenomenon in Canada's immigration

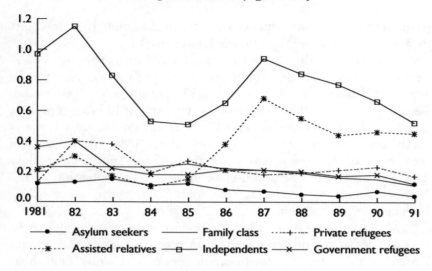

Data for plotting points

Components	1981	1982	1983	1984	1985	1986	1987	1988	1989	1990	1991
Asylum seekers	0.12	0.13	0.15	0.11	0.12	0.08	0.07	0.05	0.04	0.07	0.04
Family class	0.23	0.23	0.23	0.23	0.25	0.22	0.21	0.19	0.16	0.15	0.11
Private refugees	0.13	0.40	0.38	0.19	0.27	0.21	0.18	0.19	0.21	0.23	0.17
Assisted relatives	0.21	0.30	0.17	0.10	0.15	0.38	0.68	0.55	0.44	0.46	0.45
Independents	0.97	1.15	0.83	0.53	0.51	0.65	0.94	0.84	0.77	0.66	0.52
Government refugees	0.36	0.40	0.22	0.18	0.18	0.21	0.21	0.20	0.17	0.18	0.12

Source: Prepared by staff within EIC.

Figure 7.2   Occupational characteristics by category of immigrant: Canada 1981–91

Ratio of professionals/managers/scientists to all other occupations

program produced an intake with lower qualifications and hence (probably) with greater settlement difficulties.

The Australian experience

The Australian story in recent years offers some parallels with the Canadian experience and offers glimpses of the dynamic underlying the privatisation hypothesis: the increasing pressure over time on certain demand-driven, self-selected and sponsor-linked categories. In

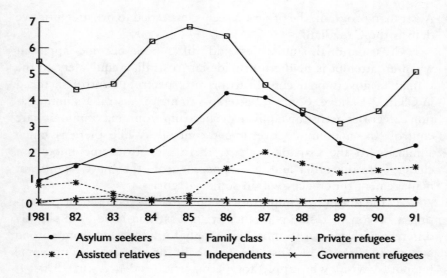

Figure 7.3 plot legend:
- Asylum seekers
- Family class
- Private refugees
- Assisted relatives
- Independents
- Government refugees

Data for plotting points

Components	1981	1982	1983	1984	1985	1986	1987	1988	1989	1990	1991
Asylum seekers	0.92	1.49	2.09	2.08	2.99	4.30	4.14	3.49	2.40	1.90	2.32
Family class	1.35	1.60	1.40	1.26	1.37	1.37	1.21	0.95	0.96	1.06	0.94
Private refugees	0.08	0.27	0.36	0.23	0.27	0.24	0.22	0.17	0.19	0.22	0.28
Assisted relatives	0.76	0.86	0.45	0.21	0.38	1.43	2.06	1.63	1.26	1.37	1.50
Independents	5.48	4.41	4.63	6.26	6.83	6.48	4.62	3.65	3.15	3.63	5.13
Government refugees	0.15	0.20	0.22	0.17	0.16	0.17	0.17	0.18	0.23	0.29	0.27

Source: Prepared by staff within EIC.

Figure 7.3   Ratio of Canadian language ability to mother tongue by component: Canada 1981–91

1988, indeed, the FitzGerald Report warned that 'without swift remedial action, current selection mechanisms will deliver many tens of thousands of immigrants more than the planned immigration program' (1988, p. 1). However, in the Australian case, the tension between privatisation, on the one hand, and immigration management, on the other hand, appears to have been less dramatic. Certainly since the FitzGerald Report warnings, important changes in categorical definitions and managerial controls have brought the Australian immigration program under tighter control. While the privatisation dynamic remains visible and is an important factor shaping the

Australian program, the program seems less ceded to private initiative than is the Canadian.

Cross-national similarities and differences become apparent when an attempt is made to provide an Australian equivalent to the Canadian government control to private spectrum control sketched in Chart 7.1 above. Chart 7.2 attempts to array Australia's immigration categories across an equivalent spectrum from 'maximum private control' to 'maximum government control'. While there is much similarity to the Canadian chart, there are also some important changes in rank order and, less apparent from the chart, significant management differences within some categories.

At the outset it is important to note that the criteria for permitting a person to reside permanently in Australia have been slightly different with respect to those who apply for admission from abroad and those already in Australia (normally having entered on some temporary visa) who apply for permanent residence. (In 1990–91, some 111 000 visas were granted to applicants abroad while some 12 700 persons in Australia were granted permanent residency.) The official immigration program, logically, covers both streams, though it is also logical to regard them as analytically separate, especially in view of this chapter's concern about the locus of control over immigration decisions. The system for granting permanent residency to those already in Australia is termed Permanent Entry Permits After Entry (PEPAE) though there are still cases being processed under the pre-1990 system known as Grant Of Resident's Status (GORS). In Chart 7.2, and in the data reported later, PEPAE and GORS statistics are lumped together and referred to, for convenience, as Residence. Chart 7.2 also includes 'New Zealand citizens' as a category though they are outside formal immigration control.

Numbers and plans

As with Canada, an appreciation of the Australian experience is assisted by a detailed statistical breakdown of immigration numbers over recent years. In order to convey the categorical information relevant to this chapter, the statistics need to be reported in two closely related but not identical forms. The first (Table 7.3) provides a better picture of the relationship between planning levels and outcomes, while the second (Table 7.4) provides a better categorical breakdown of immigrants. While it would be highly desirable to have the requisite information combined in one table, the way

Chart 7.2   Australian immigration categories by locus of control

Maximum private control

New Zealand citizens
family residence
preferential family
special eligibility
special talent
employer nominees
humanitarian residence
economic residence
business immigrants
labour-agreement entrants
concessional family
independent
privately sponsored humanitarian
unsponsored humanitarian

Maximum government control

in which the data are collected and reported does not make this possible.)

Table 7.3 reports on the planning levels and outcomes with respect to the Australian immigration program since 1984–85. Unfortunately, the data can only be broken down into broad categories (e.g. 'independent' and 'concessional family' are combined until 1988–89, and the 'skilled' intake is not broken down into its component sub-programs). The 'outcomes' reported in Table 7.3 are based on the actual award of visas. Table 7.3 includes, for both planning levels and outcomes, 'Residence' statistics. Until 1988–89, Residence planning levels can only be reported in aggregate; from 1989–90 they can be distributed across categories.

More detailed break downs into finer categories are provided in Table 7.4, which reports 'visaed settler arrivals' (visa-awarded persons arriving in Australia within a given year as settlers), along with the same Residence numbers provided in Table 7.3. Table 7.4 thus effectively reports the number of new permanent settlers (arriving from abroad or switching from temporary status) each year. Its data differ marginally from the 'outcomes' data in Table 7.3 because a small proportion of persons granted visas under Table 7.3, estimated at around 6 per cent (BIR 1991d, p. 7), do not use them and hence do not show up as 'settler arrivals' under Table 7.4. There can also be some delay between the issuing of a visa and the time at which 'settler arrival' in fact occurs. Conforming with the approach adopted with the Canadian statistics, the rank ordering of categories in Table 7.4 follows that in Chart 7.2, roughly arrayed from least to most 'government-controlled'.

A further table (Table 7.5) reports *non-visaed* settler arrivals. These are not regarded as part of the immigration program but, from the perspective of this chapter, constitute *ipso facto* probably the least 'government-controlled' category of all. Most of these arrivals are New Zealand citizens.

Discussion of the management and control implications of these statistics can usefully start with Table 7.5, which reveals the effect of the unrestricted entry rights into Australia of New Zealand citizens. The numbers involved can be significant. The 27 234 New Zealanders who arrived in Australia for permanent settlement in 1988–89 represented almost 19 per cent of settler arrivals in that year, though two years later the numbers in 1990–91 had fallen to 8338 and represented under 7 per cent of settler arrivals. The fluctuating New Zealand intake is probably an index of the relative buoyancy of the labour markets in the two countries While there has been questioning of the privileged position of New Zealanders by some academics (Collins 1991, p. 247–8) and by some elements of the Labor Party, there is little likelihood that general bipartisan support for its continuation will change.

Occupying the 'maximum private control' end of the Canadian spectrum in Chart 7.1 was the category of 'domestic asylum seekers', with the 'privately sponsored humanitarian' conceptually located nearby. The Australian case (Chart 7.2) suggests much greater managerial control over these categories, or at least over their nearest equivalent, namely 'humanitarian Residence' and 'privately sponsored humanitarian'. An explanation for the difference reveals much about the different program regulation and control experiences in Australia and Canada, and suggests that the 'privatisation' dynamic is less powerful in the former than it has been, as described above, in the latter.

Until the end of June 1990, Australia handled applications from 'domestic asylum seekers'—persons in Australia seeking permission to stay on refugee or humanitarian grounds—in a similar way to Canada (though within a different administrative and judicial structure with which this chapter is not concerned). From Table 7.6, which reports applications and approvals for permanent residence status over the 1979–80 to 1990–91 period, it can be seen that the number of applications on humanitarian grounds grew through the 1980s,

Table 7.3 Immigration Program and Outcome, Australia, 1984–85 to 1992–93

	1984–85					1985–86				
	Planning level		*Outcome*			*Planning level*		*Outcome*		
Components	*Visas*	*Residence*	*Visas*	*Residence*	*Total*	*Visas*	*Residence*	*Visas*	*Residence*	*Total*
Preferential family	28 000		22 370	4 160	26 530	26 000		25 949	6 470	32 419
Skilled	15 500		9 128	693	9 821	18 500		14 903	1 101	16 004
Independent & concessional	14 000		17 291		17 291	16 000		29 791		29 791
Humanitarian	14 000		14 207	1 115	15 322	12 000		11 700	1 936	13 636
Special & other	500		476	46	522	1 500		938	165	1 103
Total	72 000	6 000	63 472	6 014	69 486	74 000	8 000	83 281	9 672	92 953

	1986–87					1987–88				
	Planning level		*Outcome*			*Planning level*		*Outcome*		
Components	*Visas*	*Residence*	*Visas*	*Residence*	*Total*	*Visas*	*Residence*	*Visas*	*Residence*	*Total*
Preferential family	26 000		30 123	7 599	37 722	33 000		30 123	7 599	37 722
Skilled	18 500		22 083	1 346	23 429	20 500		22 761	2 420	25 181
Independent & concessional	25 000		39 479		39 479	42 000		55 144		55 144
Humanitarian	12 000		11 291	2 424	13 715	12 000		11 400	3 468	14 868
Special & other	1 500		1 542		142	1 500		1 742		1 742
Total	85 000	10 000	104 459	10 105	114 564	109 000	11 000	121 170	13 487	134 657

Table 7.3 Cont'd

1988–89

Components	Planning level		Outcome		
	Visas	*Residence*	*Visas*	*Residence*	*Total*
Preferential family	35 000		34 133	6 847	40 980
Skilled	30 000		27 826	2 387	30 213
Independent & concessional	45 500		45 563	—	45 563
Humanitarian	12 000		11 309	3 664	14 973
Special & other	1 500		2 188	2 513	4 701
Total	138 000	14 000	121 019	15 411	136 430

1989–90

Components	Planning level	Outcome		
	Visas+Residence	*Visas*	*Residence*	*Total*
Preferential family	41 000	32 914	11 001	43 915
Skilled	21 500	20 064	2 572	22 636
Independent	32 500	30 001		30 001
Concessional	30 000	22 577		22 577
Humanitarian	12 500	11 701	714	12 415
Special & other	1 000	544	258	802
Total	138 500	117 801	14 545	132 346

1990–91

	Planning level	Outcome		
	Visas+Residence	*Visas*	*Residence*	*Total*
	44 000	30 600	8 200	38 760
	19 500	12 900	1 800	14 634
	30 500	34 700	400	35 128
	20 000	22 500		22 493
	11 000	9 800	1 500	11 329
	1 000	500	800	1 222
	126 000	111 000	12 700	123 566

Table 7.3 Cont'd

| Components | 1991–92 | | | | 1992–93 | | | |
| | Planning level | Outcome | | | Planning level | Outcome | | |
	Visas+Residence	Visas	Residence	Total	Visas+Residence	Visas	Residence	Total
Preferential family	37 000	26 969	10 757	37 726	39 000			
Skilled	12 500	9 478	2 528	12 006	10 400			
Independent	30 000	29 300	54	29 354	13 400		n.a.	
Concessional	19 000	18 133		18 133	6 000			
Humanitarian	12 000	9 147	2 862	12 009	10 000			
Special & other	500	371	1 295	1 666	1 200			
Total	111 000	93 398	17 496	110 894	80 000			

Source: Adapted from BIR 1991d, pp. 14–15; BIR 1992d; DILGEA 1991c, p. 27; DILGEA 1992c; BIR 1992e.

215

Table 7.4 Visaed settler arrivals and grants of permanent residency: Australia 1982–83 to 1991–92

	1982–83		1983–84		1984–85		1985–86		1986–87	
	No.	%	No.	%	No.	%	No.	%	No.	%
Preferential family*	25 348	28.1	29 026	41.3	26 856	37.7	30 681	36.4	34 885	33.1
Special eligibility**	219	0.2	146	0.2	206	0.3	328	0.4	584	0.6
Special talents	38	0.0	34	0.0	63	0.1	31	0.0	181	0.2
Employer nominees	6 715	7.4	3 531	5.0	3 658	5.1	6 250	7.4	8 353	7.9
Humanitarian residence	955	1.1	930	1.3	1 115	1.6	1 936	2.3	2 424	2.3
Economic residence	1 441	1.6	961	1.4	693	1.0	1 101	1.3	1 346	1.3
Retiree	310	0.3	217	0.3	176	0.2	231	0.3	631	0.6
Business migration	1 079	1.2	1 472	2.1	1 561	2.2	1 649	2.0	3 535	3.4
Concessional family	6 648	7.3	12 365	17.6	18 420	25.9	25 563	30.3	31 735	30.1
Occupational shares	24 037	26.6	6 332	9.0	3 361	4.7	4 569	5.4	9 037	8.6
Independent	6 494	7.2	283	0.4	213	0.3	138	0.2	1 639	1.6
Humanitarian arrivals	17 054	18.8	14 769	21.0	14 850	20.9	11 840	14.0	11 101	10.5
Other***	229	0.3	209	0.3	46	0.1	165	0.2	–	–
Total	90 567	100.0	76 275	100.0	71 218	100.0	84 485	100.0	105 421	100.0

Table 7.4 Cont'd

	1987–88		1988–89		1989–90		1990–91		1991–92	
	No.	%	No.	%	No.	%	No.	%	No.	%
Preferential family*	37 744	28.9	38 252	29.1	41 035	34.0	39 614	32.2	38 053	33.1
Special eligibility**	549	0.4	664	0.5	797	0.6	1 701	0.9	2 698	2.3
Special talents	182	0.1	140	0.1	226	0.2	148	0.1	67	0.1
Employer nominees	8 200	6.3	8 119	6.2	10 148	8.4	6 651	5.4	3 663	3.2
Humanitarian residence	3 468	2.7	3 664	2.8	714	0.6	1 549	1.3	2 862	2.5
Economic residence	2 420	1.9	2 387	1.8	2 572	2.1	2 153	1.7	2 582	2.2
Retiree	1 084	0.8	1 007	0.8	684	0.6	46	0.0	–	–
Business migration	7 222	5.5	10 051	7.7	10 001	8.3	8 118	6.6	6 444	5.6
Concessional family	39 426	30.2	28 187	21.5	19 907	16.5	22 522	18.3	21 325	18.6
Occupational shares	7 148	5.5	8 344	6.4	–	–	–	–	–	–
Independent	12 066	9.2	17 142	13.0	22 461	18.6	33 504	27.2	30 160	26.2
Humanitarian arrivals	11 076	8.5	10 887	8.3	11 948	9.9	7 745	6.3	7 157	6.2
Other***	–	–	2 513	1.9	–	–	–	–	–	–
Total	130 585	100.0	131 357	100.0	120 493	100.0	123 751	100.0	115 011	100.0

*Aggregates 'settler arrival' and 'residence' numbers,
**'Settler arrivals' only up to 1988–89; 'settler arrival' plus 'residence' numbers from 1989–90
***'Other' encompasses grants of residence status for which the category is not stated

Source: Adapted from BIR 1991a, p. 24; BIR 1992a, p. 9; BIR 1992d; DILGEA 1992b

Table 7.5 Non-visaed settler arrivals: Australia 1982–83 to 1991–92

	1982–83	1983–84	1984–85	1985–86	1986–87	1987–88	1988–89	1989–90	1990–91	1991–92
New Zealand citizens	7 660	6 562	10 584	15 044	15 730	24 158	27 234	13 345	8 338	8 201
Others	2 619	2 505	2 299	2 556	2 233	2 234	2 136	1 934	2 274	1 675
Total	10 279	9 067	12 883	17 600	17 963	26 392	29 370	15 279	10 612	9 876

Source: Adapted from BIR 1991d, p. 17; BIR 1992a, p. 9

though less than half of these were approved. Relatively few of these cases were classified as 'refugees': in 1988–89, for example, only 529 of the 8704 applications and 51 of the 3664 approvals pertained to refugee status; the remainder of the 'humanitarian' cases are simply classified as 'compassionate' (BIR 1992f, DILGEA 1992a, p. 13.)

In 1989–90 came a very large surge in applications: 17 048 new applicants sought resident status on humanitarian grounds, 3370 of them as refugees. This surge prompted the government to institute a very significant change in the rules. Since the end of June 1990, no new applications for resident status on humanitarian grounds have been permitted (DILGEA 1992a, p. 12). Applications may be lodged for refugee status but, if granted, refugee status now results in a four-year temporary visa and not permanent residence. At the expiry of the four-year period, applicants will have the opportunity to apply for a further temporary permit or for permanent residence, but approval will be subject to demonstrating an ongoing need for refugee or humanitarian protection and to the availability of places in the annual immigration program.

The numbers seeking refugee status increased in a very startling way in 1990–91, the 13 954 applications received represented a 537 per cent increase on 1989–90. This increase in refugee applications can be 'mainly attributed to increased applications from nationals from the People's Republic of China following events in that country [viz. the Tienanmen Square incidents] in June 1989' (DILGEA 1992a, p. 13). Chinese nationals who were in Australia as of 20 June 1989 were in fact automatically awarded a four-year temporary visa.

There has been a backlog of refugee applications, with some public controversy caused by publicity given to the internment in secure camps of many illegal-entry applicants awaiting the outcome of their cases. The success rate for applicants is quite low: only 16 per cent of the 403 cases finalised in 1990–91 resulted in the recognition of refugee status (DILGEA 1992a, p. 13).

The Australian process for handling on-shore claims for humanitarian asylum thus differs significantly from that in Canada. In the terminology of this chapter, the reforms have reasserted government control in the face of privatisation pressures. With the expiry of the initial set of four-year temporary visas in early 1994 the Australian government granted, by and large, permanent residence to those in Australia prior to June 1989.

Australia's off-shore humanitarian program also appears to have been well controlled throughout the period under review. Whereas in Canada the 'privately sponsored' category has presented some

Table 7.6 Grant of Resident Status by component, Australia, 1979–80 to 1990–91

7.6.1. Applications received

Component	1979–80	1980–81	1981–82	1982–83	1983–84	1984–85	1985–86	1986–87	1987–88	1988–89	1989–90	1990–91
Preferential family	4 602	4 221	4 133	9 904	7 764	6 063	7 624	8 844	8 029	11 366	14 299	11 177
Economic	–	674	1 885	3 037	1 086	1 146	1 478	2 768	3 269	4 293	4 770	3 284
Humanitarian	322	940	2 026	1 506	2 052	2 686	4 219	5 740	8 476	8 704	17 048	117
Special	–	–	–	–	–	–	–	–	–	–	1 695	1 012
Other	4 229	1 941	174	331	79	3	13	–	–	1 200	1 147	2
Total	9 153	7 776	8 218	14 778	10 981	9 898	13 334	17 352	19 774	25 563	38 959	15 592

7.6.2. Applications approved

Component	1979–80	1980–81	1981–82	1982–83	1983–84	1984–85	1985–86	1986–87	1987–88	1988–89	1989–90	1990–91
Preferential family	3 417	3 221	3 007	5 044	7 434	4 160	6 470	6 335	7 599	6 847	11 001	8 202
Economic	–	84	915	1 441	961	693	1 101	1 346	2 420	2 387	2 572	2 153
Humanitarian	469	87	746	955	930	1 115	1 936	2 424	3 468	3 664	714	1 549
Special	–	–	–	–	–	–	–	–	–	–	258	771
Other	2 958	1 078	690	229	209	46	165	–	–	2 513	–	–
Total	6 844	4 470	5 358	7 669	9 534	6 014	9 672	10 105	13 487	15 411	14 545	12 675

Source: Adapted from BIR 1992d

management difficulties due to its sponsor-initiated character, private sponsorship has much less management significance in Australia than in Canada. Privately sponsored humanitarian entrants are managed within the overall planning level designated in advance. There is in fact little management distinction made between sponsored and un-sponsored entrants except in the sense that applicants with Australian 'connections' (such as a family member or sponsor) are more likely to be selected to participate in the program. This is regarded by Australian officials as a sensible policy which facilitates the selection of entrants most likely to settle successfully. It is not regarded in any significant sense as a 'privatisation' of program control.

Tables 7.3 and 7.4 reveal that the trend in 'humanitarian' immigration numbers since the early 1980s has been towards modest decline. Greater change is discernible when the program is disaggregated into its 'refugee' and 'humanitarian' components. Of the 17 054 'humanitarian' settler arrivals in 1982–83, fully 95 per cent were classified as refugees; of the 7745 arriving in 1990–91, just 16 per cent were refugees. There has thus been a huge swing from providing third-country asylum for refugees recognised under the UN Convention to selecting people with reasonable prospects of successful settlement from among those seeking humanitarian assistance. The change reflects the declining number of persons in the world identified by the UN High Commission for Refugees as needing resettlement as refugees, but also underscores—in comparison with Canada—the strong managerial control over the program.

The changing distribution between source countries also demonstrates considerable control at the official level. Soon after assuming office in 1983, the Hawke Labor government decided to accept more refugees from 'right-wing' regimes in Chile and El Salvador. More recently it has approved the creation of a Special Assistance category, targeted at East Timorese nationals living in Portugal, Soviet ethnic minorities, and people fleeing conflicts in the former Yugoslavian republics and in Lebanon. Selection under the Special Assistance category depends on two main elements, the degree of stress being suffered by the applicant and the extent of the person's links with Australia.

It is with respect to the balance between the 'family relationship' and 'economic' immigration streams that parallels between Australia and Canada become closer, though again it seems fair to conclude that recent management changes in Australia appear to have been more successful than in Canada in attenuating the impact of privatisation.

From the late 1970s until the early 1990s, when Australia began to reduce its target intake levels while Canada continued to expand them, the fluctuations in overall intake numbers were broadly similar in the two countries. Australian immigration numbers were steadily built up in the late 1970s and early 1980s under the Fraser Liberal–National Coalition government from the low base to which they had fallen in the years of the Whitlam Labor government in the mid-1970s.

The advent of the Hawke Labor government in 1983 saw a quick cut to the immigration intake as a response to the recession of 1982–83. In deference to trade union concerns about job competition, the cuts were particularly severe in the 'economic' categories. On the other hand, family reunion rules were liberalised, with (for example) much less weight being given to English language ability in order, as explicitly explained by the Minister, to make the process 'more acceptable to the ethnic communities of Australia' (Parkin & Hardcastle 1990, p. 319). In the terms of the privatisation hypothesis, the government was effectively choosing to cede some of its managerial and selection control.

By 1986, a new Minister (Chris Hurford) had assumed the immigration portfolio and, through his Department, sponsored both an increase in total intake and attempted to increase the overall skill level. This roughly coincided with the similar Canadian moves to increase the overall intake and was based on a similar rationale of the perceived advantages to the national economy accruing from a 'high quality' immigrant intake. The consequent changes to categories and rules upset ethnic community organisations and contributed to Hurford's demise as Minister. The FitzGerald Report of 1988 nonetheless strongly argued for a larger and more highly skilled intake.

What ensued, as in Canada, was a program expanded to encompass more skilled entrants but also to accommodate a larger demand-driven family component. The privatisation imperative was, however, held in check by rule changes with respect to 'concessional family' applicants which are further discussed below. In the early 1990s, with Australia having again suffered an economic recession, the immigration planning levels have been cut, with the 'economic' intake bearing the brunt of the reductions (in part reflecting decreasing demand). As in Canada, the 'privately controlled' end of the spectrum—specifically, in Australia's case, the demand-driven preferential family intake (see Chart 7.2)—has been largely unaffected.

Table 7.3 reveals a steady increase in 'preferential family' program numbers over the period under review. Annual planning levels were regularly exceeded until 1989–90, with the result that the planning level (or, strictly speaking, the estimated demand) was increased from about 32 000 in 1984–85 (building in an allowance for grants of resident status) to 44 000 in 1990–91. The overall upward trend was tempered by the introduction of the 'balance of family' rule for parental applicants. Since 1987–88, the number of parents being admitted has fallen by 50 per cent and the number of applications by 66 per cent. The majority of 'preferential family' immigrants are spouses or fiancees of Australian residents, with the Philippines (somewhat controversially) being the biggest single source country for fiancees and Vietnam for spouses. Birrell (1990, p. 45) predicted that numbers of spouse/fiancee applications would tend to increase in coming years due partly to the increased international mobility of Australians but mainly due to chain migration within particular ethnic communities (especially those of Lebanese, Yugoslavian and Turkish origin). The validity of this prediction has yet to be borne out.

The impact of managerial controls is even more dramatic with respect to the 'concessional family' class, which is located in Chart 7.2 towards the 'government controlled' end of the spectrum. Settler arrivals reported in Table 7.4 reveal a remarkable increase from just 6648 to 1982–83 to 39 426 in 1987–88. In the mid-1980s, planning levels were consistently exceeded. Accounting for a large proportion of the increase were large numbers of sponsored siblings (Birrell 1990, p. 3).

In response to the increasing numbers and to concern about their 'quality', some of the rules were tightened through this period, and the pass mark in the points test increased (Birrell 1990, pp. 3, 46). The current system, designating the 'concessional family' class as a residual buffer to be used only when demand has been satisfied under 'preferential family' and only to the extent that there is room left under the announced target, has been in effect since 1989–90. As both Tables 7.3 and 7.4 reveal, 'concessional family' numbers have since that time fallen significantly. While the decline in part reflects falling demand during the recession, the government has decided on several occasions not to lower the pass mark in the points test in order to meet the 'concessional family' targets; indeed the pass mark (85 points) set in December 1989 was increased (to 90 points) in January 1992. It was increased again (to 100 points) in May 1992, and at the same time greater selectivity on the basis of English language proficiency was incorporated (requiring principal applicants to be 'vocationally proficient' in English).

The 'economic' stream shows interesting developments. The categories here range from those with strong 'government control' in the spectrum of Chart 7.2 (such as the 'independent' category) to those nearer the middle of the spectrum (such as the 'business' and 'employer nominee' categories). Even these mid-spectrum categories, however, exhibit a fair degree of government control. While the use of private agents in connection with the business program arguably represented a diffusion of government control, strict criteria for admission have been applied in both the business program (until its suspension) and the employer nomination programs.

Table 7.4 reveals that in 1982–83—the last year of the Fraser Liberal–National Coalition government—the various 'economic' categories (business, employer nominees, economic Residence, Occupational Shares, and independent) accounted for 44 per cent of visas and resident status grants. Next year, as a result of initial Hawke government policies, the proportion crashed to 18 per cent, and to just 13 per cent in the following year. The policy shift noted above for 1986 then moved the proportion back upwards, though—consistent with elements of the privatisation thesis—this was accomplished largely by expanding the overall intake rather than by cutting overall family reunion numbers. By 1990–91, the proportion was back up to 40 per cent. The announced 1992–93 program, however, was targeted to return the skill categories, in which demand has been disproportionately affected by the recession, down to 30 per cent of the program. At the same time, as with the 'concessional family' stream, there has been an effort to stress English language proficiency through an emphasis on 'vocational proficiency' and the award of extra points for language skills.

Within this general story of the management of the immigration program, there is a more specific story, well related by Birrell (1992), about legislative and managerial changes since 1989 which have produced greater managerial control over on-shore applications for Residence status. Table 7.6 above gives an indication of the increasing number of these applications up to 1989. The way that applications on humanitarian grounds are now handled has already been described above. Measures were also instituted to provide better control over the other categories, the largest single class constituting applications by persons on the basis of *de jure* or *de facto* marriage to an Australian resident. Changes to the Act in 1989 (which *inter alia* reduced Ministerial discretion) and various changes to regulations have meant that 'the regulation of residence claims has overall been tightened' (Birrell 1992, p. 40).

Composition

While the Australian story thus suggests less support for the 'privatisation thesis' than found in Canada, some similar patterns are discernible with respect to the characteristics of immigrants across intake categories. Comparable data for educational and language characteristics are not available, but Figure 7.4 provides for Australia a portrait of occupational skills analogous to that provided for Canada in Figure 7.2. Figure 7.4 plots the ratio, for various intake categories, of 'professional' to all other occupations. As for Canada, it finds that the demand-driven 'preferential family' category, as well as the humanitarian category, display consistently low ratios. The points-tested 'independent' category produces a higher ratio, while the ratio for 'concessional family' entrants has increased in recent years in response to greater competition for fewer places. It is worth noting, contrary to the privatisation hypothesis, the high ratios within the 'skilled' stream which includes admission categories (such as employer nomination) located on Chart 7.2 towards the 'private control' end of the spectrum.

Conclusion

In both Canada and Australia, the dynamic underpinning the privatisation hypothesis—the propensity for immigrants admitted under all categories to sponsor relatives under demand-driven categories and for immigrants to self-select under humanitarian programs—can be discerned. The evidence in this chapter suggests, however, that Australia has been better able to adjust to privatisation pressures by implementing policy and managerial changes in recent years. This suggests that the 'privatisation hypothesis' should be treated with some caution, since the relative impact of privatisation is shaped by the particular policy and management approach of the immigrant-receiving nation. An explanation for the policy and management differences between Canada and Australia is beyond the scope of this chapter, but may include the different roles played by the respective judicial systems in asylum matters, the greater strength of pro-refugee sentiment in Canadian political culture, and the operation of executives, legislatures and political parties in the policy process. Some of these matters are explored in other chapters in this volume.

It should also be noted that in 1992 Canada introduced new legislation designed to improve its management of immigration. The

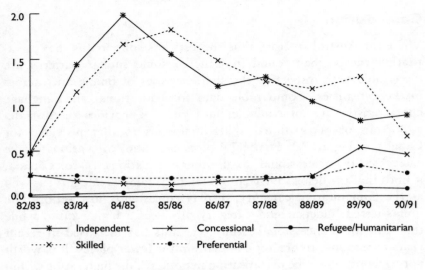

Data for plotting points

	Preferential	Concessional	Skilled	Independent	Humanitarian
1982/83	0.23	0.24	0.47	0.48	0.02
1983/84	0.23	0.17	1.14	1.44	0.03
1984/85	0.20	0.14	1.66	1.98	0.04
1985/86	0.20	0.13	1.82	1.55	0.07
1986/87	0.21	0.16	1.48	1.20	0.06
1987/88	0.21	0.19	1.25	1.30	0.06
1988/89	0.21	0.22	1.17	1.03	0.07
1989/90	0.33	0.53	1.30	0.82	0.09
1990/91	0.25	0.45	0.65	0.88	0.08

Source: Prepared by staff within EIC.

Figure 7.4 Occupational characteristics by category of immigrant: Australia, 1982/83–1990/91

Ratio of professionals to all other occupations

legislative changes (which, as of early 1993, still required regulations to be given effect) include giving Canadian authorities greater authority to limit the granting of visas and to deal with applications in various ways, including being able to compare applications in order to choose the best candidates. In a number of important ways, the proposed system will come closer to that of Australia.

CHAPTER 8

Business Migration

Allan Borowski and Alan Nash

Introduction

This chapter compares and contrasts the development, achievements and problems of the business migration programs in Canada and Australia. It also seeks to identify some of the major issues relevant to policy that flow from this analysis in relation to business migration in particular and immigration policy in general.

The chapter begins by reviewing the history of the business migration programs of the two countries and their major turning points. Consideration is then given to the scale of business migration and the source countries that have yielded business migrants to Australia and Canada.

In the third section, the available research findings on the impact of the business migration programs vis-à-vis their goals are reviewed.

Several years ago, Australia's business migration program began to face increasing challenges to its legitimacy. This culminated in a 'legitimation crisis' that, in turn, saw the replacement of the existing program in mid-1991 by a new 'business skills' category in early 1992. In Canada, however, no such negative reaction has occurred despite public concerns over what was perceived by many to be 'visas for sale' and apparent inadequacies in government monitoring of the program. The fourth section of the chapter, therefore, considers the nature and credibility of the challenges to the business migration programs.

The last section seeks to identify the lessons of Australia's and Canada's business migration programs for policy making and implementation.

History of business migration programs in Australia and Canada

Considerable interchange of ideas and personnel have always been a feature of the way Canada and Australia have run their respective immigration programs (Hawkins 1988); their business migration programs—as their similarity will make plain—are no exception in this regard. Indeed, a friendly rivalry exists regarding the origin of innovations in this field. Nevertheless, business migration became part of Canada's immigration program about a decade before Australia's program first began to provide for the entry of business immigrants. Thus, this section on the history of business migration to the two countries begins with Canada.

Canada

With the points system of 1967, business migration became a specific element in Canada's Independent Class of immigrants (Marr 1985, p. 3). Under this system independent applicants had to earn 50 or more of the 100 potential points to qualify for admission. The entrepreneur was one of the categories of independent immigrant eligible for admission and was required to show that he or she had sufficient funds to establish a viable business in Canada. Entrepreneurs were assessed like other Independent applicants except for the categories of occupational demand and occupational skill. Instead they automatically received 25 points in lieu of any points they might have received for these factors (Marr 1985, pp. 3–4).

In April 1978 greater focus was brought to bear with the introduction of regulations (under the authority of the 1976 *Immigration Act*) which, for the first time, defined a business immigration program as a separate category, and modified the point system as it applied to entrepreneurs. The program was designed to bring into Canada experienced entrepreneurs who intended and had the ability either to establish new businesses or to purchase substantial interests in existing Canadian businesses. Under the regulations the proposed business had to employ at least five Canadians other than the entrepreneur and his or her dependants and make a significant contribution to the Canadian economy. The entrepreneur was also required to be active in the management of the business (EIC 1984, p. 2; Marr 1985, p. 5).

The 1978 regulations, in addition, provided procedural guidelines to aid visa officers in Canadian posts abroad distinguish business applications that could be approved. Visa officers were also able to use a range of admission methods that were not available to non-business applicants (unconditional landing, conditional landing, and early admission with a Minister's Permit) (EIC 1984, p. 2; Marr 1985, p. 6). The 1978 regulations, therefore, introduced most of the structure and principles seen in the current legislation.

Some four years later, in November 1982, a policy review of business migration was initiated to see how the program could be used more effectively to promote economic activity and create employment for Canadians. The major result of this review was the formal implementation of a new entrepreneur immigration program in January 1984. The new policy directives were aimed at enlarging the definition of those eligible under the program and increasing the speed of their processing. Most importantly new legislation redefined the components of business migration. An entrepreneur immigrant was now defined as a person:

1 who must intend and be able to establish or purchase, or make a substantial investment in a business venture in Canada whereby employment opportunities will be created or continued for one or more Canadian citizens or permanent residents, other than the entrepreneur and his or her dependants;
2 whose business must make a significant economic contribution; and
3 who must participate actively in the management of the business (Wong et al. 1985, p. 3).

Entrepreneur immigrants were now also accorded a higher processing priority than before; they were assigned third place, after Family Class immigrants and Refugees (Marr 1985, p. 8).

In addition to expanding the potential pool of people who might be eligible for entrepreneur status by dropping the minimum employment threshold from five Canadians to one and, of course, thereby making it much easier to meet that threshold, the redefinition also necessitated the alteration of the previous definition of a self-employed person. The regulations were altered in the 1984 changes to define such an individual as:

an immigrant who intends and has the ability to establish a business in Canada and will create an employment opportunity for himself and one that will make a significant contribution to the economy, or to the cultural and artistic life of Canada (EIC, 1984, p. 27).

The new entrepreneur program's administrative guidelines emphasised the need for more careful selection of entrepreneurs, a new provisional admission procedure to supplement the unconditional and conditional visa alternatives, and a national monitoring system to ensure that entrepreneurial immigration offered significant benefits to Canada (Wong et al. 1985, pp. 4–5).

Further changes implemented in January 1986 included the introduction of one-year business visas to facilitate the admission of business people to Canada to oversee their investments or businesses. The provisional admission category was replaced entirely by the conditional category. Thus, entrepreneurs could enter Canada and have two years to establish a business while Canada's Employment and Immigration Commission (EIC) maintained the control necessary to ensure that such plans were realised. In addition, CEIC's planning level for business immigrants was increased substantially, by 82 per cent over the figure for 1985–86, to 4000 principal applicants in 1986–87—a goal to be pursued through increased promotional efforts and by according processing priority to all three streams of business immigrants (the self-employed, the entrepreneur and the investor), second only to Refugees and Family Class members (EIC 1985, pp. 2–5).

The third category of business migration just referred to—the investor immigrant—was added to Canada's business immigration program on 1 January 1986. This component was designed for qualified business people with more substantial capital than those in the entrepreneur component who might not want to be actively involved in the management of a business (EIC 1985, p. 1). In terms of program development, it was argued that the new investor category provided the legislative base to accommodate risk ventures that the provinces considered important to their regional economic development. Moreover, a select group could now be chosen who possessed the sizeable capital necessary to expand Canadian industry and who were not being attracted by the previous program (EIC 1985, pp. 2–3; EIC 1987, p. 1).

According to the 1986 regulations, 'investor immigrants' were defined as persons who had business experience and had a personal net worth of at least $500 000. (All amounts in this section are in Canadian dollars unless specified otherwise). They were required to make an irrevocable investment of at least $250 000 for a minimum of three years that would 'contribute to the creation or continuation of employment opportunities for Canadian[s] . . . other than the investor and his/her dependants'. Applicants could invest in either: (a) a business or commercial venture, (b) a privately administered investment syndicate supported by the province or (c) a government-administered venture capital fund (EIC 1986a).

On 27 April 1988 the then Minister of Employment and Immigration, Barbara McDougall, announced important revisions to the investor immigrant program's regulations. The government announced that, effective 1 April 1988, the minimum investment criterion of $250 000 would be altered and no longer apply across Canada. Instead, it was replaced with a three-tiered structure in which the net personal worth, minimum investment requirement and minimum investment term varied. For example, a qualified investor would be eligible to immigrate to Canada if he or she had a personal net worth of $500 000 of which at least $150 000 was available for investment in Newfoundland for at least three years (Tier 1) (EIC 1989, p. 1) or a personal net worth of $700 000 of which at least $50 000 was available for investment in any province for five years (Tier 3) (EIC 1988, p. 2). Subsequent amendments that came into effect on 1 October 1990 increased the minimum period of investment from three to five years, the minimum investment under Tier 1 from $150 000 to $250 000, under Tier 2 from $250 000 to $350 000 and allowed provinces that had received less than 10 per cent of business immigrants in a calendar year to be eligible for investments made under Tier 2 (EIC 1990g).

The continuing refinement of the entrepreneur immigrant category and the innovation and subsequent evolution of the investor immigrant program discussed above indicate the two essential goals of Canada's business immigration program: first, the desire to focus the program in such a way that those with the necessary skills and acumen are selected, and second, the wish to attract the full potential of risk capital that is available. These goals have guided the program through the changes describe above, while recent developments indicate a realisation that the same business immigrant cannot always meet both goals.

Australia

Compared to Canada, Australia's history of business migration is much more recent. Australia's migration program first provided a

category of entry for migrants with business skills under the entrepreneur category which was introduced in November 1976 (Joint
Committee of Public Accounts 1991, pp. v, 15). The entrepreneur
category existed until 1981 when it was replaced by the Business
Migration Program (BMP). The new BMP continued to provide for
admission under the same criteria as the previous entrepreneurial
category but added self-employed people (successful professionals and
trades-people with their own firms) who could show that they had
sufficient capital to establish a business. At the beginning of 1983
these two elements were amalgamated into a separate stream (Inglis
& Wu 1992, p. 3).

The BMP formed part of the economic stream of migration to
Australia until 1991 when it ceased operating. At the beginning of
1992 the BMP's replacement—the Independent–Business Skills category within the Skill Migration component of the migration
program—became operational.

The business migration program

The purpose of the BMP was to attract successful business people to
settle permanently and contribute their capital and expertise to commercial ventures that would benefit Australia through:

• the creation of jobs or retention of jobs that otherwise would have
been lost;
• the introduction of new or improved technology;
• the stimulation of export trade; and
• the replacement of imports.

The BMP's selection criteria were subject to a number of changes
over the 10-year life of the program. Unlike the Canadian program,
however, there was never a points test involved in selection.

The selection criteria in place between 1987 and the time the
program ceased to operate in 1991 required that applicants had had
a successful business record, intended to settle permanently in
Australia and owned assets which were available for transfer to
Australia for both business and settlement purposes. The amounts
(all in Australian dollars) required for business purposes were
$350 000 for applicants under 40 years of age, $500 000 for applicants
between 40 years and 58 years of age, and $85 000 for applicants over
58 years of age. The amount required for settlement in Sydney or
Melbourne was $150 000. If applicants intended to settle elsewhere
in Australia, they required $100 000. In addition, applicants were
required to show how they proposed to meet BMP objectives, how
they would meet other regulatory requirements, and how their busi-

ness background, their proposed activities in Australia and their understanding of the Australian economic environment would satisfy the requirements of the BMP.

On 1 January 1988, as part of a progressive process of deregulating the BMP which had begun in 1985, the Federal Government introduced the Accredited Agents Scheme (AAS) to allow agents to play an active role in assessing migrants under the BMP. The AAS involved a substantial transfer of the responsibility for receiving and verifying applications from DILGEA officers based overseas to private agents who also marketed the program (Lever-Tracy 1991). At the peak of the scheme there were about 240 agents listed, in mid-1991 there were about 130 agents in Australia and overseas. In Australia, they included major legal and accountancy firms, appropriate State Government departments and individual business people some of whom employed sub-agents overseas. They provided assistance with applications. The agent's role was also seen as involving the provision of business advice and services to help business migrants enter business after arrival.

The new Independent–Business Skills category

On 25 July 1991 the Federal Government announced its decision to replace the BMP as a separate migration category. No new applications under the BMP were accepted after 2 August 1991. However, applications which had already been lodged under the BMP criteria were processed.

The BMP was replaced by a new Independent–Business Skills category, a sub-category within the Independent category of the migration program. It became operational on 17 February 1992. The details of the new category were announced by the Minister of Immigration on 17 December 1991 (DILGEA 1991b). It is targeted at an applicant's skills and experience rather than a specific business proposal or sum of money available for transfer to Australia.

Applicants under the new category are required to prove that they have attained a certain level of business experience and success according to specific criteria. Like the other Independent applicants and applicants under Canada's program, business skills applicants are now subject to a points test. Applicants must score at least 105 points. The points test includes credit for age, English language proficiency, the size of turnover of the applicant's business, the number of employees and the possession of capital available for transfer to Australia. Applicants can gain extra points if their main business background is in a field from which Australia can derive particular benefit (the manufacturing sector, traded services or the development and use of innovative technology).

Under the new category, people seeking to migrate to Australia may be able to qualify either as a shareholder or sole proprietor of a business or as a senior executive in a major corporation. Shareholders or sole proprietors must demonstrate that they: (a) have held net assets of not less than $350 000 in one or more businesses for at least three of the last four years, (b) were actively involved in their principal business and (c) had experienced no trading losses in more than one of the last four years. To qualify as a senior executive applicants must, among other things, have worked for at least three of the last four years in the top three management levels of a major corporation (defined as one with an annual turnover of at least $50 million) and demonstrate a commitment to engaging in business in Australia.

To assist with the assessment of applications, the Department of Immigration, Local Government and Ethnic Affairs (DILGEA, now DIEA, 1993) has established a new independent expert panel drawn from the business community and federal and state/territory governments. The panel will also advise DILGEA on the overall operation of the new arrangements for business migrants.

The scale of business migration to Australia and Canada

The history of business migration to Canada indicates that, over the years, Canada has progressively adopted an increasingly inclusive definition of what constitutes a business immigrant. (It has also, as noted, raised the processing priority attached to this class of immigrants.) In contrast, the recent introduction of the Independent–Business Skills category in Australia suggests an effort to delimit this definition (Easson 1992; Lever-Tracy 1991). It should come as no surprise, therefore, that the level of business migration to Canada has been generally higher than that to Australia, although other reasons for this situation (such as Canada's proximity to the US market, a long tradition of Chinese migration to Canada, and Canada's much lower investment thresholds for business migrants) should not be overlooked. Business immigrants have also represented a higher proportion of Canada's total immigrant intake than of Australia's total intake.

Australia

The BMP experienced modest growth during the early 1980s. Between 1982–83 and 1985–86 an average of 375 principal applicants arrived annually. After 1986, however, the numbers increased markedly. This was due to such factors as first, the scheme becoming more widely known in Northeast and Southeast Asia; second, the weakening of many barriers to foreign investment in Australia, including the financial deregulation of the early 1980s, which increased the attractiveness of Australia as a destination; and, third, the initiation in 1987 of a campaign by DILGEA to promote the BMP (Easson, 1992). Thus, in 1986–87 arrivals numbered 885 (3535 including family members). In the next year, 1793 arrived (7219 including family members). In 1988–89 the number of arrivals of principal applicants had reached 2458, representing a total immigration intake of 10 039 principal applicants and their families. A similar number arrived in 1989–90.

The year 1990–91 witnessed 8118 arrivals of principal applicants and their families—several thousand below initial planning levels—reflecting a reduced demand given Australia's declining economy and, arguably, the effect of competition from other countries (particularly Canada). The planned allocation for business migrant visas in 1991–92 was 5000 out of total planned immigrant intake of 111 000, or 4.5 per cent (BIR, 1991b, p. 34; DILGEA 1991c, pp. 40, 43; Joint Committee of Public Accounts 1991, p. 20). Indeed, the numbers during the late 1980s notwithstanding, the principal applicants and their families have never represented more than a small proportion of Australia's annual migrant intake.

The major source countries for business migrants between mid-1982 and March 1990 were Hong Kong (32 per cent), Taiwan (15 per cent), Malaysia (12 per cent), the United Kingdom (8 per cent), Indonesia (6 per cent) and Singapore (5 per cent) (Joint Committee of Public Accounts 1991, p. 30). As shown below, today Hong Kong and Taiwan are Canada's top two source countries for business immigrants. However, Canada has experienced quite a marked shift in the mix of source countries during the last decade.

Canada

Some data on Canada's business migration program are presented in Tables 8.1 and 8.2.

As Table 8.1 shows, initially the main contribution to business immigration was made by self-employed immigrants who represented

Table 8.1   Business immigration, Canada, 1978–90: principal landings by component

Year	Entrepreneur		Self-employed		Investor		Total
	No.	%	No.	%	No.	%	No.
1978	29	18	130	82	–	–	159
1979	183	15	1 054	85	–	–	1 237
1980	213	14	1 343	86	–	–	1 556
1981	256	14	1 647	86	–	–	1 903
1982	436	21	1 604	79	–	–	2 040
1983	523	26	1 462	74	–	–	1 985
1984	1 015	53	886	47	–	–	1 901
1985	1 454	74	504	26	–	–	1 958
1986	1 678	77	511	23	5	*	2 194
1987	2 313	74	740	24	87	3	3 140
1988	2 948	73	816	20	249	6	4 013
1989	3 098	73	646	15	514	12	4 258
1990	2 995	65	602	13	980	21	4 577
Total	17 141	55	11 945	39	1 835	6	30 921

Notes: * denotes percentage too small for tabulation. Percentages may not sum to 100 due to rounding. 1979 data are under-estimated because some business immigrant landings were processed under other immigrant categories (Employment and Immigration, Policy and Program Development Branch, 1986, p. viii). 1990 data are preliminary.

Sources:
1978: EIC, Strategic Policy and Planning, April 1990, p. 8.
1979: Wong, Schutz and Crone 1985, p. 38; EIC 1985, p. 21.
1980–83: EIC, Immigration Statistics Group 1986, p. 48.
1984–86: EIC, Landed Immigrants Data System, unpublished tabulations, June 11–12, 1987; revised from Employment and Immigration Canada Strategic Policy and Planning, April 1990, p. 8.
1987: EIC, 23 July 1990, Schedule 4.
1988–90: EIC, 5 April 1991, Schedule 6.

85 per cent of all business immigration in 1979. By 1986, however, the balance had shifted so that entrepreneur immigrants (who had comprised only 15 per cent of business immigration in 1979) now represented 77 per cent of the total annual inflow of over 2000 business immigrant principal applicants. By 1986 entrepreneurs had become the driving force in Canada's business immigration program. The major reason for this change was the alterations in January 1984 in the regulations governing the entrepreneur component (see earlier discussion).

The 1986 introduction of the investor stream had a similar, though less dramatic effect. As Table 8.1 shows, in 1986 approxi-

Table 8.2 Leading origins of Canada's business immigrants, 1981–90, by country of last permanent residence

Rank	1981 Country	No.	%	1985 Country	No.	%	1990 Country	No.
1	UK	227	11.9	Hong Kong	785	40.1	Hong Kong	1 625
2	USA	225	11.8	W. Germany	202	10.3	Taiwan	591
3	W. Germany	207	10.9	USA	133	6.8	S. Korea	195
4	Netherlands	110	5.8	France	69	3.5	Lebanon	147
5	Switzerland	97	5.1	UK	67	3.4	Kuwait	145
6	France	89	4.7	Taiwan	45	2.3	England	119
7	Hong Kong	68	3.6	Philippines	43	2.2	Arab Emirates	109
8	Israel	67	3.5	Netherland	42	2.1	Syria	108
9	Iran	60	3.2	Lebanon	38	1.9	W. Germany	101
10	Belgium	57	3.0	Switzerland	36	1.8	Saudi Arabia	92
	Total, top 10	1 207	63.5		1 460	74.6		3 232
	Total, rest	696	36.5		497	25.4		1 352
	Total, all	1 903	100.0		1 957	100.0		4 584

Notes: Data are for principal applicants, by year of landing. 1990 data are preliminary.

Sources: EIC, Policy and Program Development Branch 19 29; 1986, graph 2, 1987, graph 2; EIC 1985, p. 22; EIC, Immigration Statistics Group, 1986, Table IM14; EIC, Landed Immigrant Data System, unpublished tabulations for 1985 (2 June 1987) EIC, Business Migration, 5 April 1991, Schedule 2.

mately 77 per cent of business program landings were entrepreneur immigrants, only a fraction of 1 per cent were investors and only 23 per cent were self-employed. By 1990, however, the investor intake had risen to 21 per cent, entrepreneur landings had fallen by 12 per cent to 65 per cent (a total of 2995 principal applicants) and the self-employed component continued it decline in importance.

These data are worth putting into the wider context of Canada's total immigration intake. Thus, the total business immigration program represented only 3.6 per cent of all immigrants in 1980. By 1986, however, business immigrants represented 7.6 per cent of all immigrants—a situation partly due to the reduction in the size of the rest of the immigration program and the effects of the 1982 restrictions on Independent immigrants, the latter designed to take account of the effects of economic recession in Canada (Kerr 1986; Nash 1987; Seward 1987, pp. 2–3). By 1989 business immigrants represented almost 9.15 per cent of all arrivals in Canada but, in 1990, they declined somewhat to represent approximately 8.55 per cent of total arrivals (EIC 1991, Schedule 1).

With regard to the origins of Canada's business immigrants, Table 8.2 presents data on the leading source nations for the three years 1981, 1985 and 1990. It can be seen from this table how the business migrant flow has always been dominated by the leading ten countries involved, representing almost 64 per cent of the total in 1981, almost 75 per cent in 1985 and 70.5 per cent in 1990. Closer inspection shows that in 1981 three countries each contributed over 10 per cent of the flow whereas by 1985 only one (Hong Kong) was responsible for 40 per cent of all business migration into Canada, its nearest rivals (West Germany and the USA) only accounting for 10 per cent and 6.8 per cent respectively of the total. By 1990 Hong Kong's leading position was somewhat reduced but still dominated the flow, and with 35.4 per cent of total business landings was far ahead of the second leading source of business migrants, Taiwan (with 12.9 per cent), and the third leading source, South Korea (4.3 per cent).

The data in Table 8.2 also indicate the changing importance of various countries. Broadly speaking, the decline of Western European and American sources and the rise of Asian and Middle East/Gulf nations are the main features to observe but, of course, the rise of Hong Kong and the other Asian Pacific Rim countries by 1990 are the most important points to note. In terms of future trends, Hong Kong's dominance remains such that it is likely that all other countries will continue to be but minor players—at least until 1997, the date when the People's Republic of China resumes control of the Territory.

The impact of business migration

Neither the Australian nor the Canadian business migration program has been carefully evaluated. Nevertheless, there are some research findings available which shed some light on the extent to which the programs of the two countries have achieved their goals.

Australian research on the BMP

The BMP was not the subject of close study during its ten-year life. DILGEA conducted surveys of the BMP in 1982 and 1985 as a means of monitoring the program (DIEA 1982, 1985) while another small survey was carried out by the South Australian Department of State Development and Technology in 1988 (Joint Committee of Public Accounts 1991, p. 32). Others have examined particular aspects of the program, including the phenomenon of split family migration (Dang & Borowski 1991; Slocombe & Lachish 1990). However, the first major study of the BMP was undertaken by MSJ Keys Young Planners (1990).

The MSJ Keys Young Planners study
This study was primarily concerned with assessing the extent to which the economic aims of the BMP were being met. It was based on a small sample of 160 BMP principal applicants.

The study painted a reasonably positive picture of the BMP. It found that respondents had transferred an average of $840 000 to Australia, substantially more than the sum required by the program at the time. (In 1989–90 the BMP accounted for $1.6 billion in transferred funds, or 43 per cent out of a total of $3.7 billion transferred by all migrants.) It also reported that business migrants were maintaining and, in some cases creating, employment opportunities in Australia. A number of principal businesses were involved in exporting goods and services, albeit on a small scale. The data generated by the MSJ Keys Young Planners study did not permit the researchers to reach any conclusions concerning the objectives relating to import replacement or the introduction of new technology. However, the report concluded that the '. . . flow of capital and entrepreneurial skill and energy into Australia under the BMP is evidently substantial

239

... and in this broader sense the survey confirms the economic value of the program' (MSJ Keys Young Planners 1990, p. 67).

DILGEA's BMP monitoring survey

Beginning 1 July 1988—after the MSJ Keys Young Planners study was commissioned—DILGEA introduced a new mechanism for monitoring the experience of BMP principal applicants *vis-à-vis* the program's objectives. All principal applicants visaed after July 1988 were given two copies of a survey form and were asked to return them to DILGEA at the 12- and 24-month marks after their arrival in Australia. Compliance with this monitoring scheme was voluntary.

The most recent monitoring survey findings are based on a response rate of 52 per cent and 50 per cent of business migrants who had been in Australia for 12 months and two years respectively at April 1992. The survey found that 44 per cent had established a business in Australia after 12 months and 58 per cent had done so after two years. The businesses employed an average of six people. About a half of all businesses were established in the services industry and over one-quarter in the export sector. Just under 30 per cent of all businesses were export-earning (DILGEA 1991c, 1992e).

Like the MSJ Keys Young Planners study, the findings of the BMP monitoring survey suggest that the BMP had been reasonably successful. However, in the view of the Joint Committee of Public Accounts (1991, p. 2), the data generated by the monitoring scheme were inadequate for the purposes of evaluating the extent to which the BMP was achieving its objectives, principally because the scheme was a voluntary one. It is important to note that at the time of the Committee's deliberations only data based on the experiences of business migrants who had been in Australia for one year was available.

Lever-Tracy et al (1991) study of Asian entrepreneurs

A recent study by Lever-Tracy et al. (1991) examined ethnic small business in the Chinese and Indian communities of Brisbane and Sydney. The study had a number of dimensions in common with Lampugnani and Holton's (1989) study of the Italian business community in Adelaide. The study included in its sample 16 business migrants. These migrants included many of the more successful and export-oriented entrepreneurs.

Although only a small number of business migrants were examined, Lever-Tracy et al. concluded that business migration should be strengthened and extended and that more assistance should be provided to new arrivals. For example, intensive courses dealing with Australian business law, company and personal taxation and business English should be made available to newly arrived business migrants.

Canada

The apparent successes of Canada's business migration program can be readily described.

The entrepreneur program

Analysis of the entrepreneur program has shown that according to their proposals, over 28 000 jobs were to be created or retained by the 4647 entrepreneur immigrants visaed between 1984 and 1986, representing an average of over six jobs per entrepreneur immigrant. More recent research indicates that the 10 964 entrepreneur immigrants visaed over the period 1987 to September 1990 intended to create or retain 55 376 jobs, representing an average figure of 5.05 jobs per entrepreneur immigrant (Nash 1987, pp. 23–29; 1991; see also Wong et al. 1985; EIC, Strategic Policy and Planning 1990, Alberta 1991).

Analysis of this program has also shown that a majority of the jobs being created or retained by entrepreneur immigrants since 1984 have been in the goods-producing sector and not in the services sector, and so have met both provincial and federal expectations of the program (Wong et al. 1985, p. 64).

Further, according to their business proposals entrepreneur immigrants intended to transfer large amounts of capital into Canada. In 1989, entrepreneur immigration was 6.6 per cent of total immigration to Canada (that is 12 761 principal applicants and dependents out of a total immigration of 19 065) while those entrepreneurs visaed in that year stated their intention to transfer a total of $3.412 billion (EIC 23 July 1990, Schedule 1; Department of External Affairs, Canada, unpublished MASENT tabulations).

The investor program

The investor immigrant program has also had some much-heralded successes. Speaking in June 1991, the Director of EIC's Immigrant Investor Program, Louis Ferguson, noted that over the period of the program's operation (January 1986 to June 1991), investment projects totalling $4.6 billion had been approved by the provinces and EIC, that to date over $1.2 billion had actually been invested in Canada by the investor immigrants; and that, as a result of this investment, a total of 7894 jobs had been created (Ferguson 1991, p. 11).

Canada has also benefited in the sense that high-risk ventures are often particularly suited to the requirements of the program. Certainly, the media are replete with examples of investment projects that are currently being developed as a result of the opportunities provided by the investor program to generate financing. For example, attempts are being made to put together the necessary consortia of investor immigrants in order to raise the estimated $1 billion needed to build a high-speed rail link between Edmonton and Calgary (*Globe and Mail* 1991: Hutchinson 1990, p. 24; Ravensbergen 1991).

A closer assessment

However, a closer evaluation of these apparent successes of Canada's business immigration program raises a number of disturbing questions. First, in terms of actual job creation, a recent major study by the ECC cautioned that much more detailed research was needed before it would be possible to say how many of the estimated 14 000 jobs that Barbara McDougall announced in 1990 had been created by investor immigrants were actually 'new' ones (ECC 1991b).

The second question relates to the regional disparities concealed within the overall achievements of the program (a problem, it will be noted below, that also existed in Australia's BMP). Thus, in 1990 82.4 per cent of all entrepreneur immigrants stated their intention to settle in Montreal, Toronto and Vancouver (EIC 1991c, Schedule 5). Even these data may understate the true patterns because significant inter-provincial migration of business immigrants occurs once they have landed in Canada. Indeed, such disparities are found in both the entrepreneur and the investor immigration programs and therefore act against one of the overall goals of Canada's immigration policy— which is, according to the 1976 *Immigration Act,* 'to foster the development of a strong and viable economy and the prosperity of all regions of Canada' (Islam 1989; Nash 1988, pp. 19–23).

Third, questions have also been raised over the nature of the investments and activities established by business migrants. The leading sectors for investor immigrant investment between 1986 and 1991 have been accommodation, food and beverage industries (with 41 per cent of investment), construction (25 per cent) and manufacturing (only 12 per cent) (Ferguson 1991, p. 10). Between 60 per cent and 80 per cent of all Hong Kong funds entering Canada are invested in real estate and a considerable proportion of this is accounted for by business immigration. The city of Toronto, for example, is currently experiencing an investment in its real estate of over Can$1 billion a year from Hong Kong. An additional problem arising from such large inflows of funds is that it has fuelled a growing anti-immigration backlash in cities such as Vancouver where, for example, it is widely believed that incoming Hong Kong money has been the cause of rapidly rising real estate prices (Nash 1991, p. 22).

Fourth, it is an unfortunate observation that Canada's business migration program has to date operated in favour of male principal applicants. Thus, government data collected over the period 1979 to 1984 indicate that fully 91 per cent of all entrepreneur immigrants to Canada were male, and only 9 per cent were female. For the years 1986 and 1987, a federal government survey indicates that 87.3 per cent of such immigrants were male and 13,6 per cent were female (EIC 1990e, p. 27; Nash 1987 p. 21). Such figures could be compared, for example, with the results of a Statistics Canada study in 1984 that showed that 27.1 per cent of the self-employed in Canada in that year were female and that this figure had increased by 20.5 per cent since 1982 (Levesque 1985, pp. 92, 99, 104). In consequence, these data suggest that the business immigration program is not supporting current Canadian trends, especially at a time when growth in female self-employment is seen as an important factor in the country's future economic growth (Levesque 1985, p. 104).

Other important problems include, first, the absence of post-arrival business advisory services to assist business immigrants and, in turn, Canada to reap the full business potential of these immigrants. A second problem concerns the lack of good publicly available data to examine thoroughly the program's economic achievements. And a third problem is the difficulties experienced in monitoring the program over time (Wong et al. 1985; EIC, 1990; Alberta 1991). Many have seen these last two factors as providing opportunities for fraud and abuse of the program (Malarek 1987, pp. 215–29; Roberts 1991).

A final impact, and one that has received little attention in the business migration literature, is the effects of business immigration upon the countries of emigration. These effects can be profound as the case of Hong Kong is beginning to illustrate (Kwong 1990; Nash 1991; Skeldon 1990–91). Analysis of these effects, however, is beyond the scope of this chapter.

Challenges to the business migration program

Several years ago Australia's BMP began to face increasing challenges to its legitimacy. Like the Canadian program, questions were raised about Australia's BMP. In Australia, however, this questioning was more intensive and extensive. It culminated in what may be described as a 'legitimation crisis' that inexorably led to the cessation of the existing program in August 1991. After a hiatus of six months the BMP was replaced by the new Independent–Business Skills category. Despite some public concerns over its business migration program, Canada has not experienced the strong negative reaction to the program seen in Australia. This section of the chapter seeks to highlight some of the major challenges encountered by both countries' programs and describe and account for the responses to these challenges.

Canada

There is by no means universal consensus in Canada concerning the merits of that country's business immigration program. While the Government has lauded the program on such grounds as its contribution to the expansion in the amount of capital entering the country (EIC 1989b, p. 1), two of the Government's investigative arms have expressed major reservations. These concern whether the program has any real impact (ECCa 1991, p. 9) and, even if it does, whether the Government can know what those impacts are (Auditor General of Canada 1990, p. 380). Other critics include journalists, commentators and academics who, over the last decade, have made a whole series of observations on the program. Therefore, the question that needs to be answered is why does the government persist in its belief in the benefits of business immigration in the face of these challenges?

In short, the thesis advanced here is that the government has become so committed to the ideology that immigrants create jobs and are good for the economy in general that it cannot allow that the selection of a group of immigrants who *prima facie* are chosen for their economic impacts can be wrong-headed or ineffective. Thus, the criticisms that have been advanced have either been trivialised, seen as inconsequential, or—because they are problems of immigration or regional development in general—ignored. This is not to say that program refinements have not been made—they have been, as previous sections have shown. However, the heart of the criticisms, that business immigration is a flawed concept, has been ignored because it is not part of the government's frame of reference.

Indeed, the current federal government has come to see immigration as a way to promote economic growth regardless of general economic circumstances. The corollary of the new policy is that immigrants must be carefully selected if they are to contribute to economic growth, because it is the current government's view that not all types of immigrant have the same potential for the economy. Thus, for example, business immigrants are increasingly favoured over refugees. Indeed, immigration and its component streams are seen, more than ever before, as strictly an economic tool—not as a demographic tool (a motive effectively ruled out by the Department of Health and Welfare's 1989 report) nor as a social or humanitarian instrument. It is this view, that the immigration of suitably selected individuals can be of benefit to the economy, that underpins the government's announcement of substantial increases in immigration levels between 1991 and 1995.

The Canadian public and the provincial governments have increasingly shared this view. Thus, a number of provinces have been keen to develop immigration agreements with Ottawa largely in order to receive more business immigrants. The complaint that the business immigration program represents 'visas for sale' is no longer heard. On the contrary, the word on the street in Vancouver now is very different from a few years ago. Business immigrants are now seen as creating wealth and 'recession-roofing' the British Columbian economy. And they are no longer criticised for driving up house prices because their involvement now guarantees condominium sales in Toronto at a time when there are no other buyers (Hiebert 1992, personal communication; Philp 1992).

In such a climate of opinion it is scarcely any wonder that the abandonment of business migration—or even a major overhaul of the program as occurred recently in Australia—is the furthest thing from the government's mind. In fact, future plans call for the expansion of business migration as a valued part of Canada's immigration program.

Australia

Although the BMP had not been heavily researched, the available empirical evidence on the effectiveness of the program painted a reasonably favourable picture. Even if this is a generous conclusion based on the small body of research, a conclusion to the contrary is unsustainable. Indeed, in Lever-Tracy's (1991) view, evaluation of the BMP is premature for at least two reasons. First, the BMP grew to sizeable numbers only in the last years of its life. Second, given the difficulties faced by the Australian economy during this period establishing a new business would be both more difficult and take considerably longer than in a more favourable economic climate.

The research findings notwithstanding, the BMP was terminated in 1991 and replaced by the Independent–Business Skills category that came into effect in early 1992. The BMP was replaced by this new category in the wake of both a Parliamentary inquiry into the BMP and DILGEA's review of the program undertaken upon the Minister's request in April 1991 while the Parliamentary inquiry was still sitting. The changes were the result of the inquiry and the review.

The inquiry by the Parliamentary Joint Committee of Public Accounts and the DILGEA review represented the culmination of a series of challenges mounted against the BMP on several fronts over a number of years.

In a recent study Nash (1988b) suggested that there were some major difficulties associated with the BMP. One had to do with the considerable regional disparity in the destinations of Australia's business migrants. Much to the chagrin of the Governments of Australia's less economically developed states and territories (South Australia, Tasmania and the Northern Territory), most business migrants had settled in the more prosperous States and major population centres, most notably Sydney. Some of the smaller States had long suggested that a form of concessional entry be introduced for people willing to settle in particular locations. Of course, this begs the question of whether those who undertake to settle in a designated location would actually remain there or could be compelled to remain against their wishes.

Another difficulty identified by Nash concerned the industries in which business migrants created their businesses. The MSJ Keys Young Planners (1990, p. 43) study found that, of the respondents who were in business at the time of the survey, about one-third were in an industry different from the industry they had planned to enter when applying to come to Australia as a business immigrant. This was problematic to the extent that the industries entered were not those desired by the Federal or State Governments. Not only did these migrants not fulfil the BMP's requirements but it also raised the possibility that the provisions of the BMP were intentionally circumvented.

But regional disparities and the entry into industries other than those initially intended or desired by the government, although perhaps problematic, did not loom very large among the factors that ultimately led to the demise of the BMP. Among the other factors at play appear to have been those of race, the alleged extensive abuses of the BMP and the BMP's supposed failure to achieve its goals to the desired extent.

With regard to the first factor, over the years the BMP became increasingly dominated by principal applicants from Asia. In 1982–83 only 25 per cent of BMP principal applicants were from Asia while in 1989–90 this proportion had reached 88 per cent. Indeed, the BMP was the migrant entry category where Asian dominance was greatest (Inglis & Wu 1992, p. 6). (The fact that such applicants came largely from one region appeared to 'disturb' the Joint Committee which examined the BMP (see below) (Easson, 1992.) Add to this a public perception that the BMP represented a means for the wealthy to 'buy their way' into Australia, then the seeds of resentment were well sown.

Another major challenge to the BMP came from those concerned that it had succumbed to a range of abuses. For example, concern was expressed that some sub-agents had been involved in supplying BMP applicants with forged documents, including police clearances (Lever-Tracy 1991). The fact that the Australian Migration Consultants Association (now known as the Migration Institute of Australia) called for the licensing of agents to protect clients and the public suggests that at least some agents were, in fact, engaged in unethical practices (Lague 1991). There were further allegations of abuse of the BMP involving some principal applicants who, after their arrival, had either returned overseas the monies they had brought into Australia or, worse still, allowed others to use the monies sent off-shore to establish eligibility for the BMP. Still other allegations of abuse included claims that the BMP had fostered tax rorts and facilitated the spread of Asian criminal Triads to the West.

There were also accusations of other questionable practices. Thus, not only was the BMP criticised for serving as a means for the rich to buy permanent residence in Australia but it was also criticised on the grounds that many principal applicants had no intention at all or only in the longer term (after 1997 for those from Hong Kong) of setting up a business (*Border Morning Mail*, 10 November 1990, p. 27). The phenomenon of the commuting 'astronaut' (applicants who settle their families in Australia but continued to conduct their businesses in their home country and periodically fly back to Australia for brief visits) was seen as an indicator that the BMP was not reaching its objectives (Ellingsen 1990). And DILGEA came in for criticisms for failing to closely follow up and monitor the scheme.

What of the evidence to sustain these criticisms? We have already referred to the research findings on the effectiveness of the BMP. What of the supposed abuses? Little evidence appears to support the contentions of abuse. Thus, for example, during 1990–91 51 cases of alleged BMP fraud were referred to the compliance arm of DILGEA. Thirty-eight investigations were launched and 19 were resolved during 1990–91. As a result two business migrants (and their families) had their resident re-entry visas cancelled (for recycling funds or submitting forged documents with the BMP visa application), two BMP agents were referred for cancellation, and three business migrants were declared illegal entrants. In 12 cases, no evidence of illegality was found (DILGEA 1991a, p. 90). This result notwithstanding, in 1991–92 a high priority of the 16 additional staff allocated to DILGEA's intelligence/investigation function was to identify those attempting to circumvent the BMP (DILGEA 1991c, p. 8).

The criticisms of the BMP were widely aired in the press. Indeed, the media's coverage of the BMP was disproportionate to the numbers entering Australia under this migration category. The source of much media attention was the inquiry into the BMP by the Australian Parliament's Joint Committee of Public Accounts. The inquiry provided a forum for the public airing of opposition to the BMP and DILGEA's management of the program (Hazeldine 1991). Consequently, the media reports emanating from the inquiry were overwhelmingly negative.

The Report of the Joint Committee of Public Accounts

The purpose of the Joint Committee's inquiry into the BMP was not to question the need for an entry category for business immigrants but rather to examine the ability of the BMP to achieve its economic objectives.

The Joint Committee's inquiry into the BMP began in a climate of growing concern about this migration category. However, the inquiry was most directly precipitated by criticisms made by the Auditor-General in 1988 and 1989 in his reports to the Parliament. The BMP was criticised on three grounds: (1) its objectives were broad, which made any performance assessment difficult; (2) the performance of accredited agents under the AAS was not monitored; and (3) the post-settlement review of the activities of business migrants was inadequate. The audit report concluded that DILGEA needed to improve its oversight of the BMP (The Parliament of the Commonwealth of Australia 1991, p. 15).

The Joint Committee tabled its report in Parliament on 21 June 1991. The Joint Committee supported the continued entry into Australia of people with business and entrepreneurial skills as part of the migration program but recommended that an entry category based on the assessment of business skills should be developed to replace the BMP. However, such assessment would no longer be undertaken by accredited agents. Indeed, the Joint Committee recommended the abolition of the AAS as this scheme made the BMP vulnerable to abuse.

The Joint Committee also investigated the extent to which DILGEA screening procedures were adequate to reveal any links between BMP applicants and organised crime and whether there was any evidence of an alleged association between organised crime and the BMP. The Joint Committee concluded that the BMP had not been the subject of a large scale assault by organised criminal groups, that there were only a limited number of cases of penetration of the BMP by identified criminals but that the 'potential' exists for criminal abuse of the BMP. The Joint Committee therefore recommended an investigation of the circumstances surrounding these cases with a view to improving screening procedures.

The Joint Committee found some evidence of money recycling (the transfer of capital into Australia for the purposes of qualifying for a BMP visa and then transferring it back to the migrant's country of origin) but could not determine its extent. Since November 1989, however, DILGEA has introduced procedures (the BMP Declaration, examination of bank accounts, etc) which the Joint Committee viewed as adequate for the purposes of deterring recycling.

Other recommendations of the Joint Committee focused upon the future monitoring of business migration and post-settlement advisory services for future business migrants.

Finally, the Joint Committee made several recommendations concerning 'business skills based' migration, the primary purpose of which would be the actual establishment of businesses in Australia.

The criticisms of the BMP together with the report of the Joint Committee resulted in a loss of public trust in the program. In an environment in which immigration policy in general was the subject of mistrust and failing consensus some action had to be taken to address the BMP's perceived or, perhaps more accurately, 'constructed' shortcomings. Hence the termination of the BMP and its replacement with the Independent–Business Skills category.

In announcing the new category of business skills migrants, the Minister for Immigration also foreshadowed the introduction of two legislative changes. The first would make participation in the business skills category monitoring system mandatory. The second would give the Minister the power to cancel the status of business skills migrants if they had not made a genuine effort within the first three years of their arrival to meet the objectives of the business skills category.

It is of interest to note in relation to the second foreshadowed legislative change that the Joint Committee's report did not recommend the introduction of conditional visas for BMP principal applicants, an approach employed in Canada and also adopted by the United States under the 'New Investor' provisions of the US *Immigration Act* of 1990. Failure to comply with the various conditions of these provisions can result in deportation from the United States and substantial penalties (Garonski 1991). The foreshadowed legislation seeks to give the Minister for Immigration the power to cancel residence status (where business skill migrants have not gone into businesses of the kind expected by the objectives of the category, or who have made no genuine effort to do so) but without making all business skills visas conditional.

The foregoing analysis underscores an interesting difference between Australia and Canada in their responses to the challenges to their business migration programs. In Australia, in the wake of the FitzGerald Report of 1988, immigrant selection had become increasingly focused on those who would bring the greatest economic benefits. This consideration, plus the legitimation crisis referred to above, played an important part in the replacement of the BMP with a much more delimited approach to business migration. (Indeed, the first nine months of the new Independent–Business Skills migration category witnessed the virtual collapse of business migration to Australia with a mere 100 potential immigrants world-wide applying for admission (Lauge 1992).) In the case of Canada, where immigrant selection had become similarly economically focused, the response to the challenges to business migration was to essentially ignore them and provide continued support for the existing program.

Lessons

What are some of the policy-relevant lessons to be learnt from the experiences of business migration in Australia and Canada? It is possible to identify at least five lessons.

1 A business migration program, like other migration categories, must ensure that it operates in a way which does not undermine, or appear to undermine, the sovereignty of the state over its borders. To the extent that a migration category comes to be perceived as a means of 'buying your way' into a country (in the case of the BMP, a process seen as aided and abetted by accredited agents), it conveys to the public an image of a program that is serving to undermine the state's control over is national borders. It would appear, therefore, that a *sine qua non* of public support for an immigration program and/or its constituent categories is that the integrity of national borders is maintained or at least seen to be maintained.

2 Another lesson is that any migration category that is seen as very special or open only to a privileged minority can expect to face public questioning. In Australia the notion of business migration appears to have been anathema to many. While migration for family reunion purposes and for economic advancement are generally seen as valid reasons for being admitted, entry by well-to-do individuals who bring substantial capital with them to set up businesses seems to go against the psychological grain of many people. It is almost as if business migrants, because of their 'wealth,' are seen as undeserving of admission while others, arguably 'battlers' in Australian parlance, have a more legitimate claim for admission.

Thus, at least in countries like Australia where cutting down 'tall poppies' seems to be so much a part of the national culture, business migration programs need to be more publicly accountable, that is, subject to close and mandatory monitoring and control. (And this despite the fact that, compared to migrants entering under other migration categories, BMP applicants and principal applicants were more carefully screened and more closely monitored.) This seems to be especially true in an environment where there have been changes in relevant socioeconomic conditions (for example, a deterioration in the economic climate) that make achieving the goals of the category, and hence maintaining support for it, more difficult (Sabatier & Mazmanian 1979).

3 Yet a third lesson appears to be that when the special or privileged minority is also a visible minority issues of race, at least to some degree, may begin to loom in debates over the program. Australia's historical antipathy towards Asians reared its head during the course of the delegitimation of the BMP. In a healthier economic climate, or at least where business migrants are still seen as making an economic contribution notwithstanding the poor state of the economy (as in Vancouver and Toronto), the issue of race seems much less likely to manifest itself.

4 It has been long recognised among students of public policy that policy implementation is a difficult task at the best of times. It

becomes even more difficult when there is a breakdown in consensus among the key actors, viz., Government Ministers and senior public servants and organised interest groups such as labour unions, agents, and so on (Pressman & Wildavsky 1979). The erosion of support for the program can be fatal unless the strongest actor—Government—has a *very* strong commitment to the program (as is the case in Canadian government's support for business migration). Where the government's support for its program starts to waver, the situation appears to be very ripe for program detractors to feed into the delegitimation of a program.

5 Business migration programs must actively encourage the application and selection of far greater numbers of female business people. If both countries' business migration programs are to avoid further public concern (in this case, over gender bias) and encourage successful entrepreneurs, then far greater emphasis must be placed on female business migrants than is currently the case.

In Australia and Canada business migration, perhaps in ways unlike the other migration categories of these two countries, has been the lightning rod for both public approval and opprobrium and clearly illustrates the effects of both careful policy decisions and broader government hopes for immigration.

As we have seen, the business migration programs of both countries have had difficulties. Indeed, it could be argued that these might be the result of inherent flaws in their design. Thus, not only are such programs aimed at only one group in society but they also concentrate the difficulties found in the other, more general categories of immigration. (The latter is particularly seen, for example, in the problem of regional disparities.) These problems cannot be easily solved at the program level. The benefits of business migration, in terms of investment, know-how and job creation, seem obvious. But in many ways they can also be illusory (as we have suggested above). Although insufficient by itself, the illusion can be difficult to dispel in the absence of a sizeable body of sound research. Moreover, the benefits of business migration sometimes can only be won at very great political cost to the governments concerned. This must be the greatest disadvantage of such programs, as the Australian case well illustrates. Whether the risk of economic gain is worth the political price is perhaps the biggest question that any country must answer when contemplating the utility of business migration.

PART FOUR

Refugee Policy Implementation

CHAPTER 9

Overseas Refugee Policy

Howard Adelman and David Cox

Introduction

The overseas refugee policies of both Australia and Canada are characterised by two very different concerns. On the one hand, refugee initiatives demonstrate compassion and commitment. On the other hand, both countries are fearful that hordes of refugees will head their way, with the result that the management of immigration and refugee programs will spin out of control.

> (M)ore people will be pressing to come to Canada, using our refugee claim route if they can. The proportion of non-European applicants will rise, perpetuated by the extended family system. If tensions in our cities increase, and if much stronger control becomes necessary, our liberal self-image, itself a unifying factor, may be damaged. (Shenstone 1992, p. ii).

Australians share the belief that large numbers of economic migrants may use the refugee system to gain entry. 'Some of these claimants have fled from countries where they have experienced persecution or violation of their human rights. Others, however, have been motivated to leave their home countries because of natural disaster or lack of opportunities to improve their lives' (DILGEA, 1992b).

Part of the reason for the difficulty in distinguishing economic migrants and refugees is that the root causes are perceived to be interconnected.

The distinction between economic and political migrants is tending to break down under pressure of numbers. The ultimate causes of migration pressure—economic underdevelopment, rapid population growth, and political oppression—are all interlocking and react on one another to produce desperate situations which millions seek to escape by moving (Shenstone 1992, p. 20).

As Dr Robyn Groves, External Affairs Officer of UNHCR, depicted the situation in an address to the Australian National Forum on Refugees in 1992, 'refugees are now one element in a mass movement phenomenon which sees up to 80 million people on the move in the world at any one time' (*Welcome Stranger* 1992, p. 25).

Further, what begins as a refugee movement may evolve into one which becomes primarily economic, as in the case of the flight of the Vietnamese. 'The question that began to arise was whether the Vietnamese asylum-seekers were refugees or economic migrants, the latter category implying that they were leaving for reasons of personal inconvenience. While it was clear that some were departing because of the economic conditions in Vietnam, there was much debate over whether they were still refugees' (Stern 1991, p. iii).

Thus, the positive humanitarian outreach, on the one hand, and the restrictive defensive approach, on the other hand, may be perceived as two very different responses to two very different but intermixed movements. However, we are concerned with situations when both approaches are applicable to refugees. The duality we refer to is one where the state attempts to protect refugees and, at the same time, exercise management controls which intentionally restrict the number of asylum cases arriving on their doorsteps, *whether those asylum seekers are or are not genuine refugees*. The same individuals may be subject to both a compassionate concern and restrictive controls. Legislation in both countries specifically requires a compassionate response to refugees for whom Australia and Canada accept responsibility. On the other hand, as sovereign states, both countries want to control whom they permit to enter their respective countries. The split in the approach may, in fact, have nothing to do with the motives individuals have for leaving their home country. The mandate of both countries requires each to be both facilitative *and* exclusive.

Government officials argue that both approaches can be complementary. We argue that they can be and often are antithetical, the direct result of attempting to achieve two very different and often contrary goals through mechanisms that overlap. The antithetical character is substantive and not merely related to the process of decision making. Examining the process of decision making may lead an observer to what we believe is an erroneous conclusion—that the consultative process for determining policy is merely a device for hegemonic manipulation. In other words, humanitarianism is considered a camouflage to manipulate public opinion to ensure that the mandarins retain control over who can and who cannot enter the respective countries. This chapter adopts the thesis that both the humanitarian and control factors are present as motivating factors and are sometimes in conflict. Civil servants attempt to implement public policy ostensibly designed to serve the public good; humanitarianism is not just a rhetorical tool to manipulate public opinion so they can retain power.

Overseas refugee policy intersects with both immigration and foreign policy. While some areas of refugee policy directly overlap with the immigration area—such as the exercise of entry controls overseas as in the imposition of visa controls and carrier sanctions, or in the selection of refugees overseas on humanitarian grounds—other areas, such as overseas aid or international co-operation to prevent refugee flows, have little to do with immigration but a great deal to do with foreign policy.

> There are vast areas of refugee policy that have nothing to do with immigration . . . Refugee policies that do not have a direct effect on immigration issues have a largely external impact, that is, they deal with providing humanitarian aid to refugees abroad who will remain abroad . . . including both multilateral and bilateral contacts that deal with root causes of refugee problems; the improvement of human rights observance, and so forth. Arrangements for voluntary repatriation to other countries of externally based refugee populations also have virtually no impact on immigration policies. I would also place in this category, aid programs directed toward refugee relief, including both short term assistance that takes care of people in the aftermath of a mass exodus and also longer term programs that deal with more substantial needs such as housing and medical care, and education. Entire debates and seminars and international conferences on issues such as enclaves, burden sharing and root causes can certainly take place without discussing immigration (Girard 1991, p. 90).

In the foreign policy area, both countries can be said to be motivated by 'confident idealism' or 'constructive internationalism', to use Canadian foreign policy terminology. In an address to an Australian National Forum on refugees in June of 1992, Senator Jim McKiernan, representing the Prime Minister, characterised Australian initiatives in Cambodia and involvement in the Comprehensive Plan of Action with respect to the Vietnamese refugees in precisely this way (*Welcome Stranger* 1992, pp. 13–14). However, many of the very same actions can be characterised as self-defence mechanisms to avoid international disorder and prevent hordes of desperate people swarming onto the shores of both countries. The antithesis not only veers between control and compassion and between self-defence mechanisms and activist constructive idealism, but between reactive responses and activist interventionism. These overlaps can be deplored (foreign policy dictates refugee intakes and even immigration policy—see Keely & Wrigley 1990). They can also be welcomed as a method of attacking root causes.

Immigration may be regarded as something entirely separate from refugee policy. Refugees can also be considered as a sub-category of migration. And, third, immigration can be considered as a necessary ingredient to the rational operation of refugee policy. Mrs Sadako Ogata, the High Commissioner for Refugees, has taken all three perspectives. 'An aggravating feature of the changing reality has been the growing movement of refugees from their regions of origin to Europe and North America, as part—sometimes even a minority—of a larger movement of migrants escaping poverty'. Mrs Ogata, in the same speech, went out of her way 'to emphasise that migrants and refugees are distinct categories, requiring different responses' (Ogata 1991, p. 31). Mrs Ogata has also urged the European countries to follow the Canadian and American examples (and, by implication, that of Australia) and integrate refugee policy into an overall immigration program because some asylum seekers are really just immigrants using the asylum process because of lack of an immigration entrée. 'European countries must examine the possible adoption of immigration policies ... A judicious mixture of asylum and migration opportunities would be important' (1992, pp. 6–7). It is this tension that emerges primarily in the issue of the bureaucratic mechanisms instituted to control migration from overseas and the obligation to protect refugees that brings this issue to the fore.

In the overlap with immigration, overseas controls need not be perceived or presented as a mechanism to keep people away. Control efforts can be presented as an effort to permit aid to go to those who need it most desperately rather than to the very few who make it to Western shores and have to be processed through a very expensive refugee determination system.

Control efforts can be presented also as an insufficient defensive measure; ostensibly altruistic humanitarian aid may be regarded as an effort to prevent millions from invading the relative tranquillity of the West. In a world of easy transportation and access to communications (which make the disparities between the rich and poor obvious to everyone) and of integrated economics, regional disparities and increasing population flows, migration can be seen as a critical factor of foreign policy. A combination of multilateral trade initiatives, aid, debt forgiveness and economic restructuring may be seen not as altruistic gestures, but as defensive ones to reduce migratory flows in the long run (Appleyard 1991).

> Migration flows have become a major world concern; they include 17 million refugees, perhaps 20 million internally displaced, and millions more seeking to find a better life. Specific flows are idiosyncratic; migrants go to where co-nationals happen to have established a beachhead, and where the easiest entry and best benefits are. But it is only a question of time before most of the developing world becomes a source of migration pressure on the countries of the North. Among the latter, the distinction is breaking down between traditional countries of immigration, and others. Much migration is now irregular; stay rates of those rejected are high everywhere, and costs of maintenance and control are enormous. Racist reactions in Europe are increasing. Meetings on migration and refugees have mushroomed, so far with little result. Governments are beginning to recognise that control measures alone do not suffice, and that a broader approach is needed, but agreement is still lacking on its nature (Shenstone 1992, p. ii).

We take the dualism between humanitarianism and controls as a given rather than an issue to be applauded, adjudicated or criticised. Our concern is to depict how it is expressed, often in contradictory or half-hearted actions in five areas of overseas refugee policy:

1 emergency and long term aid;
2 international intervention;
3 bilateral, multilateral and international mechanisms for co-ordination;
4 unilateral legal and bureaucratic mechanisms such as visa controls and carrier sanctions to limit access to entry; and
5 special programs for and direct assistance to refugees overseas to facilitate their coming to Australia and Canada.

The five areas are not as distinct as indicated above. For example, the Comprehensive Plan of Action (CPA) in dealing with the Vietnamese refugee problem is one of overseas aid, co-ordinated international action, a multilateral initiative, a mechanism of orderly control on the movement of people in order to inhibit other kinds of irregular movement, as well as a means of selecting refugees for resettlement in Australia and Canada. The very same arrangement covers all five of the areas above. Nevertheless, in spite of such overlaps, we will explore this policy area under five distinct headings and discuss programs which overlap some of the areas under the heading we believe most appropriate.

Aid

Overseas aid can be subdivided into four sub-categories: emergency aid (including food transfers); institutional aid, such as support for the UNHCR, UNRWA, UNICEF, etc.; program aid, such as assistance for repatriation of refugees; and, finally, development aid which is sometimes directed at long term assistance to refugees to enable them to become self-sufficient.

Unfortunately, neither Australia nor Canada disaggregates its statistics on overseas aid to collect together all the data on aid directed solely at refugees. In the case of some of this assistance, such as in the area of development, this is difficult to do. In general, Australia and Canada occupy the second run of foreign aid givers, below the Scandinavian countries. Per capita, Australia and Canada give about 60 per cent of the aid provided by the Scandinavian states, but well above the third ranked group which includes the United States of America.

Australia contributed US$576 583 in 1990–91 to non-government organisations (NGOs) for emergency relief and assistance to refugees and displaced persons. In the special programs category, Australia, for example, contributed US$22 million of a total US$109 million for the Cambodian refugee reintegration program, including both interim emergency relief and long-term reconstruction, using CARE Australia as the key NGO to help in transportation and logistics. The Canadian International Development Agency (CIDA) responded favourably to an appeal by the Office of the United Nations High Commissioner for Refugees by providing US$340 000 for the construction of housing in Turkey for Kurdish refugees from Iraq (CIDA News Release, No. 90–06, 12 February 1990; see also *Canadian International Relations Chronicle: January–March 1990*, External Affairs, p. 23.) CIDA offered US$1.2 million to three organisations undertaking emergency relief in Mozambique—UNICEF, ICRC and a consortium of Canadian NGOs (CIDA News Release, No. 90–12, 13 March 1990). The donations totalled over US$1.5 million for these two emergency refugee aid projects alone. In comparison, the United States Administration FY93 proposal for 1992 sought $20 million in total for Emergency Refugee and Migration Assistance (ERMA).

This aid is inseparable from the effort to deter refugee claimants. Four Cambodians, who arrived directly in Australia, were induced to withdraw their refugee claims and were returned to Phnom Penh by air, with Australia not only paying the air fare, but also a small stipend for rehabilitation. This event was explicitly connected to the Australian assistance for Cambodian reintegration through CARE Australia (DILGEA, 1992b, p. 9).

However, while providing emergency aid, and while providing strong support to international and NGO aid agencies helping refugees, there is no clear policy statement that Australia or Canada supports the creation of a UN humanitarian emergency fund, stockpiling basic relief supplies around the world, and a standby pool of international emergency experts intended to allow the UN to become more responsive to emergency aid demands. Both Australia and Canada still operate their emergency aid in a reactive rather than a proactive prepared mode.

Australia and Canada each provides institutional aid to refugee specific organisations as well as other international agencies and NGOs that assist refugees. For example, the UNHCR total 1992 appeal was $373 million for basic care and maintenance for 17 million refugees and $568 million for special programs for a total of $941 million. In 1991, Canada contributed $35 million, an increase of more than 50 per cent over 1990.

Australian institutional aid programs totalled almost A$31 million for 1991. They were divided as shown in Table 9.1, in comparison to the Canadian assistance:

Both countries also contributed to special programs for refugee assistance. For example, of the approximately twenty refugee repatriation programs underway worldwide, Canada contributed to most of them. In 1989 Canada provided a grant of Can$5 million to the UNHCR to help implement the Comprehensive Plan of Action for Indochinese Refugees, an amount that grew to Can$8.4 million over the three-year period by 1991, representing 3 per cent of the total contributed.

Table 9.1 Institutional aid program, 1990–91

	Australia (A$)	(US$)	Canada (US$)
United Nations High Commission for Refugees (admin. budget)	10 660 440	8 373 608	7 339 850
United Nations Relief and Works Agency	3 000 000	2 356 453	8 727 527
United Nations Border Relief Organisation	1 564 390	1 228 804	1 658 230
World Food Program	10 095 453	7 929 819	135 276 663
International Organisation for Migration	741 000	2 000 000	1 745 505
International Committee for the Red Cross	4 900 000	3 848 873	15 708 675
Totals	30 961 283	24 319 601	170 456 450

In addition to emergency aid, institutional aid and aid targeted for specific refugee programs, both countries provide long-term development assistance, some of which is directly applicable to relieving countries suffering from civil wars, large numbers of internally displaced as well as refugees undergoing repatriation and reintegration. This is the case of Canadian aid in Central America.

> By fiscal year 1987/88, total direct aid to the region had reached Can$55.1 million (US$47.4). Although still a modest amount, this represented a substantial increase: in nominal terms it was more than double the Can$22.1 million of 1981/82; in real terms (taking inflation into account) the increase was much less. Government-to-government aid to Costa Rica and Nicaragua—Central America's most democratic societies, with political systems encouraging equitable development and popular participation—increased most rapidly . . . Most disturbingly, however, Canadian ODA to the region during fiscal 1988/89 actually declined, to Can$50.7 million from the Can$55.1 million of 1987/88. Moreover, by mid-1989 the Canadian government was charting dramatic cutbacks in ODA that would erode the commitment made by the secretary of state. (North 1990, p. 97).

The Central American aid constituted less than 3 per cent of overseas development aid on average.

Australia concentrated its efforts on areas closer to home—such as relief assistance for 270 000 Muslim Burmese refugees along the

Bangladesh border. Australia played a particularly active role in Cambodia.

However, the assessment of the roles of both countries is mixed. Although the picture over time is uneven, nevertheless, the aid provided by both countries is relatively generous on a comparative basis. Neither Canada nor Australia ever implemented the principle of additionality enunciated at ICARA II, the African Conference organised for refugee assistance in that continent. 'Additionality' meant that countries should not only assist refugees but ensure that the assistance was over and above normal development aid as well as targeted to ensure that the local population in refugee receiving areas would be beneficiaries of assistance as well. If the overall assistance declined rather than increased when refugees were being repatriated, this suggests not only that the principle of additionality was not being followed, but overseas aid for development, and for refugees in particular, was in decline.

There have always been explanations offered for resistance to increasing aid. As a case in point, the donors at ICARA II objected to the poor project design advanced as part of the additionality concept, noting, for example, that hospital facilities were located at long distance from the refugee camps and in close proximity to the country's army bases. Additionality was perceived as a cover in many cases for diverting aid from refugees.

Lisa North (1990, p. 8) contends that Canadian aid for Latin America was given as a response to public pressure. Others see overseas aid as motivated primarily or even solely by humanitarian motives on the part of the government. Still others argue that such assistance constitutes a form of insurance and self-protection. Repatriation and local integration efforts helped minimise the pressures for resettlement and the numbers pursuing asylum in First World countries. 'Canada favours the development of an international strategy to deal with the linkage between refugee, asylum-seeker and irregular migrant flows' (Shannon 1991, p. 1).

But Canada has been inconsistent in linking foreign policy with respect to refugees and overseas aid. 'Ottawa was forced by considerations of human rights and the physical security of its personnel to suspend bilateral aid to El Salvador in November 1981 . . . Aid was restored in 1985 and then suspended again in November 1989 as the civil war exploded once again with renewed ferocity' (Foster 1990, p. 204). Thus, Canada identified El Salvador as one of only two countries belonging to the Political Prisoners and Oppressed Persons Designated Class. But Canada also suspended its moratorium on deportations to El Salvador in 1987 and did not renew the suspension when the abuses increased enormously in the latter part of the 1980s.

International intervention

The explicit endorsement of humanitarian military intervention on the sovereign territory of another state entails different degrees of involvement beyond the non-military intervention to provide humanitarian aid without permission of the state: (a) passive military intervention to protect relief supplies and relief workers (Yugoslavia); (b) active military intervention to protect relief supplies and relief workers (Somalia); and (c) active military intervention to protect refugees in flight and provide safe havens (Kurds).

Senator Robert Hill, Leader of the Opposition in the Senate of Australia, explicitly endorsed humanitarian intervention.

> We have also seen more ambitious attempts by the world community in exploring internal intervention, contrary to the traditional principle of non-interference in the domestic affairs of states. The international community found the treatment of the Kurds in Iraq so horrendous that it was prepared to intervene to provide humanitarian assistance, even without Iraqi agreement. Similarly, the international community was prepared to send peacekeepers to Yugoslavia without invitation. The consequences of the communal fighting were so horrific that they demanded an international response. Whilst respect for state sovereignty remains critical to a stable world order, the responsibility of states to their own citizens in circumstances of abuse has now been accepted as something for which states must answer to the wider international community—*and it is a development* which I commend (*Welcome Stranger* 1992, pp. 21–22).

Hill endorsed humanitarian intervention on the grounds of internal human rights abuses and not just to counteract massive outflows of refugees. The Australian Government, in its plenary statement to EXCOM in 1992, endorsed these sentiments. Referring to UNHCR's role in the former Yugoslavia, it went on to comment 'In this and other recent situations UNHCR has moved away from its traditional role as an organisation narrowly concerned with the "correct" application of the 1951 convention and issues of protection, to that of an international humanitarian organisation with a heavy operational focus.' While the attention of the government has been on assistance for massive repatriation efforts, such as the leading role Australia is playing in the peace efforts and repatriation of Cambodian refugees along the Thai border and in Australia's very active role in the Comprehensive Plan of Action directed at repatriation or resettlement of the remaining Vietnamese and Laotian refugees, it has contributed to the recent initiatives in Somalia.

Gerald Shannon, the Canadian Ambassador and Permanent Representative to the United Nations, in his address to the Plenary Session of the 42nd Executive Committee of the UNHCR in Geneva on 7 October 1991, drew a clear linkage not only between aid and the need to limit asylum flows, but explicitly with the issue of the many ways Western countries intervene to attack the causes of refugee flows. International intervention goes beyond the activities which encourage the protection of human rights in the countries so they will not produce refugees, such as diplomatic activity in the form of statements of general principles, publicly or privately expressed objections to the actions of other states, and specific actions, such as boycotts, voting in international bodies and technical assistance in peace negotiations. International humanitarian intervention refers to peace-keeping activities such as sending military forces to such hot spots as Sarajevo and military intervention as in Iraq and Somalia.

Though Ambassador Shannon referred to 'root causes', he stressed material ones—poverty and the environment—that are not the direct causes of most refugee flows. One root cause, ethnic conflict (as in the former Yugoslavia) was not even mentioned by Shannon. This may have been because, thus far at least, the Western world has not demonstrated any real capacity or strategy to deal with this rising source of refugee flows.

This omission aside, both Australian and Canadian spokespersons are correct in stressing the political/military dimension of the refugee issue which must be addressed by states and international agencies. This theme was echoed by the High Commissioner for Refugees herself. In an address, Mrs Ogata (1991, p. 32) stated that:

> the refugee issue must not be seen only as a matter for humanitarian agencies of the United Nations but also as a political problem which must be placed in the mainstream of the international agenda as a potential threat to international peace and security. The Security Council Resolution 688 on Iraq created an historical precedent by finally acknowledging the link between human rights, refugees and international peace.

The lesson Canada drew from the Gulf War was not the need to adopt a policy of humanitarian military intervention, but the need for more UN co-ordination of relief efforts as indicated by the difficulties in coping with the hundreds of thousands displaced by the initial Iraqi invasion of Kuwait. 'The Gulf War has also made it clear that there is a need for greater co-ordination in the responses of the various UN agencies to the displacement of persons' (Shannon 1991, p. 3). The Honourable Barbara McDougall, Canada's Secretary of State for External Affairs, at the UN General Assembly on 25 September 1991, called for the appointment of a senior official for humanitarian relief and disaster assistance to be given the mandate and the resources to effectively co-ordinate international responses to disaster with dispatch and compassion. In February of 1992, Jan Eliassen, with the support of Australia and Canada, was appointed as the UN's Under-Secretary General for Humanitarian Affairs responsible for precisely this type of co-ordination.

Canada did lobby 'the UNHCR to provide better protection for refugees in camps in Honduras and Mexico' (Arbour, cited in North 1990, p. 158). Canadian forces, in the forefront in such hot spots as Sarajevo as the leading edge of an international peace-keeping force, were not active in the military protection given to the Kurdish refugees. Further, General Mackensie, the leader of the Canadian forces in former Yugoslavia, vociferously advocated a non-active role for the Canadian military in Bosnia-Herzegovina. Canada's political foreign policy was cautious in another respect. While Canada opposed military intervention in regional disputes in general and in the former Yugoslavia in particular (though participated when Iraq invaded and annexed Kuwait), and gave explicit support to peace processes which would benefit the Balkans and prevent further refugee flows, Canada also avoided any explicit criticism of the United States military intervention of the opposite variety, namely US support to rebels in Central America.

As the Canadian Prime Minister once stated in bold generalities, 'We do not approve of any country supplying arms to any faction in the area ... whoever the third party may be, and regardless of its legitimate interests in the area' (Address to Inter-American Press Association, Vancouver, 15 September, 1986). Canada was in the forefront in promoting peace, not only by its generous offers of peace-keeping forces throughout the world, but in the direct assistance provided to witnesses for democratic processes, as in the election in Namibia and the refugee repatriation process underway there, and in technical assistance as well.

Australia has also become more active in the peace-keeping area in recent years, as demonstrated in Cambodia and Somalia. Moreover, some Australians have also been more critical of both the Europeans for their resistance to resettling former Yugoslav refugees and the Americans for turning back Haitian boat people without giving them an opportunity to establish whether they were Convention refugees. 'We are concerned that European states are now putting up barriers to the last wave of human misery forced out of the former Yugoslavia. We were concerned at the United States returning Haitian refugees, apparently without giving them the chance to apply for asylum' (Senator Hill *Welcome Stranger*, 1992, p. 22).

Thus, while Australians and Canadians may be critical, either explicitly or implicitly, of the failure of other states to protect refugees, and while both countries expend their prime effort to prevent refugee flows by drawing a direct link between human rights observance and foreign aid and foreign policy, neither country was consistent in applying the criticism to themselves. For example, Australia has taken no substantive political or military initiatives with respect to the 270 000 Muslim Burmese refugees on the Bangladesh border. Both countries, in comparison to the United States, exhibit great caution in adopting the new policy of humanitarian intervention.

Bilateral, multilateral and international co-ordination

In the effort to attack root causes as well as to develop co-ordinated mechanisms for dealing with flows of refugees and irregular movements, a multi-pronged approach was initiated to deal with refugees and migrants as well as the situations which gave rise to them. In a 1992 statement published by the Canadian Employment and Immigration Commission (EIC), international co-operation was endorsed, 'both to maintain effective national immigration policies and to address root causes', and to that end endorsed 'international harmonisation and co-operation, with respect to migration policies ... to achieve better management of international immigration levels' and to discourage 'asylum-shopping' (EIC 1992e, p. 5).

These approaches were enunciated the year before by the UN High Commissioner.

There is a growing recognition of the need for a broad response, which takes into account the totality of the refugee problem from its root causes to its solution, and addresses the continuum of refugee flows from exodus and relief to return and integration. I am convinced that it is only through such a comprehensive approach which includes all parties and all aspects of the problem that an effective strategy can be developed which recognises the close relationship between human rights, economic development, peace building and population displacement. This was the approach adopted by the International Conference on Central American Refugees . . . [CIREFCA] led generally to the strengthening of protection for refugees in the region. On the other hand, the durability of the solutions depends on the extent to which refugee aid can be married to development assistance and, more importantly, to the overall resolution of the complex economic and social problems facing the Central American countries (Ogata 1991).

Australia, at the 63rd annual meeting of the International Organisation for Migration (IOM) in Geneva in November of 1991 reiterated the same theme, that current global events require a co-ordinated and quick response and that there is a need to develop a specific range of harmonised and streamlined procedures for services to cope with the ever increasing movement of peoples in the world. Australia's 1991 Refugee Review strongly endorsed the need for a co-ordinated and speedy response internationally, and for national mechanisms to ensure Australia's participation within them (National Population Council 1991b, p. 54).

These co-operative efforts were sometimes regionally based, as in CIREFCA or the CPA for Vietnamese refugees or the Cambodian peace and refugee repatriation effort. At other times they involved multilateral discussions aimed at co-ordination among the First World refugee-receiving countries, such as in the multilateral Informal Consultations among sixteen western states, the trilateral American, Canadian and Mexican talks and the bilateral US–Canada talks. They all had somewhat overlapping but different agendas.

For example, in contrast to CIREFCA, 'the Comprehensive Plan of Action or CPA in Southeast Asia was fashioned by the need to tackle a mixed movement of migrants and refugees within a very complex political context' (Ogata 1991, p. 33). Put more succinctly, the CPA was overtly designed to deter the outflow of refugees from Vietnam, assisting those needing (not desiring) repatriation while ostensibly maintaining obligations to refugees in accordance with the International Convention. The Memorandum of Agreement signed between UNHCR and Vietnam in December of 1988 recognised the need for economic assistance for repatriation and reintegration of asylum-seekers returning to Vietnam. The 1989 International Conference on Indo-Chinese Refugees adopted the CPA explicitly to deter clandestine departures while promoting the Orderly Departure Program and protecting the first asylum principle and humane treatment of asylum-seekers. Refugee determination procedures were initiated with many countries agreeing in advance to resettle those refugees who were assessed as meeting the Convention requirements, but only those refugees. Rejected claimants were to be repatriated. In addition, special procedures were instituted for unaccompanied minors and other special vulnerable groups.

What were the Australian and Canadian responses to the CPA? Of the 52 000 Vietnamese to be resettled under the terms of the CPA, Canada accepted 20 per cent of the cases, second only to the USA in the numbers resettled (Stern 1991). On the other hand, only 55 of the 620 children recommended for resettlement under the unaccompanied minors program have actually been resettled. Canada did not take one in spite of its early successes and the studies on how to improve the program. Australia agreed to admit about the same numbers as Canada. In fact, Australia has already resettled the 11 000 Laotians and Vietnamese who arrived before the specified dates of 1988 and 1989 as agreed at the 1989 International Conference on Indo-Chinese Refugees. Australia also funds the special informational program and the counsellors working in the camps in Thailand, Indonesia and the Philippines to advise, ostensibly objectively, the refugees of their options, but particularly that return to Vietnam is inevitable if they are not accepted as Convention refugees. However neither country contributed in any significant way to the aid and trade packages that were to be forthcoming for Vietnam.

On another front in Southeast Asia, as stated earlier, Australia was very actively involved in the settlement in Cambodia, not only in the diplomatic negotiations leading up to the settlement, but in advising on democratic legislative elections and the rehabilitation of the country following the Peace Accords signed in Paris in October of 1991. Assistance to the return, reintegration and rehabilitation of 350 000 refugees from the Thai border area is an integral part of the peace package. It alone involves constructing staging centres in Thailand and transit centres in Cambodia, de-mining, and undertaking road and bridge repairs as well as temporary feeding programs until the land is revitalised.

For Canada's part, it has participated in a three-year effort to redraft the immigration function of the Organization on Economic

Co-operation and Development (OECD). Canada agreed to act as the convener for the OECD conference, scheduled for Madrid in March of 1993 with a focus on immigration and refugee issues. The Conference, explicitly closed to journalists and academics, divided the agenda into two major sessions, the first on migration systems, controls and selection, and the second on development assistance, trade, capital movements and aid being used in order to reduce some of the incentives to emigrate.

Canada also hosted (and Australia participated in) the Informal Consultations (more formally, the inter-governmental consultations on asylum, refugee and migration policies in Europe, North America and Australia) of the sixteen western states in Niagara Falls in June of 1992. After a review of each country's activities, many topics were discussed, including such mechanisms of control as finger-printing and the adoption of one of three contending technical systems for storing and retrieving data so that the systems in the various countries would be compatible. The most important area of discussion (though not necessarily the most interesting, which was probably the current crisis in the former Yugoslavia) was the move towards co-operation and some degree of technical harmonisation using the Dublin and Schengen Agreements as models.

Canada had already tabled its proposed new Immigration Act just prior to that meeting. The Act provided for entering into bilateral and multilateral agreements with foreign countries to 'share responsibility' for the examination of refugee claims (Clause 97 re: Section 108.1). One might interpret this as an effort to move towards common harmonisation of a refugee determination system according to fair standards. However, the models for co-ordination were the Dublin and Schengen Agreements which do not provide procedural standards for status determination or standards for interpretations of the Convention refugee definition. In short, far from attempting to promote fair and universal standards for the examination of refugee claims, the European club simply fosters a system of *collective deterrence* to limit the entry of asylum seekers by providing 'an incentive to offer only the lowest common denominator of protection, since to do otherwise will lead them to take responsibility for a disproportionate share of the collective duty' (Hathaway 1992, p. 86).

The new proposed legislation had indicated that this would also be the Canadian interpretation of 'shared responsibility'. The Act not only continued and strengthened the clauses allowing immigration officers to refuse entry and access to the refugee determination system to individuals who had sojourned in a 'safe third country'—that is, a country that was a signatory to the Convention and in which they could have made a claim—but it directly linked the 'shared responsibility' clause with the provision for prescribing countries as 'safe third' in paragraph 114(1)(s). 'Shared responsibility', became a euphemism for refusing to process claimants who could be processed in a neighbouring country. Multilateral action was thus not designed to raise refugee determination to a political level beyond the receiving state, but to increase the receiving state's capacity to control entry.

Though Canada had been pursuing trilateral talks with the United States and Mexico on co-ordinating immigration and refugee issues, and though the North American Free Trade Agreement (NAFTA) talks seemed to have reached agreement in a number of immigration areas with the goal of facilitating the reciprocal entry of citizens from the countries of the agreement for business purposes under the 'temporary Entry of Business Persons' chapter of NAFTA (as the complement to chapter 15 of the US–Canada Free Trade Agreement (CFTA)), virtually no progress on refugee issues had been realised in the trilateral talks. The Mexicans, after all, were not signatories to the Convention and their philosophical approach and absence of any developed legal system of protection and procedure made that country too different from the American and Canadian systems to move towards harmonisation at this time.

This did not seem to be the case in the bilateral talks with the Americans. The Canadian government announced in the explanatory material provided with its proposed new Immigration Act tabled in Parliament that a bilateral agreement was under discussion with the United States to discuss 'shared responsibility' along the lines indicated above. However, as of 19 January 1993, a leak appeared in the press indicating not only that no progress on this front could be expected for several months until the Clinton administration was well established, but hinted that the US under the Clinton administration might not be favourably disposed to such an agreement.

Clearly, the Australian emphasis on multilateral initiatives to stem flows and repatriate refugees and the Canadian emphasis on regional bilateral agreements and Safe First Country provisions in its legislation reflect differences in geographical locale rather than any fundamental differences in philosophy. Australia has continued to emphasise its international role, serving on the Executive Committee of the UNHCR—the advisory body to the High Commissioner on protection strategies and appropriate durable solutions—and channels much of its assistance funding through UNHCR. Canada has taken a major initiative in the Australian direction. A multilateral system requires not only common standards and procedures, which, to be fair, Shannon also called for, but a common information base. Canada had, in the documentation centre of its Refugee Board, developed the best information and data collection system thus far for using country profiles as a basis of informing refugee board members of the situations from which the refugee had fled. An initial move has begun to set up a common documentation data base and set of country profiles for the purposes of developing a common system.

Controls

Australia is less subject to accusations of singling out refugee countries for the imposition of visa controls since it requires all foreign nationals, except New Zealanders, to have visas. The Australian government has defended its policies of strict controls on entry as follows: 'To admit people into Australia who vote with their airline tickets or by simply arriving in Australia, clearly depreciates the role of responsible government and its establishment of global and equitable immigration policies and programs, including those established for humanitarian entry.' These comments by Senator Jim McKiernan were made at the 'Welcome Stronger Forum' in 1992.

The problem is that both countries have been obliged by circumstances to include, along with an emphasis on overseas selection of refugees (the dominant policy only a decade ago), a process of case-by-case refugee determination of on-shore claimants. In the above-quoted address, Senator McKiernan argued that 'case-by-case refugee determination ensure equity and enables our policy to adjust rapidly to changed circumstances.' But to undergo case by case determination, the refugees have to get to Australia or Canada, and this may entail obtaining visas through illegal auspices or under false pretences.

Efforts have been made to strengthen the Canadian visa control system, for instance, the inducements and penalties for refugee claimants who destroyed documents and the proposed new draconian penalties for carriers who transport individuals to Canada without proper documentation. The responsibility for ensuring passengers carry proper documents begins when the passengers board the carriers and end when the passengers are presented to an immigration officer for examination.

The proposed Canadian legislation did not balance the new administrative fees for carrier (a substitute for the earlier provision for fines, a process which required court action and, hence, long delays and little deterrent effect), deposit requirements and the provision for seizing aircraft, with a provision for repayment if the individual carrying improper documents proved before the Refugee Board that s/he was a Convention refugee. Fees, and very large ones at that, were to be levied on carriers for transporting individuals with improper documents even if they were genuine refugees who had to use forged documents as the only method of getting to a country where they could make a refugee claim.

The fact is, visas are geared to immigrants, visitors and business people; there is no provision for visas for refugee claimants, only for refugees selected abroad.

> The assessment of an application for a visa is based on the selection standards prescribed for the class of immigrants in respect of which the person is making the application, and is intended to determine whether the applicant and all dependents appear to meet the requirements of the Act. A visa may be issued to an applicant and to each of the applicant's dependents if the visa officer is satisfied that it would not be contrary to the Act or the Regulations to grant landing or entry (EIC 1992a, pp. 4–5).

It is *not* contrary to the law to make a refugee claim, but it is contrary to norms to issue a visa to someone who declares they want to come to Australia or Canada to become a refugee claimant even though 'Immigrants and dependents may also be granted landing for reasons of public policy or compassionate or humanitarian considerations if they are members of any class established for purpose of regulation' (EIC 1992a, p. 1). In other words, there is a catch-22 in the provisions of both countries. You need a visa to enter Australia and, in increasing numbers of cases, Canada. But if you state that you intend to come to Australia or Canada to claim refugee status, it is highly unlikely you will be given a visa to enter.

Overseas entry

The categories shown in Chart 9.1 represent the different groups of refugees.

This paper is primarily concerned with those selected abroad. In the above chart, both types of cases selected abroad can be sponsored in Canada either by government or privately. Humanitarian refugees

Chart 9.1 Refugee groupings

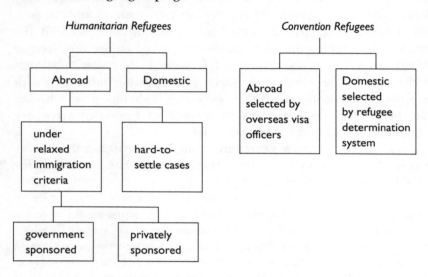

differ from Convention refugees in that the latter are determined to be refugees on a case-by-case basis, while the former are determined to be refugees on a group basis, although selection is done on a case-by-case basis. The criteria differ in that the definition for a humanitarian refugee is broader and more flexibly applied than is the case for Convention refugees. In Australia, the emphasis placed on ties to Australia make the criteria more akin to those applicable to immigrants, while the definition, even though broadened to be based on discrimination rather than persecution, is still more restrictive than the lack of such criteria in the Canadian program. In both countries, there is no system of refugee determination for deciding if an individual is or is not a Convention refugee when application is made abroad.

For overseas entry, there is no requirement to establish that a refugee fulfils the requirements of the refugee convention. Humanitarian refugees are selected abroad under relaxed immigration criteria or as special hard-to-settle cases. Some refugees selected abroad who clearly fit the persecution requirements of the Convention, are still not Convention refugees because they are not outside their country of origin. This was the case with the Political Prisoners and Oppressed Persons Designated Class in Canada. Australia made humanitarian spaces available to help a small group of refugees affected by the Gulf War. Australia also has a Special Assistance Category to assist individuals and families displaced by civil conflict as well as others who may not be able to establish that they have been persecuted, but who have otherwise been disadvantaged or discriminated against in their home country.

Australia, unlike Canada, but like the United States, has a four-year Domestic Protection Temporary Entry Permit designated for rejected refugee claimants who have a strong humanitarian claim in the US it is eighteen months. In fact, the program was specifically designed for the 20 000 Chinese students in Australia at the time of the events in Tienanmen Square.

In Australia, selection within both the Humanitarian and Refugee Categories is on a case by case basis involving a similar combination of factors—namely, factors pertaining to circumstances leading to the application for settlement and factors indicating potential to settle successfully in Australia. In practice there is often little difference between the two categories, although the Humanitarian criteria are on paper the broader and more flexible of the two categories.

While Canada was clearly intent on limiting access to the inland Canadian refugee determination system, while at the same time developing a system that was the fairest in the world, it had previously demonstrated a modest but reasonably generous program for selecting refugees abroad to come to Canada. To retain flexibility in refugee policy for those who did not fall within the strict refugee definition, both countries, as indicated above, made provision for Special Humanitarian Programs. In Australia, that policy was explicitly not made formal until 1982 'as a means of providing humanitarian flexibility' (DILGEA 1990b). Originally intended to apply to the Khmer in Thailand, it was soon extended globally. In fact, in Australia as in Canada, humanitarian programs of this nature had been part of the immigrant intake and refugee movements since after World War II. Price (1993) claims that many quasi-refugees were resettled in the 1950s and 1960s on the basis of humanitarian policy unfettered by the narrow refugee definition. Those who failed to prove they were refugees under the Convention could still be accepted on humanitarian grounds. Overseas programs of selection did not require refugees to fall within the narrow Convention definition. The Australian 1977 Humanitarian refugee policy specifically recognised this need for flexibility. 'There will be people in refugee-type situations who do not fall strictly within the UNHCR mandate or within Convention definitions. Government policy will be sufficiently flexible to enable the extension of this policy, where appropriate, to such people' (noted in DILGEA 1990, unpub.).

Some critics in both countries claimed these humanitarian programs proved that the refugee programs were really disguised
immigration programs and indicated a lack of commitment on the
part of either country to take their responsibilities seriously under the
refugee Convention. Defenders note that the program addressed the
needs of persons who do not meet the Convention definition of a
refugee. The agreement allowed 'hard-to-settle cases' to enter either
country if those cases were sponsored by churches or other agencies.
Canada went further and made provision in the 1976 Act for private
sponsorship of refugees. In July of 1978, Ron Atkey, then Minister
of Immigration, announced that after the initial intake of 8000 government sponsored refugees from Indochina, the government would
sponsor one refugee for every one the private sector sponsored to a
total of 50 000 refugees, but then with no upper limit to private
sponsorship, though even in this case the refugees would also have
to show they had a capacity to become self-supporting in Canada.
The new Canadian legislation implemented in 1993 set a limit to such
private sponsorship. The proponents of the change argued that, in
the past, there had, in fact, been a *de facto* limit based on the
processing capacity of Canadian visa officers in an area. Rather than
cope with the frustration and long waits experienced by private
sponsors and in order to undertake proper planning, *de jure* limits
were now proposed for private sponsorship.

In Australia, private sector involvement has been more restrictive
in recent decades. Ironically, this had been a major mode of entry to
Australia prior to the 1970s. In the post-war resettlement program,
there had been a significant involvement of NGOs, including the
Lutheran World Federation, the World Council of Churches and the
International Migration Committee as well as sundry Jewish organisations. A request for the organisation to sponsor a refugee often was
initiated from outside Australia, the dossier submitted to Australian
immigration, and the NGO arranged travel, reception and settlement
upon approval of the application (Price 1993). Price (1993, pp. 30–32)
notes that the Australian Council of Churches resettled 80 000, the
Roman Catholic Church 45 000, Jewish agencies 27 000, the Luther-
ans 5000 and the Red Cross 2000. By the 1970s, under a new
Australian government policy, private sponsorship came to a halt.

In the 1977 Refugee Policy and Mechanisms statement, the
Australian government announced:

> Voluntary agencies are to be encouraged to participate and indicate
> periodically or as the need arises, the extent of assistance they can

provide. Early consideration will be given to those refugees who are the subject of adequate sponsorship by appropriate voluntary bodies (noted in DILGEA 1990 unpub.).

In practice, however, and unlike Canada where no such favour-itism was demonstrated, the government revealed a stronger predisposition towards community groups as sponsoring bodies than voluntary agencies. The government established the Community Refugee Resettlement Scheme (CRSS). CRSS groups, approved and supported by government, could either nominate a refugee (usually a relative of someone already here—the very pattern that developed in the late 1980s in the Canadian private sponsorship program), or accept requests to sponsor by the department originated by an immigration officer overseas who perceived an applicant as needing and likely to benefit from such community support. The CRSS group was expected to provide accommodation, help secure entry into English classes and to secure employment, and generally assist with settlement needs. In so doing they had to be largely dependent on community funds, although a small government grant could be sought for second and subsequent sponsorships.

Whereas the Canadian private sponsorship scheme was more extensive, far exceeding the government's ambitious sponsorship program for Indochinese refugees in the years 1979–81, and entailed full financial responsibility on the part of the sponsors (though the federal government funded repayable but interest-free travel loans and language classes for privately sponsored refugees), the Australian sponsorship program tended to focus on cases perceived as likely to experience difficulty in resettlement. The scheme served to provide new arrivals with additional support, reduced pressure on the government's migrant centre accommodation scheme (a program which Canada did not have in the early 1980s), and passed some of the costs onto the community.

Defenders of the humanitarian program in general in both countries, and of private sponsorship in particular in Canada, have argued, we believe, justifiably, that the humanitarian program provided flexibility and an enhanced capacity to any refugee situation. In the 1980s, both the Australian and Canadian governments went further in accepting more direct responsibility for humanitarian cases when each participated in the UNHCR's Women at Risk Program. But the private sponsorship program for hard-to-settle cases in both countries—unaccompanied minors, refugees with disabilities, torture victims, etc.—enabled both countries to serve a few very needy individuals while maintaining mass resettlement programs, with the bulk of the costs borne by private, dedicated and overburdened volunteers.

The program of refugees sponsored by the government is another matter. In Canada (and Australia) it has recently declined as illustrated in the following table:

Table 9.2   Immigration plan for 1991–95, year two, November 1991

Actual	Planned				
1991	1991	1992	1993	1994	1995
7 300	13 000	13 000	13 000	13 000	13 000
Australia		12 000	10 000		

	Actual		Planned
Breakdown by world area	Australia 1991–92	Canada 1991	Canada 1991
Eastern Europe	124	330	300
Southeast Asia	2 834	2 188	2 600
Latin America	1 553	2 494	2 300
Middle East/West Asia	1 743	1 132	1 800
Africa	90	1 072	1 000
Other or Reserve	1 289	46	5 000
Total	7 745	7 262	13 000

Source: Adapted from EIC 1991c.

The Canadian government offered the following explanation for the lower numbers.

The number of government-assisted refugees admitted to Canada, approximately 7 300, was lower than planned, not because of any decision on the part of the government to resettle fewer persons, but for a variety of external factors: improved conditions in Eastern Europe: the relatively slow screening of asylum seekers under the UN-sponsored Comprehensive Plan of action in Southeast Asia; fewer referrals by international and other organisations than were anticipated in Africa; and, the adverse effects of wars in the Horn of Africa and the Persian Gulf on the operation of visa offices (EIC 1992c, p. 2).

The Australian government simply said that demand had fallen. This is in spite of the fact that Australia maintains posts in Nicosia and Damascus to process Lebanese nationals, seriously and directly affected by the conflict in Lebanon, who also had close relatives with permanent residence status prior to 1989 in Australia. Stateless former residents of Iraq, Afghanistan and Iran, particularly Christians and Kurds from Northern Iraq who fled to Turkey and Iran are processed at Ankara, Islamabad, Athens and New Delhi.

As a result of the dramatic changes in Eastern Europe in 1989, Canada removed Poland from the designated latter class list. Chile was removed in the next year, so that only Guatemala and El Salvador remained (EIC 1991c). In Canada only two designated classes remained in 1991: the Indochinese and the Political Prisoners and Oppressed Persons Class. Australia followed a similar path. Australia still maintains refugee processing posts in Mexico City and Santiago, but given the changes in the political and human rights situation in Latin America, the result has been 'a significant reduction in applications from this region. The trend is expected to continue' (DILGEA 1992b, p. 23).

In the 1991–92 Canadian report, the Self-Exiled Class applicable to Eastern Europe was deleted as a Designated Class, a designation not reinstated when the troubles in Yugoslavia produced 500 000 refugees and 1.7 million internally displaced persons. Of the 500 000 who have left the former Yugoslavia, almost all are scattered throughout Europe, 200 000 in Germany, 60 000 in Hungary and 41 000 in Sweden. Only 930 'Yugoslavs' claimed refugee status in Canada by the end of June of 1992, predominantly Serbs from Serbia and Macedonia rather than Croats and Muslims from Bosnia-Herzegovina. (The Canadian suspension of the landing rights of JAT, the Yugoslavian airline, ostensibly to accord with the Security Council trade sanctions against Serbia, also served to limit the number of Serbs who could fly to Canada and make a refugee asylum claim.) The Canadian government also expedited family reunification applications and sympathetically processed requests for extensions of visitor's visas. Though provision was made for 5000 persons from the conflict in Bosnia-Herzegovina with family connections in Canada to obtain visas, no significant initiative was taken, comparable to the Boat People initiative in 1979, to introduce a special program or designated class for refugees fleeing the area. As Peter Harder, the Canadian Associate Deputy Minister of Immigration, remarked, 'the priorities of the government of Canada are as follows: one, peacemaking and peacekeeping; two, the humanitarian support that

Canada is giving in the region through international organisations to—at the right time—respond with a comprehensive approach that involves protection and return.' (*The Globe and Mail*, 16 July 1992, p. A11). This emphasis is defended on the basis that 'repatriation' is the preferred durable solution, reinforced by the fact that Mrs Ogata had declared 1992 as the 'Year of Repatriation'. Peter Harder has argued that 'repatriation and local integration, rather than third country resettlement, is thus entirely in keeping with UNHCR philosophy' (personal communication, 19 October 1992). In fact, prioritising repatriation and local integration as a substitute for third-country resettlement is entirely *contrary* to UNHCR policy. Protection and return, *instead of resettlement*, had become the hallmarks of Canadian refugee policy for the 1990s, thus placing the emphasis on the overseas program.

The generosity of the early 1980s was followed by apparently more restrictive policies on resettlement and activist policies overseas by the early 1990s for Latin American countries. Canada facilitated entry for Central American refugees through the 'political prisoners and oppressed persons designated class' program. This program permitted the acceptance of political prisoners and persons from El Salvador and Guatemala who were in refugee-like situations but who applied from within their own country. A special program for Salvadoreans was announced in 1983, and for Guatemalans in 1984. These programs relaxed the criteria for the selection of refugees within El Salvador and Guatemala, allowed Guatemalans and Salvadoreans in Canada to apply for permanent residence without leaving Canada, and established a moratorium on deportations to Guatemala and El Salvador. Despite this, the number of Guatemalan refugees admitted to Canada increased from a minuscule 7 in 1982 to only a still very small 128 in 1983. Canada also initiated a program to accept Central American refugees who feared deportation from the United States. In the mid-1980s Canadian refugee policy towards Central America shifted from a generous acceptance of refugees to a less open policy and practice (Ryan 1988). In February 1987 Canada began a series of procedural changes that restricted the entry of asylum seekers, changes that had a direct effect on Central Americans. The government cancelled the special program that had protected Central American refugees from being deported to their countries of origin (Bryden 1989). Previously, Salvadoreans and Guatemalans had been automatically allowed to enter Canada and been given permission to work for one year pending the outcome of either their claim to refugee status or of their request for landed-immigrant status under order-in-council (Arbour 1990, p. 159).

While the above describes recent development in Canada, in Australia the situation was very similar in many ways. Australia has maintained a commitment to a Refugee and Humanitarian component within its overall immigration program throughout. In January 1993 it even announced 'an increase in the number of entrants under the humanitarian categories by 2000 within the overall migration program of 80 000 for 1992–1993'. That brought the total to 12 000 persons (Minister for Immigration, Local Government and Ethnic Affairs, Media Release 3/93). The Government at the same time decided to separate the humanitarian entry programs from those of the regular migration program.

There is one other major influence on the number of refugees selected from abroad either as humanitarian or as convention refugees—the number of posts in an area. Thus, although Africa holds one-third of the world refugee population, both Australia and Canada maintain few processing posts on that continent.

Conclusion

Whether in overseas aid, international action and diplomacy, efforts to establish multilateral mechanisms for co-ordination and harmonisation, efforts to develop better control systems to limit who can arrive at the border and claim refugee status or in direct admissions from overseas, both Australian and Canadian policy seemed to travel in two different directions at the same time—a policy dictated by compassion and humanitarianism that at the same time demonstrates paranoia about masses of spontaneous arrivals. This is accompanied to some degree of recent miserliness in overseas aid to follow through either on its multilateral initiatives, such as the CPA requiring aid for Vietnam, or in the principle of additionality when assisting repatriated refugees or the self-sufficiency of refugees in countries of first asylum.

The increasing efforts to restrict access to the Australian and Canadian refugee determination systems is often rationalised by saying it is necessary to retain Australian or Canadian public support for genuine refugees who are processed through the system. In Australia, the then Minister for Immigration stated in 1992: 'To maintain support for the [humanitarian entry] program, the Government has to ensure that only those with legitimate claims are permitted to stay'. (DILGEA, 1992; Preface). 'Order and control must be re-established over migratory movements. Not to do so will result in the loss of the domestic public support which is so critical in our efforts to assist true refugees. To do this, we must work collectively to discourage irregular movements' (Shannon 1991, p. 5). However, the polling data, at least in Canada, do not support such a contention.

For example, Canadian polls found that 'A slim majority (53 per cent) [accurate to + or −2.5 per cent] of Canadians believe that individuals should not have the right to claim refugee status in Canada if they have had the opportunity to claim refugee status in a 'safe third' country' (A National Survey, April 1991, p. xiv). But note that 72 per cent of those surveyed, a much larger majority than the one above, believed refugee levels were increasing when they were in fact decreasing. This misperception can be related to an increase from 39 per cent to 49 per cent who want a reduction in refugee levels. Further, the group that supports the safe third country option tends to be composed of males 45 years of age and older living in Toronto, or in cities with a population of less than 250 000, who, in either case, have little acquaintance with refugees or immigrants, and who possess a high school education or less. Note further that a much larger majority, 67 per cent, feel that Canadian rights and freedoms should *not* be extended to refugee claimants in spite of the decision of the Supreme Court of Canada to the contrary.

The surprise is not that such a slim majority supports the safe third country provision, but that the majority is so slim given the much larger majorities favouring other propositions which are based upon erroneous data or lack of understanding of the values and laws by which Canada is ruled; and, that this majority is so slim in spite of the fact that our current political leadership has chosen to eschew a positive governmental education campaign on behalf of refugees in favour of a repeated emphasis on the need to 'get tough' with phoney refugee claimants.

Even taking into consideration reactionary domestic political forces endorsing a more restrictionist and self-centred program, Australia and Canada can afford to be more forthcoming in their assistance to refugees and less defensive about allowing them to reach their distant shores. Even the new stress on overseas programs could be made with a greater generosity of both spirit and money, reinforced by a more pro-active policy. The implication is that both countries have responded to the tension between humanitarianism and control by shifting the emphasis to control.

CHAPTER 10

Illegal Immigration and Refugee Claims

David Cox and Patrick Glenn

Introduction

While sharing a common public law tradition, that of the common law, Australia and Canada have diverged significantly in terms of regulation and control of illegal immigration and refugee claims. It appears possible to speak of two distinct regulatory models—the administrative and the adjudicative—to describe the current positions of the two countries. Australia has adopted in principle the administrative model, though adjudicative methods have not been entirely eliminated and appear to be increasing in importance. Canada in the last two decades has undergone a major shift from the administrative to the adjudicative model, and while many administrative methods remain in place they are now largely subsidiary to adjudicative institutions. Adoption of one or the other of these two regulatory models has important consequences in terms of the relative number and treatment of illegal entrants and overstayers, change of status requests and refugee claims, as we shall try to demonstrate.

In very general terms, the administrative model adopted by Australia consists of a universal, complex, and differentiated visa system; a supplementary control system of entry permits; the use of administrative authority to control access to national territory; the submission of refugee claims to administrative regulation and decision-making; and resort to adjudicative methods and legal professionals in only limited and exceptional circumstances. The adjudicative model prevalent in Canada places less emphasis on conditions of initial entry, using only a non-universal and relatively simple visa system; submits all claims of entitlement to access to national territory to an adjudicative process (implying a right to entry for purposes of determination); extends constitutional procedural guarantees and legislation to refugee claimants, whose claims are submitted to a distinct adjudicatory agency; and makes extensive use of legal professionals in the decision-making process, leaving considerable room as well for resort to the courts.

In both countries, however, a similar range of problems must be dealt with. In this chapter, we deal successively with illegal immigration, change of status applications, and refugee claims, as representing the most significant subjects of interest in the Australian and Canadian regulatory and control regimes. These subjects are closely related to one another, and their relative importance appears to be a function of the regulatory model adopted. In matters of illegal immigration and change of status applications, the Australian administrative model appears to bear the greatest regulatory burden. As to refugee claims it is the Canadian adjudicative model which has attracted to itself the greatest volume of activity. In our concluding remarks we explore in greater detail the relationship between regulatory models and different forms of immigration and refugee movement.

Illegal immigration

Even in countries of immigration, illegal immigration will usually be regarded as undesirable. Politically it is unacceptable because it reveals a country as being unable to control its borders, and in a country of immigration governments will wish to demonstrate to the public that they are in control of the program, in terms of both overall numbers and selection. Socially, illegal migration is unacceptable because it tends to create a tight society in which those with no legal status are discriminated against and deprive themselves and their families of particular services for fear of apprehension. Finally it is often seen as unacceptable on security grounds because it allows into a country some who may constitute a threat to it.

Australia's illegal population is comprised mainly of overstayers—those who entered legally but did not leave again as their entry permits or entry visas required. The figure, now regarded as 90 per cent accurate due to a new computerised visa processing and records system, was put at 90 000 on 30 April 1990. In addition, there is a small number of clandestine illegals who evade border controls.

The number is put in the hundreds each year, and includes stowaways and ship crew deserters, but actual figures are of course unknown. Finally, there are some who enter the country on the basis of deception, whether intentional or unintentional. Is an illegal population of these dimensions perceived as a problem in Australia? The answer is yes, mainly because it is seen to affect the employment market, threaten the integrity of the immigration program and generally to constitute a threat to the integrity of borders. Hence in recent years government has adopted an unsympathetic approach. Part of the reason for this is the extent to which immigration in Australia touches on important issues of national identity and excites strong expressions of public policy.

In Canada, on the other hand, the illegal population is not now perceived as a major problem, although estimates of its size have ranged in the past as high as 250 000. After some debate on the issue in the early 1980s (see Hawkins 1989, pp. 205–11), it quickly merged into the issue of refugee claimants. This was because the great majority of illegal immigrants sought to regularise their situation by applying for refugee status; hence both public reaction and government attention is directed mainly to the issue of refugee claimants. This situation could, however, change in the future and illegal immigration become a matter of specific concern.

In seeking to control illegal immigration, it is logical that a government tighten its entry arrangements. This can be done in several ways, including ensuring that everyone entering does so through an established system and not clandestinely, that the system facilitates identification of bogus and undesirable applications and that measures exist that will effectively exclude those perceived to be undesirable. Overall Australia has sought to exercise greater control over entry arrangements than has Canada. Attempts to control clandestine entry to Australia include patrols of the northern shores. While the high distances have meant that effective patrols are expensive, the policy is assisted by the often inhospitable nature of the terrain, the absence of large population centres and the distance of these shores from possible take-off points. The situation in Canada renders such a policy far more difficult.

More important, however, have been the attempts to control illegal immigration by exercising control over entry, and in these endeavours Australia and Canada differ significantly. The policy in Australia is expressed in a 1990 government publication: 'It is the correctness of the initial decision to approve a [visa] application which will largely determine the level of illegal immigration in Australia'

(DILGEA 1990b, p. 31). To facilitate this policy, Australia introduced a universal visa system, forcing all applicants for entry through a screening procedure. Canada, on the other hand, has always exempted non-immigrant visitors from a large number of countries (currently more than sixty) from any visa requirement. While a report on 'illegal migrants in Canada' in 1983 recommended that 'The Government should undertake a major review of the list of visa-exempt countries and, in the absence of compelling reason, should remove all countries except the United States' (Hawkins 1989, p. 29), this approach has been rejected as extremely difficult given the large number of entrants from the USA and Great Britain.

The Australian visa system is buttressed by elaborate computerised information systems that provide profiles of overstayers and identify common fraudulent procedures in visa applications. Consequently, Australian immigration officers can reject applications from suspicious applicants within designated 'at risk' groups. While the justice of doing so is sometimes queried, the effectiveness in controlling illegal entry is undeniable. In addition, the current wide range of visa types enables different conditions to be applied to each, further assisting ability to exercise control. By contrast, Canada's far simpler and narrower visa system is cheaper and easier to implement but much less effective as a control mechanism (Wydrzynski 1983).

Both Australia and Canada have made use of carrier sanctions. Indeed the principal sanction for limiting the flow of illegal immigration to Canada is through the imposition of financial penalties on airlines which embark people without appropriate documentation onto flights destined to Canada. Although the system of fines has proved difficult to implement, it is regarded as reasonably effective. In Australia, carrier sanctions were introduced in 1979 with provision for fines to ensure compliance.

In addition to its universal visa system, Australia has in effect a second level of screening at the point of entry through a system of entry permits. Under the provisions of the migration arrangements of December 1989, the culmination of increasing control measures, a visa 'does not entitle the holder . . . to enter Australia'. Once one is the holder of a valid visa and 'physically present in Australia', the next step is to apply for an entry permit—the instrument permitting lawful entry. (Applicants who are issued entry visas initially do not need to receive entry permits. All others who have been issued with travel-only visas are subject to this second level of screening. Their visa in effect only entitles them to travel to the border and not to enter Australia.) The conditions attaching to an entry permit reflect those of the relevant visa; more significant, however, is the 1989 provision that a temporary entry permit is not valid for the purpose of granting a permanent entry permit after entry to Australia. This provision is an attempt to control change-of-status applications.

All in all, Australia has established a most elaborate system to control who is permitted to enter Australia, the objectives being to detect bogus applications but also to exclude those categories of persons determined from past experience to be most likely to remain in the country after the expiry of the temporary entry permit. Such control was purely on the basis of administrative decisions permitting very limited rights to merits review. The system, in addition to controlling entry, was effective in establishing clearly the status, and the rights pertaining to that status, of everyone present in the country. Either one possessed or did not possess a valid entry permit, and if one possessed a temporary entry permit it established indisputably one's rights in Australia, including the period during which one could remain.

Given, however, that in any country some people will enter or remain illegally, it is logical to anticipate a policy of detecting such people and removing them from the country or regularising their situation. Canada employs a relatively small number (circa 150) of immigration inspectors who are assigned apprehension responsibilities. In 1991 approximately 4500 illegal entrants were removed from Canada as a result of these apprehension methods (up from 3039 in 1990 and 2379 in 1989). In Canada the emphasis is on illegal entrants guilty of criminal behaviour or subject to deportation orders. Australia pursues a similar policy but without the emphasis on specific groups of illegals. If the relevant government department becomes aware of the presence of any illegal immigrants it will move to apprehend them. It will even undertake 'dawn raids' on places likely to harbour illegal immigrants—a policy frequently criticised in that it tends to target particular racial groups and to treat them all as possibly illegal immigrants. This activity resulted, between 1983 and 1990, in an average of 1784 enforced departures. However, 1990–91 'saw a markedly more determined approach to dealing with the record high level of over-stayers (90 000 as at 30 April, 1990) and immigration fraud' (DILGEA 1991e, p. 82). Compliance field staff were increased from 50 to 150 and investigations staff from twenty to thirty. This work resulted in '9253 illegal entrants located and 4862 forced to leave Australia. (784 of these were deported and 4078 departed under departmental supervision.)' (DILGEA 1991e, p. 83)

In such immigration work, detection (or rejection of applicants for change-of-status) is one thing but removal from the country another. Most governments desire to remove illegal entrants yet are reluctant to use severe measures against defenceless and often harmless people. Australia is one country that shows little sympathy for illegal immigrants and has no difficulty in exercising the right to deport them should they be unwilling to depart voluntarily. While an illegal immigrant who is detained is usually given the option to leave voluntarily, as a last resort and in clearly designated circumstances the government may compel the person to leave. As Crawford (1990, p. 632) outlines, a deportation order in such circumstances may be issued and, if it is, that order is mandatory, cannot be revoked and prevents the person from being issued an entry permit. While the regulations ensure that the mandatory deportation power can only be used in prescribed situations, it is the existence of that power that distinguishes Australia. The purpose behind this scheme is 'to provide incentives for illegal entrants to apply for temporary or permanent residence as entitled to by law, or to depart Australia' (Gibbons, 1990, p. 6). In other words, a person must act before a temporary entry permit expires or within the period of grace or not act at all, even if that person believes that an application would be futile.

Unlike Australia, Canada presently has no practice or policy of forcible, administrative removal or exclusion of persons seeking illegal admission into Canada. A person seeking admission at a port of entry who is believed not to be a genuine visitor or immigrant may be allowed to withdraw voluntarily or may become the object of a report which will lead to a quasi-judicial adjudication of the claim to admission. Persons arriving at the border of Canada and the USA may be directed back to the United States until such time as the inquiry and adjudicative process may commence. Voluntary withdrawal is very frequent, and occurs after advice given by immigration officials on the likelihood of success of a claim of admission. A policy of forced 'turnabouts' has been seen as contrary to the natural justice requirements of the Canadian Charter of Rights and Freedoms. In 1992, however, the Government of Canada introduced amendments to the Immigration Act (Marrocco & Goslett 1991) which would allow immigration officers to exclude from Canada undocumented illegal entrants who have not made a claim for refugee status.

Canada also differs from Australia in its treatment of detected illegal entrants in Canada. It has no provision for mandatory deportation following automatically on the absence of a valid temporary entry permit, as Australia has. Instead, if there is no voluntary departure the alien non-resident will become the object of a report to a senior immigrant official, who may either admit the applicant to Canada or cause a formal inquiry to be held as soon as is reasonably practicable. Legal aid is generally available to the illegal entrant and the proceedings assume a quasi-judicial adversarial form, usually without detention. The inquiry is held before an adjudicator appointed under the *Public Service Employment Act* for the purpose of adjudication under the *Immigration Act* (Immigration Adjudication Branch 1990), but in deportation proceedings on grounds of security the adjudicator cannot proceed until there has been review by the Federal Court of the 'reasonable' character of the security certificate filed by the Ministry.

In Australia prior to 1989 there was no legislative right of merits review for entry or deportation decisions with respect to illegal entrants, with very few exceptions and any review that did occur was internal. Illegal immigrants could request a review of a deportation order, which was no more than a reconsideration of the decision by the minister or department. Such a review involved a repeat of the same process that gave rise to the original decision, with no formal right to be heard. It was a procedure that encouraged appeals, resulted in heavy workloads but precluded a fully independent review. Should visa or entry permit refusals be at issue, illegal immigrants might have access to an administrative system of internal merits review (the Immigration Review Panel) which made recommendations to the Minister. Illegal entrants subject to arrest, search, detention, prosecution, deportation or entry permit refusals could make use of judicial review procedures through the normal court system.

The 1989 changes in Australia introduced a two tier-review system:

> the first tier being a discrete and independent Migration Internal Review Office, within the Department of Immigration, Local Government and Ethnic Affairs. The second tier, the Immigration Review Tribunal, is an independent statutory authority (O'Neil 1990, pp. 3–4).

O'Neil goes on to say that 'the objective of the tribunal is to provide a mechanism of review that is "fair, just, economical, informal and quick" '. Although the 1989 regulations as amended permitted those illegally in Australia before 19 December 1989 to apply directly to the Immigration Review Tribunal for a review of an unfavourable decision in some cases, the general trend of the new arrangements was to preclude illegal entrants from either applying for any variation in their status or appealing against a deportation order. With the amendments to the *Migration Act* in 1989, the power changed from a broad discretion (where all of the circumstances of a person were relevant, or potentially relevant), to a deportation power that focused only on a consideration of prescribed matters or procedures.

> The major philosophical change embodied in the changes [of December 1989] is to remove consideration of the merits of persons' circumstances from the deportation process and to shift the responsibility for the actions of illegal entrants back on to them (Pryles et al. 1990, p. 36).

There is thus a major difference in the procedures adopted in relation to illegal entrants. In the Australian approach, if a person enters illegally or fails to abide by the conditions of a legal entry, they must attempt within the 28-day period of grace to regularise their situation or 'be shown little sympathy except in very clearly defined circumstances' (Bitel 1990, p. 54). If they do not act, they are subject to a Deportation Order which cannot be revoked while the person is in Australia, has heavy ramifications and is subject to limited appeal rights. Associated penalties attached to this situation are, in Bitel's view, so severe that they have led already to 'an explosion in Federal Court appeals'. Canada, on the other hand, allows the illegal entrant to present a case, bring witnesses, have legal aid (in a deportation case) and have free interpreter services. At the same time, however, deportability is often relatively simple to establish in a *prima facie* manner, and a shifting of the burden to the alien non-resident then occurs to establish some ground justifying non-deportation.

A final procedure not infrequently used in relation to illegal entrants is that of amnesties. While the practice is not frequent in Canada, a number of near-amnesties were adopted in the last two decades. In 1973 the Minister announced a 60-day Adjustment of Status Program allowing those in a selected category to regularise their status.

> Applications for immigrant status would be judged in the light of such criteria as length of residence in Canada, family relationships, financial stability, and employment records, as well as compelling grounds for compassionate consideration (Hawkins 1989, p. 48).

Under this program, some 39 000 people from 150 countries obtained landed immigrant status with a further 13 000 accepted under administrative measures. The Program was widely held to have been a success. Then in 1986 a procedure known as the Administrative Review was adopted to deal with persons then in the refugee backlog. Under this policy persons then in the backlog were given permission for landing as permanent residents if they could show successful establishment in Canada or a potential for successful establishment.

Australia also made use of the amnesty strategy to control illegal immigration. The first important amnesty occurred in 1976, when 8614 persons applied and were mostly accepted. Then in 1980 a further amnesty saw some 14 000 persons apply and mostly be accepted. Hawkins (1989, p. 205) concludes that amnesties have more political significance than potential to resolve illegal immigration, and Australia's experience with them certainly confirms this. Australian policy makers are also conscious that amnesties may well encourage further illegal immigration on the assumption that ultimately there will be a further amnesty. Special provisions made in 1989–90, permitting those illegally in Australia to apply for entry permits, led immediately to the assumption that this represented an amnesty, although government was quick to deny it, and this illustrates the prevailing mood in the immigrant community.

All recent reports (United Nations 1982; Appleyard 1987 and OECD 1987) emphasise the importance within international migration of illegal migration and illustrate the marked increase in numbers. Illegal movements frequently merge with both migrant worker and refugee movements, and in particular, as Hawkins (1989, p. 195) says:

> the undocumented migrant and the claimant for refugee status are in very similar situations and can often be, at different times, the same person. An undocumented migrant can sometimes achieve entry via refugee status, while the claimant for refugee status who is turned down often becomes one of the army of undocumented migrants.

Both Canada and Australia experience the phenomenon of illegal immigration, although neither country sees it as having as yet reached alarming proportions. Many in Australia are illegal because they overstay their entry permit provisions, and many of these ultimately leave voluntarily. Some now (and possibly many more in the future) resort to claiming refugee status, if determined to try to stay or even simply to prolong legally their period of residence. Even though the situation is in no sense alarming, the decision of the Australian Government since 1989 is to adopt a tough stance against illegal immigration. The procedures discussed represent a series of barriers placed in the way of would-be illegal entrants, and, against those who succeed, a tough policy with little sense of their possible rights or sympathy for their circumstances. In Canada also the situation is not seen as alarming, but partly because the merging of this movement with that of asylum seekers is much further advanced than in Australia. What distinguishes Canada from Australia in this area of control is, however, a recognition that illegal entrants are persons with rights. Especially they have the right to be heard and, if their claim can be justified, the right to be granted landed immigrant status. Australia, by removing the very right to be considered for landed immigrant status, apart from in very limited circumstances, has effectively obviated the need or possibility for a case to be presented. If one is illegal it is through one's own deliberate act and the consequence should be deportation. In the total international situation—of extreme North–South disparity, limited legal migration opportunities, rising expectations and abuse of human rights—the justice and the feasibility of such a stance needs to be questioned. On the other hand, the political and longer-term policy consequences of the cost and so on of processing on-shore large numbers of would-be immigrants have yet to be fully revealed.

Change of status

An immigration procedure which arrangements in some countries have effectively endorsed is to enter the country on whatever temporary entry provisions are available and then apply to have one's status changed to that of permanent resident. Sometimes this represents an understandable and acceptable procedure, which is why regulations at times permit it. For example, a temporary visitor may be offered employment, may like the country and satisfy normal entry criteria, or may enter into a relationship with a permanent resident. Alternatively, a person seeking refugee status may, for various reasons, prefer not to publicise this intent until safely in the country by other means, legal or illegal. Such potentially bona fide claims might well be accommodated, but even so the procedure has undesirable consequences. It may favour certain persons or groups and lead to the rejection of other equally eligible applicants abroad; it may encourage entry on false pretences to achieve a goal; and it may result in expensive procedures with outcomes that can be difficult to enforce.

An alternative to processing such applications is to test people's bona fides by asking them to leave the country, apply from abroad and take their chances along with the majority. Such a process will, however, be resisted strongly by those who are convinced of the genuineness of their case and cannot afford the cost of going off-shore or back home and applying. It will also be resisted strongly by those who realise that their claim has little hope of success.

Both Australia and Canada have faced the need to provide for change of status claims. Today in both countries the majority of these claims are for recognition as refugees or on humanitarian grounds, so that this situation has merged largely into that of the asylum seekers. However, there remain in both countries many who still seek change of status on the grounds of either meeting the criteria for landed immigrant status and only now deciding to immigrate, or of a change in circumstances due to marriage or other such reasons.

In Australia in the 1970s a common procedure was for people illegally in the country to establish roots and then apply for a change of status on the grounds of being integrated and that it would be a denial of natural justice to force them to sever existing social ties. Change of status was the prerogative of the Minister or the Minister's Delegate, and many became permanent immigrants in this manner without, however, the number being of any concern.

In the course of the 1970s, and especially in the 1980s, the numbers grew steadily. This resulted in a massive workload for the public service and minister but also, and more importantly, to an increasing sense that the country was being used. This sense became particularly strong in the 1980s when investigations revealed whole systems of bogus marriages designed to subvert the system.

In 1980 an Immigration Amendment Bill reduced considerably the power of the Minister or the Minister's Delegate to grant change of status, introducing a list of 'categories of immigrants eligible to be granted permanent status subsequent to their arrival in Australia'. The intention of the amendments was to simplify and reduce the use of change of status procedures. However, as Birrell (1991, p. 11) points out, while the intention was to restrict access to change of status procedures,

> Instead, by stating in legislative terms that certain persons had rights to change their status, this became the launching pad for the humanitarian and ethnic communities to claim change of status rights.

The grounds of restriction came to be seen as entitlements resulting in claims which, when rejected, were in some cases contested in the Courts on the grounds of unfair, unreasonable or improper administrative judgments, appealable under the *Administrative Decisions (Judicial Review) Act* of 1977.

Throughout this period Canada avoided the problem to a large degree by adopting the tactic referred to above of not permitting an application for an immigrant visa to be made by a visitor to Canada from within Canada. Return to the country of origin was required, unless the applicant received a Ministerial Permit on public policy or humanitarian and compassionate grounds. These Permits were not regularly granted so that no expectation of such was created as occurred in Australia. The Australian situation is indeed a good example of the difficulty of any country changing its policies radically.

Of particular concern in Australia in the 1980s, and culminating in two official reviews of policy in 1990 (National Population Council and Senate Select Committee), was the possibility of applying for change of status on the grounds of marriage or a de facto relationship. 'Marriages of convenience' became a hot issue, and there were reports of 'marriage rackets' whereby people overseas paid dearly for their entry and permanent residence, to be achieved ultimately by using the provision of marriage to a citizen. The fact that in Melbourne in 1985 some 45 per cent of applications for change of status were on the basis of marriage, and 7 per cent on de facto relationship grounds, shows the trend. Birrell (1991, p. 16) argues that many of these were approved because:

> It was believed [by immigration officers] that the administrative law system was loaded in favour of the applicant, and that it was both futile and potentially threatening to one's career to reject a case.

The changes in immigration law and regulations introduced in December 1989 took cognizance of the 1988 report of the Committee to Advise on Australia's Immigration Policies, which recommended that:

> Anyone who is illegally in Australia by unauthorised stay beyond the expiry of a visa, or by illegal entry, should forfeit the right to apply for immigration while here or be automatically rejected if they have already applied (CAAIP 1988, p. 125).

While this recommendation was not adopted in full, Section 47 of the Act provided that a key condition for converting to a resident entry permit after entry be that the applicant was the holder of a valid temporary entry permit for the purposes of Section 47. It remains possible to apply for permanent residence on stated criteria (spouse, family, economic and other grounds); however, to be granted permanent residence the person must also be the holder of a valid temporary entry permit. Whether this will resolve the long-standing problem is still unclear.

In Canada, while change of status was not normally possible, as has been said, landed immigrant status could be granted by an Order in Council in exceptional cases. In 1989 there were 19 000 such orders, 12 000 of which were on marriage grounds. So numbers in Canada are not insignificant, even though the issue has not become the subject of public debate as it has in Australia.

Canada has in fact also provided an alternative change of status procedure that effectively overcomes the provision of being required to leave the country to apply for landed immigrant status. This procedure, known as the 'Buffalo shuffle', enables temporary residents to be processed fully for landed immigrant status while still in Canada. At that stage, however, they must travel across the border into the United States in order to return as landed immigrants. This procedure has tended to be quicker than the alternative Order in Council procedure. It is almost certain that among Canada's change of status applicants are many bogus marriages. This is not regarded as a major problem, however, and current practice tends to be to rely only on proof that a marriage has taken place. Most cases are thus approved unless one of the parties (or another) provides evidence that the marriage is not genuine. Contrary to Australian practice, Canada does not permit change of status on *de facto* grounds.

Depending on developments in regard to asylum seekers, pressure to allow change of status in at least selected circumstances is likely to be politically strong, and perhaps sometimes even having a basis in rights. The experience to date seems to indicate, however, that it is important to adopt a fairly tough policy in this regard.

Refugee claims

Since the mid-1980s both Australia and Canada have experienced significant increases in the volume of refugee claims. In Canada the number of claims tripled between 1983 and 1986 (from 6000 to 18 000). In 1990, 36 000 claims were received, while the volume diminished in 1991 to approximately 31 000. Australia until the late 1980s was receiving fewer than 500 claims annually; in 1989–90 the figure rose sharply to 3500 and in 1990–91 to 17 300 (largely because of the aftermath of events in China in June, 1989 and partly because of new limitations placed on the use of humanitarian and compassionate grounds for obtaining an entry permit). In both countries the increase in numbers placed major strains on existing resources and brought about major re-evaluations of institutional structures.

Both countries since the late 1970s had relied on administrative or ministerial forms of refugee determination, relying on immigration officers for interviewing and investigation and on an inter-ministerial/departmental committee as the recommending agency for the decision of the Minister or the Minister's Delegate. Both systems were typified by a combination of immigration and refugee responsibilities in the work of ministerial officials, a disjunction of investigative and decision-making functions, and an absence of any form of adjudicative procedure in the determination process. In 1985 this form of refugee determination was constitutionally challenged in Canada and the Supreme Court of Canada, in *Re Singh and Minister of Employment and Immigration* [1985] 1 SCR 177, decided that the procedural guarantees of the *Charter of Rights and Freedoms* extended to foreign, non-resident refugee claimants, and that the existing determination system was unconstitutional. While the Supreme Court did not set out a particular procedural regime as mandated by the Constitution, the existing determination system was found to be defective in not providing a hearing for the refugee claimant before the decisional authority, and in not providing sufficient notice to the claimant of the case that might be made against the claim (Casswell 1986; Wydrzynski 1986).

Canadian treatment of refugee claimants then went through a highly turbulent period from 1985 to 1989, when present legislation came into force (Adelman 1991; Crépeau 1990; De Mestral 1987; Segal, 1988). The influx of refugee claimants following the *Singh* decision brought about the Administrative Review discussed above, and by 1989 a new backlog of refugee claimants had been formed, necessitating the creation of a special (ongoing) backlog determination process. The transition from administrative to adjudicative model was therefore a difficult one, initiated precipitously by a court decision and effected under the constant pressure of a rising number of claims (Hathaway 1988, 1989, 1992; Matas 1989).

Faced with a rapid increase in refugee claims beginning in 1989, the Australian response has been one of refinement of the administrative model of decision-making, along with a much greater commitment of resources. Following reforms in 1990, which were effected not by legislation but by simple administrative restructuring, the primary responsibility for refugee determination remains with the Delegate of the Minister. Whereas until 1990 Delegates acted upon the advice of an interministerial committee (the Determination of Refugee Status—DORS—committee), Delegates now are officers of the Department of Immigration, Local Government and Ethnic Affairs (DILGEA) who, at the primary stage of the determination system decide the case on the basis of an interview or on the papers in the case of manifestly unfounded applications. In the event of a negative decision made by a Delegate, the file may be reviewed, at the initiative of the applicant, by a newly created Refugee Status Review Committee (RSRC), which in turn will make its recommendation to a Delegate. The structure of the new RSRC is similar to that of the DORS committee, but there is no longer a representative of the Department of the Prime Minister and Cabinet, and there is now a representative of the community nominated by the Refugee Council of Australia. The Australian administrative reform therefore permits faster processing of refugee claims which are assessed initially as well founded, but retains the major characteristics of the administrative refugee determination model, that is, a combination of immigration and refugee responsibilities in the work of ministerial officials, a disjunction (now however only partial) of investigative and decision-making functions, and an absence of any form of adjudicative procedure in the determination process.

Before examining some of the important features of the refugee determination process in each country, a few remarks are in order concerning the relation of the refugee determination process to broader questions of immigration regulation and control, such as illegal immigration and change of status. The Canadian transition to an adjudicative form of refugee determination occurred in the cadre of a broader immigration regulation system which itself was largely adjudicative in character and which assumed a certain measure of permeability. Put another way, it is an implicit, though usually unacknowledged, principle of Canadian immigration regulation that access to Canadian territory cannot be controlled and enforced, in a systematic manner, by the Canadian State acting through its purely administrative agencies. The visa system is therefore non-universal and simple; there are no entry permits; and all claims of access, by people within the country charged with being illegal entrants or by those seeking access, are presently subject to adjudication in an adversarial process. There is therefore no refined distinction in

Canadian law as to whether one is within the country or outside it (for example, on landing within the country at an international airport). The extension of constitutionally guaranteed procedural safeguards to refugee claimants was therefore entirely consistent with underlying assumptions of Canadian law—that some measure of international personal mobility is inevitable; that no rigid distinction can be drawn between early and late arrivals; that constitutional guarantees cannot therefore be preserved uniquely for one group; and that refugees should be treated no worse, in procedural terms, than other entry claimants.

The Canadian transition to an adjudicative form of refugee determination can thus be seen as essentially dictated by a number of other fundamental decisions taken in establishing its basic form of immigration regulation and control. In contrast, the administrative form of refugee determination re-affirmed in Australia in 1990 is entirely consistent with the overall pattern of Australian immigration regulation and control, which is affected as much by general conditions of demography, geography and history as is that of Canada. Different instruments of the common public law tradition are therefore chosen, in different social contexts.

The refugee determination system created in Canada by federal legislation following the *Singh* decision is expensive and slow in operation, compared to determination systems in other countries (Glenn 1991, pp. 37–62; Holloway 1990). The principal decision-making authority is a two-member panel of the Convention Refugee Determination Division (CRDD) of the Immigration and Refugee Board (IRB). Panel members are politically appointed by Order-in-Council for terms of from two to five years (renewable), and have no responsibilities other than those of refugee determination. The Board is the largest administrative tribunal in Canada and there are approximately 250 members active in the CRDD; approximately fifty are assigned to backlog determinations. Decisions made by CRDD members are not reviewable by ministerial authority or by a hierarchical superior in the Division. The Division granted refugee status in approximately 90 per cent of the cases referred to it in its first year of operation. The acceptance rate has now declined to approximately 60 per cent. Members must provide written reasons in the event of a refusal, and the decision-writing process is now becoming more burdensome. The Board provides model reasons for denial of claims from certain countries and members may rely on these reasons in formulating their own decision. The practice has inevitably been controversial and criticism of the practice has been based on the need to guarantee the independence of CRDD members from executive influence. Members, sitting in pairs, usually do not participate in more than ten hearings per week and in 1991 an average of ten claims were disposed of per month by individual members in normal proceedings. Processing time at this stage of the full hearing is from 3 to 5 months, depending on the region. The structure of the CRDD and its procedures therefore exemplify the adjudicative model of refugee determination—there is a clear separation of refugee determination responsibilities from those of immigration policy implementation; the investigative and decision-making responsibilities are united; and an adjudicative procedure or hearing is established in which the claimant may be directly heard by the decision-maker.

In adopting this adjudicative model of refugee determination Canada has encountered a number of problems which are absent in the administrative model. The main problem, not yet resolved, is the type of procedure most appropriate for adjudication of refugee claims. Some acknowledgment of the particular nature of refugee determination occurred in the creation of the institution of the Refugee Hearing Officer (RHO), whose task is described as that of acting as legal counsel for the Board, and not for the Ministry (Convention Refugee Determination Division Rules, s.2). It is therefore not the task of the RHO to systematically oppose refugee claims, but to assist CRDD members in adjudicating them. The determination procedure is therefore often referred to as non-adversarial in character, but in practice determination hearings have become very court-like in character. Legal aid is available to refugee claimants, at a very high annual cost (estimated at $31 million for the province of Ontario alone in 1992), and counsel are present in almost all cases in the major urban centres. Cases are begun, once formalities are completed, with presentation of the refugee claim by counsel for the claimant. There is inevitably extensive questioning of the claimant by his or her own counsel, in the detailed, formal manner of courtroom, adversarial interrogation. The RHO is authorised both to call and question witnesses, with the result that witnesses are subject to a form of examination-in-chief and cross-examination. While no burden of proof is formally placed upon the refugee claimant, the procedural system thus functions as though the claimant is to prove and the RHO to disprove. The claimant does benefit, however, from split board decisions, since an affirmative vote of only one board member is sufficient for allowing the claim. (Legislative amendments introduced by the Federal Government in 1992, however, would require a unanimous decision in order to recognise refugee status where the applicant had destroyed personal identity documents, visited the country of alleged persecution since making the claim, or came from a prescribed country which respected human rights.) The extended and conflictual nature of determination proceedings has been the major cause of delay in CRDD proceedings, and in 1990 an informal, expedited process was implemented as a means of increasing CRDD productivity.

The expedited procedure now used by the CRDD involves a fast-track procedure for claimants coming from designated countries which in the past have had high rates of refugee-claim acceptance. The expedited procedure thus depends on a presumption of refugee status for claimants from particular countries, and is heavily dependent both on a current high rate of acceptance and on political conditions in these countries. A claimant from a country designated as appropriate for expedited claims is referred to an interview with the RHO, generally accompanied by his or her counsel. On favourable assessment by the RHO, the claim will be referred to a single CRDD member, who will grant refugee status in summary fashion. Since mid-1990, approximately 44 per cent of claims before the CRDD have been dealt with in this expeditied fashion. Implementation of the procedure has allowed the Board to reduce the number of current, outstanding claims (the 'frontlog') from approximately 34 000 in January, 1991 to approximately 27 000 in September 1991.

In the future, more expeditious procedures which do not depend on presumptively high acceptance rates will have to be established if the CRDD is to fulfill its function of non-adversarial and expeditious adjudication of refugee claims. One proposal which has been advanced is to establish a more collaborative, investigative form of procedure, in which questioning is undertaken by CRDD members themselves, while retaining existing procedural guarantees of the right to counsel, legal aid, and the benefit of a split board decision in favour of the claimant. Such a collaborative, investigative form of procedure was partially adopted in the United States in 1991 with the implementation of proceedings before Asylum Officers. The Australian administrative determination procedure is in contrast highly expeditious in character, but in its present form would not be compatible with the constitutional guarantees of the Canadian *Charter of Rights and Freedoms*.

A second major feature of refugee determination is the treatment of what may be generally described as impermissible claims. Claims may be considered impermissible on a number of grounds, such as arrival of the claimant from a safe third country, security reasons, lack of documentation, or the manifestly unfounded nature of the claim itself. In neither Australia nor Canada are claims presently rejected on grounds of arrival from a safe third country, and it appears to be the manifestly unfounded claim which gives rise to the greatest pressure for expedited dismissal. Canada does so once again through cumbersome, adjudicative procedures; Australia does so through a more expedited form of its administrative procedure.

All refugee claims in Canada are subjected to a preliminary refugee inquiry, the object of which is to determine whether the claimant is ineligible and whether the claim can be said to have a 'credible basis.' Preliminary inquiries are held before a joint panel, composed of one adjudicator from the Adjudication Branch of the ministry and one member of the CRDD. The procedure is explicitly adversarial and counsel are present on behalf of the claimant in approximately 80 per cent of hearings, by virtue of legal aid and a system of designated counsel. The institution of the joint panel was created for purposes of deterrence and for purposes of screening out applicants from safe third countries, when it was thought that this ground of exclusion would be implemented in Canadian law. The joint panel has proven to be inefficient for screening purposes and is now avoided in over 90 per cent of cases through use of a Simplified Inquiry Procedure (SIP), which allows referral to the CRDD of refugee claims having a credible basis, following only a simple examination of the written file. Where a claim is contested for lack of a credible basis at the preliminary inquiry, the inquiry has tended to degenerate into a full hearing on the merits of the claim, since counsel for the claimant must adduce all available evidence to support the claim. A large proportion of ministerial resources is therefore committed to preliminary merits adjudication in a very small number of cases which may require re-litigation at the CRDD level if a credible basis is found to exist. Removal of the preliminary inquiry is now being discussed in Canada and was proposed in legislative amendments introduced by the Federal Government in 1992. The amendments would also confer on senior immigration officers (a return to the administrative model) the power to rule on the eligibility of refugee claimants to have their claim determined by the CRDD, notably in terms of whether they have come to Canada from a prescribed county whose refugee determination system respects the UN Convention Relating to the Status of Refugees. The amendment, if adopted, is likely to be resisted in the courts on constitutional grounds (Brun & Brunelle 1988; Brunelle 1987). Its removal would entail dismissal of manifestly unfounded cases by the CRDD itself.

Australia has integrated treatment of manifestly unfounded

claims into its existing institutional structures. A claim thought to be manifestly unfounded will be assessed on paper and without interview by a Regional Immigration Officer at the primary stage of the determination system. This Officer will make a summary report to a Delegate and, on confirmation of its manifestly unfounded character by the Delegate, the claimant will be excluded. Through implementation of this policy in 1990, Australia appears to have renounced its use of administrative 'turnabouts' which may have occurred prior to that time. The new procedures entail some limitation of primary level administrative authority, though 'turnabouts' will remain possible if highly expeditious procedures are adopted for confirmation of initial judgments that a claim is manifestly unfounded. In the absence of legislation relating to such questions in Australia, practice will depend on ministerial direction.

It should be noted that Australian practice in recent years has involved the detention of one category of refugee claimants. Claimants who arrived by boat or aeroplane and were detained by immigration officials, before being deemed to have technically entered Australia, were classified as Prohibited Non-Entrants. As such they were covered by Sections 88 and 89 of the *Migration Act*, which was interpreted as allowing for their detention for the duration of the determination process. Some classified as Illegal Entrants under Section 92 of the Act have been detained in the same manner. For some boat people that detention, as at mid-1992, had lasted for two and a half years. Although lawyers, some NGOs and the Human Rights Commission have rejected this interpretation of the Act, the Government has consistently upheld it, presumably as a necessary safeguard against a perceived potential flood of boat arrivals. This procedure is not applied to any other refugee applicants (except in very exceptional circumstances) and they remain at liberty in the community.

The relatively open Canadian adjudication system for refugee claims appears therefore to have drawn to itself a great deal of the primary burden of immigration and refugee regulation and control. Making a refugee claim allows a foreign non-resident to regularise his or her status during the process of adjudication, and the delays attendant on the procedurally complex process of preliminary and subsequent full hearings have provided a further incentive to make a refugee claim. The Australian procedures clearly provide less incentive, though the recent surge in Australian applications indicates that any procedure for refugee application will be preferred to exclusion or deportation. Before any conclusions can be drawn with respect to refugee determination procedures, however, a number of their incidental features should be noted.

A refugee claim in Australia in itself provides the claimant with no incidental benefits such as welfare payments, an employment permit, medical care or family allowance. Entitlements to these benefits have been made more restrictive in the last two years, although where the applicant was entitled to a benefit because of the status held prior to lodging a refugee claim, that entitlement remains. Health and income support benefits are now available only after determination has been effected; an employment permit is in principle available after a refugee claim is determined not to be manifestly unfounded, but obtaining the permit itself is often subject to considerable delay. These provisions are consistent with the general administrative model of regulation and control. To the extent that the measures of control assume a sharp division between internal and external population groups, and an expeditious determination process, it would appear even perverse to extend benefits to a potentially unlimited external population group, which could not be seen as suffering hardship from an extended determination process. In effect the Australian Government does assume some responsibility for the welfare of applicants, but it has preferred to do so not by granting any rights of access to assistance, but by providing selected NGOs with funds to which refugee applicants can apply.

In contrast, and again in a manner consistent with the general pattern of regulation and control, a claim for refugee status in Canada will attract significant benefits to the claimant. Refugee claimaints are entitled to social security or welfare payments and in the largest province, Ontario, some 24 000 claimants are presently receiving welfare, at a total cost of some $155 million. The number of welfare recipients is increasing, and funding is a matter of ongoing discussion between the federal, provincial and municipal governments. Payment of welfare will begin from the date of arrival or from the date of completion of the Personal Information Form necessary for completion of the refugee claim, depending on the province. A work permit may not be obtained, however, as in Australia, until completion of the preliminary refugee inquiry at which the credible basis of the claim is established. Given delays of three to four months in Canada for completion of this initial stage, and possible earlier delays prior to completion of the Personal Information Form (depending on the province), a refugee claimant will usually be on welfare for six months or more before a work permit may be obtained. There is therefore discussion of the creation of welfare dependency and accumulation of unnecessary cost, but current economic conditions do not ensure employment opportunities for the refugee claimant. Elimination of the preliminary inquiry will expedite granting of work permits. Health care is available subject to generally applicable initial residency periods, usually in the order of three months. Unemployment insurance is also available but benefits are dependent on having accumulated a number of weeks of gainful employment.

A determination that a person is a refugee is followed in Australia by grant of a temporary stay for a period not exceeding four years (rather than resident status as was the case until 1991). The individual then has the opportunity to apply for further temporary stay or permanent residence, subject to an ongoing need for protection and the availability of places in the migration program. This new provision in Australian law has been criticised as creating a 'four-year regime of suspense' (Hardy 1990, p. 4), and an 'uncertain sanctuary' (Murray 1990, p. 624). Canada has maintained the historical position that grant of refugee status is followed in almost all cases by landing for purposes of permanent residence.

There have also been substantial differences between Australia and Canada in terms of recourses against, and enforcement of, refugee determination decisions. Australia, consistently, allows no merits review by the courts from a refugee determination. The preclusive effect of denial of a court appeal on the merits is offset in some measure, however, by the very broad terms of judicial review in Australia, including whether denial of refugee status can be said to be 'unreasonable'. Although in 1978 the Full Court of the Federal Court of Australia held that a decision pertaining to a person who had not entered Australia was was not a decision under an enactment, and hence not reviewable under the *Administrative Decisions (Judicial Review) Act*, the courts have always had the power under the *Judiciary Act* to hear such cases. Then in 1991, the Full Court of the Federal Court defined refugee status decisions, in respect of persons who have not entered Australia, as conduct engaged in for the purpose of making a decision under an enactment. In this way such decisions can be heard under the *Administrative Decisions (Judicial Review) Act*. Judicial review may be difficult in the absence of eligibility for legal aid, however, and under the current legal aid system very few refugee applicants will receive aid.

In Canada appeal against a negative determination made by the CRDD is possible to the Federal Court of Appeal, with leave of the

Court. There is no appeal from a decision at a preliminary inquiry that a refugee claim has no credible basis, though here judicial review may be sought. Seeking leave to appeal to the Federal Court of Appeal, and making such an appeal, suspends any measure of deportation until exhaustion of all rights of appeal. The number of applications for leave to appeal is now increasing rapidly, given the increased rate at which decisions are being rendered by the CRDD. In 1990, 2242 applications for leave to appeal were received, of which 28 per cent were granted. Applications in 1991 more than doubled, to over 4500 applications, and this figure is expected to rise still further. The Court has been allowing approximately 55 per cent of appeals. The overall success rate of appellants has therefore been in the area of 15 per cent. Legislative amendments introduced in 1992 would bring the Canadian position closer to that of Australia. The amendments provide for elimination of the direct appeal to the Federal Court of Appeal and a single means of recourse (by way of judicial review, broadly drawn to parallel that of Australia and approximating the previous grounds of appeal) to the Federal Court, Trial Division, with leave.

Finally, given a refusal of a claim for refugee status, there remains a potentially important difference between Australia and Canada in terms of the granting of permission to stay on humanitarian and compassionate grounds. Such an application may be made at any stage of proceedings in Canada prior to a deportation order, by way of application for a Minister's Permit, and the Supreme Court of Canada has held that the Minister is under a duty to consider applications for exemption from the provisions of the *Immigration Act,* on humanitarian and compassionate grounds. In seeking to establish a more precise administrative regime in Australia in 1990, it was decided to eliminate the use of humanitarian grounds and to adopt a policy of 'mandatory deportation' in the event of an illegal entrant being refused refugee status and having failed to exercise the right of leaving Australia voluntarily. This provision appears never to have been given effect, however, and in 1991 it was announced that ministerial discretion could still be used to allow stay in Australia following rejection of a refugee claim. However, rigorous guidelines for the exercise of the discretion have been established ('exceptional cases presenting features of threat to personal security and intense personal hardship'), and the Minister must make twice-yearly statements to both Houses of Parliament on the exercise of this discretionary authority.

Conclusion

Adoption of an administrative or adjudicative model of regulation and control appears to be dictated not by careful estimates of the consequences of adoption of one or the other model (since this appears to be very difficult to do), but by underlying assumptions as to the nature of the state, the role of executive authority, and the nature of international population movement. The Australian concept of the state appears more dominant that that prevailing in Canada; the role of executive authority in policing its territorial limits is more accentuated; and international population movement accordingly is sought to be controlled in more affirmative fashion. One outstanding question is whether the administrative model provides a more effective means of regulation and control than the adjudicative model.

We are not convinced that this is the case. To the extent the adjudicative model invites challenge to administrative authority it is evident that this model cannot purport to systematically control immigration and refugee movement. On the other hand the grounds of entry and the criteria for granting refugee status are still defined by the state (subject of course to the requirements of the Refugee Convention of 1951), and adjudicative authorities, themselves subject to various forms of judicial review, will act according to law in granting or refusing entry or according refugee status. The process of entry and refugee determination is a transparent one and there are clear disincentives to going underground or effecting an illegal initial entry. Control is likely to be lost in the adjudicative model not initially or in the process of adjudication, but following adjudicative refusal of a claim to entry or claim to refugee status (usually the latter given its availability). At this critical stage, however, the possibility of control is enhanced by the previously transparent character of proceedings and the identity and contacts established by the claimant. Whether deportation is effected appears to depend more on the use made of humanitarian and compassionate grounds than on considerations of physical whereabouts or policing ability.

In the administrative model there are evident reasons why the questions of illegal entry and change of status dominate. Given external population pressure and the absence of available and transparent adjudicative procedures, illegal entry or overstaying is the only means of establishing a territorial connection, or perhaps even of making a refugee claim. There is therefore a major, front-end incentive to acting illegally or going underground, which is unlikely to be offset by denial of particular benefits. The administrative model therefore creates its problems of control *ab initio*, and the continuing problem of overstayers in Australia indicates that the means have yet to be found to correct this front-end problem. Change of status is also a problem and, given the possibly draconian consequences of departing the country once entry has been effected, Australia has been unable to prohibit change of status applications from within the country, as Canada has largely done. European states, faced with the impossibility of regulating entry to national territory, have extended regulatory authority to conditions of residence, and have been facilitated in so doing by the existence of national policing powers and widespread use of obligatory personal identity papers. In countries of the common law tradition, however, such internal regulatory authority has never been exercised, and this lack of internal regulatory authority presents what appear to be insuperable difficulties in term of control of internal movement by illegal entrants. The social costs of a large, intractable illegal population must therefore be assumed.

A second important question is whether a system, whatever its nature, conforms with the requirements of justice as expressed in human rights conventions (Glenn 1991). Any system which places selected categories of persons as beyond the mandate of accepted rights regimes, as far as that state's responsibility is concerned, is to be questioned. While the Canadian system does not do so, the Australian treatment of Prohibited Non-Entrants and Illegal Entrants would seem to constitute such a case. Moreover, the Australian exclusion of refugee applicants from health and welfare benefits for what is often in practice a lengthy period would seem to be a denial of justice.

Finally, the procedures used for the assessment of applications need to be examined in terms of their conformity to acceptable standards of justice. In Australia questions arise with respect to the assistance given to applicants in preparing their claim, the right to counsel in the primary hearing, the right to appeal a decision on the merits of the case, and the very location of the assessment procedure within the immigration bureaucracy.

Some claims are made that in each of these areas the Australian system falls short of the requirements of justice. In defence of the prevailing model, however, some would argue that in the interests of expediting processing of claims, maintaining costs within acceptable limits and retaining public support for the system, compromises are necessary. Clearly many Western countries are likely to struggle with such dilemmas for at least the remainder of this decade, as the movements of asylum seekers test sorely the processing model adopted, government budgets and public patience. In such circumstances, governments may find it difficult both to maintain control over the process and to conform to human rights requirements.

An adjudicative model which is implemented in an expensive, cumbersome and procedurally unsuitable manner will, however, exacerbate problems of control and not meet demands for procedural justice. In the absence of international agreement on population movement, the establishment of appropriate mechanisms for implementing a political community's definition of itself remains a major challenge. The criteria of natural justice are clearly relevant to this process. In their absence it is impossible to assert that a claim has been fairly treated, and impossible to know more generally whether the collective definition is being respected.

CHAPTER 11

Refugees and Other Migrants, International Instruments and Future Options and Dilemmas

Stuart Harris and Morton Weinfeld

Introduction

This chapter will develop three themes. First we present a critical overview of the current international regime which affects the world's refugee population. This section focuses on the Australian and Canadian responses within the international system as well as some general issues. Second, we explore the option of a regional approach, with particular reference to Canada, the North American Free Trade Agreement (NAFTA) and into Latin America as well. Third, we explore the possibility that the principle of state sovereignty itself may be challenged by other forces.

Current trends and contexts

For various reasons—armed conflicts, civil wars, political, ethnic or religious persecutions and mass abuse of human rights, environmental and other natural disasters, and economic and social deprivation—the extent of international movements of populations has grown substantially, causing a variety of social, political and economic problems.

Most of the movement has occurred 'spontaneously', if by that we mean migration outside authorised national migration programs or international resettlement arrangements. Such migration has, of course, been massive in the developing world. Most of the around 17 million people that the UN High Commission for Refugees (UNHCR) estimates live, through fear and force, outside their countries of nationality are in developing countries. Since the causes and nature of these movements are varied but interlinked, a many-layered solution involving international co-operation is similarly needed to prevent or deal with those problems.

The numbers that want to migrate to the developed world are large. The annual migration intake into the major migration receiving countries is less than 1 million a year. A similar number of migrants is in practice taken each year into Europe, despite an absence of formal immigration programs. In relation to the demand, however, the opportunities for authorised migration are limited. For those wanting to escape from generalised political oppression, from economic and social and political deprivation or simply from lack of economic opportunities, migration opportunities are too few, and barriers to their movement too high.

Particularly since the mid-1980s, in the face of more restrictive immigration procedures and reduced labour market needs for temporary migrants, there has been growing pressure to circumvent existing legal arrangements; migrants either cross borders illegally or enter legally as visitors or students but overstay after their authorised time has expired.

In 1990, estimates suggest there were at least 1 million illegal migrants in Europe (Martin, Honekopp & Ullman 1991, p. 591; Widgren 1990).

In addition, administrative difficulties have been exacerbated by the substantial growth in numbers of those overcoming the barriers to authorised migration by whatever means possible, and then seeking political asylum. Worldwide, asylum applications increased from 94 000 in 1983 to 660 000 in 1991, mostly in Europe.

These pressures, and the problems they raise, increased substantially with the movement of eastern European migrants into Western Europe since the lifting of the Iron Curtain. The growing inflow of undocumented migrants from Africa and the Middle East was also raising political concerns in Europe.

Recent Canadian legislation, notably Bill C-86 (1992), has been directed in part at the problem of controlling the influx of asylum seekers (refugee claimants) in Canada. Over the past few years, the backlog of 85 000 earlier refugee claimant files as of 1989 has been drastically reduced. But whatever intake system is established, the pressures on Canada may well persist.

Australia in 1992 had a waiting list of some 24 000 asylum seekers although, as in Canada, applications are now falling from their peak to average about 500–1000 a month.

For Australia, the existing problem is relatively small and the potential is less immediate than for Canada. It is seen as particularly significant, however, given the presumed pressure in its geographic region, in addition to spillovers possible from the changing European scene. One study suggests, for example, that: '. . . as a country of perceived wealth, opportunity and political stability, Australia will increasingly become a prime destination country for . . . intra-regional population flows . . .' that will result from growing emigration pressures in the Asia–Pacific region (National Population Council 1991a, p. 96).

From a global population perspective, and that of actors in the population system—individual migrants and/or refugees—the previous category distinctions have become blurred. In particular, the term asylum seekers increasingly encompasses those wanting to escape from personal persecution (for whom at least formally the international system provides institutional mechanisms and safeguards), generalised political oppression, economic, social and political deprivation or simply from lack of economic opportunities.

Clearly, migration has increasingly become less of a solution to world population problems. From 1881 to 1910, migration to North America and Australia took 20 per cent of Europe's population growth. During the 1970s, only 4 per cent of Europe's population growth and less than 2.5 per cent of that in Asia, Africa and Latin America was absorbed through migration (Brundtland 1987, p. 102). But declining percentages may still correspond to large absolute movements of population now and in the future.

Nevertheless, for refugees, including those referred to generally as refugees but having no formal international status as such (see below), resettlement is not only the least preferred solution but it is not feasible in almost all cases. Nor indeed do most of those leaving their country under duress want to be resettled. Of the seventeen million or so of such refugees, UNHCR sought resettlement in 1990 for just 150 000; of these less than half were actually relocated and resettled (UNHCR 1991, p. 12). The numbers of refugees actually resettled in 1989 were 84 000 in the United States (US Dept of Commerce 1991, p. 8), 37 000 in Canada (including refugees and designated classes) (EIC 1991a, p. 8) and 12 000 in Australia (Australian Bureau of the Census 1991, p. 144). For the United States the number is a drop from the 100 000 average level in the 1980s; for Australia, the 1989 figure marks a steady decline from the level of 22 000 in 1981. Only for Canada do we see a systematic increase corresponding to increases in general migration levels. The lower

American and Australian refugee figures may seem somewhat surprising given higher total levels of migration though in the latter case at least the rundown of Indochinese migration is a partial explanation.

The links between economic disparity and population movements are complex (Appleyard 1992) and, in the Asian region for example, economic development has reduced the extent of economic disparities. The virtual end of the independence process, and the political settlement of major conflicts such as Indochina, Afghanistan and possibly southern Africa may dampen flows. Moreover, the international interventions that contributed substantially to most major refugee situations (Zolberg, Suhrke & Aquayo 1986) were mostly linked to the now past Cold War superpower competition.

The common belief, however, is that pressure for future movements is likely to be stronger, a belief that, while needing qualification, has to be taken seriously.

UN population projections suggest that an additional 2.5–3.0 billion people will inhabit the planet in 2020, compared with 1990 estimates (UN 1986). This population growth could itself encourage substantial economic refugee movements from developing areas, despite the absolute material progress that has been made. Climate change, inducing drought, flooding and other ecological disasters could exacerbate this influx; one recent estimate, admittedly likely to be an upper limit, of the number of potential world environmental refugees reaches 10 million (Brown 1989, p. 60). And finally the impact of the end of the Cold War on regional and local conflicts is as yet unknown. Possibilities exist of political instability and the emergence of localised ethnic and religious disputes, civil wars and smaller interstate wars.

In short, there are reasons to presume that population pressures will be substantial on immigrant-receiving countries like Canada and the United States, Western Europe and Australia. The emergence of the next large refugee situation, in particular, is likely to be largely unpredictable—the Kurds, Afghans and eastern Europeans are a few (not easily predictable) past examples.

It may also be sensible to accept that given such pressures, and with increasing temporary migration, full control of inwards population movements would be impossible without resource-intensive and unacceptably intrusive administrative procedures. For despite Australia's advantage of a sea frontier, and Canada's buffer of two oceans and the United States, they will have a rapidly growing tourist intake and continued growth in business exchanges. They will need, therefore, to balance sensitively frontier control with the encouragement of temporary entry.

The potential problems that such population flows offer in regionally integrated areas introduce further policy questions. Thus, in the European Community following Europe 1992 and in the North American free trade area, especially with the proposed inclusion of Mexico, the greater freedom of internal population movement is likely to lead to tougher controls at the external border. For the Australia–New Zealand free trade area, where free movement has been in force for some years, there has been an increase in Pacific Island migrants into Australia through their open access to New Zealand. Overall, however, apart from some move towards commonality of Australian and New Zealand policies, the Australia–New Zealand link has not been significant in Australia's total immigration program.

In receiving countries, the seeming lack of control over inflows of spontaneous movement of large numbers of asylum seekers has created tensions about the capacity for social integration of the migrants. The consequent political hostility reduces support for humanitarian approaches to refugees and reinforces assistance fatigue for aid to refugees. As well as this concern, there is the problem of the additional administrative resources needed to maintain a nation's control of its immigration intake and retain its sovereignty as the pressures of spontaneous migration grow.

Sudden large-scale migration exerts indirect effects as well. It poses potential security problems. These may be linked to border, ethnic or other disputes between countries. In Australia's case, public security concerns arise from the potential for large numbers of boat people to arrive from such areas as Hong Kong, China (Australia's traditional fear, exacerbated with recent arrivals of mainland Chinese by boat seeking entry) and the Philippines. In such circumstances, Australia may be forced to take restrictive measures that could expose it to politically or economically damaging reactions in the region. Such migration also has broader foreign policy implications as a cause of hostility in itself or in relation to the measures taken to deal with it—either in accepting or rejecting refugees or with the continually vexed question of visas.

The responses of developed countries, even those of once liberal countries, to what is seen as an uncontrolled flow of asylum seekers, have increasingly been unilateral measures to keep refugees out through tougher conditions of entry. Legal opportunities for entry have been tightened, support while asylum claims were investigated reduced, and related regulatory provisions intensified, including more restrictive visa requirements and penalties for transporting undocumented migrants. Firmer action to expel particular groups, such as the large-scale expulsion of Romanian Gypsies from Germany, may become more widespread. The tightening of the administrative approach to asylum seekers has been parallelled in both Australia and Canada, although not to the extent of some European countries. Nevertheless, Australia has returned undocumented migrants to China and to Cambodia.

These developments affect existing international refugee and migration arrangements. From an international perspective the common receiving-country argument—that these were not political refugees needing a humanitarian response but economic migrants— threatens to put undocumented migrants outside the coverage of existing international arrangements based on an acceptance that political refugees are entitled to help. There are fears that genuine refugees will suffer under the new arrangements being introduced, because of the greater difficulty of reaching a safe haven and, once there, through the imposition of tighter conditions. The UNHCR has, in consequence, been exhorting governments to ensure opportunities exist for asylum seekers to establish their status as refugees.

Problems of international migration and of international refugees are increasingly converging. More specifically, in practice, the issues of migrants, temporary workers and refugee flows have increasingly merged with those of asylum seekers. In particular, it is not always easy to distinguish between asylum seekers escaping from unacceptable conditions and those seeking to improve their situation. Moreover, a refugee may become a migrant through seeking asylum, and those refused permanent settlement on refugee grounds may become illegal or undocumented migrants (Hawkins 1989, p. 195).

Existing administrative arrangements seem to have been sufficiently open that even after they have failed to achieve refugee status, apparently on average some 75–80 per cent remained in the country of reception (Anon 1991, p. 18). In some contexts, this reflected an acceptance that the general fears of the refugee were broadly justified even if not judged sufficient to meet the specific legal requirements for refugee status. Nevertheless, even though the institution of asylum has been overburdened and at times misused, the process of claiming asylum appears in the past at least to have been a reasonably effective mechanism of migration.

Given the global reach of movements of spontaneous migrants or refugees, and because of the administrative as well as political problems of unilateral measures, the need to deal with the problem on a collective basis internationally is widely argued and generally accepted. It is also acknowledged that existing arrangements cannot respond effectively to the current problems. The then UN High Commissioner said that '. . . it was time the international community took a fresh look at the legal instruments available, and identified a political means to address the problem more effectively' (Hocke 1989, p. 6).

Before considering the new requirements, we need to put the existing arrangements into perspective. The many international and regional conventions covering refugees, temporary workers and involuntary migrants provide a limited degree of protection for those involved. Nevertheless, the international regime for the handling of migration and refugee issues is limited in at least two respects. First, the various factors important in the global approach to population movements are dealt with separately and discretely in the official international system. As well as the UNHCR, the International Labour Organisation (ILO), and the UN itself deal with particular aspects, as does the International Organisation for Migration (IOM) and a substantial number of regional official or informal forums, Western and non-Western.

Second, and perhaps more fundamentally, the international regime for refugees is incomplete and dated. The existing arrangements were based on a limited post-World War II view of world population movements as taking place within authorised migration programs of displaced persons or consisting of refugees being resettled because of persecution. The later emergence of temporary migration (guest-workers) could, it seemed at least initially, be handled within this view, although this became increasingly in doubt over time. The wider deficiencies of this incomplete and western-oriented view have become increasingly apparent (Loescher 1989, p. 9).

In formal terms, this situation has not changed much although the UNHCR, in the face of major international refugee problems of a different nature emerging, has expanded its role despite constraints placed upon it. It means, however, that among other things there is no commonly accepted response to refugee problems, nor are all refugees treated similarly. Refugees are not easily defined and do not know what protection ultimately they can reasonably expect. Although the existence of state control at the border makes all acts of migration nominally political acts, more substantial foreign policy and political factors, rather than objective factors, have in the past been major determinants of how particular groups of migrants have been treated within the system.

There are now three broad categories of refugees relevant to our interest here. The first consists of those fitting the definition of the 1951 UN Convention (and 1967 Protocol) on the status of refugees. The Convention's definition of refugees, which remains the formal definition today, was essentially in terms of persecution (Coles 1989, p. 374). It was associated with a concern with the individual rather than groups, while refugees were by definition outside their home country. Perhaps as fundamental was the protection against coerced return to the home country (refoulement).

The convention based on this framework became the basis for specific legal obligations by Convention signatories. Since it also reflected the political perceptions and dynamics of the early postwar years, it contributed subsequently to political factors, particularly Cold War ideology, becoming important in determining whether or not persecution existed. This has come into salience again with the US treating spontaneous migrants from Haiti and, earlier, Salvadoreans as not suffering persecution, with those from Cuba being more readily assumed to be victims of persecution. Such political differentiation had also been a factor in the acceptance of Indo-Chinese migrants.

The gaps in the formal regime led, in practice, to the development of a second category of refugees: those not statutory refugees but accepted as 'persons of concern' to the UNHCR. These, termed 'extra-Convention refugees' by one High Commissioner (Hocke 1989, p. 6), are defined on a group rather than individual basis, are usually victims of warfare, civil strife or natural disasters and are normally expected to return to their country of origin. They are usually outside their own borders, although exceptions, notably the Iraqi Kurds, exist. Much of the international discussion, at least until the last five or so years, has concentrated on this category.

The third category, variously termed spontaneous, undocumented or illegal migrants, has become the focus of concern to developed countries and the centre now of much international attention. It contains within it the asylum seekers and illegal migrants in the developed countries. Because of the greater interest in seeking asylum as a way to gain entry to another country, those in this category are not easily distinguished from the second and perhaps the first categories.

There are a variety of motivations for movements outside planned migration programs. Unplanned migrations include sizeable national groups who, being temporarily resident in another country at a time of upheaval (political, social or ecological), do not wish to return home at least while conditions remain unchanged. USA, Canada and Australia have all had this experience with People's Republic of China (PRC) nationals and all have implemented specific domestic measures to prevent unsafe return to the PRC of those with claims arising from the 1989 tragedy in Beijing. All three countries, although to different degrees, have seen their existing onshore refugee determination system considerably taxed by increased numbers of asylum seekers from various sources. Of course, there is also 'spontaneity' behind the decision of many people from developed countries, Britain and Europe, to come as visitors to the USA, Canada and Australia and overstay with the intention of starting a new life.

And there are the obvious profiles of sudden, involuntary mass movements requiring emergency action on the part of the inter-national community. Again, these can have a variety of causes—political, environmental or economic—and they can be of an internal or external nature, such as the sudden arrival of tens of thousands of Albanians in Italy in 1991; more than 120 000 'Marielito' Cubans on US shores in 1980–81; the Kurds in Iraq in 1991; the hundreds of thousands of Salvadorans displaced and dislocated in the past twelve years; and in Africa, estimates of up to 4.5 million in Sudan; 300 000 in Chad; more than 1 million in Ethiopia; 800 000 in Somalia; and over 4 million in South Africa.

In addition to the 17 million or so international refugees there are also substantial numbers of internally displaced persons, with estimates as high as 20 million (Shenstone 1992, p. 18). Their signif-icance in the present context is that in the absence of remedial action, many of them may be forced to seek safety and protection in neigh-bouring states—adding to the already unwieldy numbers of extra-Convention refugees.

Action by the Security Council in the Gulf, Somalia and Yugoslavia has placed the issue of internally displaced persons firmly on the international political agenda, and although many are sceptical, there is a hope in some quarters that the CSCE (Conference on Security and Co-operation in Europe), with its new conflict prevention procedures (1990) could provide a framework to address the inter-national security aspects of mass displacements at least in Europe.

The relevant international organisations are increasingly finding it necessary to clarify and identify the categories of mass population movements in order to begin to define options for more appropriate and expeditious solutions. A logical adjunct to this defining process is to look at the full cycle of movements from their causes through to their outcome (such as ethnic or internal conflicts) causing people to flee to nearby countries, the sudden socio-economic challenge for the receiving countries, the immediate humanitarian and protection needs of the displaced, and longer-term solutions including 'safe return' to the country of origin, or reintegration or resettlement where necessary.

The problem is that measures to restrict asylum seekers are seen as threatening policies and attitudes towards those genuinely needing help. The question for Canada and Australia, as for other receiving countries, is how to balance on the one hand, the wish to protect their sovereignty and their public's undoubted wish to have a clear say in who joins their community with, on the other hand, the wish to maintain the humanitarian institution of asylum.

Australian and Canadian approaches internationally

Australian and Canadian current approaches to international discussions about collective solutions reflect this growing problem of control of national borders and the administrative problems associated with the large increase in asylum seekers.

Historically, with only small differences of approach, both countries had large immigration programs, and generally supported the development of the existing international regime. Both countries, although with some delay, ratified the 1951 Convention and signed the 1967 Protocol, and both have been active members of the UNHCR's Executive Committee (Hawkins 1989, p. 156). As Hawkins has described, Australian and Canadian reactions to past refugee flows have been mixed. The overall record of both countries on refugees is impressive but, while the Canadian response to the Ugandan Asians was positive, neither was quickly responsive to the Chilean refugee situation. Initially, Australia's response to East Timorese refugees was limited as was its early response to Vietnamese refugees. Both Canada and Australia, of course, eventually became major recipients of Indochinese refugees.

Both countries in international discussions of the issues have given support to the need to deal with the issues in a global context and to the UNHCR's mandated objectives for refugees. The latter, apart from an added emphasis on prevention, remained those of the earliest international (NGO) discussions in 1921 (Smyser 1987, p. 6)—that is, the need, in order of preference, for voluntary repatriation, integration in the country of first asylum or resettlement in third countries.

Like other Convention parties, Australia and Canada have accepted specific obligations towards those formally defined as refugees, including an obligation not to forcibly return those meeting the Convention criteria. Consequently, it is not surprising that support for limiting the term to those meeting the Convention definition of refugees has been increasingly strongly articulated, with 'extra-Convention refugees' being referred to simply as 'internationally displaced persons' (Walker 1990, p. 4).

Both countries have articulated specific refugee policies, recognising their importance as part of their international relations, for Australia particularly in Asia, as well as constituting an important component of the immigration program. For its part, however, Australia has increasingly stressed that its acceptance of Indochinese refugees was part of a burden-sharing exercise rather than a population-building process of migration.

With the emergence of the problem of asylum seekers, Australia and Canada have been closely involved with extensive discussions in Europe to co-ordinate international action to exercise greater border control. A recent statement by the National Population Council in Australia affirmed the importance of a fundamental commitment to an active refugee policy that accepts third country resettlement in the absence of a durable solution, but that also addresses root causes, seeks to resolve temporary refugee situations and facilitates repatriation and integration through aiding political, economic and social development goals (1991).

The Council also argued that Australia has no moral obligation to accept for settlement those seeking refugee status in response to environmental or economic causes. The inclusion of the term environmental is significant. For example, were ocean levels to rise in the event of global warming, the possibility of a regional exodus of environmental refugees from the Pacific Island Nations or from countries such as Bangladesh, would be strong.

The reference to resolving temporary refugee situations is also important for Australia (although less so for Canada) since its interests differ substantially from those of European countries. The European authorities are concerned with what they term 'irregular movements' of asylum seekers since, apart from many Eastern Europeans, they see asylum seekers as moving from a country of first asylum to a developed country. This is also largely the case for Canada. Of course, all countries are countries of first asylum for those who overstay their lawful temporary entry. More important for Australia, however, is that it could be the country of first asylum for any spontaneous migration from Asian or Pacific Island countries. Hence a high priority given by Australia in the late 1970s to the issue of temporary asylum, responding to the outflow of Indochinese refugees.

From Australia's national interest viewpoint, the need to obtain international help in the event of a large flow of asylum seekers of this kind would seem to be the first priority of any international discussions involving understandings on temporary asylum and burden sharing. Yet an articulation of Australia's policy proposals based on the lessons of the Comprehensive Plan of Action (CPA) for handling Vietnamese refugees, does not indicate this as the priority. The emphasis is directed more to issues of basically economic or South–North movements of migrants, with an emphasis on 'temporary assistance and care and maintenance while awaiting return' (Anon 1991, p. 17).

The CPA was important in that, as a comprehensive package, it achieved an overall resolution of the various issues. It distinguished between refugees under the Convention definition and migrants; it looked at cases individually, it provided for resettlement on a substantial scale and included a sizeable orderly departure program from Vietnam with access to developed countries to reduce incentives to exit as asylum seekers. It also involved enforced return for those judged to be economic migrants This is what some see as its attraction as a model and what gives others problems, partly because of the difficulty of defining when involuntary return is appropriate.

The Vietnamese refugee situation offers other lessons, however, apart from Australia's potential as a country of first asylum. It demonstrated that the difference between a refugee and an illegal migrant was often simply a political value judgement.

It also raised the issue of what constitutes a durable solution. In the case of Indochinese refugees in the late 1970s, a rigid approach to durable solutions led to several ASEAN countries rejecting or threatening to reject refugees from Indochina, towing them back out to sea. A move which Australia initiated in the Thirtieth (1979) Session of the Executive Committee of the UNHCR achieved a degree of agreement on temporary asylum (or temporary refuge) which acknowledged, in effect, that countries of first asylum were not expected to provide for permanent settlement. That agreement, which provided for international help, contributed to reducing this problem. Following this move back from where non-return had come increasingly to mean, by all but the ASEAN countries involved, asylum in the sense of a durable solution, the exclusion of refugees was largely discontinued. This not only met more effectively the humanitarian need of the refugees themselves but also the national interests of Australia since the refugees frequently headed, or were pointed, in its direction.

The question of how far the CPA offers a model is difficult to judge without further research—and a study of the CPA is currently underway (Coulombe 1991). There were several special factors, however, which made it possible but which will be difficult to repeat. Achieving Vietnam's co-operation was crucial; the ideological component of the conflict that gave rise to the refugees made definition of persecution simpler than likely in other contexts; and the major co-operative effort from resettlement countries will also be difficult to replicate. The experience also illustrated the difficulty of framing comprehensive solutions that did not provide incentives to further refugee flows.

A satisfactory solution of the temporary asylum problem does depend upon a more systematic collective approach to other problems. Without this, the essential achievement of, for example, an orderly resettlement program, such as for the Vietnamese (or Chileans) would be difficult. Collective international solutions, however, depend upon reconciling two major areas of difference. The first is the difference between those emphasising the need for control—the national perspective; and those emphasising international or human rights concerns. The international perspective also frequently overlaps with the second difference, which is the difference between the developed and the developing countries.

These differences lead to considerable difficulties in obtaining a meeting of minds on how to deal with those who fall between the Convention refugee and the explicitly economic migrant. Although it is partly a financial resources issue, it does not stem from economic differences. Migration, at manageable levels, is generally thought to benefit the receiving country (National Population Council 1991) while also being beneficial to the source country (Appleyard 1992). It is the political factors that are crucial and have to be addressed. The need to co-operate with the source country on the refugees is emphasised but is not helped by a definition which, being based on persecution, is necessarily offensive to the source country. The OAU definition of what constitutes a refugee in Africa—someone 'who is compelled to flee' avoids this problem, whatever its other limitations, as does that relating to Palestinian refugees, accepted by the West in 1949, as those 'who had lost their home' (Coles 1989, p. 375).

The various themes of international discussions continue to emphasise such concepts as 'global approaches', 'root causes', and 'durable solutions'. The logic in looking at the problems globally stems from accepting that transport and communication changes make it possible for asylum seekers to come from all continents, from other world-wide interdependencies, and from the commonality of many of the causal factors. There are also limitations, however, if it confuses the different nature and specific causes of particular population movements and varying characteristics of receiving countries. It would be easy to forget, for example, that the overwhelming majority of those currently displaced would want to return to their own country or, as with the large numbers of illegal Indonesians in Malaysia, want at least a compatible socio-cultural environment.

A regional alternative to the global approach has at times been put forward by some developed countries, which proposes that countries in each region accept responsibility for solving the problems of refugees in their region. This leads to major problems in a context of global interdependence, and a multilateral approach to such things as protection of refugees and burden-sharing. It would also pose major problems for Australia. The possible consequences for Canada in NAFTA are discussed below.

The need to deal with root causes reflects a need to deal with underlying social and international forces—such as poverty and institutionalised violence—that generate major population and refugee flows to reduce the number of potential asylum seekers. The Canadian government has emphasised targeting potential areas with development aid as one means of dealing with root causes.

The desirability of durable solutions rather than short-term solutions that might create more problems than they solve would seem to be self evident. Yet the Indochina experience indicates that defining correctly what in fact are durable solutions is important. Perhaps even more important is how the burden is shared internationally.

Elements of solutions around which discussions are taking place internationally include:

1 encouragement to governments in source countries to control migrant outflow and to provide reasonable conditions for the return of refugees, including provision of financial assistance for reintegrating returnees. For reasons we have given, the belief that these objectives can be achieved in other than exceptional cases may be drawing unduly optimistic conclusions from the Vietnamese case.

2 clearer international arrangements for the second category of refugees (possibly another protocol to the 1951 Convention). While widely supported as a general objective, its specifics reflect wide divergences

322

of position. Australia has argued that it should be based upon enshrining the important human right of individuals to leave their country and return, but should also reinforce the right of receiving countries to reject entry and enforce return (Anon 1991, p. 18). The question is whether the international community would accept unchallenged such an exercise of national sovereignty.

Suggestions have also been made for generalising from the 1984 Cartagena Declaration dealing with refugees in Central America. There is no general agreement on that, however, nor on an African (1967 OAU Convention) model, both of which extend refugee status to groups rather than individuals and emphasise burden-sharing as well as elimination of the problem.

Such solutions are not greatly welcomed by humanitarian interests which reflect wide unease at sending back potential refugees to situations of civil, social and cultural disadvantage. Others in the international community fear the Cartagena and OAU principles would increase the numbers of unfounded asylum seekers.

Discussion of these ideas continues in the Working Group on Solutions and Protection under the UNHCR as well as in an 'informal group' of various largely European countries in which Australia and Canada participate. This has the disadvantage (or maybe to some participants the advantage) that developing countries are not involved.

UNHCR has for some time thrown out a challenge to member countries to think about the protection and other needs of 'persons of concern' to the UNHCR who fall outside the 1951 Convention—essentially displaced persons. UNHCR officials acknowledge that this category of 'humanitarian' extra-convention refugees accounts for up to 90 per cent of persons currently under UNHCR's care. It is also accepted that the ultimate goal for 'persons of concern' is return to their country of origin. The difficulty is that the nature of the problem has changed since the international regime was established. Only a small proportion of those in need of humanitarian assistance today are covered by the 1951 Convention definition. The problem is how to retain effectively the important provisions regarding prohibition of refoulement while dealing effectively with those who have left their homes not because of persecution as defined in the 1951 Convention but because they are victims of generalised violence, civil disturbance or political instability, often compounded by severe economic hardship.

Two components of this include, as indicated earlier, a recognition that for many outflows temporary asylum may be desirable while accepting that integration or resettlement may not. Associated with this might be a shift in the emphasis on return, with less weight put on its voluntary nature and more on how to ensure its safety.

A further shift in thinking is a recognition that population movements cannot be dealt with in isolation. A holistic approach is seen as necessary, bringing together UN and other international agencies dealing with such disparate issues as human rights, population policies, environmental policies and global economic development. The mechanisms for bringing about such a coordinated approach have yet to be determined. In that context some suggestions have been made for regional approaches.

From regions, blocs and hemispheres to international approaches

The present patterns of international migration in general, and refugee movements in particular, are affected in some cases by geographic proximity and, more likely, by contiguity. We have focused on Australia's experience with Asian migration. Consider now the case of Hispanic migration in the Americas. Looking at Mexico, we note that the volume of Mexican migration to the United States has been large and growing absolutely from the 1960s to the 1980s, though the percentage have been relatively constant, from 13.3 per cent in the decade of the 1960s to about 12 per cent in the 1980s (about 14.8 per cent in 1988). A similar pattern applies for total Hispanic immigration from all sources to the United States. The major transformation in American migration patterns has been the drop in European migration and the increase in Asian migration.

In Canada, we note that the percentage of Hispanic migrants rose from 0.2 per cent for the years 1946–55 to about 8–9 per cent for the years 1985–87 (Mata 1988, p. 16). Looking at immigration by country of last permanent residence indicates an increase in the proportion of Canadian permanent residents from Central and South America from 7.0 per cent in 1982 to 10.6 per cent in 1991, with a high of 12.9 per cent in 1986. The proportions of *refugee claimants* (or 'asylum seekers') from South and Central America are even higher, ranging from 15.5 to 17.2 per cent for the three years 1989–91 inclusive. Almost all this movement has been northward; relatively few immigrants and refugees from Central and South America have reached Western Europe and Australia.

Similarly in Europe, we note that the percentage breakdown of extra-EC foreign employees in the twelve EC nations in 1988 was 22 per cent other European countries, 22.6 per cent Morocco, 22.3 per cent Algeria, 13.2 per cent Turkey, 7.1 per cent Yugoslavia. 1.2 per cent Tunisia, and 11.5 per cent all other countries (Commission of the European Communities 1990). There are relatively few recent migrants from Latin America or Asia.

Asian migrants, including refugees, are most mobile. During the 1980s they have comprised 30–40 per cent of the total immigrant proportion to Australia. But these percentages are similar to those for the United States, and lower than those for Canada, where Asian immigrants comprised 40–50 per cent of the intake throughout the 1980s and into the early 1990s. On the other hand, black Africans move least and if anywhere to Europe, though increasing numbers of Somalis are arriving in Canada.

Despite the Asian pattern noted above, as a general rule, we are not surprised that refugees from Argentina, Chile, Haiti or Cuba move to the United States (and Canada), that it is in Hong Kong that we have large concentrations of Vietnamese and others in refugee camps, that North Africans and eastern Europeans move to Europe, and that Ethiopian refugees are concentrated in Sudan and Somalia and Afghan refugees in Pakistan and Iran.

It is inherent in the nature of the crises which create spontaneous migrants, from wars and ethnic repression to natural disasters, that geographic proximity and contiguity play some role in the location of refugee camps and other refugee concentrations. The question arises as to whether proximity and contiguity will likely play increasing roles in an eventual enlargement of the role of resettlement as one refugee option, and in seeking greater international co-ordination of approaches to these problems.

One factor which may enhance a regional or hemispheric approach to resettlement, and indeed to population movements generally, is the trend toward regional trade blocs. In some cases, such as the EC, international agreements include clear stipulations encouraging the free movements of goods, capital, ideas, and labour (that is, people). For a review of the evolutionary process of freedom of movement given to EC member states, see Seche (1988).

Whatever the future of Europe, the EC momentum is clearly toward increased intra-regional migration. While the nationality breakdown of the twelve EC countries reveals that there has been more migration from non-EC sources than other EC countries, the non-EC sources are those of greater contiguity or proximity, as seen above. But by definition, refugees from an EC member would have preference over others in the queue.

In North America, the negotiations for a tri-partite North America Free Trade Agreement (NAFTA) have been proceeding. While most of the public and private discussions have focused on trade matters, informed opinion suggests that at some point the freer (not absolutely free) movement of people would be a logical consequence (Hart 1990; Ostry 1991). Indeed, some have argued that an eventual hemispheric free trade arrangement might ensue, as a counterpoint to the European bloc, and to growing integration in the Asia–Pacific region, building on a NAFTA. Surely any such eventuality would likely increase the possible intra-hemispheric flows of migrants in general, including possible refugee claimants under a NAFTA regime, economic planners might begin to think of regional or continental labour markets.

The question which emerges is whether a move towards greater regional economic interdependence, including greater movements of peoples, would translate into greater regional responsibilities for refugee resettlement, or immigration generally.

This type of sectoral approach is already embedded in regional structures of the UN or ILO. Thus a recent ILO meeting dealing with non-EC migrant workers to the EC reflected a configuration which was a European–Mediterranean–North African one; along with six EC countries were Yugoslavia, Turkey, Morocco, Algeria, Tunisia, and Poland (International Labour Office 1990).

Geographical proximity should theoretically play its major refugee role for those refugees able somehow to lay their claims in the receiving country. For example, in 1989, roughly 13.2 per cent of all immigrants to Canada, including refugees, were from Central and South America and the Caribbean. These regions provided only 10.9 per cent of all those admitted specifically as refugees or designated classes, reflecting perhaps that these three regions in 1989 were less likely to serve as refugee source countries. Of the top ten refugee source countries in 1989 only one, El Salvador, is in the American hemisphere.

However, of those individuals who claimed refugee status *in Canada* in 1989, fully 19.2 per cent were from these three proximate source regions (Stibernik 1992.) Thus one wonders whether under an expanded NAFTA regime immigrants and/or refugees from Latin America might be advantaged. This is already the case regarding certain types of cross border movements of Canadians and Americans covered under the North America Free Trade Agreement. As such special considerations would flow from bilateral or multilateral treaty arrangements, they might likely also escape the charge of discrimination against other immigrants or refugees; treaties by definition discriminate in favour of citizens of one country over citizens of another. But it should be clear that the degree to which regional free trade agreements could or should evolve into broader linkages involving freer movements of peoples is a question whose resolution lies more in the future.

Any evolution toward greater regionalisation in dealing with refugee movements might have a variety of effects. One analyst has claimed that regionalising the international protection of refugees might 'Balkanize' any universal, truly international system (Winter 1990, p. 41). In some cases, a North American focus on hemispheric integration might marginalise further the masses of refugees in Asia and Africa, and reinforce the subtle and open racial biases reflected in recent movements of immigrant restrictions, and comparatively favoured treatment of the (white) eastern European refugees found in North America and Western Europe.

On the other hand, regionalisation may provide a useful point of departure on the way to a more global approach to world population systems, of which refugees are only a part. The processes of transportation, resettlement, and refugee integration may become less costly and more successful. Moreover, discussions of global, interdependent, approaches to these problems often founder on the rocks of national sovereignty; yet greater regionalisation along the lines of that in EC or NAFTA may have a long-run effect of modifying claims of national sovereignty, even with regard to movements of peoples.

Countries like Canada, the United States, Australia, and to a lesser extent Western Europe are doubly fortunate. While they are the countries with the greatest economic ability (and land mass) to absorb refugees and additional population, they are also farthest removed from the source countries. Other affluent countries, like Japan or the Gulf States, which cannot or will not integrate large numbers of refugees, might be expected to play a greater financial role in any interdependent approaches. Yet it is possible that the future will see greater examples of refugee claimants overcoming the barriers of distance to lay claims in these developed western societies. (It is of note that claims laid in Canada declined from 36 000 to 30 000 from 1990 and 1991. It remains to be seen if this represents a trend.) The actual number of admissions depends on the number of claims and the acceptance rate, and here we see conflicting forces at work in Canada. Consider the evidence since the introduction of the new refugee processing system for claims made in Canada, beginning in January of 1989. For the years 1989–91, over 95 per cent of claims made were judged credible at first hearing. At second hearing, the ratio of those accepted as refugees to those denied (ignoring those claimants who withdrew) was 4744:562 or 8.44 to 1 in 1989, 10 710:2913 or 3.67 to 1 in 1990, and 19 425:7516 or 2.58 to 1 in 1991. The acceptance ratios are declining, but the applications are increasing at an even greater rate, which leads to an increase in overall admissions (Stibernik 1992).

How do these acceptance rates compare with those obtained for refugee applicants abroad, whether in camps or elsewhere? Consider the statistics for the period September 1990 to August 31 1991. Of 14 521 applicants for private sponsorship, 9256 were accepted; the ratio of acceptance to denials was 9256 to 2374, or 3.90 to 1. For government sponsorship, 5828 applied and 3327 were accepted; the ratio of acceptances to denials was 3327 to 1612, or 2.06 to 1. Overall, the ratio was 3.15 to 1. (Note that some applications were withdrawn.) This is roughly comparable to the rates cited above for claims made in Canada for similar time periods; the evidence does not suggest that refugees improve their chances dramatically by laying their claims in Canada. It is also not clear whether the overseas acceptance ratios are declining in a fashion comparable to those within Canada (Trottier 1992). (It should be realised that, in all of the statistics given above, acceptances in one time period may refer to claims made in a previous period.)

The determination process within Canada of course differs widely from the determination and selection process which takes place outside Canada, often in camps, and under the supervision of External Affairs. It is thus difficult to compare figures on 'acceptance rates', particularly since the nature of Canada's obligation to those refugees is far different than the obligations under international law for those claimants in Canada (Grushman 1992). But it is clear that more and more claims are being made from Canadian soil, where claimants may have access to more legal representation, and media reporting of varying degrees of sympathy. Further analysis breaking down the previously cited figures by specific source countries would shed light on the effect of proximity to Canada, inter alia, on acceptances of refugee claims.

The likely increase in refugee claims made from within Canada or Australia, the political and demographic pressures, and the humanitarian imperatives, pose a severe challenge to territorial sovereignty.

Sovereignty: possible limits

Sovereignty becomes the answer to the following question: according to what principles of natural justice do the citizens of Canada, and Australia enjoy their immense endowments of land and natural resources? The question is particularly germane to environmental refugees, since the creation of democratic stable societies might be seen as a man made construction, *vis à vis* claims of political refugees. For those achievements perhaps citizens of liberal democratic societies might take some credit. It is impossible to 'blame' Bangladeshis for the global warming and sea level rises which potentially threaten them. (We should note as well that many convention refugees, or those fleeing generalised violence and chaos, are not its instigators but its victims.)

Sovereignty is thus the last frontier, and is challenged when refugee claims are made. 'Coerced and other uncontrolled population movements challenge that aspect of sovereignty subsumed within the principle of community and self-determination' (Goodwin-Gill 1988, p. 169).

There may well be forces at work which can weaken sovereignty as an acceptable justification for those societies which seek to keep refugee intake at low or declining levels.

Many precedents already exist for the potential restriction of sovereignty. While these cannot all be reviewed, it is important to list some of them. First we have rights of passage through water, land, and air space of various sovereign states by other states, though it is not clear whether a generalised right of innocent transit through such space has yet developed in final form (Delupis 1974). Certainly the inviolability of foreign embassies and consulates is another example, which would include the right of some sort of asylum in these protected areas. Foreign military bases, generally established through mutual consent, also represent a case of restricted sovereignty of the host country over a part of its territory.

More intriguing for our argument is that of the equitable use of water. While states have the right to use water in their own territory, that right has historically been limited to what has been considered 'reasonable and equitable' use. Such use must take into account the right of downstream states to use such water for irrigational or other purposes (Delupis 1974, pp. 95–7).

We also have the existence of refugee camps in various countries of the world. These camps occupy the land mass of various countries. Under international law, these countries, usually adjacent or near the refugee homelands, may not forcibly evict refugees, under the non-refoulement principal. However, the issue remains that for as long as they persist, these camps and camp members encroach upon the sovereignty of the host state. They add financial and administrative burdens. While generally the criminal law of the host country applies, administration of the camps, including law and order, often involves extra state entities such as the UN. The host countries may be required to endure a variety of social, economic, or political consequences from this presence which may not be salutary. Yet it is not clear that any jurisprudence within international law has firmly established any legal or customary entitlement for these camps.

Western states are used to seeing refugee camps located at some remove. Thus the special camps set up in Florida for the detention of Haitian refugee claimants, like those earlier for the Mariel Cubans, represented a rather traumatic initiation to mass refugee realities for North Americans.

One might note two points. First, on many issues, such as clashes over water rights, or recently, alleged overfishing by Portugal and Spain in Canadian waters, international law may be a far weaker instrument than power politics. Second, the case of refugee camps may represent a somewhat voluntary ceding of sovereignty.

The newly emerging field of environmental law may yet pose the greatest challenge to sovereignty. This may develop from a number of lines of argument.

First is the distinction among convention refugees, environmental refugees and other spontaneous migrants. Is there any basis for expanding the notion of refugee to include those seeking safe haven from generalised violence, chaos, or the ravages of drought and flooding? Certainly, a conceptualisation of refugee issues as those of human rights, rather than immigration, sustains this argument on the basis of the right to life itself, which is the basic human right. Death by torture, as distinct from death by random bombing, flooding, or drought, is still death.

We also have the question of sovereignty as it relates the disposition of land and land-based resources. States may not deliberately or negligently cause damage to the territory and inhabitants of other states, through actions like acid rain or a Chernobyl-like accident, or through what is called a 'wrongful act'. Yet while international law is one thing, political will and pressure is at least as important. Thus, not a single state has actually pressed forward successfully with litigation against the former USSR for the Chernobyl accident (Bronfman 1991, p. 15).

Perhaps the basic principle of emerging international environmental law is the 1972 Declaration of the United Nations Conference on the Human Environment, known as the Stockholm Declaration. Principle 21 states: 'States have . . . the sovereign right to exploit their own resources pursuant to their own environmental policies, and the responsibility to ensure that activities within their jurisdiction or control do not cause damage to the environment of other States or of areas beyond the limits of national jurisdiction'. This statement attempts to balance state sovereignty over natural resources with state responsibility for extra-territorial damage.

A case in point concerns the Brazilian rain forest. The destruction of these forests can cause major global ecological degradation. (A similar claim has been made concerning the planetary importance of British Columbia's forests (Lush 1991).) As yet the Brazilian deforestation does not contravene international law. The closest legal avenue would be reliance on 'strict liability' which focuses on liabilities which derive from the *result* of state action. Here strict liability has been limited to 'ultrahazardous activities', such as running nuclear reactors. However, at some future point states may wish to strengthen this remedy. Some evidence suggests that the government in Brazil has become more sensitive to international concerns on the rainforest (Dillon 1990).

Yet while the law lags behind, the ecological evidence grows concerning the harm which may arise from deforestation. The principle which may emerge is that sovereignty over territory may yet be limited where a compelling international or global interest can be demonstrated. New emerging notions such as the 'common heritage of mankind' have been applied to areas where sovereignty is indeterminate, such as Antarctica, deep sea beds, and the Moon, but not—yet—to where there is any permanent sovereignty of states.

Some observers might possibly argue that land itself, not just trees, or water, can be seen as a finite resource with international obligations. This applies particularly to land which may be actually or potentially arable, and on which people may enjoy freedom from persecution or violence. The advantaged position of Canada and Australia bears repeating. Each country has a very low density, three per square kilometre. Many of the currently non-habitable or uninhabited areas may still be judged to be preferable alternative sites for refugees, particularly when adequately financed and perhaps developed. Of course, there would be enormous expense associated with making parts of Canada and Australia habitable for large populations, and encouraging settlers to remain in the presently uninhabited areas.

FAO data for the mid-1980s on measures of per capita arable land favour Canada and Australia by seven to one over Africa and Latin America, and forty to one over Asia (Weinfeld 1988). Environmental refugees are projected to increase in number, both from land degradation and sea level rise (Jacobson 1989). If—and it is still a big if—the world is evolving to the point where the weight of international law and political pressures might limit state sovereignty in matters such as the use of fresh water, or use of forests, would land use—and access—be far behind?

To be sure, many of the advantaged states are powerful, and constraints of realpolitik have always proved decisive in the evolution of international law. (It is interesting to note that Russia would qualify, like Canada and Australia, as a highly advantaged state in terms of a land resource base. Perhaps a reformed Russia might become a destination rather than a source of refugees and immigrants generally!). We ought to note that this moralistic debate may take place within a context of rising general population pressures, as well as the possibilities of nuclear proliferation and regional instability.

Conclusion

There has been at no time a fully satisfactory international regime on refugees, nor one dealing with the various aspects of the international movement of peoples. Nevertheless, although the definitional problems of refugees or persecution are important, there is an accepted process for handling individual cases of persecution. Less successful, given the constraints of the underlying political circumstances that have caused the problem, has been the handling of extra-Convention refugees. In addition, there is a clear understanding that economic migrants do not warrant international protection other than normal human rights entitlements, and protection against undue economic exploitation within an ILO framework.

The major gap in the system has reflected the emergence of problems not anticipated, or if anticipated not seen as requiring collective international action, at the time of the regime's formation. Two major streams of population movements, extra-Convention refugees and guest workers, have emerged largely outside the system.

Although we have not discussed the guest worker issue, the convergence of the various elements of international population movements manifesting itself in the problem of asylum seekers will make it more difficult to achieve a coherent, workable regime.

In particular, proposals for collective action have not overcome, and seem unlikely to overcome, the essential international dilemma. Countries will continue to exercise the right to say who will be part of their community, a number far less than those wishing to join.

The particular problems still to be faced and likely to continue unresolved, are the problems of the definition of persecution, and the ambiguity about involuntary return. Clearly the question of numbers will ultimately determine the outcome and definitions and processes will be adjusted accordingly. Communities will react if there is an apparent lack of control and strains appear on social cohesion. Yet, too strong a control may generate unpredictable political reactions, whether domestic or in terms of foreign policy. More differentiated access, like Australia's recently introduced four year temporary asylum visa, will help but not solve the problem. Ultimately, however, states will limit the inflow in one way or another but as the Vietnamese experience showed, political and ideological factors will influence the extent of such limits.

This paper has also discussed two broad types of forces which may be acting to reduce the power of state sovereignty to justify restrictive immigration and refugee determining policies: regionalism and ecological imperatives. At the same time there are clearly political forces at work in Canada, the United States, and Australia, and more notoriously in western Europe, which seek to reduce the intake of immigrants and refugees. Moreover, the forces of borders and sovereignty can continue to assert themselves, whether in the EC or—perhaps—in the defence of Canadian cod stocks against foreign offshore fishing. A new equilibrium is evolving, which will affect refugee issues as well as many other policy domains.

The numbers of refugees actually able to reach Australia or Canada and make claims are small when compared to the global refugee population. In the future, it may be more and more difficult to maintain the viability of the distinctions among convention refugees (and designated classes), environmental refugees, economic migrants, and migrants seeking security of the person, whether from an immigration or human rights perspective. Refugee issues may well come to be seen as *more* than human rights issues, and along with immigration as part of a broader population agenda. Regional approaches may or may not play expanded roles in this context.

Global population pressures are likely to increase the numbers of all such groups, and increase the numbers who will be arriving at Canadian and Australia borders, unless tighter measures of security and control are adopted. Such defensive/aggressive measures would be inevitably sending mixed signals from the North to the South.

The privileged positions of countries like Canada and Australia will come under closer scrutiny in the next century. While there will be no easy solutions, recognising and discussing some of the forces which may be shaping the future context is a good place to begin.